T0384718

DEAR JOHN

Are "Dear John" letters lethal weapons in the hands of men at war? Many US officers, servicemen, veterans, and civilians would say yes. Drawing on personal letters, oral histories, and psychiatric reports, as well as popular music and movies, Susan L. Carruthers shows how the armed forces and civilian society have attempted to weaponize romantic love in pursuit of martial ends, from World War II to today. Yet efforts to discipline feeling have frequently failed. And women have often borne the blame. This sweeping history of emotional life in wartime explores the interplay between letter-writing and storytelling, breakups and breakdowns, and between imploded intimacy and boosted camaraderie. Incorporating vivid personal experiences in lively and engaging prose – variously tragic, comic, and everything in between – this compelling study will change the way we think about wartime relationships.

Susan L. Carruthers is Professor of US and International History, University of Warwick. The author of six books, including *The Good Occupation: American Soldiers and the Hazards of Peace*, she taught for fifteen years at Rutgers University-Newark, and has held visiting fellowships at Harvard, Princeton, and the Woodrow Wilson Center. She was a finalist for the 2017 PEN Hessell-Tiltman prize.

DEAR JOHN

Love and Loyalty in Wartime America

Susan L. Carruthers

CAMBRIDGE
UNIVERSITY PRESS

CAMBRIDGE
UNIVERSITY PRESS

University Printing House, Cambridge CB2 8BS, United Kingdom

One Liberty Plaza, 20th Floor, New York, NY 10006, USA

477 Williamstown Road, Port Melbourne, VIC 3207, Australia

314–321, 3rd Floor, Plot 3, Splendor Forum, Jasola District Centre, New Delhi – 110025, India

103 Penang Road, #05–06/07, Visioncrest Commercial, Singapore 238467

Cambridge University Press is part of the University of Cambridge.

It furthers the University's mission by disseminating knowledge in the pursuit of education, learning, and research at the highest international levels of excellence.

www.cambridge.org
Information on this title: www.cambridge.org/9781108830775
DOI:10.1017/9781108913867

First published 2022

Printed in the United Kingdom by TJ Books Limited, Padstow Cornwall

A catalogue record for this publication is available from the British Library.

Library of Congress Cataloging-in-Publication Data
Names: Carruthers, Susan L. (Susan Lisa), author.
Title: Dear John : love and loyalty in wartime America / Susan L. Carruthers.
Other titles: Love and loyalty in wartime America
Description: Cambridge, United Kingdom ; New York, NY : Cambridge University Press, 2022. | Includes bibliographical references and index.
Identifiers: LCCN 2021024899 (print) | LCCN 2021024900 (ebook) | ISBN 9781108830775 (hardback) | ISBN 9781108823326 (paperback) | ISBN 9781108913867 (ebook)
Subjects: LCSH: United States – Armed Forces – Military life. | Soldiers – United States – Correspondence. | Rejection (Psychology) | Unmarried couples – United States – Correspondence. | Military spouses – United States – Correspondence. | Soldiers – United States – Psychology. | Man-woman relationships – United States – Anecdotes. | World War, 1939-1945 – Social aspects – United States. | United States – History, Military – Miscellanea. | BISAC: HISTORY / Military / General
Classification: LCC U766 .C37 2022 (print) | LCC U766 (ebook) | DDC 355.10973–dc23
LC record available at https://lccn.loc.gov/2021024899
LC ebook record available at https://lccn.loc.gov/2021024900

ISBN 978-1-108-83077-5 Hardback

For Joseph Romano, Again

Contents

Illustrations

Picking Up the Pieces

I N SEPTEMBER 2011, gay, lesbian, and bisexual Americans were permitted to serve openly in the US armed forces for the first time. A few months earlier, President Barack Obama had terminated the policy in place since 1994, whereby "homosexuals" could serve in the military, but only if they kept their sexual orientation hidden. For their part, commanders were not meant to enquire into servicemen's and servicewomen's sexual identities. Nevertheless, a policy initially dubbed "Don't Ask, Don't Tell, Don't Pursue" quickly became truncated to "Don't Ask, Don't Tell" (DADT) in everyday usage. This abbreviation reflected the reality that some commanding officers remained in covert pursuit of closeted gay personnel. An estimated 13,000 men and women were discharged from the military in the DADT era as a result of their sexuality – or presumptions about it.[1]

The Onion greeted the demise of DADT with a droll satirical story, its stock in trade, headlined: "First-Ever Gay 'Dear John' Letters Begin Reaching U.S. Troops Overseas." With a dateline of Bagram, Afghanistan, the spoof report noted the arrival of "hundreds of Dear John letters" addressed to "newly outed troops overseas this week, notifying soldiers for the first time ever that their same-sex partners back home were leaving them and starting a new life with someone else." The story quoted a fictitious first lieutenant, delightedly announcing: "This is what we've waited so long for ... My boyfriend wrote that he didn't love me anymore, that he wasn't sure he ever really had, and that he never wanted to see me again. Those are words earlier generations of gay soldiers never had the opportunity to read." *The Onion* relished the perversity of service-men and women hailing heartbreak as a civil rights victory. "Now all troops, regardless of their sexual orientation, are free to have their entire lives ripped out from underneath them in a single short note," hurrahed an imaginary gay rights advocate. This humorous take on the repeal of DADT underscored the fact that, hitherto, queer service personnel could share neither the ecstasy of new love nor the agony of lost love with their comrades at arms.[2]

The Onion offered a wry critique of homophobia in the military. By using the breakup note as its vehicle, the paper also attested the Dear John's status as a rite of passage – as predictable a feature of military life as the "high and tight" buzzcut, Kitchen Patrol drudgery, and drill instructors' profanity. *The Onion* invoked several well-worn tropes. It stressed the callous brevity of breakup notes, with their twin revelations that the sender wasn't only ending things with the recipient but begin-ning a *new* romance – rejection and betrayal rolled into one. And the story highlighted the military's concern over the impact of imploded intimacy on operational efficiency. *The Onion* included a spurious soundbite from Senator John McCain. A well-known opponent of DADT's repeal, McCain was quoted warning against the havoc "gay Dear John letters" would wreak in the field: "Allowing so many utterly lonely, dejected, and newly single troops to serve on the front lines would only impair our combat capabilities and place our nation at risk."[3]

To illustrate its story, *The Onion* used a photograph of a serviceman crouched in the desert, helmeted head bent disconsolately over a letter. Leaving aside this soldier's camouflage jacket – sleeveless to better dis-play his impressively sculpted biceps – the image could've been drawn from any US war since GIs first coined the term "Dear John" during World War II. The precise origins of the phrase are shrouded in obscur-ity. Dictionaries of slang and standard American English supply an array of possible derivations and early exemplars. Some propose the coinage took its inspiration from a popular radio serial, *The Irene Rich Show*, broadcast nationally from 1933 for a decade. This anthology of mini-dramas used the epistolary form as its hook, each episode beginning as

0.1. Irene Rich greets a canine fan of her "Dear John" radio show at CBS KNX radio studios, Columbia Square, Hollywood, May 1, 1942. (Courtesy of CBS via Getty Images.)

though Rich were reading aloud a letter she'd penned. (Hence the show's alternative name, *Dear John.*) But though the letters began with this salutation, they weren't what would soon become known as Dear Johns.[4]

As a synonym for a breakup note sent by a woman to a man in uniform, the Dear John letter made its debut in a major national newspaper in October 1943. Milton Bracker, at twenty-four already a seasoned correspondent stationed in North Africa, wired a story back for publication in the *New York Times Magazine*. His feature ran under the didactic headline: "What to Write the Soldier Overseas." "Separation," Bracker observed, was the "one most dominant war factor in the lives of most people these days." Regrettably, however, absence wasn't making all hearts grow fonder. Wherever "dour dogfaces" – from "Maine, Carolina, Utah and Texas" – found themselves in "places as unimaginable as Algiers," "Dear John clubs" were springing up. These, the reporter explained, were mutual consolation societies formed by officers and enlisted men who'd received letters from home "running something like this:

'Dear John: I don't know quite how to begin but I just want to say that Joe Doakes came to town on furlough the other night and he looked very handsome in his uniform, so when he asked me for a date –'"[5]

Yank, the Army weekly, had reported on "Brush-Off Clubs" months earlier, in January 1943, offering illustrative examples of these letters without yet calling them Dear Johns.[6] Many press stories in the same vein followed, dotting the pages of both civilian and military newspapers over the course of this war and beyond. Excerpts from archetypal specimens of this newly named genre were a common feature of reportage. According to journalists, women composed brush-off notes in a variety of registers, ranging from the naively clueless to the calculatedly cruel, but invariably beholden to cliché. When Howard Whitman explained the Dear John to readers of the *Chicago Daily Tribune* in May 1944, he had his imaginary female writer string hackneyed phrases together: "Dear John – This is very hard to tell you, but I know you'll understand. I hope we'll always remain friends, but it's only fair to tell you that I've become engaged to somebody else."[7] Formulaic words, Whitman implied, would do little to soften the blow. Trite sentiments might even exacerbate the pain caused by a revelation that was both belated and perfunctory.

War correspondents who brought these letters to civilians' attention were keen to preach a particular sermon about mail and morale, love and loyalty. Hyperbole was the order of the day. "It is doubtful if the Nazis will ever hurt them as much," Whitman opined, referring to the emotional wounds inflicted by women who sent soldiers Dear Johns. This was quite a claim under the circumstances. Neither the loss of limbs, sight, hearing, sanity, nor death itself – which the German Wehrmacht inflicted on millions of Allied personnel – caused as much damage as a letter from a wife or girlfriend terminating a romantic relationship. So Whitman and others insisted. But, to these commentators, it was precisely the circumstance of being at war that made rejection more tormenting – and more intolerable – than in civilian life. Since many contemporaries agreed that a broken heart was the most catastrophic injury a soldier might incur, "jilted GIs" garnered widespread sympathy, including from their COs. While the brass still tended to regard "nervousness" in combat as an unacceptable manifestation of weakness, officers often extended a pass to servicemen who responded to romantic loss with tears, depression, rage, or violence.[8]

Among other things, a Dear John issued servicemen a rare license to emote. That stricken soldiers would act out, and be justified in doing so, was a widely accepted nostrum in civilian circles too. Here's Mary Haworth, an advice columnist, indignantly addressing her readership in the *Washington Post* in July 1944:

> a bolt of bad news that strikes directly at their male ego – telling that some other man has scored with the little woman in their absence – can lay them out flat, figuratively speaking; and make them a fit candidate for hospitalization. This is no reflection on their manhood, either. It illustrates, rather, their civilized need of special spiritual nurture while breasting the demoniac fury of modern warfare.[9]

Like Haworth, many female opinion leaders condoned men's emotional disintegration under the duress of a Dear John. Eager to shore up vulnerable male egos, they joined the chorus condemning women who severed intimate ties with servicemen as traitors – worse than Axis enemies because American women were (or *ought* to be) on the same side.[10]

In World War II's gendered division of labor, it fell to women not only to wait but to *write*. Men battling Axis forces were fighting "for home" – as innumerable propaganda posters, movies, and other patriotic prompts reminded them. Women may have symbolized the home front, but their role was neither passive nor mute. The wartime state, along with legions of self-appointed adjutants, regularly reminded women that to "keep the home fires burning," they had to stoke the coals of romance with regular loving letters to men in uniform.[11]

For their part, many soldiers endowed mail with magical properties. Facing the prospect of life-altering injury or death, men readily sacralized objects they believed might serve as amulets against harm. Some took this faith in mail's protective power so literally that they pocketed letters next to their hearts, as though note-paper – or the loving sentiments committed to the page – could deflect bullets.[12] But the magic could also work in reverse, or so some soldiers feared. For if loving letters could ward off danger, mightn't unloving words invite it? Pulitzer-winning poet W. D. Snodgrass recalls harboring these suspicions as a Navy typist during World War II: "Mail call was the best, or worst, moment of each day; you approached carefully any man whose name had not been called. Only a 'Dear John' letter was worse – we felt, mawkishly no doubt, that with no one to come back to, a man was less likely to come back."[13] Similarly, Vietnam veteran Michael McQuiston remembers his platoon sergeant's reluctance to let him go out into the field after he'd received a Dear John: "Their rule was that they didn't do that. It was bad luck." (McQuiston pestered his way into a mission only to sustain an injury, thereby confirming the wisdom of superstitious belief.)[14]

From Homer's *The Odyssey* onwards, soldiers have been haunted by – and taunted themselves with – the specter of female infidelity, associating disloyalty with fatality. Penelope, whose constancy Odysseus put to the test by disguising himself as a beggar when he returned home after long years away at war, ultimately demonstrated her steadfastness to her husband's satisfaction. By the time of his return, she had already fought off more than 100 suitors with her cunningly unraveled and rewoven yarn, except in an alternative version of the legend which has Penelope sleeping with them all.[15] That this revisionist myth-maker preferred not to copy Homer's portrait of Penelope – a model of connubial chasteness – hints at a larger phenomenon. Soldiers' and veterans' recollections have tended to accentuate the unfaithful few, not the devotedly loyal many. Dear John stories exemplify this trend, commonly treating as "universal" an experience that, though not unusual, was far from inevitable.

American men in uniform began to broadcast tales of being "given the air" by mail long before GIs conjured the term "Dear John" in World War II. Some of these notes, or perhaps apocryphal versions of them, swiftly found their way into public circulation. One Civil War specimen, an uncanny harbinger of things to come, appeared in September 1863, in Point Lookout, Maryland. The *Hammond Gazette*, a hospital newspaper, excerpted a letter that had apparently just been received by a rebel soldier, "Henneri," then recovering on the ward: "Kind Sir – I received your letter – glad to hear from you. We have been corrisponding for some time together. Now we will have to quit our corrisponding to each other, as I have placed my affections on one I wasn't dreaming of, and soon will be joined in wedlock."[16] Civil War scholars have identified several Dear John letters (anachronistically so-called) sent to both Confederate and Union soldiers.[17]

What's often billed as the "most famous" Dear John in history was sent to another hospitalized invalid shortly after the end of World War I, a quarter century before the phrase was coined.[18] In March 1919, nurse Agnes von Kurowsky wrote to tell "Ernie, dear boy," that their dalliance during his recuperation in a Milan hospital was over. For her, it had been an immature and platonic infatuation: "Now, after a couple of months away from you, I know that I am still very fond of you, but, it is more as a mother than as a sweetheart." Agnes's opening salvo anticipated that her words would "hurt," but she expected they wouldn't harm the recipient "permanently."[19] Literary scholars have debated the acuity of her prediction ever since. Some insist that Ernest Hemingway, the "dear boy" in question, never did recover from this blow to his adolescent ego. ("Ernie" was nineteen at the time; "Aggie" a venerable twenty-six.) Hemingway suffered bouts of severe depression throughout his life, committing suicide in 1961. He did, however, exact his revenge early on. In one of Hemingway's first pieces of published fiction, "A Very Short Story" (1924), a nurse jilts the narrator, whom she'd pledged to marry, sending him a note that theirs had been merely a "boy and girl affair." She is in love with a major and expects to marry him. But this union does not come to pass. The nurse is betrayed by the major on his return to Chicago, and the story ends with his contracting gonorrhea "from a sales girl in a loop department store while riding in a taxicab through Lincoln Park."[20]

If Dear Johns existed *avant la lettre*, why weren't they recognized as a distinct genre and given a name until World War II? This book doesn't provide a definitive answer to that question. Since the term emerged from oral tradition not bureaucratic decision, no official memorandum filed in an archive can tell us precisely who invented the term, when, and why. Enlisted men did this work unbidden. We might speculate, though, that the Dear John's crystallization resulted from several factors that set World War II apart from previous conflicts.

This globe-spanning cataclysm required mobilization on an epic scale. All told, about 16 million American men served in uniform, along with nearly 400,000 women in the auxiliary services. Of this total, around 73 percent were shipped overseas. Although the average period of service abroad was sixteen months, many spent far longer away from home, including months as occupation troops after the war ended.[21] With hindsight, knowing the dates of VE Day and VJ Day, we tend to forget just how much uncertainty Americans in uniform and their loved ones lived with during a war that stretched on and on across multiple fronts. Even in early 1945, as the Third Reich crumbled, many War Department planners expected that Japan mightn't be beaten into "unconditional surrender" until 1947. Separation, as Milton Bracker noted, was indeed the most formidable aspect of wartime life. Not knowing when – or, yet more achingly, whether – a lover, husband, or father would return home severely tested emotional ties between "here" and "there."

Unlike in World War I, when fewer Americans served overseas for a shorter period, millions of married men were mustered into the ranks in the 1940s. Marriage, already corroded by the increasing incidence of divorce, became yet more precarious.[22] Despite, or perhaps because of, the greater number of husbands in uniform, romantic love achieved pre-eminence as a "sinew of war" in this conflict. "Mother love" had been the Great War's most valorized bond between the home front and men at war. "The emphasis somehow has been on the mothers, or sometimes the wives the youths were leaving," sighed a writer in the *San Francisco Chronicle* in September 1917. "Nobody has been talking about the sweethearts, although everybody must have known that draft age and enlisting age was also lover age."[23] No one could convincingly have made the same complaint in the 1940s. In the sentimental culture of World War II, intimacy between men and women – whether between husbands and wives, or young men and their girlfriends or fiancées – sidelined maternal affection.[24] With more emotionally attached men sent off to war, the probability that some relationships would not survive separation exponentially increased, as distance, danger, uncertainty, and unreliable lines of communication strained even the strongest connections. The Dear John condensed – and confirmed – pervasive fears that love mightn't conquer all.

If it's impossible to pinpoint categorically why the Dear John came into existence when it did, it has undoubtedly remained a fixture of American war culture ever since. Five years after World War II ended, the younger siblings of the greatest generation – along with some veterans – were drafted to fight another war, this time in Korea. The armistice that ended what the Truman and Eisenhower administrations had dubbed a "police action," signed in July 1953, coincided with the Dear John's inaugural etching onto vinyl, courtesy of Jean Shepard and Ferlin Husky's hit, "A Dear John Letter." In the duet, Shepard's character plaintively writes to her former beau, John, serving far away in Korea, to break the difficult news that she no longer loves him:

> Dear John oh how I hate to write
> Dear John I must let you know tonight
> That my love for you has died away like grass upon the lawn
>
> And tonight I wed another dear John

As if this weren't bad enough, it's his brother, Don, she plans to marry – and Don wants John to return her photograph! The record soon topped the Billboard country charts, making nineteen-year-old Shepard the youngest country musician to score a number one hit, and remained on the charts for twenty-three weeks. The song, along with the coinage it helped popularize, became a fixture of the Country music canon, recorded many times over by various artists as a timeless anthem for doomed love. In 1990, the song was still believed so emotive that some local radio stations banned it from the airwaves, fearful that it might cause too much dejection among men in uniform bound for the Persian Gulf.[25]

America's war in Vietnam elevated the profile of Dear John letters yet higher, while further lowering the reputation of women who wrote them. In 1969, prominent forensic psychiatrist Dr. Emanuel Tanay (an expert witness at Jack Ruby's trial) announced that more wives and girlfriends were sending these notes to men in uniform than in any previous conflict.[26] The fact that he couldn't substantiate this claim didn't stop many soldiers and veterans from repeating an anecdotal assertion, then and thereafter. As a statement about the faithlessness of women at home, it evidently rang true, whether empirically verifiable or not. "Everybody gets a 'Dear John' letter at some point," Vietnam veteran Tom Nawrocki recalls in the continuous present tense of war memory. The 48th Army Postal Unit even named itself the "Dear John Express," embroidering this legend onto its patches.[27] Of course, nearly three million American men who served in Vietnam were *not* all jettisoned or betrayed by their wives or girlfriends. But to some more jaundiced observers, Dear John letters seemed of a piece with other forms of treachery on the home front, like antiwar protestors who spat at returning veterans – a widely recounted experience that has been challenged as a myth.[28]

The Dear John letter imparts a bitter tang to many poems, plays, novels, and memoirs Vietnam veterans wrote on return to "The World," as well as innumerable books written about grunts. Hollywood's dramatizations of the Vietnam war also commonly accord the Dear John a bit-part, if not a starring role. Movies such as *Hamburger Hill* (1987), *Platoon* (1986), and *Love and War* (1987) tapped into a longer tradition founded by celebrated veteran-novelists of World War II, like Norman Mailer, Leon Uris, and James Jones. Their semi-autobiographical blockbusters and the movies subsequently based on them – *The Naked and the Dead* (1948/1958), *Battle Cry* (1953/1955), and *The Thin Red Line* (1962/1998) – all feature soldiers or marines receiving Dear John letters while serving overseas.[29]

The Dear John tradition has been kept alive over subsequent decades. Participation in the Persian Gulf War (1990–1991) inspired Marine Corps veteran Anthony Swofford's *Jarhead* (2003), which, like Sam Mendes's screen adaptation, made considerable play with female infidelity and the technologically inventive Dear Johns that alerted marines to their cuckolding.[30] More recently, the "forever wars" – America's military operations in Afghanistan and Iraq, launched in the wake of 9/11 – have ushered the Dear John into the twenty-first century. Nicholas Sparks's novel and Lasse Hallström's lachrymose movie, *Dear John* (2010), introduced this expression to a new generation of "born digital" Americans, ensuring it wouldn't become as unfamiliar as the practice of letter-writing itself.[31]

Over the decades since World War II, a lexical counterpart to mission creep – the unplanned expansion of an operation's objectives – has been evident. Locution creep has seen the Dear John proliferate in non-military settings, just as fresh meanings for the term have mushroomed. By the 1960s, if not before, a note terminating employment might, with dark humor, be referred to as a Dear John. In January 1973, cartoonist Reg Manning imagined Henry Kissinger being sent a pre-emptive Dear John by the President of Harvard, warning the National Security Adviser not to let multiple rounds of peace talks with the Vietnamese detain him from his academic duties too long. Young missionaries, sent out into the world to proselytize on behalf of the Church of the Latter Day Saints, have also found the Dear John to be a regrettably common rite of passage. LDS channels on YouTube offer teenage Mormons advice on how to cope with this seemingly unavoidable accompaniment to their mission.[32] Giving the phrase a different twist altogether, anti-prostitution campaigners, operating in many US towns and cities in the early 2000s, accosted the consumers of commercial sex with the sardonic salutation, "Dear John." The city of Atlanta led the way, with the Mayor's office issuing posters warning sex-workers' "johns" that they were "abusing our kids, prostituting them and throwing them onto the streets" when they were "done." Some local police departments sent "Dear John" letters to men whose cars were regularly seen in, or clamped and towed from, red-light districts with a warning to cease and desist from procuring sex.[33]

As these examples suggest, Dear John letters have surfaced in diverse contexts and for divergent purposes. Sometimes they provide a comic hook, as when hapless sit-com characters for whom romance presents particular challenges receive their marching orders, like *M*A*S*H*'s Radar or, before him, Sgt. Carter from *Gomer Pyle: USMC*.[34] But despite their humorous applications, Dear Johns have – from the outset – also been associated with depression, self-harm, and suicide. Bill Mauldin, the army enlistee responsible for *Stars and Stripes*' wildly popular Willie and Joe cartoon strip, noted darkly in 1945: "A man feels very fine fighting a war when his girl has just written that she is thinking that perhaps they made a mistake. He might figure: What the hell, the only thing I was living for was that I knew she would wait for me. He's going to feel pretty low and he might get a little careless because of it, at a place where he can't afford to be careless."[35]

0.2. Henry Kissinger, having tarried too long at peace talks in Paris, receives a "Dear John" from the President of Harvard. Reg Manning, Saturday Republic, January 27, 1973. (Courtesy of the Reg Manning Collection, Greater Arizona Collection, Arizona State University Library.)

The dire outcomes Mauldin hinted at have been made explicit over the past fifteen years, as the Army and Marine Corps have tried to arrest an alarming rise in the rate of suicides committed by active duty personnel and veterans. Numerous military investigations, as well as testimony delivered on Capitol Hill, have linked Dear John letters to these deaths of despair – a topic explored at greater length in this book's final chapter. The enduring nexus between ended relationships and ended lives has entered public consciousness in more exploitative ways too. For instance, visitors to the *USS Hornet*, berthed at Alameda, California, can pay to go on a night-time "history mystery" tour that includes a "ghost hunt for the spirit of a sailor who supposedly hanged himself after receiving a 'Dear John'" – personal tragedy appropriated to inject a ghoulish frisson into this commercial venture.[36]

Given the ubiquity of the Dear John in American military life, veterans' lore, and popular culture, it might seem surprising that no previous author has charted its history. This book offers the first full-length study. Other types of wartime correspondence – love letters and last testaments, soldiers' mail to mothers and children's scribbles to soldiers – have received their due share of recognition in print. Published collections of war letters have appeared during and after all the United States' major conflicts.[37] Soldiers' missives have also figured prominently in documentary films: none more memorably than Sullivan Ballou's majestically lyrical paean to his wife, Sarah, written in July 1861, shortly before the First Battle of Bull Run. This love letter – also a last testament, albeit unbeknownst to its author – was etched into national memory by the first instalment of Ken Burns's *The Civil War* series.[38] In September 1990, when this program was broadcast, thousands of American troops were massing in the Saudi Arabian desert bordering Kuwait, part of a vast Coalition "Shield" assembled before the launch of "Operation Desert Storm" in January 1991. The United States Postal Service would later produce a compilation volume, sold together with four commemorative 29 cent stamps, entitled *Letters from the Sand*. Mail to and from service personnel in Vietnam had already received their turn in the spotlight in Bill Couturié's documentary *Dear America* (1987), based on an anthology of the same name.[39]

War letters form a recurrent focal point of public history exhibits, online and in more tangible locations. Since 2011, the Smithsonian's National Postal Museum, adjacent to Union Station in Washington, DC, has devoted a permanent exhibit to "Mail Call." Strikingly, however, "Mail Call" – in both its physical and digital variants – contains no mention of the genre that soldiers and veterans have memorialized with more feeling than any other type of letter: the Dear John.[40] Anthologies of wartime correspondence tend to fight similarly shy. The dust jacket illustration of *Dear America* is a photograph taken by David Burnett that belongs to the collection at Salt Lake Community College. In its archival setting, the image – which depicts a forlorn young GI holding a letter – is labeled, "American Soldier Reads a 'Dear John' Letter from Home." *Dear America* uses the photo, and attributes its creator, but makes no mention of the Dear John.[41]

The sentimentality of American commemorative war culture helps explain these strategic omissions. Dear John letters invert the Platonic ideal: the loving letter that reassures men in uniform, facing mortal danger far from home, of the sender's constancy, love, and gratitude. In the patriotic imagination, mail and morale march together in unbreakable lockstep. Inconveniently, however, as the Dear John attests, some types of mail can have the opposite effect on soldiers' esprit.

If it's readily guessed why many federally subsidized initiatives prefer to omit Dear Johns in their celebration of the ties that bind home and fighting fronts in shared commitment to duty, honor, and country, it requires more explanation why a phenomenon otherwise so richly recorded in soldiers' stories, and so well preserved in numerous popular cultural forms, should have escaped other authors' attention. After all, historians boldly go – and sometimes even prefer to venture – where patriotic flag-wavers fear to tread. Why not, then, to the scene of soldiers' experiences of emotional desertion?

The answer hinges on evidence. Professional historians are creatures of the archive, and Dear John letters are simply not to be found en masse in box files on the shelves of climate-controlled vaults. Most men in receipt of Dear Johns brooded on their contents at leisure, but disposed of the letters themselves in haste. A whole strand of soldiers' story-telling documents the inventive ways in which they've consigned these missives to oblivion: tearing them to shreds, throwing them overboard, igniting them or, in cruder versions, using these notes as "bumf" (shorthand for "bum fodder"). In January 1971, Specialist 3 Roger Hicks submitted a verse on this subject to the *Los Angeles Sentinel*, a Black weekly newspaper, while he served in Vietnam:

> What is left at the end
> A crumpled envelope
> A misting of the eyes
> Thirty-eight pieces of her letter.[42]

Like Hicks, few recipients preserved hard evidence of rejection for later inspection. It takes a certain kind of personality – precociously endowed with a grandiose sense of self, like Ernest Hemingway – to retain a Dear John for posterity, imagining that future greatness would imprint an early heartbreak with historical significance.

Whatever else they may have done with Dear John letters, veterans have not bequeathed them to posterity. Most, after all, did not exist to be handed down to descendants, along with other war memorabilia, and donated to archives for permanent preservation. As I discovered early on while researching this book, libraries and historical societies instead contain phantom Dear John letters. Several archivists I approached for assistance, including at the Marine Corps History Division, Archives Branch, the US Army Women's Museum, the Center for American War Letters Archives at Chapman University, and the Institute on World War II and the Human Experience at Florida State University, expressed initial certainty that their collections contained specimens, only to come up empty-handed after further digging.

A collection of women's letters from World War II assembled for publication by historians Judy Barrett Litoff and David C. Smith, now housed at Bryant University, boasts just one Dear John.[43] A stinging one-liner, this note is characterized by both brevity and irreverence, unlike the cliché-laden apologias of journalistic reportage. It takes the form of a V-mail: pre-printed stationary that was microfilmed for despatch overseas, introduced by the government in 1942 to speed the flow of supportive sentiment between men at war and loved ones at home. And it was written by twenty-one-year-old Anne Gudis of Newark, New Jersey, to her soldier boyfriend then stationed "Somewhere in Britain."[44] Enraged by a string of insulting messages he'd sent her, she dashed off a furious zinger. Stripping him of rank, Anne addressed herself to "Mr. Kramer." Then she got straight to the point. "Go to Hell!" runs the body of the text, at a diagonal slant expressive of pent-up rage. Its recipient, twenty-six-year-old Corporal Samuel Kramer, was so piqued that he promptly sent Anne's missive to the editor of *Yank*'s "Mail Call" feature, claiming to have received the "shortest V-mail letter" in the European Theater of Operations (ETO). Three weeks later, the army weekly reproduced the offending V-mail in facsimile under the headline: "The Importance of Being Terse." Anne's return address was clearly legible in the top right-hand corner, ensuring that she received dozens of letters from *Yank*'s readers – some eager to chide her, others to chat her up.[45]

Yank published Anne's "Go to Hell!" message just days before the *New York Times* introduced readers to Dear Johns and the associated phenomenology of heartbreak in uniform. As World War II veteran and literary scholar Paul Fussell subsequently glossed the term, "This was the feared letter from home beginning harmlessly enough but exploding finally with the news that the beloved female writer has (of course, experienced soldiers would say) taken up with someone more accessible."[46] Gudis's V-mail upended that paradigm. It began explosively, but ended affectionately, "With Love." That "something doesn't quite jibe" prompted curious GIs to write to *Yank* for elucidation. In its issue of October 10, 1943, the magazine published a note from two soldiers, also stationed in Britain, wanting to know what Cpl. Kramer had "said to the girl." Those more eager to satisfy their curiosity than to garner publicity addressed their inquiries directly to Anne herself.[47]

Gudis preserved all the correspondence she received in response to a message she'd never intended for publication. The letters and V-mails strangers sent her offer sharp insights into how Americans processed issues of love and loyalty in wartime: the intricate quickstep between observing rules and breaking them. The story of Anne Gudis and Sam Kramer's public/private, love/hate relationship runs through this book's chapters. Anne (or rather Sam) provided third parties with something remarkably rare: a Dear John whose provenance is beyond dispute. The young Newarker told her boyfriend to "Go to Hell!" Not just categorically, but indisputably. Moreover, we know what scores of Americans, and a few bemused Brits, made of Anne's note.

If Gudis's V-mail was an unorthodox breakup note, Kramer's sharing it was much more typical of how Dear Johns traveled from servicemen's hands into the public sphere. Men who'd been "Dear Johned" regularly passed these letters around among their peers. Critiquing the composition, defacing the note-paper, destroying or "recycling" Dear Johns was often a collective activity undertaken in solidarity with the recipient to aid his recuperation. The Air Force University's library contains one bona fide but second-hand Dear John, duplicated in a former POW's scrapbook. Received by a fellow American airman in German captivity, this rejection note had done the rounds, with scathing annotations penciled in the margins by its recipient.[48] Wider dissemination offered a way to alleviate the sting of rejection. Men in uniform sometimes submitted

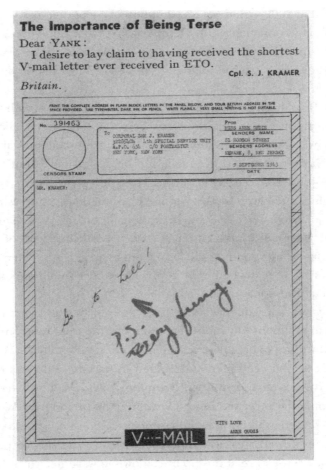

0.3. Anne Gudis's V-mail to Sam Kramer as published in *Yank*, annotated by a stranger, and mailed to Gudis in Newark, New Jersey. (Courtesy of Cornell University, Kramer Family Papers.)

their Dear Johns to military newspapers for publication, as Sam Kramer did, or gave them to the Armed Forces Radio Service for broadcast on air. Several veterans of World War II, including celebrated novelist James Salter, recall having heard Dear Johns read aloud on the radio, sometimes to the accompaniment of a sobbing string section. *Variety*, the Hollywood trade paper, published a story about this phenomenon in 1946.[49] More recently, an anthology of women's breakup notes published in 2002 includes a transcription of a lengthy Dear John letter, received by an unnamed GI in Vietnam, who read it aloud over a military PRC-25 radio. He was recorded doing so by his buddy, Dave Syster. Like many other artifacts of the analog age, this recording can now be listened to online.[50]

How Dear John letters became common currency – their absence from the archives, but ubiquity everywhere that servicemen talk or write of their war experience – tells us something fundamental about this genre. Namely, that *men* invented, authored, and have kept rewriting the Dear John. GIs coined the phrase. Then they verbed it. Men could be (and quite often were) "Dear Johned." Sometimes, they referred to authors of such notes as "the Dear John ones," as though the term denoted a certain kind of woman, not a particular type of letter.[51] Rather than understanding the Dear John as an exclusively female epistolary form, we'd do better to approach it as a predominantly male vernacular tradition.

Dear John is consequently about both letter-writing and story-telling. It has less to say about why individual women wrote Dear John letters than about why other people have had so much to say about the severance of romantic ties between men and women in wartime. Why has the Dear John served as such a durable lightning rod for soldiers' feelings of alienation, grievance, and injury? Spanning the period from World War II to the present, this book examines the precariousness of romantic love in wartime. It explores how American civilians and service personnel have made sense of relationship breakdown in wartime: why it happens, who or what to blame, and how to mitigate the consequences, or (better yet) prevent the occurrence of men's emotional injury. Examining how the armed forces have attempted to make heterosexual coupledom serve martial purposes, *Dear John* illustrates the fraught and failure-prone nature of efforts to channel feeling in approved directions. The book also highlights how many different individuals and institutions have been – and remain – invested in trying to discipline and dissect the emotional lives of soldiers and their romantic partners. Not only members of the military establishment but civilian opinion-leaders, journalists, advice columnists, social workers, religious authorities, as well as "psy-" professionals, psychologists and psychiatrists who serve in uniform or practice as civilians.

On all these topics, there's an abundance of evidence. *Dear John* draws on a wide array of source material: declassified official documents that detail military policy on marriage, mail, and morale; Chaplaincy records; the papers of the American Red Cross; military psychiatric reports and other professional literature dedicated to fathoming the mysteries of why women break up with men at war, and why men break down as a result. Movies, novels, memoirs, and popular songs chart the contours of the Dear John letter's public reputation. Letters and private papers reveal how Americans *actually* wrote to one another in wartime, while the civilian and military press convey copious instructions on what they were *meant* to say, and to suppress. Women's magazines issued a torrent of prescriptive advice on matters of dating and mating, waiting and writing.

Above all, research for this book involved listening to hundreds of hours of oral history testimony recorded by veterans about their military service. The Veterans History Project at the Library of Congress has amassed the largest repository of such material. Well over 100 taped interviews include Dear John vignettes, apocrypha, and jokes. Other collections, such as the National World War II Museum in New Orleans, the Rutgers Oral History Archives, and Texas Tech University's Vietnam Center and Sam Johnson Vietnam Archive, all contain veterans' recollections of the Dear Johns they, or their unfortunate buddies, received.[52] These stories are narrated in distinct registers – tragic, comic, and all points between – by servicemen of every rank, race, and class. Romantic rejection was an experience shared by men across otherwise firmly entrenched divisions. In successive wars, Black, Chicano, and Puerto Rican soldiers received, and lamented, the arrival of Dear Johns, as did their white ethnic peers. Officers who took a dim view of how young enlisted men crumpled on receipt of a Dear John were sometimes surprised to find themselves served notice of divorce proceedings by the wives they'd believed unwaveringly loyal. On occasion, they were also chastened by the discovery that maintaining their own emotional equilibrium wasn't easy.[53]

I listened to women's voices, too, where they've been recorded. Most archival collections, however, contain significantly fewer oral histories featuring female veterans or women who served in civilian capacities in America's wars since the 1940s. The Betty H. Carter Women Veterans Historical Project at the University of North Carolina-Glassboro is one of a handful of exceptions to this general rule.[54] The imbalance in part reflects an undeniable statistical truth: far more men than women served in uniform. Collections of private papers – letters, diaries, scrapbooks, unpublished memoirs – also tilt heavily in favor of male-authored ego documents (as historians call these personal materials). Far more letters written by, rather than *to*, soldiers survive in US archives. This lopsidedness could also be attributed to wartime circumstance. Soldiers often destroyed letters, not just Dear Johns, soon after reading them. During World War II, and again in Vietnam, officers sometimes encouraged, or even ordered, men to destroy mail from home. Among the many "things they carried," in Tim O'Brien's phrase, letters could be an unnecessary burden. Worse yet, correspondence could fall into enemy hands, inadvertently betraying valuable intelligence.[55] But neither of these matter-of-fact explanations for archival asymmetry does justice to more purposeful issues of preservation practice.

A more fundamental reason why male testimony predominates is that archives (and the publics they serve) have tended to value front-line combat as *the* quintessential war experience to be celebrated and preserved. If this gendered imbalance is starting to break down, as more archivists seek to incorporate a broader spectrum of experience into their collections, inclusivity often remains more aspirational than achieved.

Yet, despite these caveats, women's voices reverberate more loudly through this book's chapters than might be expected in the absence of bona fide breakup notes. My proposition that men carved and embellished the Dear John totem is not meant as a denial that some women did indeed write to men in uniform announcing the end of unsatisfactory relationships. We know they did – not only from men on the receiving end, but because women sometimes acknowledged authorship in public commentary on the phenomenon. They did so almost as soon as the term was coined, not because they found writing Dear

Johns "empowering" – a claim later made – but attempting to redress the balance of culpability.[56] Men too, they wanted fellow Americans to know, were unfaithful to the women they'd left behind. Yet male soldiers enjoyed wide latitude for sexual "adventurism" emphatically denied to women. Men sometimes penned breakup notes. Tellingly, however, the phrase "Dear Jane" trailed more than a decade behind the "Dear John."

Where some women raised their voices in protest against pronounced double standards surrounding love and loyalty in wartime, demanding both greater equality and greater empathy, others sided with men in uniform. Many of the busiest disciplinarians of female behavior and affect were other women, particularly those empowered to issue commandments and deliver judgment from the advice columnist's lofty pulpit.

Dear John encompasses several different kinds of relationships: romantic bonds between men and women; comradely bonds between men; and interactions (often tutelary, sometimes sisterly) between women. The book's focus on heterosexual love reflects the military's insistence – until the repeal of DADT – that this kind of intimacy was the *only* permissible variety for uniformed personnel. Before 2011, same-sex relationships necessarily had to remain under wraps in the services. Although they undoubtedly occurred nevertheless, they weren't the target of prescriptive military and civil advice. These partnerships weren't, after all, meant to be happening. For decades, all branches of the armed forces policed sexuality intensively, though not always identically. Many scholars, activists, and veterans have documented these repressive practices, and resistance to them, in print.[57] They remind us that the military is a peculiar institution, embedded within yet also set apart from civilian society. Thus while the armed forces draw recruits from the country at large, they also draw up different rules for their conduct than those enshrined in civil legal statutes. The military's governance of sexuality strikingly illustrates this fault-line. The Uniform Code of Military Justice still outlaws "adultery," long after it ceased to be illegal in most states, and for decades the UCMJ made "sodomy," which it linked with "bestiality," a crime.[58]

It would be easy to imagine that an institution which, for so many decades, outlawed gay and lesbian partnerships must have perennially encouraged heterosexual conjugality – not just as a mandatory norm, but a celebrated ideal. For years, the army has boasted its "family friendly" credentials, recently bringing non-traditional families under that extended umbrella. Yet, as this book shows, the armed forces have long struggled with romantic love in *all* its iterations. And they still do.

This claim may seem paradoxical: how can maritally oriented institutions simultaneously harbor profound mistrust of marriage? Or, perhaps more specifically, of *wives*? Going back to the very first press reports on Dear John letters we find indelible traces of this skepticism – expressed by soldiers and amplified by journalists attuned to their emotional tribulations – about whether romantic relationships with women were either worth saving or deserved mourning. Woman-hating courses through these reports, sometimes a subtext, but often on the surface. Correspondent Hal Boyle, reporting on Dear John clubs in Algiers in 1943, noted that, amid the "lovesick GI Joes," "A lot of the soldiers are grateful to the Nazis for postponing the day when they have to return to meet the loving arms of some girl friend they have since decided has a face 'like a pailfull of worms.'"[59] For their part, female authority figures could be just as quick to berate "philandering war wives" as men in uniform. Prominent advice columnist Dorothy Dix had this to say on the subject of "flighty women" in August 1943: "Their hearts are not flesh and blood. They are made of flimsy. It is not in them to have any deep feeling, or any loyalty, or sense of duty or responsibility. All they want is pleasure, excitement, pretty clothes, and they will change to any man who will give these to them ..." Lest any reader missed her point, she concluded with an admonition that "the man who grieves over losing one of them is as foolish as if he spent his days weeping over a broken doll."[60]

Misogyny and heteronormativity make an awkward, if not uncommon, pairing. Where the latter mandates heterosexual coupledom, the former remains mistrustful of the women to whom men in uniform are flimsily tethered. To the misogynist, wives and girlfriends pose a severe "flight risk," liable to take off – and tear up men's morale – at any moment. Viewed this way, the only bonds that men in uniform can *truly* trust are those between male comrades-at-arms – a mystical communion far more durable than any conjugal union. For misogynists, Dear John letters offer proof that mistrust of fickle females was warranted all along. As both a harbinger of bad news and an emblem of romantic love's unreliability, the Dear John has stimulated male solidarity: homosocial bonds strengthened by heterosexual ties' severance.[61]

This book begins with a fuller exploration of the tensions and paradoxes that mark wartime attitudes toward heterosexual romantic love and marriage. Like the chapters that follow, the first one draws illustrative material from several of America's twentieth- and twenty-first-century wars. *Dear John* ranges across the decades from World War II to the present, with some contextual nods back to earlier conflicts. The material is organized thematically, not in chronological sequence, to better capture the layers of feeling that surround the central subject. Since recurrent preoccupations are more evident than linear evolution in the realm of military intimacy, the book is conceived in onion-like fashion. At its core, sits a chapter dedicated to the stories men tell about women's Dear John letters and the issues women have attempted to make audible in response – revelations about unhappy relationships, betrayal and abandonment by men at war, and what would belatedly become known as "Dear Janes." But we reach this center by first peeling back the outer skin of wartime romance: how men and women were encouraged to get together (or remain apart); the prescriptions surrounding couples' communication, and anxieties generated by technologies that let distant partners remain in touch – or call things off.

Where the first half of the book concerns couples getting together, the second deals with relationships breaking up and men breaking down. Chapters 5 through 7 examine the consequences of severed ties as service personnel and the armed forces have made sense of romantic loss and its ramifications. In these chapters, military psychiatrists come to the fore. We examine how, in the Vietnam era, they began to probe the psychology of "waiting wives" and, more urgently, of women who rejected that mantle. During the Vietnam war, as well as conflicts that preceded and followed it, psychiatrists, padres, lawyers, comrades, and commanders – along with former partners and bystanders whose paths intersected with those of stricken men – have run headlong into the consequences of relationship failure. These have ranged from alcoholism to absence without leave, and from domestic violence to homicide, prompting the military judicial system to ponder the circumstances under which a "Dear

John defense" might be warranted. Since Dear Johns have also been associated with self-harm and suicide, the military has repeatedly – and increasingly – had to grapple with how to make service members, spouses, and marriages more resilient.

Making romantic intimacy serve the cause of victory has never been straightforward for the military. Nor has making love work in wartime been simple for individuals and couples. The reasons why can be discerned by reading the subtexts and contexts of Dear John letters, and by listening attentively to what men and women have had to say about the fragility of love at war.

CHAPTER 1

The Marital and the Martial

I N MAY 1942, twenty-year-old Anne Gudis took the bold step of introducing herself by letter to a man she'd never met: Samuel Kramer, the brother of a friend of a friend, who was then stationed at Fort Niagara, New York. Twenty-five-year-old Sam had joined the army, having failed to make his way through college, while Anne, a recent graduate, worked at the Army Signal Corps Inspection Station in her hometown of Newark, New Jersey. She lived with her family in the Weequahic section later immortalized by Philip Roth. (Born in 1933, Roth grew up just a few blocks from the Gudis home on Hobson Street.) Sam was evidently impressed by Anne's pluck, and the exchange of letters soon escalated in tempo and temperature. By the time Anne scribbled her V-mail on September 9, 1943 to a civilianized "Mr. Kramer," the two had been corresponding for seventeen months. Surviving papers hint that the pair had yet to meet in person when Anne fired off her intemperate injunction.[1] Much circumstantial detail remains murky, however, as Sam did not preserve the letters he received. Indeed, he seemed to enjoy informing her that he'd burnt them all. Anne's V-mail survives only because he submitted it to *Yank*'s "Mail Call" editor, who then saw fit to publish it, not quite three weeks later.[2]

The couple's erratic, sometimes highly erotic, courtship unfolded against the backdrop of a clamorous national conversation about the situation ethics of wartime romance. Were soldiers better off, in terms of their emotional and psychological wellbeing, with or without romantic partners? And were the armed forces better served by married men or single personnel? These questions were probed relentlessly over the war years, with the ideal relationship between Mars and Eros forming a persistent preoccupation of national commentary and cultural production. Answers diverged. But the relationship between Gudis and Kramer was emphatically *not* the sort of interaction most opinion leaders encouraged. As during earlier conflicts, correspondence between single women and soldiers unknown to them struck some observers as indelicate at best, indecent at worst – a throwback to nineteenth-century modes of epistolary courtship, minus the constricting corset of Victorian values.[3]

Sam, however, relished indecency. No respecter of social convention, he needed little encouragement to pick up pen and paper after receiving Anne's introductory message. Soon he was regaling Anne with tales of his innumerable sexual conquests, before, during, and after his abandoned college career; the marriages he'd nearly sundered, and the offspring he'd narrowly avoided fathering. Telling Anne that she was his equal – "almost" – he laced the salacious content of his letters with pedantic criticism of her prose style. "You use the word nice and its derivations too much ... Nice comes from the Latin verb nescio which means know nothing, be ignorant."[4]

The frisson of their early correspondence, electrified by an unmistakably carnal charge, lent urgency to the couple's desire to meet in person. A rendezvous was duly planned for Penn Station, New York as soon as Sam received a furlough from training. "You may be the one to realize the fury of my passion – circumstances providing," Sam wolfishly warned his new pen-pal.[5] But it was not to be. Perhaps distracted by lustful fantasies, he forgot to telegram word of when his train would arrive. Anne, who had already taken a reputational risk in agreeing to a night-time encounter in the first place, couldn't loiter indefinitely. If it was in questionable taste for a "nice girl" to go and wave off her soldier-boyfriend when he shipped out, as some advice columnists cautioned, it was a bold step indeed to agree to a rendezvous with an unknown man in uniform. The couple understood the socially hazardous nature of Sam's proposition. "Gee whiskers," Sam mused, "what does your mother think about you going to NYC at what may be a very late hour to see a lad you know only from correspondence?"[6] When Sam failed to show up at the appointed spot outside Savarin's restaurant, Anne eventually gave up, and returned home across the Passaic. He later prowled Penn Station furious at having been (as he saw it) both stood up and shown up in front of his army buddies. A second assignation also came to naught. This time the missed connection was calculated. Intent on teaching Anne a lesson, Sam failed to materialize at the appointed hour. A hiatus in the correspondence ensued, though this breach was mended before he shipped out to Britain.[7]

The X-rated content of Sam's letters may have been atypical of wartime correspondence, or at least of the standard *imagined* content of soldiers' letters to sweethearts. However, the speed with which this interaction between two strangers turned to conjugal conjecture serves as a reminder that flirtation, sex, and marriage weren't easily disentangled in the early 1940s, even by as dedicated a convention-flouter as Sam. Within weeks of starting to write to one another, the pair began to speculate not only whether they would "click" in person, but if they would subsequently tie the knot. "If we had met prior to my induction and hit it off," Sam mused in June 1942, "I would marry you before going for the big boat ride." Had he and Anne done so, his commanding officer would almost certainly have disapproved.[8]

From the War Department's perspective, the single soldier represented a Platonic ideal. But this war, like those both before and after it, put civilian Americans' and the armed forces' ideas about romantic love – and the institution of marriage – to the test. Despite their lexical proximity, the marital and the martial proved enduringly hard to align.

"WAR HYSTERIA MARRIAGE" AND OTHER PERILS OF WARTIME ROMANCE

Familiar with the twenty-first-century armed forces' promotional boasts of "family-friendliness," we might imagine that the services in World War II were similarly invested in marital coupledom as the bedrock of a disciplined fighting force in which morale, matrimony, and monogamy marched in perfect formation.[9] Yet in the early 1940s, the military viewed the marriage of enlisted men with grave apprehension, if not outright disapprobation. Writing in the *Ladies' Home Journal* in March 1942, Gretta

Palmer explained the prevailing mentality to her female audience: "The Army has never looked with a kindly eye upon the marriages of men in the lower ranks . . . [A]mong the officers, there is an unofficial belief that 'a colonel must have a wife, a major should, a captain may and a lieutenant mustn't.' The Army has discouraged the marriage of low-ranking soldiers, both of the regular forces and of the draft. The Navy, too, frowns on marriage for sailors."[10]

Although the military establishment tacitly expected women to provide servicemen with emotional, sexual, and practical support, the War Department struggled to determine what kind of male–female relationships were likeliest to ensure that women's love would boost martial esprit without simultaneously jeopardizing or depleting it.[11] Senior officers feared that wives constituted an alternative pole of attraction, pulling enlisted men's attention away from martial duty and discipline. Marriage was a potentially disordering condition, making husbands both answerable to and responsible for wives and, in many cases, children too. Domesticity could readily distract married soldiers if they became mired in financial troubles or sucked into a vortex of marital strife. Far off and unable to provide domestic back-up, uniformed husbands were liable to fret fruitlessly about a spouse's mood, a child's illness, a malfunctioning boiler, a rent check delayed, or a mortgage payment unmet. Palmer's article warned that "a worried soldier is an inefficient soldier": a well-worn theme in military musings on the perils of matrimony.[12] In short, marriage saddled young men with excess baggage that the military preferred neither they nor the services should have to carry.

Palmer's article did not overstate the case. Indeed, the armed forces didn't simply express certain preferences about recruits' marital status, they issued regulations designed to deter junior enlistees from marrying. Army Regulation (AR) 615–360 (1935) established that all soldiers were required to gain their regimental commander's approval before marrying. A more punitive postscript followed in the form of AR 600–750 (1939), which decreed that enlisted men who married without permission could be refused re-enlistment. Non-commissioned officers (NCOs) of "excellent character" were exempt. Rank had its privileges, though not without qualification. NCOs with bad manners or questionable morals were seemingly destined to remain bachelors. In 1942, with thousands of American servicemen stationed overseas and more setting sail each month, the War Department further extended its veto power over marriages commanders considered unwise. Circular No. 179 (June 8, 1942) required all personnel stationed abroad to secure the permission of the overseas commander if they wished to marry, regardless of whether their intended spouse was a foreigner or a fellow US national – a member of the Army Nurse Corps, for instance, or a Red Cross "Donut Dolly." Despite a Supreme Court ruling, issued the same month, that decreed marriage one of the "basic civil rights of man," the Judge Advocate General (JAG) of the Army insisted that marriages entered into by members of oversea commands must be prohibited, "except with special permission."[13]

The JAG invoked "military efficiency" to justify encroachment on a fundamental human right. In wartime, this capacious catch-all was (and is) invoked to rationalize many expedient practices of questionable legality. In what ways, though, did spouses threaten "efficiency"? As we've seen, the armed forces feared that wives added to, rather than subtracted from, soldiers' psychological burdens. Devoted husbands would be loath to undergo separation from home, missing their spouses to the point of distraction, while unhappily married soldiers would remain hobbled by marital dysfunction from afar. But if the War Department hoped to insulate soldiers from emotional stress by ensuring they entered the service single and remained so for the duration, that aim was just one element of a more complex equation. Romantic intimacy was enmeshed with issues of economy as well as "efficiency." Put bluntly, married soldiers cost more money for the state to maintain. Servicemen's wives would have to be supported during their husbands' absence; and widows provided for in the event that absence became permanent. (The War Department assumed that the male head-of-household was the primary, if not exclusive, breadwinner.) To deter maritally minded recruits, the War Department reminded men poised to enter the junior ranks that their meager salaries – more akin to pocket money than a living wage – wouldn't suffice to support a wife, let alone any offspring. Employers rarely issue such public reminders about their employees' threadbare wages. However, early in World War II, the War Department wanted to avoid an insupportable burden of "welfare cases" that it would have to shoulder if married men enlisted en masse.[14]

Ideological common-sense also tilted institutional preference toward single soldiers. In a nation that loudly celebrated marriage and family life, it wasn't an easy proposition to pluck husbands and fathers from the safety of home and place them in harm's way. Drafting married men was an especially tricky maneuver when the state deployed romanticized images of "hearth and home" to legitimate military action, as Woodrow Wilson's administration had during the Great War. While the president proclaimed a need to make the world "safe for democracy," propaganda artists primarily conjured American participation in a far-off war as a crusade to save *domesticity*. This motif had the added virtue of being much easier to depict than a political abstraction. "Home" featured prominently as the imperilled site to be secured, no matter how distant brigades of Prussian troops remained from American hearths.[15]

This sentimental framing of wartime purpose militated against the call-up of married men to serve overseas. "All American life is built around the marriage status, and great effort should be made not to dissolve the home ties," trumpeted the provost marshal in 1918.[16] The Selective Service machinery that set to work in 1917 began by mustering only single men into uniform. But exempting husbands from the draft entailed a substantial risk: that young men and women would rush to marry for opportunistic reasons. When the War Department started to suspect that some service-averse men were getting hitched with a shrewd view to getting themselves exempted from enlistment, they changed the rules. Newly wed husbands suspected as draft-dodgers were returned to Class I status, rendering them liable for call-up. All told, about one in ten men who served with the American Expeditionary Forces was married.[17]

Twenty-three years later, the War Department replayed the same drama over the span of a few months as President Franklin D. Roosevelt nudged a reluctant populace toward entry into another global cataclysm. By the summer of 1940, newspapers noted that conscription's looming reimposition had stimulated a nation-wide marriage boom after a long Depression-induced dip. In the nation's capital, young men "swarming into the marriage license clerk's office at District Court" set an all-time monthly record in August 1940, the month in which Congress debated the Selective Service Act.[18] This mass dash for the altar – or its civic equivalent – reminded older observers of 1917, only on a grander scale. Conservative social critics greeted this development warily. The author of a grouchy *Los Angeles Times* editorial, "'Martial' Spelled 'Marital,'" noted with evident *schadenfreude* that the honeymoon for draft-dodging "new benedicks" was about to end as the government revised Selective Service eligibility criteria. Henceforth, newly wed husbands would be treated as available for induction, just like bachelors. Only married men with children remained less likely to be called on to serve, though they too might be (and were) summonsed at a later date. The *Times*' editorialist wasted no sympathy on men who made "hasty and ill considered excursions into matrimony." They deserved to repent at leisure – and in uniform. But he regretted that matrimony should have been debased into a "funk-hole for slackers."[19]

In less abrasive language, First Lady Eleanor Roosevelt echoed the view that men who married to evade military training – victims of "cupid's bad luck" – should not be spared from service.[20] Others felt that Cupid had less to do with many of these unions than misguided calculation. In their view, the specter of conscription hadn't simply accelerated couples' existing wedding plans, it had implanted ideas among men and women with *no* prior intention to marry. Before long, newspapers started running cautionary tales about couples who rued their insincere vows rather hastily. In June 1941, Mrs. Charlotta Rutledge Marshall sued for divorce from Lockwood Marshall, scion of a prominent St. Louis family who was rumored to be the nephew of Army Chief of Staff George C. Marshall. Her claim for alimony rested on the "grievous mental suffering" she'd endured during an abusive eight-month marriage that, Charlotta alleged, Lockwood had entered into solely to avoid being drafted into the army.[21] (A month later, he reversed his estranged wife's charge and announced that this dodge had been all *her* idea, foisted upon him against his better judgment.)

Even when it became clear that marriage offered husbands no immunity from conscription, American couples continued to tie the knot at an unprecedented rate. The year 1942 set a national record with 1,758,000 marriages contracted.[22] But while these couples weren't suspected of marrying to shirk military obligation, they weren't necessarily entering the connubial state for the *right* reasons either – or so many military chaplains, marriage guidance counselors, social workers, and psychologists warned. Together, these professionals turned "war hysteria marriage" into a new national malady. From the pages of newspapers, magazines, and advice manuals, a slew of experts enumerated – and often excoriated – young people's motives for seeking to cement romantic commitments before men were mustered into uniform. Many couples, noted Evelyn Millis Duvall (director of Chicago's Association for Family Living), believed marriage would provide "a comforting port of personal security as the seas of crisis run high." In their eagerness to find a secure berth, though, soldier-spouses risked tethering themselves to the flimsiest of moorings. Young wives, especially those who barely knew their husbands before the latter went to war, were liable to drift. Duvall noted that in some cases it wasn't long after husbands departed before young wives were "dating other soldiers." Alarm bells sounded even louder when demographers noted that a significant number of 1942's 400,000 "surplus" marriages were entered into by teenagers. Chicago's Cook County reported more sixteen- and seventeen-year-old girls marrying "than ever before."[23]

Champions of marriage set to work sandbagging what they saw as an endangered institution. The army chaplaincy's radio drama series, *Chaplain Jim*, which began broadcasting in 1942 with a view to reassuring "mothers, wives and sweethearts" that their soldier's "moral and spiritual well being" was in safe hands, featured recurrent plot-lines illustrating the perils of whirlwind romance followed by protracted separation. "The Case of the Soldier, the Ring and the Girl" explained (in Jim's folksy speech) that: "'A so-called war hysteria marriage is one in which a girl meets a soldier, an' marries him after a few days because she feels she owes it to him for what he's doin' for his Country . . . or maybe the girl an' the boy both feel they've got to grab whatever happiness they can from life . . . Both reasons are wrong, an' such marriages often lead to a good deal of unhappiness . . ."[24] This four-part serial resolved felicitously. The young woman in the scenario – recipient of a ring bestowed by an ardent suitor after a fleeting acquaintance – agreed that it would be wisest to defer any big decisions until he returned home. Meanwhile, neither party would harbor expectations of future commitment.

1.1. *Can War Marriages Be Made to Work?* This American Historical Association pamphlet from 1944, aimed at enlisted men, joined the wartime chorus urging conjugal caution. (Courtesy of the American Historical Association.)

Many advice columnists endorsed the fictional Chaplain Jim's counsel. Gretta Palmer concluded her *Ladies' Home Journal* homily by informing readers that the "consensus of informed opinion is that a single man should delay his marriage if he is at all likely to be called to the colors." A pamphlet published by the American Historical Association in 1944, *Can War Marriages Be Made to Work?*, written with enlisted men in mind, answered its own question with a highly qualified affirmative. Yes – but only if men chose wives wisely, letting time prove the wisdom of spousal selection before they rushed to exchange vows.[25]

A mere half-decade later, cautionary notes sounded loudly again as eligible males were drafted to serve in Korea, leaving them and their girlfriends to ponder the vexed question of "war marriage" anew. "A sharp increase in marriages always has been as accurate a barometer of war as rising steel production or rising prices," observed Stanley Frank in the women's magazine *Redbook* in December 1950, decrying the concomitant rash of "quickie" marriages entered into by "men who hoped to escape the draft."[26] Advice columnist Muriel Nissen received "many, many letters" on the issue of wartime weddings, referring readers of the *Hartford Courant* to Dorothy Dix's free leaflet, D-8, "Hasty Marriage." Nissen's own view couldn't have been clearer: "Young teenagers to whom 'responsibility' is merely a long word difficult to spell are strongly urged to establish a waiting period before exchanging wedding rings." Impetuous couples who disregarded their elders' advice had better beware. The "waiting wife" would soon decide not to martyr herself for the "sake of a man she may not see for another year." The *dénouement* was inevitable: "another 'Dear John' letter."[27]

SEX AND THE SINGLE SOLDIER

During World War II and the conflict in Korea that followed, magazine feature writers and advice columnists rarely broached concerns uppermost in the minds of many young Americans contemplating marriage: whether the man would return home unaltered – or, indeed, at all.[28] Fear of life-altering injuries and death impelled some couples toward marriage, while premonitions of impotence, paralysis, or widowhood deterred others. But whether they intended to marry or not, the prospect of lives cut short by war encouraged couples to consummate romantic relationships sooner rather than later, jettisoning peacetime behavioral norms that seemed increasingly outdated.[29] Pitched at a female audience of approximately four million listeners, *Chaplain Jim* remained reticent on two of the commonest manifestations of "war hysteria:" pre-marital and extramarital sex.

Others were not so coy. Psychologist Samuel Tenenbaum, writing in the *American Mercury*, announced that war had created "a pathological interest in sex." At a time when pre-marital sex was widely frowned upon, some couples saw marriage as a way to make "last fling" liaisons respectable, while others tumbled heedlessly into bed with near-strangers. Tenenbaum outlined several common *carpe diem* scenarios in which such misbegotten unions occurred, including one that roughly approximated Sam Kramer and Anne Gudis's near-miss rendezvous: "A college girl carries on a correspondence with a soldier she has never seen. When he is about to be shipped, she meets him at a railroad junction, and between trains they become man and wife." In Tenenbaum's eyes, and those of many others invested in the long-term institutional health of marriage, unions entered into for erotic gratification were less laudable – and likely to be even less durable – than unions contracted in search of emotional security.[30]

Professional experts cast back to World War I to add empirical heft to their grim projections. Just 5 percent of couples who wed during the Great War "could be described as happy," prominent psychologist Dr. David Seabury warned. How he presumed to know the state of these marriages was unclear.[31] But it wasn't pure speculation to point out that a spike in America's divorce rate had indeed followed hard on the heels of the armistice, reaching a peak in 1920. Where conscription acted as an accelerant to marriage, demobilization boosted divorce rates. This cycle couldn't be permitted to happen again, critics warned. Columbia sociologist Willard Waller, one of the country's foremost experts on veteran affairs, predicted that as many as 38 out of every 100 marriages were likely to collapse when World War II ended.[32]

Opinion-leaders tutted and sighed about young people justifying pre-marital intercourse as a prerogative owed to potentially doomed youth. They blamed both men and women for "sex delinquency," but tended to indict the latter more than the former.[33] "It is the girl who generally takes the initiative in these telescoped courtships," Tenenbaum huffed.[34] In popular discourse, "patriotutes" and "victory girls" emerged as objects of moral censure: young women who promiscuously had sex with soldiers, believing they were raising morale by lowering their morals.[35]

Worst of all, "downright sinister," as Tenenbaum saw it, was the bounty-hunting woman who preyed on emotionally insecure young men, not for carnal gratification but in search of the $50 monthly sum (termed an "allotment") the government gave soldiers' wives. Some criminally conniving women – without scruples, but with superior organizational skills – were reported to have lured multiple naive soldiers into polygamous unions. A few apparently managed to schedule more than one wedding on the same day. "Allotment Annie" became a vilified hate-figure of wartime culture: her notoriety set in celluloid as a B-movie anti-heroine.[36]

The Office of the Chaplain grew increasingly troubled by War Department strictures meant to deter enlisted men in the lowest three grades from marriage. Religious leaders viewed the conjugal state as both a civil right and a divine sacrament. Only up to a point, however. Chaplains were also in the business of deflecting soldiers from inter-racial marriages, citing the anti-miscegenation statutes several states maintained.[37] Since the armed forces themselves upheld segregation as an organizing principle, until President Truman desegregated the military in 1948, racialized prejudice wasn't simply foisted on a reluctant military from without. But some chaplains *did* challenge legislation designed to prevent men and women of different races from marrying. One Catholic padre, stationed at Fort Ord in California, drew his superiors' attention to the plight of many members of the First Filipino Regiment, to whom he ministered. The state of California refused to grant licenses for Filipino soldiers to "marry what the state calls 'white women.'" "It just happens that there are very few Filipina girls here and consequently they have to go out with white girls," Chaplain Noury explained to the Chief of Chaplains. "As I said there is a great number of our Filipino soldiers who are now living for several years with white girls and were never married ... and they have children." These men, desperate to formalize their unions, would soon be sent overseas, leaving "common law wives" and children unsupported.[38]

Noury's dismay over racist objections to "miscegenous" marriages intersected with another conundrum posed by soldiers' intimate relationships: namely, pregnancy outside wedlock. Should pregnant single women be denied an opportunity to legitimize their unborn children? And was it conscionable that babies begotten in the throes of "war hysteria" be punished for their parents' disregard of convention or misplaced patriotism? In January 1942, William R. Arnold (Chief of Chaplains) addressed the Adjutant General on a topic of growing concern:

> Chaplains of all denominations are placed in a serious predicament by
> their attempt to comply with the principle involved in these orders and
> regulations [discouraging marriage] and at the same time satisfy the

obligations which their churches place upon them to solemnize the marriage ceremony with a religious ritual for all those men of any grade and women who meet the civil requirements and come to them and request it.

In a roundabout way, Arnold alluded to the growing number of pregnancies for which unmarried men in uniform were responsible. There were, he proposed, many cases where marriage should be encouraged rather than discouraged "because of the *immediate necessities of the situation* and for reasons of military and civilian morale" [emphasis added]. While military chaplains disapproved of pre-marital sex, they tended to dislike the prospect of illegitimacy even more. In certain cases, army chaplains went beyond advocacy of a right to conjugality. Some padres prodded soldiers with no desire to marry pregnant girlfriends – or women who'd already given birth – to "do the right thing."[39]

As the pace of basic training and overseas deployment quickened, soldiers who wanted to marry found their opportunities curtailed. Furloughs simply weren't long enough to travel home, secure a license, have blood tests performed, arrange a ceremony, and attend it. Then there were men who discovered their girlfriends' or fiancées' pregnancies only *after* they landed overseas. Long-distance separation further complicated the military's conflicted stance on conjugality. One potential solution was "proxy" or "absentee" marriage: a wedding ceremony conducted either with a stand-in spouse or with the husband connected from afar via a radio-telephone hook-up. Staff of the American Red Cross (ARC), the charitable organization dedicated to connecting family members with loved ones in uniform, fielded an escalating number of requests for assistance with proxy marriages. A Red Cross meeting in September 1942 noted: "Most of the cases are the same and run about as follows: A girl, living in a local community, goes to the R.C. Chapter and says that she is expecting a baby and that the father of the expected child is a serviceman. She requests that the serviceman be communicated with to see if an absentee marriage can be arranged." Unlike some military chaplains, Red Cross field workers didn't think they should be in the business of trying to cajole reluctant men into marriage. Heavily dependent on volunteer labor, good will, and public donations, the Red

Cross worried about damaging its own reputation by facilitating ceremonies that local communities might regard as shot-gun affairs.[40]

Then there was the issue of legality. ARC representatives made repeated requests of the War Department for clarification on this score. Surveying the nation's crazy quilt of marriage laws, military legal advisers found that almost every state refused to accept the legitimacy of such unions. Since the War Department's Allotment Division didn't regard proxy marriages as lawful either, women who married husbands in absentia would find themselves denied the monthly payments that other wives received.[41] Proxy marriage encountered further stiff opposition from senior Catholic authorities, who let the Red Cross know that Rome did not approve of absentee ceremonies enabled by radio-telephone: an ethereal arrangement that made administration of the sacrament impossible.[42] Bishop John F. O'Hara, appointed by Pope Pius XII as an auxiliary bishop to the US Military Ordinariate in 1939, felt "these marriages had some of the aspects of a stunt such as the performance of a wedding ceremony in a balloon or at home plate in a ball park." But O'Hara wasn't concerned about the sacrament alone. He clearly sympathized with soldiers who'd never contemplated marriage when they became sexually involved with girls who "all too frequently," as he saw it, were not "of a caliber to warrant marriage."[43] O'Hara's disdain for unwed mothers left in abeyance the unborn child's right to legitimacy.

Discouraging omens and disparaging attitudes didn't prevent some women from heading to Kansas, one of two states that did recognize proxy marriages, and trying their luck. In Kansas City, one middle-aged trial lawyer became "the most-married man in America," as *Yank* put it. A contented husband for twenty-one years, Thomas Finnegan had acted as a stand-in groom for no fewer than thirty-nine brides by the war's end. He took the role seriously, *Yank* reassured its soldier readership, though the magazine's levity mightn't have mollified Bishop O'Hara. Sporting a dapper gray-flannel suit with a carnation in his buttonhole, Finnegan ensured that "his" brides carried a bouquet and enjoyed a festive lunch after their unorthodox wedding. Only once had he apparently experienced a twinge of bigamous guilt, when some tipsy guests at a reception began congratulating him, seeming to have forgotten that Finnegan was merely playing the absent husband's part.[44]

One way or another – near or far, in civvies or in uniform – Americans continued to wed during the war years at a prodigious rate. The swelling pool of husbands included those who married just prior to induction as well as a significant number of men who, once in the ranks, ignored the army's attempts to discourage matrimony. National census data reveal that a higher proportion of women under the age of twenty were married in 1944 than had been married in 1940. Three-quarters of these young wives had husbands in uniform.[45] All told, about half of the sixteen million American men who served in World War II were married.

Those minded to marry would have found plenty of reassuring prompts in patriotic war culture. For every Cassandra warning darkly of a postwar dash to the divorce courts, there was a defiant magazine feature about couples who "married anyway," revelling in the triumph of young love over wartime adversity. Numerous romance novels, department store window displays, and Hollywood movies celebrated conjugality and glamorized "war brides": a term first applied to American women before being redeployed to connote the foreign spouses of US soldiers overseas. In 1943, the pages of Anne Gudis's local newspapers, the *Newark Ledger* and *Newark Evening News*, overflowed with photos of beaming young brides and notices detailing betrothals between civilian females and uniformed fiancés. No wonder, then, that the more transgressive elements of Anne and Sam's courtship were tempered by the tug of marriage, with its patina of permanence amid so much uncertainty and flux. And if marriage promised emotional reassurance, it also made sex respectable. Early on in their relationship, Sam ruminated aloud on these matters: "Some fellows marry just for ?? Others marry to make it legal. Some have to – some for the real and sacred reasons – Wonder what mine will be."[46]

LOVE IN A COLD WAR CLIMATE

Military attempts to shape the marital decisions of men in uniform didn't end with the war, nor were they restricted to personnel serving in the continental United States. Efforts to steer soldiers away from what commanders viewed as ill-considered romantic choices were, in fact, more persistent and prolonged overseas than strictures against marriage initially applied stateside. If senior officers imagined that single men would make better disciplined soldiers – less encumbered by concerns about home, less apt to pine for distant partners or fret about their fidelity – their suppositions would soon be challenged by the behavior of GIs overseas. Men of every rank, regardless of marital status, proved eminently distractable when presented with opportunities for female companionship in the many foreign countries where Americans landed during and after the war, first as liberating or conquering forces, then as armies of occupation.[47]

Whether in Europe, Australasia, North Africa, or Asia, GIs lost little time in finding women with whom to have sex. The voracious enthusiasm of American servicemen for erotic experience came as no surprise to their commanding officers. Indeed, the latter sometimes made it their business to help facilitate soldiers' access to sex-workers, even overseeing the management of brothels in locations as far-flung as Hawai'i, Italy, France, and Japan. Several prominent generals shared George S. Patton's bluntly put view that fucking and fighting were complementary activities. They just had to shield this reality from American public view as best they could, for while some civilians tacitly accepted the proposition that men in uniform both needed and had earned carnal compensation, others expected soldiers to remain chaste. Social purity campaigners, responsible for the 1941 May Act that debarred prostitution from around US military camps, strove to keep sex and soldiering as far apart as possible.[48]

Senior commanders were neither shocked nor appalled by the carnal appetites of men under their leadership. Their major concern, other than trying to mask the military's involvement in the brothel business, was how to curb sexually transmitted diseases as they swept through the ranks.[49] What seemingly caught the brass more off-guard was that, for tens of thousands of American soldiers, sex wasn't the whole story – or perhaps even a substantial part of a story that was about love, companionship, and dreams of long-term commitment. GIs' eagerness to marry local women quickly became evident everywhere American troops landed in 1942 and 1943, from Britain to Australia, Iceland to Italy. More unexpected yet was the speed with which GIs petitioned to take

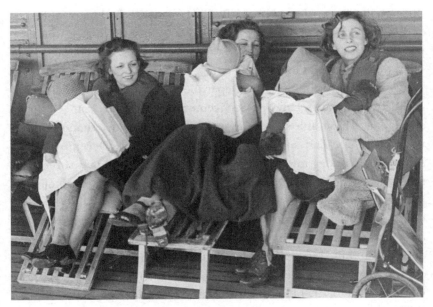

1.2. By 1946, British war brides and their babies were sailing across the Atlantic to join these women's husbands-in-uniform. (Courtesy of Picture Post/Hulton Archive/Getty Images.)

German and Japanese women as their brides – sometimes before hostilities had formally ended and while bans in former enemy territory on "fraternization" (a euphemistic substitute for a shorter F-word) remained in place.[50]

American soldiers' desire to wed foreign women shouldn't have taken their officers aback. Many doughboys sent overseas with the AEF in 1917, fathers and uncles of the current crop of GIs, were similarly smitten with French women and other foreigners they encountered in Europe. Some had petitioned for the right to marry overseas, as an historical report hastily compiled by Lt. Col. Albert B. Kellogg of the Army War College Historical Section attested.[51]

A quarter century later, amidst another world war, a fresh wave of marriage applications flooded in. Although War Department Circular 179 decreed that no soldier could marry overseas without his commander's consent, the directive didn't outright *prohibit* marriage. Instead, it presented couples with a formidable thicket of red tape they'd have to cut through in pursuit of permission. By 1944, many GIs had married British and other "war brides," looking forward to the time when it would be possible for these spouses to sail to the United States, and couples could build postwar futures together.[52]

It took longer for the War Department and civilian US leaders to authorize marriages between servicemen and women from Germany and Japan. These unions were more politically sensitive than weddings that involved Allied nationals, though, as early as December 1946, American attitudes toward their former foes had softened sufficiently that GIs were permitted to wed Germans.[53] Soldiers who hoped to marry Japanese brides confronted a different obstacle: longstanding barriers blocking Asian immigration to the United States. This ban on Asian "war brides" was lifted briefly in 1947 and again in 1950 by special presidential decree. But these temporary easements were far from a free pass. On the contrary, servicemen seeking permission for "alien spouses" to enter the United States in 1950 had to furnish proof that their partners were not "idiots, paupers, tubercular or other diseased persons, mental or physical defectives, draft evaders, criminals, polygamists, prostitutes, procurers or pimps, contract laborers, public charges, people previously deported and illiterates" – a catalog that reprised just about every anti-Asian trope in circulation since the nineteenth century.[54]

Several considerations underpinned prohibitions against servicemen marrying local women without commanders' approval: directives that remained in place into the 1980s. In some locations, the military recognized that feelings ran high in host countries where American men "taking" local women provoked nationalist hostility – sharpened by racial animosity when the GIs in question were Black.[55] The armed forces were also responsive to, and often shared, American civilians' judgments about foreign women and their acceptability (or otherwise) as prospective immigrants and putative citizens. But, more fundamentally, commanding officers mistrusted young soldiers' ability to make sensible decisions about their own emotional and financial wellbeing. And they worried that bad individual choices would have costly knock-on effects for institutions burdened with supporting foreign wives and widows. During the Korean war, Eighth Army commanders carefully stipulated how long after a soldier's death his "alien" widow would be permitted to shop in the PX, receive army medical care, and remain in married quarters before being relegated to a second tier of widowhood that wouldn't just debar her from access to American military facilities but from entry to the United States. (Sent into battle to Korea from occupation duty in Japan, the Eighth Army included many GIs with Japanese wives.) Thirty days into their bereavement, Japanese wives of American soldiers received a six-month "death gratuity" and were on their own. Widows lost entitlement to US citizenship along with their husbands and homes. By command of General Ridgway, Japanese women who'd lost their soldier-husbands were ineligible to enter the United States under Public Law 717, on the grounds that "a widow" was no longer a deceased US citizen's "spouse."[56]

The military shouldered responsibility for "alien" widows grudgingly and, as a result, only fleetingly. But what about divorcées? Military leaders worried that many marriages between American men and foreign women would rapidly end in divorce – as soon as the couple's fundamental incompatibility became clear. Marital dissolution would strain units forced to deal with distressed young men in the throes of emotionally wrenching separations. Taking a dim view of the maturity of lower ranking enlisted men, commanders harbored darker suspicions about the kind of females they thought set out to lure guileless American boys into marriage: women in pursuit of personal enrichment and fast-tracked admission into the United States.[57]

Racialized prejudice undoubtedly colored American attitudes toward foreign women. Asian girlfriends and fiancées of GIs were often damningly stereotyped as scheming predators: presumed to be bar girls, taxi dancers, and brothel workers looking to escape the sleazy entertainment districts that encircled US bases in South Korea, the Philippines, and Japan.[58] But white European women weren't free from stigmatizing judgment either. The Commander in Chief of US forces in Heidelberg cabled the Department of the Army in 1952 to complain about grasping German women who "attempt to entangle our pers[onnel], many of whom are young and impressionable and vulnerable to the blandishments of the 'wrong' people into marriage." His plea was that the Pentagon retain its restrictive policy on GI marriage overseas.[59]

The assumption that marriages between American men and foreign women were doomed to failure rested on insubstantial, often anecdotal, evidence. The same year that the Commander in Chief in Heidelberg was wiring his jaundiced views back to Washington, DC, a military chaplain in Japan undertook a study of 183 marriages between American servicemen and Japanese brides. Gomer Rees expressed surprise at several of his own findings, including the number of Japanese American husbands among his sample. He was "amazed at the length" of most couples' courtship. With only seventeen couples having known each other for less than a year prior to marriage, these unions weren't the product of "sudden infatuation." Musing on the fact that only one in four American marriages succeeded, Rees speculated that these Japanese–American partnerships enjoyed a "much higher possibility of success," based on the length of courtship, "favorable intelligence equality," and "sincerity of the parties."[60]

Between 1947 and 1959, 43,197 American soldiers fought their way through a daunting obstacle course to secure permission to marry Japanese women.[61] Yet the military's objections to biracial marriage didn't dissolve when it became clear that men in love wouldn't readily be deterred by voluminous paperwork or obligatory counseling by chaplains; nor would these relationships all unravel as soon as lust faded or the bride's allegedly avaricious aims became clear. In the 1960s, the locus of anxiety shifted as US involvement in Vietnam escalated, transporting an ever greater number of young American men to southeast Asia. Soon, US Military Assistance Command, Vietnam (MACV) was wrestling with the same dilemmas that earlier confronted the Eighth Army in Japan. According to military chaplains in Vietnam, "oriental war brides" constituted a "foremost problem" by 1965.[62]

That year it took an estimated four months for soldiers wishing to marry Vietnamese women to complete all the necessary forms. Additionally, they had to amass evidence attesting their fiancées' moral character and good health, including notarized supporting statements from parents (if the prospective bride was under twenty-one) and a police "certificate of good conduct."[63] A study made by Captains William Kenny and Albert Kastl of sixty-four GI marriage applicants in 1967 offered evidence for those striving to deter men from marrying by demeaning their character and fitness to make sound choices. There was, the captains proposed, "a definite kind of individual who is prone to marry a Vietnamese woman": an under-educated man, likely from a broken home, possibly with a prior broken marriage, who had a "marked fear of American women," preferring Vietnamese because he regarded the "oriental woman as passive and understanding."[64]

As more GIs arrived in-country and the number of petitioners rose, so too did the bureaucratic hurdles. By 1971, aspiring husbands had to submit no fewer than nineteen different pieces of corroborative evidence alongside Form 2029, "Application for Permission to Marry." If the applicant hoped to wed during his twelve-month-long tour, rather than revisiting Vietnam to complete the process, he needed to move swiftly. A system intended to curb "impetuous marriages" perversely encouraged men to rush toward matrimony with women whom they'd met in the first six months of their tour. Wait any longer and the GI risked having to make a return-trip most enlisted men could ill-afford.[65]

This wasn't the only paradoxical aspect of the military's relationship with marriage during the Vietnam era. As in previous wars, the army favored young, single men as draftees – only then to fault teenage GIs for their immaturity in forming romantic attachments to "inappropriate" women they encountered overseas. Stateside, the Pentagon's initial reluctance to draft married men again prompted some couples to marry quickly, hoping the husband would be spared service in Vietnam. A lengthy *New York Times Magazine* analysis of the draft in 1965 noted that the "tendency to teen-age, or at least exceptionally early, marriages has added another large, deferrable category," alongside college students.[66] Of 10.1 million American men aged from nineteen to twenty-six who hadn't yet seen military service, 3,226,000 were classified III-A (a hardship designation that included married fathers).[67] Alert to the rise of perceived "draft-dodger marriages," Johnson's administration changed tack. On August 26, 1965, President Lyndon B. Johnson revoked the ruling under which childless married men would be called for induction only *after* the pool of single men aged between nineteen and twenty-six had been drained. LBJ's executive order, intentionally issued just hours before the policy change went into effect, set off a stampede to marry.[68]

Anyone familiar with the events of 1917 and 1940 could have predicted that couples would flock to cities in which no "cooling off" period was required between securing a marriage license and the ceremony itself. The morning after Johnson's announcement, the *Washington Post* reported a "bridal wave" that had slammed Las Vegas the night before. One Justice of the Peace alone performed sixty-seven "I do-and-dash" ceremonies. All told, this JP and his colleagues conducted 171 ceremonies, of which 112 took place between 10pm and midnight, with couples flying in from as far afield as Chicago, Kansas, and New Jersey. The *Post* conjured a tragicomic scene, noting that many couples – in their haste to wed at warp speed – neglected even to bring rings with them. Brides appeared in dungarees, and one more traditionally attired newlywed loaned her veil to five other women who'd come without. Some husbands-to-be were accompanied by mothers who, to the JPs involved, appeared more eager than either the bride or the groom for the ceremony to go ahead – desperate that their sons "wouldn't have to go off and fight in that stupid war," as one woman put it. If anxious moms felt relieved when a slipshod knot was tied, the young women their sons married didn't all revel in a shared sense of malign fate averted. "Some of the brides were backing off. The mood was very rushed," noted James Brennan, the JP who clocked up the largest number of ceremonies. "Not all of the fiancées were ready for the 'till-death-do-us-part' stuff."[69]

Almost overnight, it became clear that these fast-moving couples hadn't necessarily evaded fate after all. Some *were* subsequently parted by the draft. Conservative columnist Drew Pearson noted gleefully that the "first married men without children will be ordered to duty after Christmas." New husbands could expect to find themselves in Vietnam in 1966. This, he hoped, would stamp out the greatest epidemic of draft dodging since the Civil War. Only married men with children would continue to be deferred, but even fathers became eligible for the draft in 1970.[70]

By the 1960s, marriage was under pressure from changing sexual mores, hastened by the licensing of the birth control pill in 1963. At the same time, second wave feminism encouraged women to prioritize educational and professional goals before they married and began families, or to flout society's conjugal expectations altogether. "The New

1.3. Bill Bradley, twenty, and Patty Mason, eighteen, both of Glendale, California, formed part of a "bridal wave" that hit Las Vegas on August 26, 1965, as couples tried to beat President Johnson's edict that men married after midnight on that date would become eligible for the draft. (Courtesy of Bettmann/Getty Images.)

Left, the antiwar movement, black power, women's liberation, and gay liberation – along with the hippies and flower children who constituted themselves the counterculture – all fused dissident politics with purposeful cultural disobedience and devil-may-care hijinks centering on defiance of sexual norms," notes historian of marriage Nancy Cott.[71] Yet the draft introduced countervailing pressures. An unpopular war with voracious military manpower needs impelled young Americans toward marital vows they mightn't otherwise have made, which some spouses regretted or found impossible to honor. Some couples were pulled by the draft toward marriage, swimming upstream against the tide of social change. As the war lengthened and US involvement deepened, "war marriage" once again became a compound noun with an ironic edge more suggestive of volatility than permanence.

THE "MOST MARRIED MILITARY": THE ALL-VOLUNTEER ERA

Marriage was one of the ruinous war in Vietnam's many casualties. Social commentators and professional experts made this observation while US troops served in southeast Asia, doubling down on their verdict after the last units were withdrawn in 1973. Their judgment – that war was good at stimulating marriage rates, but bad for sustaining relationships – repeated a familiar pattern. Both world wars, as well as the conflicts in Korea and Vietnam, were followed by instant post mortems into the military's "divorce crisis." Crisis-talk in turn gave way to prolonged debates among demographers about whether veterans' marriages were in fact more unstable than civilian couples' unions. If so, which "variables" did the most damage to what, exactly?[72]

Like many marriages, the US military also emerged broken from the war in Vietnam. With the armed forces demoralized and in disarray, the Pentagon pondered the dynamics that had fueled attacks by enlisted men on their officers ("fraggings"), racial strife within the ranks, rampant drug use, and high rates of desertion.[73] A major institutional overhaul followed. Henceforth, the United States would populate its armed forces and fight its wars with volunteers: men and women for whom military service was a profession, not an obligation. But first the services had to recruit fresh personnel or persuade those who'd passed muster in Vietnam to re-enlist. To attract and retain soldiers of higher caliber (as the brass saw it) than the often poorly educated, indisciplined, and increasingly mutinous draftees swept into the ranks during Vietnam, the armed forces needed to make their terms of service more attractive. Over the next couple of decades, higher salaries, less spartan accommodation, and better welfare provision for married soldiers and "dependents" (spouses and children) would emerge as part of this package.[74]

The 1980s marked the onset of a more avowedly "family-friendly" military: an aura the army, air force, and navy have continued to project and burnish over half a century. Where the War Department had earlier tried to discourage junior enlisted men from marrying, the post-Vietnam services increasingly made a boast of accommodating couples with children. For the first time, these appeals addressed soldiers in the lowest three ranks (E1–E3) hitherto denied benefits enjoyed by more senior ranks, such as commissary privileges, dependents' medical care, and on-base family housing or subsidized privately rented accommodation. The proportion of married personnel in uniform grew rapidly. By 1978, nearly 60 percent of soldiers were married – a rapid rise from the Vietnam-era nadir of 46 percent just a decade earlier.[75]

Army wives, married women soldiers, and female veterans played a major role in pushing the institution toward more generous welfare provision, healthcare benefits, and other policies that would enable pregnant servicewomen and soldiers with children to combine parenting with career advancement.[76] Their activism helped prompt the abandonment of longstanding Pentagon policy that took pregnancy to be inimical to military service. Even though women were permitted to marry while serving in the Women's Army Corps during and after World War II, between 1951 and 1975 female service members could be – and were – discharged for pregnancy or parenthood. (The latter stipulation meant that women could neither adopt children nor become step-mothers and remain in the service.) Formal discrimination against pregnant women soldiers ended in the mid 1970s, and by 1983 the "military family" encompassed one-and-a-half times as many dependents as personnel in uniform.[77]

The Marine Corps alone bucked the "family-friendly" trend. General Carl E. Mundy announced on August 11, 1993 that the USMC would phase out enlistment of married applicants by 1995. The reasoning behind this policy change was familiar. In a service that required low-ranking personnel to undertake long tours away from home, "an inordinate number of marriages" ended in divorce, "disrupting the individual's concentration level" and denting the operational readiness of the institution they served. So said a Directive announced in Mundy's name.[78] Just like the paternalism that underpinned the War Department's former directives against marriage overseas, the Marine Corps' logic combined expressions of concern for the wellbeing of immature men with mistrust of the wives they chose, or who (some Marine generals suspected) chose *them*. "Getting married at age 18 and 19 – and in many cases the men marrying girls who were younger – in our profession that's just very difficult," opined General Walter E. Boomer, the Marine Corps assistant commandant.[79] The Corps feared that policies intended to incentivize marriage had paradoxically succeeded so well that "family friendliness" itself contributed to a doubling of divorce rates for marines since 1983. With married privates who had dependents earning approximately $17,100 in salary and benefits, as opposed to the $9,770 for single privates, young couples married hastily in pursuit of material perks. But then they struggled to make their relationships work. The average failed marriage lasted just two years.[80]

Mundy's directive came under instant and heavy fire. Some commentators bristled that, with the "Don't Ask, Don't Tell" policy in place, LGB personnel could serve in the military, albeit not openly, yet the Marine Corps now wanted to debar married heterosexuals. Taking a different tack, Representative Patricia Schroeder, the third-ranking Democrat on the House Armed Services Committee, pointedly asked: "If [marines] are not allowed to be homosexuals and they're not allowed to be married, what are they supposed to do, take cold showers?" Before the day ended, however, Defense Secretary Les Aspin had thrown cold water over Mundy's directive, about which neither he nor the Commander in Chief himself had apparently been consulted. The Marine Corps hurriedly backed down. Married men and women continued to enlist. But despite its tactical retreat, the USMC announced that it would step up its chaplaincy-delivered program of pre-marital counseling aimed at encouraging marines to delay marriage plans, or drop them altogether.[81]

Military prescriptions governing *servicewomen* and marriage were even more fitful and capricious than rules for enlisted men, emerging from a tangled web of concerns about sexuality, respectability, and maternity. The army's traditional preference for single male recruits combined economic hard-headedness – wives and widows cost money to maintain – with worries about the psychological pitfalls of marriage for military men. Uxorious husbands were liable to yearn for spouses to the detriment of professional focus, while men in less felicitous marriages were (as commanders saw it) apt to fret over their wives' fidelity, excessive spending, or neglectful parenting, perturbed by the prospect – or fact – of divorce. Army and Marine Corps commanders viewed servicewomen's spouses quite differently, however. They seemingly feared husbands less as emotional distractions than as potential inseminators of female soldiers who, once pregnant, would be useless to the services. Thus, as the official history of women marines crisply noted of the period from 1948 to 1964, "marriage was indeed acceptable; husbands and children, however, posed some problems."[82] This problem was tallied in women's discharges for pregnancy, not the cost of allotments payable to servicewomen's spouses. Until challenged by a Supreme Court ruling in 1973, the prevailing military ethos remained that husbands were *ipso facto* household breadwinners.[83]

For much of the twentieth century, the armed forces construed women's military service as a brief professional sortie prior to marriage, or certainly before motherhood, rather than a long-term vocation. From its founding in 1901, the Army Nurse Corps (ANC) accepted only single women. The ANC lifted its ban on married recruits during World War II to meet the exponentially greater need for trained nurses, a move the Navy Nurse Corps replicated – but not until January 1945.[84] If the Women's Army Auxiliary Corps (or Women's Army Corps as it became in 1943) appeared more liberal in permitting married women to serve, this ostensible progressivism owed a good deal to the Corps' pressing PR problems. A slander campaign instantly engulfed the WAAC on its inception in 1942. Wildfire rumors spread, fanned most strenuously by disgruntled GIs, that this novel outfit was a hotbed of lesbianism and/or a corps of "camp followers" mustered as sexual "playthings" for the officer class. Recruitment of respectable married women, including those with children no longer "dependent," promised to help dispel the thick pall of sexual immorality that hovered over the new organization, choking the supply of recruits.[85] An Army Signal Corps promotional film for the WAC, *We're in the Army Now* (1943), featured a matronly applicant with grown offspring who wasn't deterred by the prospect of having to "reduce" a little in order to meet the body-mass criteria for eligibility, promptly shedding some pounds and re-presenting herself for induction. As for single Wacs stationed overseas, they were permitted to marry (with commanders' consent) in North Africa, the Mediterranean, and the Middle East. But if a Wac married another soldier in the ETO, one spouse was immediately transferred out of theater or to a distant post within it – a zero-honeymoon policy intended to deter pregnancy.[86]

After 1945, the military executed a sharp about-turn, making itself inhospitable to women in general, and wives with children in particular. By 1946, the ranks of the WAC had dwindled to a few thousand women. Married nurses were permitted to serve in the ANC for just six months after the war ended. Strikingly, when the Corps started accepting male recruits for the first time in 1955, the latter *could* be married, for much the same reason that married Wacs were acceptable during World War II. The WAC and ANC wanted to reassure social conservatives that there was nothing alarmingly "mannish" about female soldiers, nor "effeminate" about male nurses – with all the connotations of sexual "inversion" implied by these loaded epithets – despite the gendered role-reversals their recruitment seemed to signal. Not surprisingly, many women in the ANC bristled at the inequity. But it took the Vietnam war to push the services to level the marital field for straight men and women, not just for the duration but for good. Starting in December 1964, married women were permitted to enlist in both the WAC and the ANC. By October 1967, nearly a quarter of ANC personnel were married.[87]

Since the Vietnam war, the number of women serving – and the roles open to them in the armed forces – have both greatly expanded. In 1973, when the All-Volunteer era began, women represented just 2 percent of enlisted forces and 8 percent of officers. In 2020, women comprised 16 percent of enlisted personnel and 19 percent of officers, with some marked variations between the different services.[88] Marriage has become normative in the "army family," but it's striking that a higher proportion of male soldiers are married than are female personnel. By the 1980s, while men in uniform were statistically *more* likely to be married than civilian peers of the same age, this demographic trend was inverted for women in the military. In the twenty-first century, it remained the case that fewer women in uniform were married than were their male peers. (DoD statistics from 2010 tabulated this female : male differential as 46 percent to 58 percent.) It's also telling that married men in uniform were more likely to have children than their female counterparts: an imbalance indicative of the greater challenges women soldiers confront in meeting the gender-specific demands of two "greedy institutions," the military and family.[89] Women soldiers are more likely to be separated from their spouses due to military assignments, and are more often married to other soldiers in so-called "dual service couples." Most revealingly of all, the marriages of female personnel fail at a significantly higher rate than those of male soldiers.

During the recent wars in Iraq and Afghanistan, military researchers have repeatedly revalidated this finding.[90] As divorce became an ever more pressing concern for the overstretched and serially redeployed military of the twenty-first century, the armed forces devised a battery of new programs aimed at shoring up couples. Yet even though servicewomen's marriages statistically appear more insecure, interventions like the army's "Strong Bonds" initiative and its Comprehensive Soldier Fitness 2 (CSF2) program, to promote "resilience" in military couples and families, primarily target the wives of men in uniform, not the husbands of female soldiers. That, at any rate, is the message signaled by promotional materials and websites showcasing men who wear uniform and women who do not.[91]

The military's angsty ambivalence about marriage has long focused on wives as the disorderly force to be managed. "While a wife is a partial contributor to her husband's success, she can be the principal cause of his failure," noted the (female) author of a guidebook for army wives in 1958, encapsulating the time-honored conviction that whatever psychological and practical support a wife might provide her husband was outweighed by the greater harm she could inflict.[92] But then, and arguably still now, there's no reciprocal understanding that the spouses of women in uniform can torpedo their wives' careers, divert their focus, and throw their emotional equilibrium off balance – unless husbands internalize rules for playing appropriately supportive and subordinate roles in their marriages.

Just as there's no "male war bride," except as a figure of Hollywood fun, so the "army husband" remains a socially unrecognized figure.[93] By the same token, the "Dear Jane," a phrase not coined until the 1950s, remains a pale shadow of the "Dear John," although female soldiers' divorce rates suggest that some women must surely have been left by their husbands – whether the notification came by mail or otherwise. To trace the history of the "Dear John" and the charged force field around it is thus to chart uneven terrain. Men's emotional needs have existed on a higher plane than those of women, in uniform or out.

"IF THE ARMY ..."

"... had wanted you to have a wife, it would have issued you one." This quip is at least as longstanding as the Dear John letter. Marines make the same joke, simply substituting "Marine Corps" for "Army." Although for decades the armed forces have proclaimed themselves hospitable to, and nurturing of, couples and families, members of the services still repeat an adage that suggests otherwise. Marriage remains hard to combine with military service, particularly when periods of long-distance separation are a fact of professional life.

Military attitudes toward romantic intimacy – within and outside marriage – have been snarled in various binds throughout modern history. In wartime, the United States' draft machinery targeted young, unmarried men as the forces' preferred labor power. Wives seemingly spelled trouble: ideological, economic, and emotional. And foreign fiancées sounded even louder alarm bells, posing risks to security, diplomacy, and citizenship. Yet, however much they feared "entangling alliances" between men in uniform and women, American or "alien," senior commanders regarded male soldiers as "red-blooded" and libidinous. Their sexual needs required gratification – so long, that is, as men's preferences ran in approved heterosexual directions. And if sex was part of the package of soldiering, then women had to be, too.

In August 1965, a week before LBJ's attempt to quash "draft-dodging" marriages, the estimable *New York Times* reporter James Reston, then stationed in Saigon, offered an observation on MACV's lavish efforts to make the Republic of Vietnam as luxurious a posting as wartime circumstances could permit:

> The Pentagon has provided most of the conveniences of home. It has picked up America and moved it to the South China Sea. It has brought along not only its planes, ships, bombs, cars and trucks, but also its refrigerators, air-conditioners, movies, radio networks, newspapers, preachers and psychiatrists – everything that makes life tolerable except its women, who are the one problem of power the Pentagon has never solved.[94]

Not for want of trying, however. Waging "war on boredom," MACV introduced five-day Rest & Recuperation leaves for men who'd been in country for six months, with enticing destinations such as Thailand, Okinawa, Australia, Hong Kong, Japan, and Hawai'i. Married soldiers could fly their wives out to join them, with airfares and hotel rooms sufficiently subsidized to put R&R within reach of enlisted men. But, for many men, the recreational sex that was R&R's biggest draw was provided by commercial sex-workers. Reston's proposition that life was "intolerable" without American women was countered by hundreds of thousands of GIs who took advantage of R&R opportunities. Foreign women could seemingly make a tour in Vietnam at least temporarily bearable.[95] "The R&R program gives him visions and memories of another world," boasted MACV's 1967 Command History.[96] It was unfortunate, then, that a publicity stunt to celebrate the "one millionth R&R" enjoyed by a serviceman in Vietnam – intended to stress the respectably conjugal pleasures it afforded – fell apart when the wife of the serviceman in question failed to appear in Hawai'i. Instead, she sent him a Dear John letter.

Over the course of the twentieth century, the military oscillated between promoting chastity and providing sex; sometimes preaching abstinence while medical officers surreptitiously supplied condoms or facilitated soldiers' access to commercial sex-workers. The armed forces, and their civilian champions, have likewise bounced between attempts to deter marriage and to promote conjugality. "War marriage" would end in tears, young Americans were warned: a claim repeated in both world wars, Korea, and Vietnam. Rushed weddings held out the prospect of "prolonged misery during the period of reconstruction and cannot be assumed even to be of benefit to the married couple while separated in the emergency situation" one marriage "expert" warned in World War II.[97] Yet constant repetition did little to impede couples intent on marrying. Men who wanted to avoid military service, taking advantage of exemptions draft boards initially extended to married men, rushed to marry. Others wanted to exchange vows prior to long, hazardous, perhaps permanent, separations.

The military's exclusionary policies that debarred queer Americans from openly serving until 2011 shaped both romantic commitments and sexual identities in curious ways. Some straight men looking to avoid the draft (in World War II and Vietnam) presented themselves as gay. Draft boards duly trained a suspicious eye on men who seemed too eager to announce their homosexuality, suspecting them as "hoaxosexuals" who were merely performing a masquerade.[98] Meanwhile, some gay men and lesbians who enlisted despite screening procedures intended to keep them out, entered into opposite-sex relationships – including marriages – to provide "cover." Others invented fictitious partners. One lesbian sergeant who served in Operation Iraqi Freedom got caught up in an extended pretence involving an imaginary boyfriend her colleagues became increasingly curious to meet. Exhausted by the charade, she ended it by telling them she'd sent him a Dear John.[99]

The armed forces have exerted extraordinary – often contradictory – pressures on the romantic lives of Americans. With the approach or condition of war hastening many couples' courtships, the military has

1.4. The 1,000,000 R&R "prize-winner," wearing a black beret on the left, is pictured shopping for his wife. Having expected her to join him in Hawai'i, he received a Dear John letter instead. "Boy was the army PO'd when this happened to this poor SOB," recalled the photographer, "plus all the work we had done was down the drain." (Ted Acheson Collection courtesy of the Vietnam Center and Sam Johnson Vietnam Archive, Texas Tech University.)

found itself in the business of trying to keep these unions intact for the duration, no matter how ill-advised commanders may have considered them. More worrisome even than a married soldier was a man in uniform whose romantic relationship was sliding toward dissolution. That goal meant stemming the tide of Dear Johns that repeatedly threatened to overwhelm men at war.

CHAPTER 2

Rules of Engagement, or "Write Right!"

WE RECOGNIZE THE IMAGES FROM HOLLYWOOD MOVIES, old newsreels, and wartime photojournalism. Soldiers gather in an expectant throng; spirits are high, exuberance playfully hammed for the cameras. At the center of the crowd, a junior NCO calls out names, cracking jokes as he hands over envelopes and dispenses parcels. Hastily torn open, letters are read with rapt attention. Buddies lean in to share news over one another's shoulders, while a few hunker down alone at the edge of the crowd to snatch a moment's solitary communion with loved ones back home. The men might be naked from the waist up, simmering in the thick tropical soup of the Marianas or the Mekong Delta, or they might be buttoned into olive drab woollens, stacked up on bunks in chilly barracks. Although the tableau could have been captured in any decade since the camera first froze soldiers on the battlefield and off during the Civil War, the name for this scene has remained unchanged. A hallowed ritual of military life – a staple of patriotic iconography – this is unmistakably "Mail Call."[1]

Orchestrators of wartime sentiment have long touted the symbiotic relationship between mail and morale, employing an array of similes to convey the potent properties of letters from home. Mail forms a "bridge" or a "chain" linking distant loved ones. "It is the letter, coming and going, that alone makes the separation of war endurable," editorialized the *Los Angeles Times* in June 1917.[2] Like food, letters supply sustenance craved by perennially hungry soldiers, giving them "a whiff of home."[3] They energize like a pep-pill, but also provide insulation from harm like protective armor. "A woman's letters to a man abroad are a proven secret weapon," *Vogue* reminded readers in June 1944.[4] No wonder, then, that in successive twentieth-century wars the government should have intervened to facilitate the flow of caring words – and more tangible care packages – between "here" and "there." During World War II and later conflicts in Korea and Vietnam, Congress authorized free mailing privileges for uniformed personnel, while significantly cutting the cost paid by civilians to send letters and parcels to men and women serving overseas.[5]

Federal agencies, commercial advertisers, and a host of interested parties bombarded Americans with sharp reminders that the primary obligation of civilians on the home front wasn't buying war bonds, digging for victory, or retooling for work in defense-related industries. It was writing letters to men in uniform. "Ask a service man what his biggest single morale booster is and he will probably reply that it is mail from home," opined an editorial in the *New York Times* in May 1951. By then, the eleven-month-old Korean war was mired in a stalemate that would persist for another two years, while the combatants haggled over POWs and their repatriation. GIs already considered themselves the neglected footsoldiers of a "forgotten war" in a country few Americans knew anything about. Dug in against North Korean and Chinese forces, US troops were waging an "unnecessary extra battle against despondency, lonesomeness and the terrible feeling of being unloved and forgotten by the folks back home," one sergeant darkly warned. "A letter or package from home may at times be more welcome than a whole boatload of vaudeville performers," the *Times* exhorted readers who might've neglected to put pen to paper recently.[6]

Mobilizing legions of letter writers on the home front was only one part of the equation, however. The twin challenge lay in ensuring that civilians "wrote right." For if mail could do more than steak, ice-cream, beer, and Bob Hope to boost morale, then the corollary also stood to reason. Few or no letters from home – or dispiriting messages from loved ones – threatened to deflate individual esprit and corrode group cohesion. As one journalist put it in 1953, "the man without a letter" at mail call was "like a puppy without a bone or a baseball fan without his peanuts."[7] Worse yet, "blue moods" were contagious, one man's gloomy

2.1. Mail Call for Marines on the road to Changkin Reservoir, Korea, November 15, 1950. "There is no soldier who isn't delighted to receive mail from home," ran the original caption. "They show a kind of reverence as they eagerly scan the letters from the U.S." (Courtesy of Bettmann/Getty Images.)

withdrawal or sullen demeanour quickly poisoning the unit's atmosphere. The "secret weapon" touted by *Vogue* might, if mishandled, prove lethal. Civilians were thus repeatedly tutored in the delicate, yet vital, art of how to write to soldiers. And since the armed forces regarded the provision of emotional support as an essentially feminine duty of care, their instructional efforts targeted women in particular, as did those of civilian attitude-shapers who lent their services to this disciplinary effort.

Military policies aimed at shaping soldiers' romantic choices found a counterpart in wartime efforts to accelerate the flow and regulate the tenor of women's correspondence with men in uniform. How to dissuade female letter writers from giving voice to their own gnawing anxieties and troubles, ensuring they produced only the kind of cheery, newsy missives soldiers apparently craved? And how to make sure that women's love, once proffered to a man in uniform, wasn't withheld or withdrawn in a devastating letter? The tricky business of sustaining intimate relationships across geographic distance – and over often unknown expanses of time – repeatedly vexed the military establishment at war, beginning with the seemingly simple question of who should write to whom.

SOLDIERS AND "STRANGE GIRLS"

Given the cyclical calls for civilians to set pen to paper and boost the morale of lonely soldier boys far from home, it might seem peculiar that some women who responded most avidly to these pleas should have been told to desist. Unease over soldiers' correspondence with females unknown to them was palpable during the Great War. Clues as to the nature of this wariness can be found in the pages of the *Indianapolis Star*, which, like many other local papers, sought to channel civic participation in the war effort. In August 1917, the *Star* trumpeted a novel plan to provide the name of "a Sammy for any patriotic backer who would lighten the burden of a soldier training or at the front." ("Sammy," a uniformed representative of Uncle Sam, was a nickname for soldiers serving with the American Expeditionary Forces – more common than the better-remembered term "doughboy.") Sammy Backers would not just send letters to doughboys but keep them supplied with "magazines, Thanksgiving boxes, Christmas and birthday presents, 'smokes' and the thousand and one other little things that will readily suggest themselves" – myriad modest luxuries "no reasonable man could expect state or nation to furnish." In short order, a "Sammy Backer Club" sprang into existence, complete with its own theme tune that swelled to a rousing finale: "Don't you be a Slacker, Come, be a Sammy Backer, Cheer a Fighting Lad!" But there was one catch. The first rule of eligibility stated bluntly, "You must be a man."[8]

Female readers of the *Star* soon protested. One disgruntled nineteen-year-old scolded the editor that she was just as capable of meeting the interests of Sammy as any man, and would gladly brief him on national

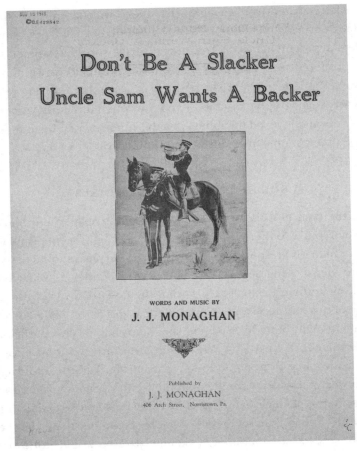

2.2. Sammy Backers – male-only volunteers who wrote to doughboys serving with the American Expeditionary Forces during World War I – had their own theme song, with lyrics and music by J. J. Monaghan. (Courtesy of the Library of Congress.)

events as well as matters dearer to the Hoosier's heart. Since Sammy was going to France "to fight for me and those of my sex," women were more indebted to doughboys than were their male peers, yet had fewer ways to do their "patriotic bit," this unnamed writer lamented. "Girls are 'cowardies,' so the men say," another scoffed, insisting that if repressive and misguided gender norms prevented them from fighting, then women should surely be permitted to do more writing. A twelve-year-old, "knitting wash cloths now for the boys who love Uncle Sam," pled her case for admission to the club, while older women also rebuked the paper for its discriminatory policy. Their petitions insisted that they had no desire to "write foolishness" to a young man; nor were they drawn to the "romance" of corresponding with a soldier or sailor.

These matronly protestors, disavowing the dubious motives they ascribed to thrill-seeking flibbertigibbets, only reinforced the *Star*'s resolve. The men-only membership policy was shared by other newspapers that sponsored Sammy Backer clubs. The *Star* continued to insist that Hoosier doughboys wanted, above all, "the friendly interest of an older man" – even when the paper's initial appeals to men above draft age failed to produce sufficient volunteers. Sammy "doesn't want any of the flowery stuff about the 'balmy breezes' and the 'calm and placid lake,'" the like-minded *Arizona Republican* chimed, disparaging what it regarded as the ineffable whimsy of feminine letter-writing style. "Sammy wants letters, a man's letters, man's ideas, man's comfort." Women could assist this effort, but only relegated to the rear echelon of "Sammy backer-backers," knitting socks, parting with some "pin money" for tobacco, and chivvying older men to sign up for club membership.[9]

The underlying concern exceeded matters of literary style. The *Star* feared that women mightn't just fill their letters with frivolity, but would subvert the paper's patriotic venture for their own sentimental purposes, seeking not so much to support Sammy as to seduce him. As historian William Kuby has shown, the 1890s and early 1900s witnessed a backlash against what critics deemed a crude "commercialization" of the sacred institution of marriage. These conjugal crusaders took aim at the people, institutions, and practices they deemed responsible. Their targets ranged from matrimonial advertisements – and the women who responded to bachelors' and widowers' solicitations for female companionship – to the alarming spread of spurious marriage bureaus. The latter inveigled solitary men into parting with significant sums on the promise of a prospective spouse's photograph and contact information. Invariably, however, the pictures turned out to be portraits of glamorous actresses, not eligible spinsters: a bait and switch that left swindled lonely-hearts to nurse their wounded pride and emptied pockets alone. The first decade of the twentieth century saw several well-publicized trials of fraudsters involved in the fake fiancée racket, with a number of unscrupulous female entrepreneurs ending up behind bars.[10]

The cloud of suspicion that enveloped women whose only crime was answering personal advertisements didn't quickly dissipate. Newspapermen found women's eagerness to volunteer as Sammy backers indecent. The more passionately women asserted their patriotic bona fides, the higher they stoked these fears. Surely, they protested their unsentimental interest in Sammy too much. A chaplain with the First Infantry at Schofield Barracks in Hawai'i confirmed the wisdom of the *Star*'s single-sex policy in a letter the paper reproduced at length. Correspondence between "soldiers and strange girls would, in the majority of cases, soon 'smack of piquancy' . . . and would eventually do more harm than good," the vexed padre warned. If "girls" were to write to soldiers at all, they should be young ladies known to the soldier – and his mother. A "mere" state of war, the chaplain reasoned, provided insufficient reason for "overthrowing convention."[11]

Since the military establishment shared this mistrust of "strange girls," the convention remained in place not only throughout the Great War but also during the World War that followed it. In May 1942, the War Department announced that its "approval would not be given under any circumstances to plans to encourage correspondence between soldiers and unknown civilians." The American Red Cross, the agency dedicated to facilitating contact between home and fighting fronts, was put on notice, while the *Army Guide for Women* (1942) reminded "letter-writing enthusiasts" that the army forbade servicemen from replying to mail sent by those "not really known to them." Letters opportunistically addressed to "The Private Who Receives No Mail" – invariably from "girls wishing to correspond with soldiers," tutted one journalist – went straight to the morale officer for destruction.[12]

In the very same month that the War Department publicized its disapproval of "unknown civilians" writing to men in uniform, Anne Gudis did exactly that. Initiating a correspondence with a man she'd never met, she was well aware that there was something unorthodox – untoward, even, in skeptics' eyes – about a single woman presuming to address a soldier she didn't know. In this case, the taint of impropriety was mitigated by the fact that Sam Kramer was the brother of a friend of

Anne's closest female friend from college. For several weeks she teasingly kept him guessing as to which mutual acquaintance had played the role of Cupid in providing his APO address. But, as Sam pointed out, "to tease by means of a letter is mild compared to a 'tease' in other expressions."[13] Within a fortnight, Sam was writing both regularly and racily to Anne, even though "it is slightly on the difficult side to continue a correspondence with one who one has never seen, nor held in one's arms, either kissed or tenderly embraced with full affection." Sam followed this rhapsodic riff with a cautionary warning he was writing not only to Anne but "about seven other girls." So, she needn't start forming any premature notions of exclusivity.[14]

The brass's fear that surreptitious romances might distract servicemen's attention intersected with civilians' concerns that they would simultaneously detract from young women's reputations. But these weren't the sole considerations behind the attempted embargo on correspondence between soldiers and strangers. During World War II, as in earlier and later wars alike, the military establishment stopped worrying that civilians weren't writing enough letters only to start fretting that too *much* mail would inundate the military postal service. Sammy backers and women who independently attempted to "adopt" soldiers in France during World War I must have been disappointed to find that censorship rules soon prohibited servicemen from corresponding with strangers on the grounds that excess volume would "choke" the mail, delaying important communications.[15] The War Department offered the same rationale during the next world war, and certainly the quantities of mail Americans dispatched were prodigious. Over the course of this conflict, the number of items handled by the postal service ballooned from approximately 28 billion pieces in 1940 to almost 38 billion in 1945.[16]

Official strictures may have tamped down civic initiatives to muster pen-pals for servicemen during World War II, but soldiers used private initiative to seek out women with whom they might exchange letters. Many of the GIs who sent notes and V-mails to Anne Gudis after *Yank* published her riposte to Sam Kramer did so with a view to securing a new female correspondent. Anne evidently had some prior experience in the business of writing to soldiers, even if the published specimen of her handiwork left something to be desired in terms of both length and tone.

Some requested not only a response but the promise of a long deferred date when the war finally ended. "As long as you told your old boyfriend to go to hell, how about me putting in an application?" inquired one hopeful staff sergeant.[17] Others professed themselves wholly unconcerned by Anne's relationship status. They just wanted a pen-pal or prospective girlfriend who'd send them a longer, sweeter V-mail than the one Kramer got, preferably accompanied by that other much sought-after wartime commodity – a photo. To improve the odds on receiving an affirmative reply, inquisitive GIs included compliments on Anne's *chutzpah*, as well as plaudits for the boost she'd provided to men in the ETO. "While you must have torn up the morale of one soldier and broken his heart you make thousands of us laugh," gushed a private stationed in North Africa, well aware of the double-edged relationship between mail and morale. One man's heartbreak could inspire other men's horseplay.[18]

Some of these strangers in uniform exhibited an unapologetic air of entitlement. As far as they were concerned, Anne *owed* them a reply because they demanded one. But many of her unknown interlocutors recognized that letter-writing was an intensely rule-bound activity, even if the protocols regarding who was eligible to address whom, how, and with what expectation of reciprocity remained rather fuzzy. Several more circumspect correspondents expressed concern that they might have violated social niceties in presuming to address a young woman they'd never met. They duly tried to justify what might otherwise seem inexcusably brash behavior. A number of the GIs who wrote to Anne invoked shared Jersey origins, or their identical hometown of Newark, to underscore a degree of familiarity between male writer and female addressee: two people who might actually have crossed paths in person if they only knew it. Perhaps they'd attended the same high school or synagogue, or frequented the same downtown cafés and clubs.[19]

Reaching for familiar templates, several GIs appropriated the phraseology of the personal ad, offering Anne cameos of their distinguishing features the better to ingratiate themselves. One of Anne's most persistent unknown admirers, Phil Seriffignano, introduced himself with droll self-deprecation unwittingly heightened by duff spelling:

I am 22 years old, 5 ft 7 inches tall, I have dark wavey hair and a neat little mustash under my nose. This description would lead you to beleive that I am rather handsome. The truth of the matter is that I am very far from being just that. I have a nose that looks as if I were continually eating on a banana. The reason I mentioned the latter fact is that I'm truthfull and hate to give people the wrong impression of what I look like.

When this note failed to elicit a reply, Phil waited two months and tried again, beginning with an apology for having "broken some sort of unwritten law concerning correct etiquette to use when writing to a girl that I neither rightfully know or even been introduced to, formally or otherwise." Then Phil changed tack, conjuring shared urban kinship to legitimize his forward behavior: "We all, the boys in the barracks and myself, figured that since you and I were of the same native state and even city, it would be strictly according to rules for me to be the one to write and ask you why you sent that V-mail to Kramer in which you told him to 'go to hell.'" His persistence was rewarded. Anne kept hold of both a Christmas card and a Valentine from Phil with references to her replies, attesting an ongoing exchange that, however lopsided, wasn't completely monologic.[20]

As time passed, correspondence between "soldiers and strange girls" ceased to seem too spicily "piquant" and became instead a vanilla staple. By the time American draftees were sent en masse to Korea, newspapers routinely printed personal ads posted by letter-hungry GIs, even if the mode of self-presentation sometimes betrayed residual traces of anxiety over questions of respectability. In the pages of the *New Journal and Guide*, an African American weekly, 1st Lt. Lonnie W. Williams announced himself a graduate, twenty-six and single, who enjoyed "photography, dramatics and music": "In music I like Chopin and hot records too. I also like to write letters about the things I see over here." For his part, Pfc Samuel Evans publicized his particular yen to hear from girls who attended basketball games. "It would give me a real big bang to get a letter from a girl in the states that I don't even know," he enthused, uninhibited by any notion this might be an indecorous desire. More relaxed social norms also extended to women who sought to initiate correspondence with servicemen. In June 1951, *Stars and Stripes* printed seventeen-year-old Janice Pendur's request for "addresses of fellows serving in Korea who'd appreciate mail." Within a week she amassed 213 letters. "They asked about everything from the color of my eyes (hazel) to the gauge of my father's shotgun (12)," Janice confided to a *Los Angeles Times* reporter, adding the guilt-inducing coda that most of her new pen-pals in uniform "sounded bitter about folks back home not writing."[21]

Both the Korean "police action" and the United States' later, longer war in Vietnam gave rise to numerous private initiatives to make sure GIs didn't lack for mail because loved ones at home had failed to do their part. Most of these ventures – or at least the ones that garnered press attention – were started up and staffed by women: an ever-lengthening roster of patriotic mothers, widows, wives, and co-eds eager to ensure that no man was left behind at mail call. Prominent among them was Mrs. Maynard ("Mom") Jenkins of Huntington Beach who turned her pen-pal drive into a California non-profit corporation in 1967. By then, her "Operation Mail Call" boasted a network of 60,000 letter writers, with Jenkins having personally shipped 10 tons of parcels to servicemen in Vietnam in 1966 alone. Taking her cultural cues from World War II, *Los Angeles Times* reporter Linda Mathews billed "Mom" as "neither a Mata Hari nor a Marlene Dietrich," but nevertheless "the most popular woman among troops in the bunkers and billets of Vietnam." At a time when newspapers regularly reported the high incidence of Dear Johns being sent to GIs in Vietnam, Jenkins's efforts supplied a romantic rejoinder. She had personally attended nine weddings between civilian women and soldiers who'd been put in contact through "Operation Mail Call."[22]

"WRITE RIGHT!"

Servicemen were right to perceive letter-writing as an activity constrained not only by invasive military surveillance but also by a thick hedge of social prescription. They were wrong, however, if they believed these rules unwritten. During World War II, guidance on how to compose appropriate missives came from numerous quarters. *The Infantry Journal*'s *Handbook for Army Wives & Mothers* (1944), a title that revealingly elevated wives over mothers, and whose subtitle squeezed sweethearts between sisters and grandmothers, devoted a chapter to "Keeping in

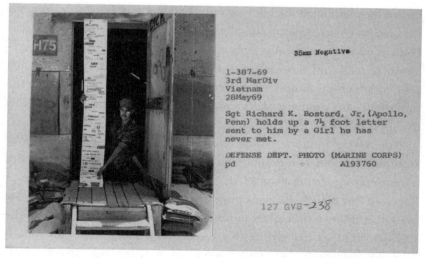

Within the image:
```
35mm Negative

1-387-69
3rd MarDiv
Vietnam
28May69

Sgt Richard K. Bostard, Jr.(Apollo,
Penn) holds up a 7½ foot letter
sent to him by a Girl he has
never met.

DEFENSE DEPT. PHOTO (MARINE CORPS)
pd                            A193760

127 GVB-238
```

2.3. Once prohibited by the War Department, correspondence from strangers became a routine feature of "mail call" in Vietnam. Women competed to outdo one another in bravura displays, like the unnamed sender of this 7.5'-long missive to a marine in Vietnam. (Courtesy of the National Archives and Records Administration.)

Touch with Your Soldier." Newspaper and magazine advice columnists, aptly termed "agony aunts" in British parlance, maintained a steady barrage of prompts. Girls who agonized over whether they should sign letters to soldier acquaintances "affectionately yours" or "sincerely yours" could send off for Emily Post's booklet, "The Etiquette of Letter Writing."[23] Entire volumes like G. A. Reeder's *Letter Writing in Wartime* (1943) and Ethel Gorham's *So Your Husband's Gone to War* (1942) strove to resuscitate what their authors billed as a "lost art." Since the telephone had supplanted letters in the interwar era as a mechanism for arranging dates and staying connected, Americans apparently needed intensive remedial instruction. Reeder duly included chapters on "How to Write a Love Letter," "A List of Salutations for Love Letters" ("My Galahad"; "My Sweet Brave One"; "My Super-Duper Love Maker"), "A List of Closing Terms of Endearment for Love Letters," and a dauntingly long list of "Do's and Don'ts for Sweethearts."[24]

Meanwhile, best-selling novels like Margaret Buell Wilder's *Since You Went Away* (1943), soon adapted as a silver screen blockbuster by David

O. Selznick, modeled the effervescence that was mandatory for women's wartime mien in general and their mail to servicemen in particular. Hollywood enthusiastically took up the drumbeat that sought to synchronize mail and morale, whether by including scenes of crestfallen soldiers left empty-handed at mail call or reminding audiences about the importance of "laughs, lookers and letters" – and civilians' responsibility to supply the latter while the studios delivered the former.[25]

Not to be outdone, radio chimed in too. The Office of War Information's didactic drama series, *Chaplain Jim*, made its debut with a pilot episode unsubtly entitled, "The Case of the Soldier Who Never Received Any Mail." This five-episode saga hinged on a lonely GI who, to mask the absence of mail from home, tried to pass off a famous movie star's portrait as his girlfriend's picture – a fabrication that nearly exposed the soldier to public humiliation when the actress made a surprise visit to his camp. Fortuitously, Chaplain Jim intervened, asking the movie star to play along with the charade to spare the GI from his comrades' ridicule. But since real-life padres couldn't always be relied on to work such timely miracles, women on the home front needed to step up their efforts. The "case" was closed with a blunt rhetorical inquiry to listeners: "Are you writing to your men in the Army every day? Are you writing regularly and cheerfully?"[26]

Levity and frequency were the watchwords of guidance angled at women in the 1940s, reprising themes from World War I and the Civil War before that, when women had been warned that men could actually *die* for want of mail.[27] Thoughtlessly written letters could do almost as much damage. "[O]f all the horrors inflicted on the man at the front he characterizes the 'sob letter' as the hardest to bear," cautioned an editorial in the *Los Angeles Times* in June 1917, alluding to notes in which the writer self-indulgently bemoaned wartime conditions, whether commodity shortages or concerns over the distant soldier's wellbeing. As more members of the AEF reached France and as life in the trenches worsened, with prospects for doughboys' unscathed return growing more precarious, calls by the civic custodians of morale for more self-censorship on the part of letter-writers grew louder. "Write to him often and always cheerily. In Heaven's name, don't mope," admonished the *Boston Daily*

Globe in 1918, five months before an armistice concluded the Great War.[28]

Etiquette gurus repeated the same mantra relentlessly during World War II. Reeder even encouraged women to illustrate their letters with quirky stick figure drawings and happy faces, anticipating the "Smiley" and emojis by several decades. "Cute little sketches liven up a letter and increase its value to the receiver immeasurably," Reeder proposed, encouraging women to cultivate their artistic talents.[29] Like other morale-minded Americans, he conceived wartime correspondence as an enterprise that, first and foremost, served the cause of victory. As some would-be Sammy Backers had surmised during World War I, writing was a gendered counterpart to fighting. The prime mandate, thus construed, was to bolster the spirits of men at war, not to foster intimate relationships that both partners found reciprocally satisfying. That women had emotional needs of their own figured nowhere in this division of labor. While composing artful missives could "improve personality," making women "more tolerant and attractive," the *Atlanta Constitution*'s Violet Moore reminded female readers that "it's not what [letter-writing] does for you that really counts. It's what it does for the man who's out there fighting for you." To this end, elevation of male self-esteem was a vital art to master. "Girls, your most important job is to keep up Bill's ego and his moral," entreated Mary Lee Smith in the "Soldier's Letter Box," a feature run by the *Call and Post*, Cleveland's African American weekly newspaper. "In the army, your hometown hero is merely a wart in a barrel of pickles. Say it isn't so. Make him feel that he is still a mighty important person in this world – especially to a certain girl back home."[30]

For women, letter-writing required a constant negotiation between expression and suppression of feeling. Dispensers of advice, anticipating (or amplifying) Johnny Mercer's hit lyric of 1944, urged women to "accent-tchu-ate the positive," "eliminate the negative," and not "mess with Mister In-Between." "Are you feeling lonely and upset and vaguely suicidal?," Ethel Gorham caustically quizzed wives who consulted her volume *So Your Husband's Gone to War*. "Don't put it into written words unless you're prepared to jump out of the window and this is your last message on it all." A like-minded, albeit more tempered, contributor to the *Ladies' Home Journal* urged women, when down in the dumps, to "take your tears

2.4. Advertisements for V-mail, like this one designed by Lejaren A. Hiller in 1945, simultaneously promoted this more efficient form of correspondence and tutored women in the appropriate demeanor for composition of cheery notes. (Courtesy of University of North Texas, Digital Library, Government Documents Department.)

to a stirring movie . . . Then when you have got it all out of your system, go home and write your husband the swellest letter you can compose, with not even a hint of a sob in it!" Official censors scrutinized civilians' mail to excise indiscreetly divulged information, squelch rumor-mongering, and catch those who attempted to write in private code. Censorship cast a long shadow over wartime letter writers. But women heard time and time again that the most vital omissions were those they authorized *themselves*, not because the offending material would violate formal censorship codes but because "trouble, complaints, grief, fears" would "raise havoc with morale and reduce the soldier's margin of safety."[31]

Although many edicts issued in World War II reprised those of the previous global conflict, the home front assumed a different, and decidedly less domestic, aspect in the 1940s. Women entered the paid workforce in unprecedented numbers. This phenomenon unnerved more conservative men, changing the character of many households that servicemen left behind, as mothers, sisters, wives, and girlfriends took up jobs in factories and offices or themselves enlisted in the women's auxiliary services. Thousands of women struck out for far-flung destinations, leaving home altogether – or shifting its location – to seize opportunities offered by an invigorated war-oriented economy.[32] But if greater mobility, more money, new skills, and wider social circles raised many women's expectations about the horizon of their lives, these developments also complicated the female correspondent's task. Letters to distant soldiers, women frequently heard, should attest the timeless, unalterable character not only of her love for the absent man, but also of that mythic destination longed for by every man in uniform. "Home may seem far away to him; but he thinks of it often – and your vivid descriptions and anecdotes can make it real to him," Frances Fenwick Hills prompted readers of *Good Housekeeping*. "Then he'll be sure that home – and you – are still there, waiting for him."[33]

Overlooking men who entered the forces from unhappy or abusive households, columnists and counselors framed their prescriptions as though all soldiers overseas clung to the same vision of home as a source of security and a reassuringly fixed compass point: an image women should strive to sustain. But maintaining the façade of domestic permanence was an especially tall order at a time of epic demographic upheaval. Men in uniform were well aware that the needle had swung in the direction of women's greater autonomy from male-headed households supported by male-earned wages. Although many soldiers approved of women undertaking war-related work, at least for the duration, not all servicemen took such a sanguine view. Some married men with children fretted that wives with jobs might be forced to abandon responsibilities for child-care. Military mail censors in the Pacific found a good deal of grumbling inspired by rumors that the federal government was poised to conscript *all* women into war work.[34] Some husbands-in-uniform doubtless feared returning home to a less malleable partner who'd relished greater freedom and was loath to retrain as a "clinging vine," in the words of one disgruntled wife. Other men may have feared that paid employment outside the home, a change likely to enlarge women's social networks, would provide wives and girlfriends with more opportunities to meet, flirt with, or date other men.[35]

Infidelity loomed large as the most corrosive of servicemen's anxieties. Soldiers traded tales of mass female defection from the home front at mounting volume and with greater vitriol as the war lengthened.[36] By 1945, *Stars and Stripes* buzzed with reports that seemed to corroborate the escalation of women's disloyalty. Two stories garnered a particularly ferocious response from aggrieved GIs. In June 1945, lawmakers in California proposed altering legislation to allow married women to put up illegitimate infants for adoption without informing their absent husbands: a move intended to curb a "black market" in babies. Egged on by headlines like "Licensed Infidelity?," servicemen vehemently protested proposals they saw as condoning – and hence encouraging – extramarital affairs conducted behind servicemen's backs.[37] GIs were perhaps even more upset by press reports that some American women were dating, and even clandestinely *marrying*, Italian prisoners of war encamped in the United States. How was such disloyalty possible when American men had risked, and sometimes lost, their lives fighting against these same Axis soldiers, GIs demanded to know. "The way I look at it is, I blame it completely on the American public and women," announced one enlisted man serving with the 59th Ordnance Ammunition Company in the Pacific theater, voicing widely shared sentiments. "If they want their daughters to go around with a P of W who has probably killed one of their friends or relatives in Tunisia or Silicia [sic] it's their fault ... Us fellows over here are really burnt up about the situation."[38]

The more convinced GIs became that American women were betraying them en masse, the more justified some men felt about their own sexual encounters overseas. Rationalizations for male transgressions were not, however, hard to come by. A 1943 handbook, *Psychology for the Fighting Man*, pointed out that servicemen who failed to receive "constant reassurances of undeviating faithfulness, expressions of pride in what her man is doing for his country, and gifts and letters in abundance," might be driven "to seek sexual satisfaction with other women" – "especially if he half-consciously wants to make his own girl suffer for her neglect of him." This observation, a warning shot to "waiting women," issued a tacit permission slip to "fighting men" looking to cloak infidelity with righteous indignation.[39]

Taken together, recommendations for correct composition of letters to soldiers mandated a delicate (if not impossible) balancing act. Women had to maintain an upbeat tone, but without striking any false note. No man wants letters filled "with forced good cheer," intoned *Vogue*, a magazine dedicated to flawless appearances. Wives and girlfriends had to reassure absent soldiers that they were missed, but not to the point of female incapacity; that women were getting along fine with their jobs, but not becoming overly independent; that they remained buoyant, but without having too much fun. As a cautionary tale, the *Afro-American*'s Will Neely alerted readers on New Year's Day, 1944, to the letter one poor soldier had received from his wife, "telling him that she was a little woozy from a night of drinking gin, and therefore her missive would be short." An evening of solitary boozing would be worrisome enough, but any reference to gin-guzzling was likely to conjure a night out on the town, and that broached the riskiest topic of all. Rule-makers warned that soldiers had no wish to hear of wives' and girlfriends' social interactions with other men. Yet the absence of *any* male figures in a woman's correspondence would arouse suspicion, Reeder's primer suggested, so the prudent female letter-writer should throw in the odd reference to a self-evidently harmless male – "some 50-year-old uncle" – by way of reassurance.[40]

All this guidance was more easily dispensed than espoused. Many women divulged to their partners feelings of anxiety, including worries about whether relationships would endure and men overseas would remain faithful.[41] Like many ordinarily mortal women, Anne Gudis failed to observe the cardinal rule of eternal good cheer in her correspondence. As a family friend later explained to Sam Kramer's chaplain, "Although we in the States are told to be very cheerful, when corresponding especially to someone overseas, there was a time when Anne was feeling blue and could not help but put that feeling into one of her letters." From Sam's response, it seems Anne had violated another cardinal principle, bemoaning the advances of a lecherous, married boss – palpably not the asexual avuncular type. Whatever inspired a note of complaint in one of Anne's letters, it elicited a ferocious put-down. "If you become too despondent why don't you try committing suicide, or some other way to an end," Sam taunted, pre-empting Ethel Gorham's similarly worded recommendation. A few days later, he warned her, "You really are in a rut. Get the hell out of it."[42]

Kramer evidently did not expect to be on the receiving end of a similarly sharp rejoinder. While Anne did indeed "keep it short" – as the snappy promotional motto for V-mail urged – her injunction didn't sound at all sweet. When Sam's self-described "chaplin" wrote to Anne, chastising her for the blow she'd dealt her boyfriend's esprit, he drew particular attention to her reprehensible language. But his telling-off, unlike some of the harsher criticisms lobbed Anne's way, was laced with unmistakable irony. Lieutenant Leonard Paul couldn't have been serious when he insisted that Anne's V-mail had caused its recipient a "terrible shock" since her phraseology was "definitely not the type of language that Sam hears in the army." Writing in 1946, psychiatrist Henry Elkin pointed out that profanity was "perhaps the most striking feature of Army life" – something Anne knew very well. Some of Sam's choicest curses had, after all, been aimed at her. However, in matters of diction, as in so much else relating to male–female relationships in wartime, double standards were the order of the day.[43]

"AND PLEASE, GIRLS, NO 'DEAR JOHN' LETTERS"

In World War II, GI slang dubbed notes from sweethearts "sugar reports," emphasizing the preferred key ingredient.[44] Anne Gudis's V-mail, by contrast, seemed to exemplify a new and more dangerous type: the Dear John. Just a week after *Yank* published Anne's V-mail, the *New York Times* carried its first reference to "Dear John" letters with Milton Bracker's Sunday magazine story on October 3, 1943.[45] Bracker helped establish a template that quickly became paradigmatic. A Dear John didn't simply end a relationship. This poison-pen letter announced that its author had transferred her affections to the rejected serviceman's rival, often excoriated as "some 4-F or defense worker." 4-F referred to the draft board categorization of men deemed unfit for service, often used as a derogatory term for men assigned this label (also referred to by GIs as "four-effers"). By September 1944, four million of thirteen million

American men examined for military service had been rejected as 4-F.[46] Among enlisted men, the most reviled "four-effer" was undoubtedly Frank Sinatra. With his perforated eardrum, silken voice, and shady connections, Sinatra struck many soldiers as the very personification of the entitled string-puller who'd managed to shirk military service on spurious grounds.[47] Being jettisoned by women in favor of men that soldiers considered too frail, feeble-minded, elderly, or cowardly to serve added insult to injury. "The girls in the states aren't to be trusted," griped one enlisted man with the 172nd Infantry. "I know that from the way the girls are throwing these guys [serving in the Pacific] over, over here to marry some 4F jerk." Not surprisingly, the *Handbook for Army Wives and Mothers* warned that, above all else, soldiers did not want "to hear that you're engaged or married to somebody else."[48]

Unmoored from their emotional anchors, men were seen as vulnerable to emotional injury in a variety of forms, from mild bruising to the ego to life-threatening broken-heartedness. "Loneliness is hard enough – isolation from hope is unendurable," intoned a Red Cross field director in New Guinea from the pages of *Vogue*, while Bracker told his *New York Times* audience that the effect of a Dear John on its recipient was "always the same. He is browned off – and a deep, dark, blackish sort of brown it is." Some men found external outlets for their rage. One private stationed in Italy, responsible for sorting his unit's mail, was reportedly so distraught by being jilted that he ripped up his comrades' love letters to ensure that, if he went unloved, others should suffer likewise.[49] More often, however, journalists highlighted cases in which feelings of rejection turned dangerously inwards. Celebrated novelist and war correspondent John Steinbeck, having warned readers of the *Boston Daily Globe* that "a good letter can make the difference between a good soldier and a sick man," hinted that heartbreak wasn't simply a figurative proposition. Romantic reversal could prove fatal. A letter from a "returned wounded soldier now doing time in an Army hospital," printed in the *Washington Post* in July 1944, made the point less obliquely: "a large number of servicemen are in hospitals today as a result of such letters. And many others are known to have committed suicide as a result of being jilted by a girl back home."[50]

With Dear John letters identified as an alarming new trend, women were warned emphatically not to break off relationships with servicemen or, in some cases, not to lead young men into unwarranted expectations of love in the first place. Dating advice aimed at teenage girls admonished them not to alleviate the longueurs of life without a full quota of beaux with "a little hot talk by mail." Penning fervent letters – motivated by a misplaced sense of patriotism rather than genuine devotion – risked encouraging romantic hopes that would necessarily later be dashed. Such masquerades could only end badly for the girl or the boy, if not both, columnist Maureen Daly and other like-minded advisers counseled. The boy might come home on furlough and expect the girl's words and deeds to align, perhaps (*sotto voce* undertones hinted) even attempting to *force* this alignment into existence. Or the flighty young woman would write a Dear John at some later date, telling the soldier she'd found some other fellow she *really* cared for. "You send him a well worded brushoff with that 'but I'll always consider you as one of my best friends' lead. And you do it feeling righteous, upstanding, and womanly. You forget to consider that the boy to whom you are writing may read that letter sitting in an empty barracks after a hard day's work, with his shoulder muscles aching from rifle drill."[51] A *Chaplain Jim* story-line reinforced the same point: "the Army wants the folks back home to write ... But, it's not necessary to pretend you feel very close to someone, just because you believe it might make him happy."[52]

Press stories about Dear Johns aimed not only to inform but to deter. Whether implicitly or explicitly warning women against their despatch, these moral fables exposed the contradictions riddling wartime prescriptions around love, letters, and loyalty at their starkest. Women could perhaps be forgiven for confusion over when and whether it was acceptable for feelings to be falsified. After all, the key tenet of wartime letter-writing mandated the adoption of a perpetually chipper persona. Even if a woman was feeling rather glum or careworn when she sat down to pen her daily missive – and no matter how sparse, self-involved, or suspicion-laden her partner's letters may have been – she should exude high spirits, optimism, and affection. At the same time, girls were also sternly instructed *not* to feign romantic sentiments where none were felt. But what if a woman's feelings, once genuinely loving, altered over the course of long months and years of separation from a soldier spouse or boy-friend serving overseas? How should this change of heart be conveyed?

The most common answer was that it should not. Although faked feeling was unacceptable in some circumstances, it was seemingly obliga-tory in others. Some journalists introduced the plaintive voices of love-lorn GIs to stress that women *must* sustain romantic bonds with soldiers come what may – or at least to perpetuate the motions convincingly for the duration. "A kid from Staten Island whose sweetheart married a shipyard worker stated the case this way," the *Chicago Daily Tribune* noted: "'You can't make a girl stay in love with you. Nobody's asking that. But any girl who calls herself an American ought to have the character – or call it patriotism – not to stab a soldier in the back. Let her at least wait until the guy gets back home before giving him the gate.'"[53] Women whose love had faded for partners serving overseas were routinely advised to maintain precisely this charade. Counselors elevated the *performance* of attachment – however hollow women's utter-ances of reassurance may have been – over authenticity of feeling. The furthest some guidance-givers went toward licensing the severance of an outworn or misbegotten relationship was to suggest that women grad-ually reduce the heat of their epistolary outpourings if they lacked the self-discipline necessary to defer the *coup de grâce* until the man's demobilization.

During later conflicts in Korea and Vietnam columnists continued to insist that women either not send Dear Johns at all or turn down the thermostat, hoping that the soldier would not notice the lower tempera-ture or respond to the cooler air with good grace. In March 1952, a perplexed young woman wrote to Elizabeth Woodward's "Column for Teens" printed in the *Daily Boston Globe*, uncertain how to handle the fact that her male pen-pal had "suddenly got much more serious when he went in the service." With the prospect of deployment to Korea looming, he'd started to write twice daily, developing burdensome emotional needs and unrealistic aspirations. Suddenly, and unilaterally, he expected to "get married!" "Every time I try to break it gently, he counters with, 'a Dear John letter would really finish me.'" Woodward agreed that things had snowballed, but weren't "necessarily headed toward the complete smash of a 'Dear John'" – so long as the girl adopted "a few slowing-up tactics," like writing weekly rather than daily. Nor should she "pour on the goo."[54] In Woodward's view, this delaying strategy had the additional advantage of allowing the girl's own feelings to develop. Perhaps, in time, hers would match his.

"Agony aunts" made similar recommendations to "cool down the letters gradually" to teenage girls whose boyfriends served in Vietnam a decade and a half later.[55] A retrospective reading of advice columns from the late 1960s offers few hints that a sexual revolution was reshaping the contours of romantic intimacy in the United States. On the contrary, young women with boyfriends or husbands serving overseas received the same counsel their parents might have heard in the 1940s. In September 1968, at the height of the war in Vietnam with half a million US service personnel in country, the Baltimore *Sun*'s "Teen Forum" featured an especially loaded column with a letter from a female reader who corroborated the paper's caution against Dear Johns. This unnamed woman volunteered her own experience of having sent such a letter and its tragic upshot: "He scrawled an answer on a piece of paper and sent it to me. In the note he said he hoped to die. Two months later I read in the local paper that he was dead." The woman had later married and begun a family, but still vehemently asserted that she would "never forget the boy in Vietnam I'd fallen out of love with and the cruelty of my letter to him." Just as "cheerful" served as the stock epithet for the ideal tone of women's wartime letters, "cruel" formed its antithesis: the adjective invariably used to characterize Dear Johns. The "Teen Forum"'s Jean Adams urged her young readers to "save the cruel news," waiting until boys had returned from Vietnam, when they were "likely to have a higher morale."[56]

To reinforce the message, battalion chaplains in Vietnam submitted their own letters on the subject to prominent national papers, the small-town press, and African American weeklies. In November 1967, for instance, Lt. Clyde Kimball, Navy chaplain of the 1st Medical Battalion of Marines at Da Nang, told the *Afro-American* that Dear Johns were "the major problem" facing chaplains in Vietnam, the "bane of fighting men." This claim was enunciated again and again in the war's later years. Not all servicemen agreed with the prohibition against Dear Johns, however, even when the warning came from military padres. One GI responded to Abigail Van Buren, whose "Dear Abby" advice column was widely syndicated, by telling her that the chaplain whose moralizing sermon she'd just printed should "go soak his head." Admittedly, a breakup note wasn't "the greatest letter in the world to receive." Yet, as this soldier saw it, the alternatives were even worse: either "sweet loving letters pretending all's well," or a sudden absence of mail from a girlfriend who wordlessly "just quit writing." He'd experienced the latter situation first-hand: "when you're expecting a letter every day and don't get it, it's like getting a Dear John every day. When a guy gets a Dear John at least he knows what's happened."[57] A mysterious void was no better for morale than a verbalized rejection.

"COWARDS" AND "TRAITORS"

This anonymous grunt's opinion didn't represent a complete generational shift against the verities of an earlier era. During World War II, some GIs had also bristled at the idea that women should write tepid letters rather than candidly state the fact of changed feelings. Some took to the pages of the servicemen's newspaper, *Tropic Topics*, to rubbish advice on "gentle jilting" recently dished out by *Modern Screen* magazine. In particular, they resented the suggestion that men would buckle under the pressure of long-range rejection.[58]

Some servicemen twinned this perceived affront to their masculinity with attacks on women's "cowardice" in sending Dear Johns rather than breaking up in person. Men weren't alone in delivering this damning verdict. Women writers were sometimes just as harsh in upbraiding the weaker sex's weakest members, who employed mail as a long-distance missile because they lacked the stomach for close quarters combat. "There are wives," *Vogue* magazine chided, "who have not had the courage to face estrangement at home while the man was there, but wait until he is overseas and then write, 'I knew all along it could not last, and now I want my freedom.'" Like other strictures against long-range breakups common during World War II, this attitude resurfaced during the Vietnam war. "Why do these girlfriends and wives wait until the man is gone to break the bad news?," one soldier undertaking his second tour in

Vietnam grilled *Sun* columnist Mrs. Mayfield in 1969. "Are they too cowardly to tell them face-to-face? I think they are."[59]

Was it always cowardice that impelled some women to wait until a soldier was overseas before announcing that she wanted to dissolve an unsatisfactory union? And was it wise for a woman to dissemble when she knew a relationship was irredeemably broken? Emotional deception of the kind recommended by many advice columnists and chaplains spelled trouble – in a variety of ways. What superficial stuff could a woman fill her letters with if she had embarked on a new relationship with someone else during her former partner's tour of duty? And how long could the semblance of unaltered affection be sustained? (How this pretence might undermine a new relationship wasn't a question publicly aired since the illegitimacy of such unions was taken as read.) Even if a woman's evasively up-beat notes managed to pull the wool over a distant man's eyes, there was always the danger that he'd hear the news from someone else back home, a "helpful" family member or friend. As Red Cross workers and chaplains repeatedly pointed out, pernicious "thought-you-should-know" letters, dishing dirt on spouses' and girlfriends' alleged infidelities, were a scourge of life on the front lines in each of the United States' twentieth-century wars.[60] "I don't want to hear none of this bull – about Joe or John running around with Sue," one Black GI in Vietnam bitterly informed the *Afro-American*'s Mike Davis in 1967.[61]

Purveyors of relationship wisdom were signally silent about the deferred moment of revelation when the soldier returned home and found the woman he'd considered "his" now in love with, perhaps even living with, another man. This scenario was fraught with peril – the pain of betrayal likely aggravated by a prolonged pretence of fidelity. Recommendations that women deliver the knockout blow on the demobilized man's return appear blind to the prospect of retribution when veterans belatedly discovered the truth. To imagine that such revelations would be received with equanimity by men making the fraught transition back to civilian life was to ignore both the evidence of history and the intuition of empathy. World War I was followed by a number of well-publicized homicides involving doughboys who returned home to find their wives or girlfriends with new lovers and then killed one or both.

Some veterans concluded their killing spree by committing suicide, like the demobilized man reported on by the *Chicago Daily Tribune* in September 1919 under the headline "Soldier Slays Girl and Self." This veteran shot his former fiancée, "so no one else shall have her," because she'd formed a new attachment and refused to marry him. He then turned the weapon on himself.[62]

During the final months of World War II, GIs' mounting hostility toward the home front, accompanied and accelerated by rage about women's rumored disloyalty, bristled with intimations of retaliatory violence directed against men and women alike. Officers overseas documented this simmering fury in morale reports based on what they found in enlisted men's mail. "Those men there that prey on wives of men over here deserve to be shot as mush so as a Jap and there's lots of 'em that will be too," one enlistee in the 1st Infantry predicted in an injudicious letter home. But while military censors tasked with tracking the ebb and flow of servicemen's moods noted dark fantasies of payback, they didn't always excise such sentiments from the outgoing mail they scrutinized. Pronounced traces of this animus linger in archival collections of wartime correspondence.[63]

One revealing example of how misogynistic ire mounted over time, transcending divisions of rank and race, can be found in the letters Leo Dykes sent home to his brother, Lawyer, in Akron, Ohio. A Black private with the 5th Marine Ammunition Company, and self-styled "'wolf' in marine's clothing," Leo maintained correspondences with several women during his period of wartime service. But he favored a certain Velvene. Her beauty made "Lena Horne and Marva Louis look silly," and Leo nurtured "great plans for the future if God is willing." So he claimed in May 1944, shortly before embarking for the Pacific. By the following January, Leo's tone had changed markedly. Not having heard from Velvene for a few weeks, he informed Lawyer: "I do know that she will never hear from me again until she writes me, and then she won't want to read it. I know she isn't sick. Boy, am I glad I'm not married now, because I know women." In Leo's opinion, some of his fellow servicemen hadn't yet wised up to the antics of wives and sweethearts in their absence. A few lotharios, he reckoned, would be unconcerned, having played the field themselves. "But for the boys that do care, watch out. These things aren't going to happen just in one city or country, but all over, just wait and see." Precisely what Leo anticipated had already been broached in an earlier letter: "I bet when some of these guys come home, there's going to be more divorces and cracked heads and jaws. (Ha-Ha.)"[64]

Dykes's prediction turned out to be grievously accurate. In April 1945, a soldier in Kansas City made the headlines when he killed his wife to prevent her marrying someone else. Questioned by the police, he darkly warned, "There's gonna be more women killed for stepping out on their husbands than all the Japanese put together."[65] His extravagant boast was, of course, hyperbolic. But this homicidal veteran was far from being the only demobilized serviceman to enact a lethal scenario that some particularly disenchanted GIs had collectively scripted while overseas. A number of veterans returning from Korea in 1953, from Vietnam in the 1960s and early 1970s, the Persian Gulf in 1991, and Iraq and Afghanistan in the first decades of the twenty-first century later killed wives and girlfriends, and/or the men they believed responsible for alienated affections. They, too, justified lethal force with reference to female infidelity. In some cases, these men's lawyers mounted what they termed a "Dear John defense," even when no such letter had been sent, and the defendants had acted on rumor and suspicion of broken vows, not direct word of a breakup.[66]

Woman-hating soldiers serving overseas perhaps enjoyed more in common with the reviled home front than they knew. Attacks on disloyal women – the ones who had affairs, gave birth to illegitimate babies, fell for Italian POWs, and sent Dear Johns (or didn't) – reached a shrill crescendo in the summer of 1945, with Germany defeated and Japan's surrender still frustratingly elusive. Opera singer Grace Moore denounced unfaithful wives as "the greatest criminals in the world," who should have their heads shorn as a "mark of shame and disgrace."[67] In Anne Gudis's hometown, Newark, New Jersey, Judge James Pellecchia proposed meting out the same punishment for female adulterers.[68] These propositions added a domestic twist to the motif of women's sexual treachery in wartime. In newly liberated Europe, French men took it upon themselves to punish French women accused of sleeping with Germans by shaving their heads, stripping or tarring-and-feathering them. In turn, German vigilantes did likewise to fellow countrywomen they condemned for "fraternizing" with US occupation soldiers.

General George Patton upped the ante, denouncing the very despatch of a Dear John as a capital offense. Never one to mince his words, Patton informed journalist Adela Rogers St. Johns that women "who began letters Dear John, I don't know how to tell you – should be *shot* as traitors."[69] In the eyes of Patton and his ilk, a broken heart was the least tolerable injury an American soldier might sustain in wartime: a wound that ought never to be inflicted, and that might prove fatal. Those who administered such devastating blows deserved to die. In his trademark style, Patton stated the case with singular bluntness. Over the course of later decades, verdicts against women who wrote Dear John letters remained consistently damning, if less viciously worded. But while condemnation of the messenger has remained a historical constant, the media through which news – good, bad, and intolerable – reaches men at war have constantly evolved, infusing commentary on Dear John letters with the technological angst of successive eras. Rules about "writing right" have been supplemented by prescriptions about how to tape, talk, and text right.

CHAPTER 3

Technologies of Proximity

L OVED ONES SEPARATED IN WARTIME COMMONLY MEASURE distance in units of both space and time. Not just miles apart, they're sundered by the months, days, and hours that have elapsed since the soldier left home, as well as the yawning expanse of time yet to tick by until the couple's reunion. During all the United States' twentieth-century wars, mail took several days, if not weeks, to traverse the void between "here" and "there." This time-lag in communication provided another measure of separation. Staying "in touch" – a perversely tactile figure of speech – required patience. Wartime letter-writers constantly confronted the asynchronous nature of the enterprise. Correspondence often seemed less a back-and-forth conversation than a syncopated sequence of monologs as letters leap-frogged over one another in transit. Long, unpredictable interludes between writing, delivery, and response made it hard for correspondents to know quite what to commit to paper when the fresh ephemera of the moment might well seem stale on arrival.[1]

For the transmission of intelligence, orders, casualty reports, liaison with civilian war managers, and other internal command purposes, the twentieth-century armed forces employed faster and more reliable means of communication than the mail. Successive conflicts in the twentieth and twenty-first centuries brought innovations in both the uni-directional relay of information and two-way conversation between distant individuals, from the telegraph and radio to telephony by way of wires, cable, and satellite. Which of these constantly evolving technologies would be made accessible to soldiers to sustain private connections proved a vexed issue for the military. The services juggled considerations including cost, logistics, and security risks. Eager to make life harder for eavesdropping enemy intelligence-gatherers, commanders favored modes of transmission that let American officers monitor what their own enlisted personnel said and sent to folks back home.[2] But these practical concerns were always entwined with more imponderable factors relating to the *psychological* dimensions of technologies that claimed to collapse the distance between "home" and "away." How much, and what sort of, contact between separated partners was desirable for operational efficiency, and for couples' own durability? Which modes of communication were best suited to sustaining intimacy, and which imperilled it? Or did all technologies of proximity carry simultaneous dangers of disconnection – whether alienating romantic partners from one another or detaching service personnel from professional duty?

The modern US military has repeatedly turned to civilians to provide uniformed personnel with the emotional reinforcement that would help them withstand the privations, dangers, depersonalization, and intermittent boredom of front-line deployment. But as the arrival of Dear John letters during World War II and subsequent conflicts made clear, the connection between mail and morale was no more invariably positive than were relationships between soldiers and their partners. All news was emphatically *not* good news. Unwelcome word from home could be devastating to soldiers serving overseas. And, conceivably, bad news cut deeper the faster it arrived from home – an anxious hypothesis running through military deliberations about how service personnel should communicate with distant loved ones.

Veterans' Dear John stories hinge on questions of time and timing. They're about the harmful impact of time spent apart, the fragility of a shared imaginary future, and the ill-considered timing of termination notices issued while servicemen are overseas, already adrift and insecure. But recollections of romantic severance often channel angst about both the message and the *medium*. From the telegram to the telephone, the tape recorder to the text, innovations in communication have seemed to promise greater proximity with home, yet have sometimes served to make separation harder and the severance of romantic ties more wounding. Dear Johns haven't arrived by mail alone. Breakup messages have mutated in tandem with evolving technologies available to service personnel and their loved ones. Veterans' recollections of being "Dear Johned," along with popular culture's depictions of ended wartime affairs, are often expressive of larger anxieties about new modes of communication and their consequences for human connectivity.

"MAKING LOVE BY V-MAIL!"

It's no coincidence that Anne Gudis's message to Sam Kramer – the object of much contemporary conjecture and some historical attention – should have been a V-mail rather than a conventional letter. Sam sent it to *Yank* with a rather mannered boast: "I desire to lay claim to having received the shortest V-mail letter ever received in ETO."[3] He evidently hoped that the weekly army newspaper would publish Anne's message as a novelty item. And so it did.

"Victory-mail," more commonly abbreviated to V-mail, represented World War II's most distinctive innovation in personal communication. The US government, borrowing a British invention, introduced it in June 1942, looking to slim the bloated bulk of paper that hogged an ever-increasing amount of space on cargo ships and planes. Notes written on pre-printed, one-page forms, with accompanying windowed envelopes, were microfilmed before aerial despatch overseas. They were then delivered to addressees in a shrunken 4″ × 5.5″ photostatic format. Eighteen hundred letters could be photographed onto a single roll of film. By one reckoning, 85,000 V-mails weighed a mere 20 pounds, whereas the same number of paper letters tipped the scales at 2,000 pounds – a significant efficiency saving for an overstretched military postal service. But the format also had advantages for users in terms of accelerated delivery and reduced cost. Civilians could pick up two free V-mail forms from their post office daily, along with the three-cent stamp required for despatch overseas. For their part, military personnel acquired the stationery and sent messages home for free.[4]

The Office of War Information (OWI) undertook several promotional campaigns to boost the uptake of V-mail use. They needed to cajole skeptics put off by the number of prying eyes they imagined would be privy to personal messages as they were photographed and then developed at the other end of their journey. (Perhaps they forgot that soldiers' and civilians' mail was already read by censors?) More prolific or verbose letter-writers bridled at the restricted space offered by a single page, the margins of which were *not* to be exceeded, OWI posters and instructional films emphatically reminded users. Those with poor hand-writing would need to acquire neater habits, or a typewriter, if their messages were to be legible after being smudged and shrunk by micro-film. But government propagandists, working in cahoots with private commercial advertisers, were quick to tout V-mail's many pluses. Together they tirelessly issued jaunty reminders to "Keep it Short!," "Write Often!," and avoid smearing the forms with lipsticked kisses – a "scarlet scourge" that clogged up the microfilm apparatus.[5]

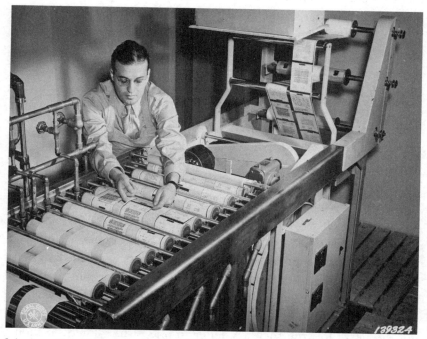

3.1. An unidentified man operates a continuous paper processing machine to develop, fix, wash, and dry paper reproductions of microfilmed V-mails at the Pentagon, Washington, DC, February, 1943. (Courtesy of U.S. Army/PhotoQuest/Getty Images.)

Boosters regarded V-mail as the ideal vehicle for female letter writers to fulfill the trinity of commandments that mandated brevity, levity, and frequency. Long letters *should* still be sent, advice-givers urged, but these might now be written weekly. V-mail, by contrast, lent itself to despatch daily "or oftener." "Write it while it's fresh – get it to him fast!," entreated the company that produced V-mail "envo-letters." The form's restricted space more than sufficed for the kinds of bright and breezy notes that seemingly almost wrote themselves. Manufacturers who hitched their product's star to promotion of V-mail commissioned advertisements that depicted women performing household chores while dashing off an affectionate note, or putting to use "moments you usually waste" – "riding on a bus, waiting for an appointment," or trapped under the immobilizing dome of a hairdryer at the beauty salon. No matter how tenuous the connection between the commercial product and this new boon to communication, companies of every stripe wanted in on the act: not just Kodak (supplier of the microfilm onto which V-mail was photographed) or Sheaffer's, which sold a special black "skrip" for use penning V-mails, but the manufacturers of Drano, Windex, and Scotch Tape. Meanwhile, the advertising agency hired by Charles H. Fletcher, maker of Castoria, a children's laxative, cautioned young mothers against filling their V-mails with constipation woes – until the child's blockage (and her writer's block) had been dissolved with their product. Tidings any father in uniform would gladly receive![6]

As this ad implied, however, V-mail's advantages could readily become demerits if the medium were abused. Its very ease-of-use triggered concern that female correspondents might dash off impetuous notes rather than more carefully composed missives. Old-fashioned letters demanded a degree of contemplative forethought easily neglected by writers of V-mail. Anne Gudis's intemperate message to Sam Kramer underscored these dangers, as some of her unknown detractors were quick to point out, using V-mail to expedite their rebukes. Four privates, stationed "somewhere in England," sent Anne a collective dressing-down: "We don't know the soldier but it makes our blood boil to think some dame got the nerve to write such a V letter to one of us soldiers." Echoing promotional claims that the format was the "surest – fastest – and most patriotic" way to reach boys overseas, these men reminded Anne that "V letters are meant for friendly letters, not insults."[7] Another corporal and staff sergeant wrote sarcastically to decry her note's vulgar haste. "It must have taken a great deal of time to compose a letter of that type," they jibed. Hailing from Jersey City, the pair professed themselves all the more bitter because she had "let the state of New Jersey down with that note."[8] Others, including Sam's chaplain, harped on themes of Anne's squanderous selfishness. "It was dreadfully wrong for you to waste paper in such a distasteful manner," Lt. Leonard Paul chided.[9] Her misuse of V-mail stationery had ignobly contributed to the wartime paper shortage, while her abusive words monopolized transportation space more fittingly claimed by an affectionate note – as though in the zero-sum game of wartime correspondence one curt message more necessarily meant one loving letter less. "You should be saving instead of wasting paper, ink and government time like that," scolded one private first class. "Some poor soldier would have liked that sheet of paper you used just to write those darn words like you did."[10]

Would Anne have told Sam to "Go to Hell!" had she been reliant on traditionally delivered mail? Quite possibly not. The conventions of letter-writing – the opening salutation, an inquiry into the recipient's state of health, responses to queries in a letter received, an update on the writer's own situation – might well have checked Anne's temper. A barbed one-liner just wouldn't have looked right on a sheet of standard stationery. Time-honored formulae for the composition of letters required *paragraphs*. Perhaps unconventional Anne might have broken the mold and committed her fury to a sheet of note-paper in the absence of V-mail. But had she done so, it's likely that no one other than Sam would ever have known. Sam didn't keep Anne's mail, and seemed to delight in telling her that he burned everything she'd sent. Her "Go to Hell!" message remains preserved for posterity solely because Sam sent it to *Yank*, and the latter decided to print it. Conceivably, *Yank*'s "Mail Call" editor felt less compunction about publishing Anne's note because V-mail didn't just have the novelty value Sam touted, but also seemed less private than the "proper" letter. Certainly, those who wrote to castigate Anne enjoyed an opportunity to talk back only because V-mail required the sender to place their address in the top right-hand corner, and *Yank* reproduced Anne's message in facsimile form. Anyone who read this item duly knew that she lived at 81 Hobson Street, Newark, 8. Like many subsequent Dear John stories, Anne's was tethered to the technology of its day. Her message was seemingly both facilitated and exacerbated by the medium.

Letters and V-mail were not the sole channels by which separated lovers, friends, or family members could communicate during World War II. Within the continental United States, both civilians and soldiers turned to telegrams for swift delivery of perishable information, like when to expect a man home on furlough. Telegrammed greetings, which cost more to send but arrived faster than letters, underscored the specialness of birthdays, holidays, and anniversaries. Conversely, though, telegrams wired from overseas often conveyed the worst of all possible news: terse notifications of injury, ill-health, or death. On occasion, Sam made use of the telegram in his fitful pursuit of Anne. But the Western Union was only as reliable as its users. The couple failed to meet in person before his departure for England when he neglected to send Anne the telegram he'd promised, alerting her to his anticipated hour of arrival at New York Penn Station when he headed north on leave from training at Fort McClellan, Alabama, in August 1942.[11]

Before they shipped overseas, service personnel could also call home during off-duty hours. But the telephone's utility as an aide to romantic intimacy was severely restricted. Phone calls were expensive. For servicemen, using the telephone could dent morale as well as finances. Placing a call through switchboard operators required waiting in line, sometimes for hours. And unless the soldier and his civilian caller had agreed a (necessarily approximate) window for their telephonic rendezvous in advance, the time spent queueing might prove to be in vain. Sam pointed out how frustrating this experience was in a letter to Anne after he'd tried calling one evening, only to find that she wasn't in. "When you wait around a damn but hot telephone booth for a certain period of time and the results are negative your temper grows rather short," he huffed. Anne had evidently not received – or failed to heed – a command he'd wired earlier in the day: "SHALL CALL THURS 830PM STAY HOME FOR A CHANGE." Men who harbored suspicions about their partners' fidelity were apt to jump to dire conclusions if their call went unanswered, as though absence from home could only mean one thing. Even when calls were successfully connected, conversations were generally limited to a few minutes. This was hardly enough time to resolve delicate relationship issues, even if the soldier wasn't deterred from broaching tender topics by the impatient throng of peers snapping at his heels.[12]

Overseas, the situation was even more challenging. A press story from December 1942 noted that the average call "costs Pvt. Johnny doughboy more than $10" – almost a week's wage for the lowliest enlistee, whose monthly pay was just $50. Depending on their location, soldiers willing to spend such exorbitant sums weren't necessarily in a position to do so. Those stationed in Britain, Africa, and Australia could forget about calling home altogether. It wasn't permitted.[13] In extremis, telephone connections could be made under the auspices of the American Red Cross, but even this crisis service wasn't a guaranteed entitlement. It was too costly. In October, 1944, the Red Cross estimated that, with approximately 30,000 injured men returning to the United States each month and calls costing $3 each, the annual bill would be $1.08 million.[14] Not until later that year did Congressional bill HR 5344 authorize federal funding to allow wounded soldiers to make one five-minute phone call as they journeyed home.

In locations like Hawai'i, Panama, central and south America, where able-bodied soldiers *did* enjoy access to telephones, they encountered the same pitfalls that beset those calling home from stateside military camps: tedious waits to use over-subscribed equipment, the possibility of a missed call, lack of privacy, poor sound quality, and the truncated duration of long-distance conversations. All this, only at greater cost and with a higher likelihood of failing to connect across different time-zones. Soldiers sometimes employed the telephone for choreographed occasions beloved of hometown newspapers, like one Passaic GI who used a three-minute call from Hawai'i to propose to his childhood sweetheart – worth every cent of the $19.80 charge, he jubilantly insisted, presumably having satisfied himself in advance of an affirmative answer.[15] But dramatic gestures aside, the telephone played only a minimal role in the routine maintenance of long-distance romantic relationships during World War II.

The phone remained marginal to deployed service personnel and their loved ones during later twentieth-century conflicts and into the early years of the new millennium. Veterans of the war in Vietnam remember rarely using the phone, even while stationed in the continental United States, "because it was just too much money," recalls Tom Nawrocki. Once in country, calling home became even more cumbersome and costly. Dennis Brodkin, another Vietnam veteran, had just two phone conversations with his wife while in Vietnam. Lasting three minutes, and with "not a lot of privacy," calls home sometimes felt less like a special treat than a tense ordeal. This could be all the more deflating when spouses anticipated that talking in real time would foster closeness rather than heightening distance.[16]

Operation Just Cause, the codename for the US invasion of Panama in 1989, was the first military operation in which deployed personnel enjoyed authorized use of telephones. But since access was still haphazard and calls made through official channels remained expensive, especially for enlisted personnel with modest salaries, some soldiers resorted to public payphones in Panamanian supermarkets. For their part, officers noted – as they would again during Operation Desert Shield the following year and in peacekeeping operations of the 1990s – that access to phones was as liable to dent soldiers' esprit as to elevate it. "Bad calls" left men feeling edgy and unsettled, unable to fix things without placing another call that threatened only to do more damage. Meanwhile, back at stateside bases, rear-detachment officers found that some wives who felt less connected with their husbands blamed the military for insufficient access to phones, not their partners' failure to call home regularly.[17]

Telephone calls may have done little to enhance soldiers' romantic relationships. Yet they've rarely been the medium women chose to sever intimate ties with distant servicemen. Soldiers and veterans infrequently tell stories of breakup phone calls.[18] Indeed, the idea of a telephonic Dear John seems rather oxymoronic. As men relate the experience of being "Dear Johned," many stress the case-closed one-sidedness of communiques that left them reeling. Dear John letters, by definition, don't appear invitations to dialog, but notifications of a mind unalterably made up. According to soldiers' lore, women have conveyed news of romantic rupture not only in a fashion but also under circumstances that deny the recipient any opportunity to respond, let alone negotiate. This explains the association between the vernacular expression "that's all she wrote" – connoting "we're done" finality – and the Dear John: coinages that emerged in tandem during World War II.[19]

The compounding aggravation of being unable to answer back forms a common motif of Dear John stories. "Many a soldier broke under the double blow of losing a loved one and not being able to fight to keep her – because he was thousands of miles from home," noted Eli Ginzberg in his three-volume postwar disquisition on *The Ineffective Soldier*.[20] Confronted with Anne Gudis's irate message, Sam Kramer couldn't do what he might've done had their courtship occurred in peacetime: namely, pick up the phone to demand an explanation or, in a more conciliatory vein, talk through their misunderstandings. Instead, he sent the V-mail to *Yank*, which published it not quite three weeks after Anne wrote it – a circuitous testament to the speed of mail service both across the Atlantic and within the ETO.

"TALKING LETTERS"

In the mid 1940s, the moment when soldiers overseas could call home more or less at will lay far in the future – another century's revelation. But World War II did witness early attempts to permit military personnel and loved ones to *hear* one another without actually conversing. Just months after the United States officially entered the war in December 1941, various commercial enterprises and entrepreneurs, typically working in conjunction with the United Service Organizations (USO) or American National Red Cross, advertised services permitting servicemen to record messages for their loved ones onto phonograph discs. In Harlem, Chappie Willet, jazz composer, arranger, and director of the Willet Music School, pioneered a service for soldiers and sailors to "photo-graph" their voices, as he put it. Men would compose letters and then speak them into a microphone connected to a recording device that would etch their voices in wax. These "wax letters" were the "latest fad for soldiers," gushed an enthusiastic reporter for the *Afro-American* newspaper.[21] Other initiatives soon followed that allowed not just men in uniform to record phonographs but spouses, sweethearts, and family members to do likewise. However, production of these audible souvenirs was curtailed when the War Department announced in July 1943 that it would prohibit the sending of such discs either to or from soldiers overseas: a regulation "necessary to safe-guard against the transmitting of secret military information through this medium."[22]

It seems unlikely that soldiers or family members, unless very brazen, foolhardy or ingenious in devising illicit coded forms of communication, would have attempted to convey operationally sensitive information by disc. The circumstances of production meant that these recordings were hardly clandestine. Several people were involved in the staging and recording process. This remained true of subsequent ventures to relay "talking letters" between soldiers fighting in Korea, then Vietnam, and loved ones at home. Typically, recording sessions were either pre-meditated or scripted performances: family members arrived at a local Red Cross chapter office, sometimes posing for a photograph in front of a festive backdrop (Christmas being the biggest catalyst for such projects), before recording their messages. The Red Cross encouraged civilians using the service to sing songs, play musical instruments, perform sketches, and even bring the family pet along, hoping animals or birds would lend a well-timed chirp or bark to the proceedings. Ten minutes was, after all, a long stretch to fill with impromptu musings. Red Cross workers wanted to avoid extended pauses in which tearfulness might well up, though one branch apparently kept a "Kleenex detail" on stand-by. Discs, and later tapes, were then mailed overseas, where servicemen listened to their recordings in quiet spaces set up by the USO for precisely this activity. In turn, soldiers could record messages for dispatch back home.[23] Champions of the aural turn proposed that hearing the recorded voice did far more to keep the distant loved one in felt proximity to the listener than the written word. In the phraseology of another promotional tag, these were "living letters." And living letters were indisputably better than dead letters.

By 1965, the Red Cross "Voices from Home" program had gained considerable momentum – only to succumb to rapid technological obsolescence. American military involvement in southeast Asia lasted so long that several innovations came and went between the initial despatch of "advisers" in the early 1960s and the final departure of US troops in 1973.

Phonograph discs and record players previously used in Korea became passé, supplanted by new tape recording devices. In turn, open reel tapes quickly ceded pride of place to encased plastic cassettes. As in World War II, commercial manufacturers seized brand-enhancement opportunities, pushing their products in the name of patriotic service. 3 M, makers of Scotch Tape, took the lead in producing and promoting "living letters" to and from servicemen serving in Vietnam.[24]

With some reason, the *Boston Globe* announced in 1968 that tapes provided "this war's cherished link between home and Vietnam." Spouses and other family members could send domestic updates and words of endearment to servicemen "over there" for just six cents, while fathers in uniform were now able to record bedtime stories for far-off sons and daughters, mailing tapes home at no cost at all. The rapid evolution of technology also cut out the need for third-party facilitators.

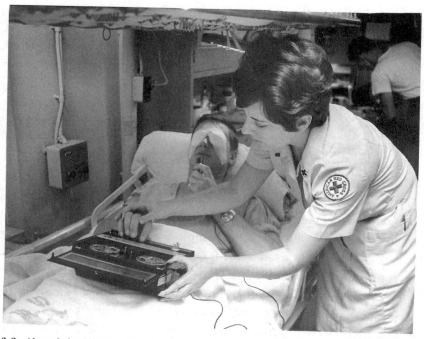

3.2. Aboard the US Navy Hospital Ship *Sanctuary*, American Red Cross worker Bridget Gregory helps a seriously wounded man tape record a message for his family in Austin, Texas in January 1969. (Courtesy of the National Archives and Records Administration.)

Anyone who could push a button and talk could make a tape recording. "The technician gave way to the average American consumer," observed the *Globe*'s Robert Taylor. And since servicemen in Vietnam were markedly *above*-average consumers – "armed with abundance," in historian Meredith Lair's apt phrase – GIs fueled the trend by buying two tape recorders at the PX (for two-thirds of the stateside price) and mailing one home.[25] Ralph Henry, serving with the American Red Cross Far Eastern Area Head Quarters, noted in 1965 that it was "quite extraordinary" how many GIs "own tape recorders of every description." Cassette tapes were, though, emphatically on the ascendant. By 1971, an estimated 90 percent of service personnel relied on tapes to maintain contact with home.[26]

The Red Cross found its gigantic stockpile of tapes and clunky recording equipment moldering unwanted in Vietnamese warehouses. Not everyone in the Red Cross regretted that they were getting out of the recording business, however.[27] As had (and has) been the case with every wave of technology that's aspired – or threatened – to transform human communication, critics regretted the dwindling primacy of the written word. Letters, they insisted, were better suited to fostering close bonds than tape recorded messages. Marie Youngberg, national director of Red Cross Services for Military Families, lamented in April 1965 that, "many servicemen and their families do not write each other regularly or frequently." Stateside Red Cross workers fielded frequent requests from GIs' family members to investigate why men in Vietnam weren't writing home more often and, more importantly, to *do* something about this deficit. Youngberg didn't agree with colleagues that recordings represented an adequate substitute for letters. "Rather, as part of our Communications Service we should give increasing emphasis to the values of direct correspondence in keeping family ties strong when members are separated by military service. We further should emphasize that nothing can take the place of letters between family members – Voices from Home recordings can only supplement, not supplant them."[28]

She had a point. At least until GIs and their intimates came into possession of their own portable equipment, recording and play-back arrangements were too cumbersome for regular use, and too intrusively engineered for intensely felt forms of expression. Recorded messages were perhaps better understood as audible mementos than "living letters." (Often, though, tapes weren't preserved as souvenirs, but recorded over and sent back into circulation.) Taped messages were good for turning absence into audible presence, but less well suited to the daily sharing of news and affirmations of love.[29] Although some soldiers and civilians who struggled with written self-expression may have found it easier to record messages onto tape than paper, the process didn't lend itself to deeply personal disclosure. Recording monologs has become commonplace in the age of social media, but to Americans in the 1960s and 1970s being taped while speaking aloud to an unseen inter-locutor was a peculiar situation that must have felt unnatural to more self-conscious or less eloquent servicemen and civilians who tried to adapt to changing times.

Imperfect conveyers of sentiment, records and tapes surely had little role to play in the Dear John's evolution – or so one might imagine. If it was challenging to compose a conventional letter breaking off a romantic relationship, wouldn't it be much harder for a woman to record a message to that effect at her local Red Cross chapter? Would volunteers even consent to assist in such a venture? The records of the American National Red Cross (housed in the National Archives at College Park, Maryland) contain no evidence that women ever approached the organ-ization with such a mission in mind, only the reverse. On at least one occasion, workers coached a woman to record reassuring messages to her husband in Vietnam after he became despondent and sent home letters broaching the topic of divorce. Apparently, her recorded voice worked its reassuring magic, and the marriage was saved, or at least bandaged for the time being.[30]

Yet the Dear John *has* been associated with disc and tape recordings in both popular culture and psychiatric literature. An episode of *M*A*S*H*, the Korea-set military medical sit-com that aired on CBS from 1972 to 1983, played for laughs the hapless corporal Radar's receipt of a Dear John via phonograph disc. Conveniently for comic plot-thickening pur-poses, the record allowed Radar's romantic misfortune to be broadcasted to the mobile medical unit as a whole, prompting the intervention of captains "Hawkeye" Pierce and "Trapper John" McIntyre, desperate to fix him up with a wildly unsuitable new girlfriend. Perhaps the writers were drawn to the unlikeliness of a Dear John being recorded onto a disc and mailed to Korea, injecting an element of surreal improbability into the proceedings. But it's possible that the show's scenarists didn't pluck this plot-line from thin air alone. By the time the ironically entitled "Love Story" episode aired on January 7, 1973, it had become axiomatic that the Vietnam war had spawned more – and also more hostile – Dear John letters than any previous conflict.[31] Although set in Korea, *M*A*S*H* functioned as an oblique commentary on the current conflict in Vietnam. Its characters' manners, mores, and modes of attire owed more to the 1970s present than the early-1950s past they ostensibly inhabited. As the show's creators were doubtless well aware, Dear Johns were a common fixture of news media reports and vernacular war story-telling of the late 1960s and early 1970s. Not only that but, according to one authority, women sent breakup messages to grunts in Vietnam using the latest gadgetry of the "electronic age."[32]

This proposition was popularized by Dr. Emanuel Tanay. The prominent forensic psychiatrist had been in the public eye before, testifying at the trial of Jack Ruby in 1964. In 1969, Tanay delivered a paper at the American Psychiatric Association (APA) annual meeting where he introduced a psychopathology he dubbed the "Dear John Syndrome." Although scholarly presentations rarely make for good copy, Tanay's thesis gained instant traction in the press – boosted, no doubt, by his more startling claims. Had there ever been an age in which young women composed regretful breakup notes to men at war, that era was definitely past. Nowadays, Tanay announced, women's letters weren't apologetic or abashed. Despite the youth of their authors and the brevity of their marriages, these women were shockingly "bitter" and "full of hatred." "Some send photographs of themselves with other men in compromising positions," Tanay told an Associated Press reporter. More callous yet, "Some send tape recordings of intimate exchanges with another man." In the published version of his APA paper, Tanay characterized one woman as a "true child of our technological age; she tape recorded an amorous session with the new boyfriend for the benefit of the old boyfriend."[33]

Tanay claimed he'd amassed copious evidence corroborating the "syndrome" on a visit to Vietnam in January 1969. Officers had bombarded him with letters sent to "distraught and desperate men," and despite many of the specimens being "taped together after having been torn to bits, or smoothed out after they were crumpled into a ball and heaved at the nearest wastebasket," the psychiatrist preserved them for analysis. Regrettably, Tanay's collection of written and recorded Dear Johns has not survived and found its way into the Walter Reuther library at Wayne State University to which he posthumously bequeathed his papers. That deficit makes it impossible to know whether Tanay found evidence that just one woman – the "true child" of the electronic era – had tape recorded herself with a new boyfriend to make her former lover's betrayal all the more woundingly felt, or if this was (as his earlier remarks to the Associated Press implied) a more widespread practice. If it were indeed commonplace, the taping of Dear John messages – whether "amorous sessions" or spoken-word breakup announcements – has left remarkably few traces elsewhere, other than scholarly articles all indebted to Tanay as their source. Dozens of Vietnam veterans' oral history interviews, as well as myriad letters, diaries, and memoirs, contain no mention of Dear John tapes but abundant references to more conventional letters.[34]

Perhaps Tanay extrapolated from one incident to strengthen his case: that there was something qualitatively and quantitatively different (and worse) in the Dear Johns sent to servicemen in Vietnam than those despatched in any prior conflict. We will return to Tanay – his trip to Vietnam and his clinical judgments – later. But, for now, the most salient point about his claims is that they evidently resonated with contemporaries who were minded to believe the worst about women and their back-stabbing mistreatment of soldiers in Vietnam. What's more, in the view of Tanay and his acolytes, these developments were intimately bound up with the power of new technology to bring distant parties together, but also tear them apart with unprecedented efficiency.

FROM THE ELECTRONIC AGE TO THE DIGITAL ERA

The image Tanay conjured of a young woman tape-recording herself *in flagrante* with a new boyfriend and sending the cassette to an unsuspecting ex established what would become a recurrent trope. Each iteration has inserted its moment's latest technology into the scenario, giving the tableau of betrayal a contemporary spin.

Although these stories often smack of the apocryphal, the most prominent version presents itself as autobiographical. *Jarhead*, Marine Corps veteran Anthony Swofford's memoir of the Gulf War (1990–1991), offers readers a vignette of marines sitting down to watch a "homemade porn film spliced into a Vietnam flick." Sent to one grunt by his wife in a "care package," the video turns out to be anything but caring. As Swofford describes the scene, the marines are initially "elated that the amateur smut had made it past the censors." But the husband has an altogether different reaction when he realizes the woman in the recording is his wife, "fucking the neighbor, a goddamn squid!" Weeping hysterically, the cuckolded grunt is hurried out and placed on suicide watch at sick call. Reworked by Sam Mendes in the screen version of *Jarhead*, the woman (hooded in Swofford's memoir, hence recognizable only to her husband) acquires a motive but also appears more calculatedly malicious. The grunts *imagine* they're settling down to watch *The Deer Hunter*, as pirated and sent to one marine by his wife. But even as the opening bars of "Cavatina" still linger, the marines unexpectedly encounter raw footage of a woman (naked and unhooded) having sex with a man. Realizing what he's seeing, the husband starts crying and yelling, "I want to go home!" His buddies bundle him out of the room before the woman on the tape delivers her *coup de grâce*. Turning to the camera, she asks, "Who's fucking around now, Brian?," and gives him the finger. This was "revenge porn" before that coinage came to denote the antithesis: not female-produced porn intended to hurt an ex who realizes his ex-ness only in the viewing, but graphic images of women made public by aggrieved former husbands or boyfriends to disgrace and shame women with whom they'd been intimate.[35]

Mendes's "enhanced" version of Swofford's original text illustrates the ease with which Dear John scenarios acquire more outrageous embellishments in the retelling. Similar stories circulate online, encouraged by the internet's evidentiary lawlessness: an electronic wild west where anyone can post more or less anything and pass it off as true. Since some websites purport to sift the chaff of urban legend from the whole-germ wheat of truth, it's no surprise that the fact-checking site snopes.com should have investigated whether any serviceman in the Gulf War *really* received a "surprise 'Dear John' video from his home." Nor is it surprising that what's billed as a search to verify or falsify this mythic tale – posted in 2005, as *Jarhead* made its cinematic premiere – should offer an opportunity for online sharing of yet more salacious variations on Swofford's theme. Snopes's co-founder and author David Mikkelson skeptically notes that, "Very few claim to have seen the video themselves. Most who swear by it base their belief in the tale on the word of someone of their acquaintance who says he was there." But many online surfers, one suspects, may be less invested in the truth-status of these graphic anecdotes than gratified by their X-rated content.[36]

Other online sites go further. Some give visitors the opportunity to view servicemen's unfaithful wives *in flagrante*, billed as footage captured by returning veterans who walked in – camera-phone in hand – on cheating wives or girlfriends. When one marine (or someone claiming to be a marine) posted a video of this sort to boost his GoFundMe venture, an online story reporting on the "viral" video attracted 445 comments in July 2015. Misogyny grows vigorously on this ever-expanding trellis of invented, exaggerated, or autobiographical material. In the analog era, the specter of female infidelity served as a goad to, and justification for, woman-hating. But the desire to police and punish women's sexually errant behavior has been made more potent by technologies that allow instantaneous sharing of footage, pictures, and text with unknown numbers of prurient strangers online. Viewers' comments (posted by men and women alike) frequently echo Patton's injunction that unfaithful women – the senders of Dear Johns to servicemen – "should be shot."[37]

Stories of women's cruel and unusual exposure of their unfaithfulness represent the outer extreme of ubiquitous concerns about the impact of digital technologies on twenty-first-century relationships between deployed personnel and their distant partners. Initially, the military was reluctant to embrace "new media" or "web 2.0" technologies in any guise – from MySpace to Facebook, Skype to FaceTime, email to SMS, blogs to Twitter, Flickr to Instagram. Not surprisingly, the DoD and individual services feared losing control over the communicative channels used by active duty personnel. The military had been hesitant to permit personnel overseas access to telephones in the 1980s and 1990s. During the Gulf War, soldiers enjoyed only intermittent access to secure satellite phone-connections. When cellphones and personal laptops became ubiquitous over the next decade, the DoD bridled. In the name of preserving Operational Security (OPSEC), the Pentagon initially tried to prevent uniformed personnel from entering the digital era in lockstep with civilians, banning access to social media sites including Facebook, Twitter, and YouTube. Instead, it experimented with a parallel online military universe complete with its own more secure variant of Facebook, a "milblog" space on which posts would be monitored by officers, and an idiosyncratic hybrid dubbed "Motomail" (short for motivational) by the Marine Corps and "Hooahmail" by the army, which briefly followed suit. Motomail provided same-day delivery to deployed personnel of messages that family members logged onto a secure online site to compose. Sent encrypted to Iraq, these notes were then printed and sealed into tear-strip envelopes to ensure confidentiality. Launched in 2004, this service fell victim to DoD budget cuts in 2013.[38]

Sooner or later, and often sooner rather than later, successive maneuvers to keep service personnel away from the perilous online world came to an end. From a present-day perspective, failure seems a foregone conclusion. Even during the life-time of these ventures, military attempts to move not so much with as *alongside* the times encountered skepticism from uniformed men and women deployed to Afghanistan and Iraq in the early years of those operations. And even as it banned access to social media sites, the DoD spent more than $165 million between 2004 and 2006 to construct cybercafes in Iraq alone, completing 170 by July of that year.[39]

With access to networked computers enabled by the DoD and non-profits like Freedom Calls, which raised funds for satellite links and communications hardware for soldiers in Iraq, more and more service personnel took to documenting their tours and connecting with distant friends and family online. By 2007, Facebook had become the primary way in which soldiers overseas maintained contact with home, supplemented with web-cam conversations, and later video-chats via Skype or FaceTime. Rather than persist in trying to divert online activity into approved channels, the DoD surrendered to the inevitable. In 2010, the Pentagon issued a new policy, authorizing access to social networking sites from the military's non-classified computer network, but with some caveats. Commanders would continue to "defend against malicious activity," attempt to stop cyber attacks, and safeguard missions, and could monitor internet and social media use by men and women under their command, though the onus remained on individuals to observe OPSEC.[40]

This intensification of connectivity reinvigorated long-running debates about the character and consequences of communication with home. Was more frequent contact between separated partners always a positive development – for service personnel, couples, and the armed forces? Over the past decade, the answer to this question at both an individual and institutional level has frequently been either a flat negative or a qualified formula, invoking the "mixed blessing" or "double-edged" properties of technologies that permit more ongoing to-and-fro between soldiers and partners than in any prior era, as well as affording novel modes of interaction, such as real-time video conversation.[41]

For deployed personnel, "family" shifted from an "abstract to concrete concept" during the wars in Iraq and Afghanistan, proposed military sociologists Dr. Leonard Wong and Colonel Stephen Gerras.[42] At first blush, romantic partners' enhanced palpability might appear a welcome development. During World War II, after all, some advice columnists ascribed the writing of Dear John letters to a form of "forgetfulness" they twinned with fickleness. "You let distance rob him of all the assets that once made him seem so wonderful," tutted Maureen Daly from her *Chicago Daily Tribune* column, addressing female readers whose amnesia might lead them into romantic temptation. Trivializing the many reasons why wartime relationships unraveled – frayed by protracted separation, coupled with uncertainty about when, whether, and in what condition the serviceman would return – Daly implied that demobilized men would return home unmarked by the experience of war. "You forget that if you spent one evening with him, talked to him a while, danced with him just once – everything would be just as it was before."[43] The trick, then, was to freeze the missing man's likeness for the duration, projecting ahead to the day when the veteran seamlessly rejoined the civilian world.

Where distance spelled danger in the 1940s, twenty-first-century commentators focus instead on the pitfalls of excessive digital proximity between separated loved ones. Digital era expectations of constant accessibility – that texts should be responded to immediately, calls answered on the spot – can feel burdensome to uniformed personnel. Likewise, divergent notions of what constitutes good or sufficient communication can generate friction between partners. Military deployment manuals counsel couples to establish ground-rules about how much and what kind of contact they would prefer prior to departure, stressing the merits of "old-fashioned" letters. A soldier's non-responsiveness may aggravate a stateside spouse's fears over his safety and also, perhaps, his fidelity (and vice versa). Anxiety over an incommunicado spouse's whereabouts can quickly metastasize into existential dread over death or divorce, as partners entertain worst-case scenarios to explain why a text or call went unheeded, dismissing more mundane reasons for silence or delayed responses. Even in the digital age, active duty doesn't permit constant connectivity. The pressures of the job are many, as may be demands on over-subscribed communications equipment. But even where soldiers enjoy reliable, round-the-clock access to phones and laptops (rarely the case for personnel serving in Iraq and Afghanistan), they don't always wish to be available "on demand." Pressure to be present while absent is difficult to manage when the very terms of engagement prohibit candid discussion of what the soldier does and sees from day to day. Some experience this as a form of frustration that there's "nothing new to say." And rather than confront awkward pauses – liable to be read by partners as evidence of emotional unavailability – they retreat from daily communication.[44]

In the judgment of some military psychologists, the key challenge facing present-day service personnel isn't so much absence from home as "incomplete separation."[45] Personnel deployed overseas remain physically distant, but find themselves expected to be constantly involved in maintaining intimate partnerships and, frequently, in parenting too. Occupying the distinct roles of lover/parent/soldier demands head-spinning switches of affect, demeanor, and register from one moment to the next. It's one thing to read "Stuart Little" onto a tape that'll be mailed back to an infant in the States, a scenario sentimentally conjured by the *Boston Globe* in 1968, and another proposition altogether to tell bedtime stories via Skype before, say, heading out on patrol or manning

3.3. A young man calls home from Camp Echo, Iraq, cradling the handgun he has just reassembled. According to *The Denver Post*, which published this photograph on December 7, 2008, cell phone service was one perk enjoyed by soldiers at the "Ritz-Carlton" of forward operating bases. (Photo by Craig F. Walker/*The Denver Post* via Getty Images.)

a checkpoint in Baghdad. Being a loving partner, an affectionate parent, and a focused soldier all at once requires prodigious feats of emotional discipline. Some Vietnam veterans count themselves lucky to have relied on letters and tapes alone. "I cannot imagine comin' in off an ambush and callin' my wife," Joseph Oltman mused in an oral history interview in 2014. "That's really got to be a circus goin' on in your brain . . . How can those two things fit together?"[46]

Thomas Stefanko, an army colonel who served in Iraq, concluded that they did *not* fit together – at least not without detriment to both deployed personnel and their unit's operational efficiency. Having cellphones in combat was "a very bad thing," Stefanko told an interviewer. "You have to stay mission focused all the time, 24/7 and that's impossible when you just got off the phone with your wife and you found the water heater blew up and the basement flooded and the kid really had a bad time his first day at school, and uh, by the way, dad, you weren't there so you're a SOB anyway."[47]

In more tender moments, technologies that let partners hear and see one another – to talk, smile, laugh, joke, or cry in real time – provide reminders that, although "connected," they are achingly not *together*. For some, this frustratingly disembodied "concreteness" represents an anguishing state of suspension: a holding pattern in which touch-down seems endlessly deferred. For others, it's such an unendurable tension that they sever contact with home altogether.[48]

With serial redeployments exacerbating the ordeal of "incomplete separation," all branches of the military now offer explicit counsel to couples in preparation for time apart. Some of this advice is decades-old, like the recommendation that partners number their letters so that the recipient can retrospectively order them in chronological sequence, even if delivery is erratic – a practice common among letter-writing couples in World War II. Other tips contained in the *U.S. Army Deployment Cycle Readiness: Soldier's and Family Member's Handbook* likewise hark back to pre-digital times. The recommendation to "write with your Spouse's picture in front of you, as though you were talking directly to him/her" evokes iconic images from the 1940s that depicted young women gazing reverently at their absent partner's portrait, pen poised in mid-air. Similarly, advice that letter writers not commit anything recklessly to paper replicates a familiar motif from V-mail ads. With regard to email composition, army-issued instructions take on a sharper, cautionary tone: "Be careful of using this method of communication for an emotionally laden message. It is better to compose it, park it for a few hours, review it for clarity and kindness, and then send it." For its part, the Fleet and Family Support Center counsels against "sending an email when you are angry," an emotion military spouses were urged to repress altogether in previous conflicts.[49]

Echoing complaints about the tape as an inferior mode of connection made during the Vietnam war, the twenty-first-century armed forces concur that email "does not replace the letter for personal and romantic communication." "Letters can sometimes be more powerful than other forms of communication," the Pentagon reminds uniformed personnel and their loved ones. And indeed several military studies over the past decade have found anecdotal evidence that some soldiers still cherish letters as more potent emissaries of home, and a more intimate form of communication than easily monitored online exchanges. Unlike emails, which require a computer and internet access to be read and re-read, letters are portable. They provide service members with "something tangible to carry with them throughout the deployment," the DoD's *Military Deployment Guide* points out. For some soldiers, love letters continue to be endowed with talismanic properties, an amulet against harm.[50] But most evidence gathered over the past decade suggests that such sentiments – like the paper objects that inspire them – are increasingly rare.

NO MORE DEAR JOHNS?

Pundits in the digital age often treat breaking-up as a humorous phenomenon. In the late 1990s, when the internet was entering puberty, various online services popped up offering to help dissatisfied partners split up for a modest fee. Politesubtlehints.com promised to send users' soon-to-be-exes anonymous notes and trial-size products, like bug repellent and Preparation H, by priority mail, while lifer.com touted a more direct approach, sending "evil Ex-greetings" to unwanted boyfriends and girlfriends. A decade later, gossip sites routinely divulged news that a certain celebrity had dumped another celebrity by text. But plenty of "ordinary" people also learned they'd been ditched by SMS. When comedians Eva McEhrue and Mel Owens invited their fans to submit read-aloud versions of final texts received from former partners, their YouTube video featuring these valedictory messages received more than 1.5 million views in a week. This viral phenomenon in 2015 prompted ABC Nightline presenter, Dan Harris, to pronounce the death of an obsolescent form: "in the old days people either broke up with you in person or with a handwritten note sometimes called a Dear John letter. Suffice it to say those days are over."[51]

The jocularity of these breakup sites and memes stands in marked contrast to the somber tenor of much commentary on how the digital revolution has destabilized intimate relationships in military circles. Behavior that may seem comically cavalier in the civilian world – a reality TV star's text telling her husband she wants a divorce –

reverberates with different force when the recipient is a soldier serving overseas.

In military psychology literature, online discussion boards and veterans' testimony, the dangerous velocity of electronic communication is a theme that recurrently surfaces in connection with Dear Johns sent by email, social media, or text. Stationed in Balad, Iraq in 2007, Captain Glen Wurglitz, a psychologist with 785th Medical Group, told *Stars and Stripes*: "Back in the olden days, a 'Dear John' letter used to take three months to arrive. With instant messaging it's 'I'm selling the house.' Send."[52] Wurglitz exaggerated. Even during World War II, letters rarely took three months to arrive. As for the simultaneous announcement of divorce and property sale by text, we can only guess whether many SMS messages took quite such a brutal form. But some stateside partners certainly *did* use instant messages to terminate relationships, with or without a real estate transaction appended. Airman Robin Ault recollects the electronic Dear John he received while serving in Iraq:

> I actually – when I first got over there, I had a girlfriend, and – it was a new one on me – I got blown off via text message, which was a new shootdown. I had never been – you know, hey, can't see you anymore, and I'm like, wow, technology, isn't it wonderful?

Others relate that they, or those serving with them, had relationships ended via MySpace messages and Facebook chats while serving in Iraq or Afghanistan. Some soldiers report having called home only to overhear, or intuit, the presence of another man with their wife or girlfriend.[53]

Many commentators on digital breakups in the military tacitly endorse a ballistic theory of communication. They hypothesize that the faster "bad news" travels, the greater the damage it inflicts on impact with its target. Put differently, a Dear John delivered almost instantaneously by text, email, or social media leaves a messier exit wound than a conventional letter. This proposition implies that mail, which may hitherto have taken days or even weeks to reach its destination, lost some of its force by dawdling along the way. Delayed communication stung less, lacking the sharp edge of immediacy.

Whether recipients of mailed Dear John letters would agree that greater velocity equates with deeper heartbreak is a moot point.

Servicemen in World War II, Korea, and Vietnam may well have felt that speed of delivery had little to do with the pain caused by a breakup note, even (or perhaps especially) if the *fait accompli* was days or weeks old by the time men discovered they'd been rejected. Personnel deployed overseas in those conflicts faced a now largely eliminated obstacle to sustaining intimate partnerships: tardy and inconsistent mail delivery.

For troops serving in the most insular and isolated theaters of World War II, not knowing what was going on at home – why they'd heard nothing for weeks at a time – could prove a nagging distraction from duty. Imagination readily filled the void left by silence with fretful, or more morbid, speculation. Military morale reports compiled in the Southwest Pacific bulged with complaints about the parlous condition of the mail service. In January 1944, one disgruntled GI vented in a letter home: "You know the old s–t they dish out in the States, 'Keep up the Soldiers' Morale, Write regularly.' Well if they'd worry less about those posters and try to do a little more about getting our mail over here I might feel just a little bit better about 'doing my part.'" Another enlisted man suggested to his girlfriend that "she might as well cast her letters off in a bottle and throw them into the river after a heavy rain." Their arrival could scarcely be any less speedy or certain than through the army postal service. Embittered soldiers often seethed over the agonizingly slow pace of mail delivery, while half-empty planes flew back and forth, and mailbags sat moldering undelivered in New Guinea warehouses.[54]

These comments have been preserved because morale officers kept a beady look-out for anything in GIs' letters that cast doubt on the "sanctity of the mail," supposedly an inviolate principle. But while it was forbidden for enlisted men to voice complaints about censorship in letters home, some officers violated their men's mail in more egregious ways. One enlisted man explained to his wife how hard it was to express loving sentiments in his letters when these heartfelt outpourings elicited the mockery of his college student officer. The latter had scornfully asked whether she believed everything in the letters. "'I really admire your wife if she does,' jibed the officer." The humiliated GI continued, "So darling if my letters don't sound so good it is because of the reasons above." Not uncommonly, enlisted men noted in letters home how they'd seen officers chuckling together in their mess hall as they censored mail, reading

3.4. Censorship was sometimes a social occasion for officers. Here, Lt. Speckles and Lt. Williams censor enlisted men's mail while Capt. Warwick and Lt. Smith play cribbage using a caribou horn in the Aleutian Islands, November 24, 1943. (Courtesy of the National Archives and Records Administration.)

"choice bits aloud so they can all laugh." Some officers even took their subordinates to task for poor "sentence structure, grammar and continuity of thought," as though they weren't screening letters but grading papers. Officers who compiled morale reports were clearly troubled that some of their brethren plundered supposedly sacrosanct mail for purposes of humiliation. Yet historians can quote verbatim from aggrieved enlisted men's letters only because complaints about officers' violations were themselves censorable: a salutary reminder that archival researchers, no respecters of the "sanctity of the mail" either, are guilty of secondary acts of trespass.[55]

Two or more decades later, sluggish mail delivery remained a dampener of morale during the earlier years of America's Vietnam war. Prior to 1966, surface mail could take as long as sixty to ninety days in transit – an untenable situation MACV worked hard to address, reducing the transit time for airmail letters and packages to just three or four days in major base areas.[56] Public Law 87–725 (authorized in November 1966) boosted efforts to expedite mail by authorizing the airlift of all letters and personal tape recordings between the continental United States and Military Post Offices overseas at surface-rate postage. That a choked system had been unblocked was attested by a huge increase in postage stamp sales on US military bases in Vietnam, nearly doubling from 4,534,162 in 1966 to 8,360,176 the following year.[57] Even if mail still took longer than a few days to reach remote bases, GIs didn't have to compose love letters with the inhibiting knowledge that an officer would later read their words, and perhaps ridicule them. Personal correspondence wasn't subject to censorship in Vietnam. During the recent wars in Iraq and Afghanistan, officers have been empowered to monitor their subordinates' online activity and social media use, but have not scrutinized outgoing "snail mail" or listened in on phone calls.[58]

Rather than trying to determine whether today's soldiers are uniquely cursed by remaining digitally within the orbit of home while deployed overseas, it's perhaps more judicious to note that sustaining love in wartime is – and always has been – an immensely demanding proposition. Individuals experience these demands in highly personal ways. Technology that makes separation bearable to some can make it unendurable to others. There is, in short, no ideal distance between "here" and "there" that resolves intrinsic tensions between being at home and being at war; remaining in love and participating in conflict. Each generation of American soldiers has faced the challenge of how to be emotionally present in one location while remaining professionally focused in another. "A good soldier can't have a divided mind," warned Cpl. Roscoe A. Rogers in the *Afro-American* in 1943.[59] Contemporary commentators often imagine the digital era presents more severe challenges of split consciousness than soldiers experienced hitherto. Slow-moving communications, they imply, facilitated compartmentalization and, with "home" sealed in its remote airtight box, uniformed personnel must have found deployment less stressful.[60] But in the 1940s minds were commonly divided by anxious imaginings prompted by too *little* connection with home. And Dear Johns mailed across oceans sometimes felt just as wounding as texts pinged over the ether.

CHAPTER 4

"That's All She Wrote": Telling Dear John Stories

BEFORE ANY GIS HAD SHIPPED OVERSEAS IN WORLD WAR II, and months before they coined the term "Dear John," men in uniform had already begun to buffer themselves against the prospect of romantic rejection. That female affections would flutter off and alight elsewhere, like butterflies in search of fresh pollen, struck some soldiers as an immutable law of nature. The odds of desertion appeared so high to a group of draftees at Camp Callan in California that they established a mutual fund, "Love Insurance, Inc.," which would offer fiscal compensation to the brokenhearted. In February 1942, just two months after the Japanese attack on Pearl Harbor, the *Los Angeles Times* delightedly pounced on this venture, reporting that draftees paid a monthly premium of twenty-five cents (a rather modest downpayment, given the magnitude of the stakes) to "insure themselves against loss of the affection of their sweethearts back home to young men as yet unclaimed by the forces." The $15 pool would be payable to one who can "prove he has lost his erstwhile sweetheart to a rival."[1]

Mere days later, the dividend was claimed by a "tall, handsome former Texas ranch hand," twenty-four-year-old Cpl. Wallace Butcher, newly in receipt of a distressing communication from his fiancée. As reported in the press, Butcher had "no inkling" that anything was awry until his engagement ring dropped from an envelope, heralding unwelcome news before he'd even unfolded the note. "I've known her for three years, and this was quite a shock to me," Butcher confided to reporters. "Some bounder must have take advantage of my absence." This was hard to take. But to sweeten the pot, another bonus accompanied the cash pay-out: a date with starlet Janet Blair, whose picture appeared on the scheme's policy papers to remind subscribers that she'd promised a tour of Hollywood nightspots to the first beneficiary of Love Insurance. Butcher's night out on the town with Blair – to "help mend his broken heart" – made perfect Valentine's Day press fodder. The *Times* pictured the attractive pair making eyes at one another over a shared milkshake. "NOT SO BAD," ran the caption. "Corp. Wallace Butcher, Camp Callan, doesn't seem so downhearted over losing his girl as he dines with Janet Blair, actress, at expense of film studio."[2]

This sequence of stories about GIs expecting their love to be lost, looking for consolation from brothers-in-arms, and finding it in the arms of other women established a template reused throughout the war. Anticipation, rejection, compensation, and recuperation looped around in an endless chain of bonds broken and reforged.

Camp Callan's premium-paying draftees soon found a counterpart in the "Brush-Off Clubs" inaugurated by GIs overseas. *Yank* reported in January 1943 that soldiers in India had started this organization for purposes of "mutual sympathy" – to "exchange condolences and cry in their beer while telling each other the mournful story of how 'she wouldn't wait.'" The accompanying photograph showed four soldiers crouching around a low table on which sat the black-bordered portrait of a young woman. Others stood at a slight distance from this devotional object, holding candles. With towels draped over their shoulders or worn in turban-style, the soldiers engaged in mock ceremonial activity befitting a club in which key officeholders styled themselves "chief consoler," "chief sweater," and "chief crier." A special category of pending membership was reserved for "just sweating members," who expected, but hadn't yet received, Dear Johns. These were "guys who can't believe that no news is good news," *Yank* columnist Sgt. Ed Cunningham explained. For men who'd sworn to "provide willing shoulders to cry upon, and join fervently in the waiting and weeping," they seemed to be having an awful lot of fun. And since these hijinks hinted more at hilarity than tragedy, it's not surprising *Yank* soon ran a follow-up. This one included "how-to"

Pfc. Frank Platt of Atlanta, Ga., is inducted into the Brush-Off Club in India.

4.1. With mock solemnity, members of the inaugural "Brush-Off Club" in India gather to mourn their romantic losses in 1943. (Courtesy of *Yank*/U.S. Army.)

instructions on setting up local affiliates of the Brush-Off Club, complete with a template application form.[3]

GIs' ingenuity at play was too good a story for civilian journalists to pass up. Like the Camp Callan insurance policy, the Brush-Off Clubs attracted nation-wide attention. The rapid proliferation of branches across different theaters of war from India to North Africa to Italy – "wherever Johnny Doughboy goes to war – or to wait," as Associated Press reporter Kenneth Dixon put it – gave correspondents an opportunity to wire home news of GIs' lighthearted response to the serious business of being brokenhearted while fighting overseas. By 1944, this news didn't have to be cabled back home. Brush-Off Club branches were sprouting up stateside. The *Washington Post* announced that New York's swanky Hotel Astor kept a table permanently reserved as the city's branch HQ, so that "victims of blasted romance" could "enjoy each other's company."[4]

Stories in this playful vein spanned successive years of World War II, and far outstripped it. Soon after the Korean war, marines formed a club for "cast-off Romeos who were rejected by their Stateside gals," as *Leatherneck* put it. Eligibility depended on an applicant's having received "at least one Dear John letter while in Korea." Fittingly, the club adopted Jean Shepard and Ferlin Husky's hit, "A Dear John Letter," as its "official marching song."[5] Fifteen years later, marines serving in Vietnam used their magazine, *Sea Tiger*, to publicize a "Dear John of the Month" competition, with winners chosen for "originality, effectiveness or subtleness."[6]

Beneath the jocular bonhomie, reports on Brush-Off Clubs and their many derivatives – almost invariably authored by men – aimed a sharper point at women. Neither sympathetic sobbing nor emotional recuperation was the clubs' exclusive order of business. Readers didn't have to scratch too far below the surface for the subtext: namely, that deterrence and retaliation featured high on the agenda. Press stories rarely failed to make apparent that finding other women was integral to the Brush-Off Clubs' mission. GIs responsible for the original branch in India styled it a "womanpower mobilization organization," and a "Good Hunting Committee" convened "as often as two or three men can get leave anywhere females are in evidence." Women who might've been tempted to break off a romance with a soldier should beware. They could expect to be reviled and replaced in short order – "shorn of their glamour," as the *Washington Post* put it in a story about Hollywood starlets assisting Camp Callan draftees bounce back from rejection.[7]

Stories about Brush-Off Clubs formed a main artery by which the Dear John – as a phrase and a phenomenon – entered into cultural circulation, flowing from GI parlance into everyday American vernacular. Fittingly, Milton Bracker's introduction of this new slang expression to readers of the *New York Times* in October 1943 began with a reference to a "Dear John club."[8] Bracker's intention, like that of other journalists covering the same beat, was didactic. To remind women to keep their letters to soldiers fond and frequent, reporters included ostensibly verbatim excerpts from women's breakup letters. These snippets provided object lessons in how *not* to write to a man at war. Over the course of World War II, civilian and military journalists introduced readers to specimens of the genre that have proven remarkably long-lived, and even more remarkably under-scrutinized.

Historians who reference Dear John letters in World War II almost invariably cite the same handful of examples, as do compilers of dictionaries of historical slang. There's the nameless GI who received a six-page letter from his fiancée in Texas, the final paragraph of which breezily announced, "'I was married last week but my husband won't mind you writing to me occasionally. He's a sailor and very broadminded." Another soldier, Ahmed S., also surfaces regularly in historical scholarship. His wife's letter, announcing the end of their marriage, apparently concluded like this:

> The time has come to clear things between us. You will have realized, before now, that our marriage was a mistake. I beg of you to put an end to this mistake and get a divorce ... As a matter of fact, I have never been yours, but now I belong to someone else, and this finishes things between us.

And then there's Sam Kramer, with his notorious V-mail from Anne Gudis.[9]

These examples share something in common. They all initially appeared in the pages of *Yank*, submitted by men who wanted to publicize their partner's disloyalty to a wider audience. The GI whose fiancée had married the easy-going sailor was featured in *Yank*'s story about the inaugural Brush-Off Club in India. Ahmed S. notified *Yank* of his wife's cruel desertion and how she'd broken it to him, just as Sam submitted the "shortest V-mail letter in ETO" for the army weekly magazine's consideration. Because the V-mail format facilitated reproduction, Gudis's brush-off was published in facsimile form, unlike the other two letters, which *Yank* merely quoted. As a result, while we know that Gudis did indeed tell Kramer to "Go to Hell!," we can't be sure exactly what the wife of the "broadminded sailor" and the seemingly heartless Mrs. "S." wrote to their former partners.[10]

It's curious that historians, trained to verify provenance and approach evidence gingerly, should be so trusting when it comes to Dear John letters. Scholars have treated the specimens quoted above as authentic samples of this genre, ignoring red flags that signal caution would be in order. Like many printed specimens of the

Dear John, these examples made their public debut in press stories about the ludic ways in which soldiers responded to heartbreak. Reporters not only celebrated the newly minted traditions GIs invented to help restore their spirits, they employed correspondingly fanciful language. Hal Boyle, for instance, characterized a Brush-Off Club as "made up of mournful soldiers who were given the hemlock cup by femmes back home." His colleague, Kenneth Dixon, referred to members as "jilted gents and sorrowing and suspicious swains."[11] Perhaps it's no wonder that the exemplary Dear Johns cited by historians and lexicographers often appear apocryphal: brush-offs so cavalier in their disregard for the recipient's feelings that they strain credulity. Like the journalistic hyperbole wrapped around them, these snippets from women's letters seem contrived to elicit gasps of horror or mirth from readers.

Whether women *really* wrote the words ascribed to them, or whether hurt GIs embellished or invented the contents of purportedly genuine brush-off notes, we can only guess. It's striking, though, that female voices were almost always introduced into wartime Dear John stories by "jilted GIs" or civilian journalists ventriloquizing the male soldier's viewpoint. Women, in other words, did not speak for themselves. They got quoted – or perhaps merely parodied. The authors of the Dear Johns reproduced or excerpted in the wartime press (and subsequently referenced by historians) never consented to having their words publicized. Anne Gudis was mortified to find her private note to Sam Kramer published in *Yank*. For weeks, she desperately tried to intercept the mailman on his daily round so her family wouldn't notice the sudden flood of mail she received from strangers as a result. And she was horrified when the *Newark Ledger* showed interest in running a story about her V-mail's infamous invective in its Sunday supplement. Where Anne wanted to evade a spotlight she'd never sought, recipients of Dear Johns commonly wanted to amplify the wrong done them. Sharing breakup notes was a way to court public sympathy while simultaneously punishing the sender.[12]

Some men, we might speculate, were surely tempted to improve on the original brush-off notes they received. The recurrence of certain plots, jokes, and punchlines gives veterans' Dear John story-telling a folkloric quality. Although men commonly frame tales of romantic rejection as though retrieved from direct, unmediated personal experience, Dear John memories often share formulaic elements typical of a collective oral tradition. Modified through repetition, these stories unsettle categorical distinctions between invention and recollection, fantasy and fact. Memory, as historians who study it point out, is socially constructed. In other words, what's remembered, and how memory is articulated, is always the product of an interaction between past and present, and between individuals and communities. The anecdotes veterans relate are thus shaped not only by the tales *other* veterans have told about Dear Johns, but also by larger cultural narratives about men, women, and war: all of which are in constant flux, as the past comes to be refracted through the corrective lens of the present.[13]

It's tempting to think of the Dear John as having two distinct moments of production: first, as Dear John letters were received, processed, and publicized in wartime, and then again in retrospect, as veterans revisited past experience in life writing and oral histories. But this linear sequence doesn't capture the circularity of the processes by which soldiers, veterans, reporters, and an array of cultural producers have collectively authored, and kept rewriting, the Dear John. They've done so in oral story-telling, through the written word, in song, and on film. Veterans of every US war from World War II to the present thus have a rich tradition of broken bonds and brokenheartedness into which to tap. Strikingly, though, many tropes apparent in the 1940s still remain in circulation today, with minimal modernization.

FORMS OF WORDS

How, then, have veterans written the Dear John? What's most immediately striking from oral testimony is how often men looking back on their wartime service invoke this letter's arrival as a matter of routine. They talk of receiving a Dear John as though it weren't so much an individual misfortune, or even a common rite of passage, as a bureaucratic process – like getting issued a termination of employment notice, or a "pink slip" in the military. The intransitive verb form, being "Dear Johned," sounds (and may have felt) akin to being served: a standardized procedure in which a messenger hands over unwelcome paperwork drawn up by someone else.

Listen carefully to how an academic linguist recorded his first encounter with what struck him as a novel locution in 1947. Professor R. M. Duncan, chair of the Department of Modern Languages at the University of New Mexico in Albuquerque, submitted the following item to a scholarly journal, *American Speech*, that tracked shifting patterns of idiomatic usage. The professor had been flagged down "at a windy highway junction in the New Mexico desert" by a veteran, still in uniform, hitching his way home to West Texas. The demobilized soldier was relieved to have escaped the army of occupation in Korea, but uncertain of the reception he'd find at home. His wife had written asking for a divorce soon after he landed in Korea. The veteran told Duncan: "'I had been there for several weeks without a letter from my wife and I was worried. Finally one came and sure enough, it was a 'Dear John.' Quite a lot of the fellows had already had their 'Dear Johns,' so I wasn't much surprised.'" Duncan continued, rather pedantically, that further questioning had confirmed his hunch that "a 'Dear John' letter is a letter received by the soldier from his wife in which she requests a divorce."[14]

Had the professor spent more time conversing with GIs – or reading the wartime press – he mightn't have needed to ask. Perhaps his uncertainty about what the phrase meant prevented Duncan from noticing *how* the unnamed veteran marked this letter's appearance. Other fellows, the demobilized soldier reported, had already gotten *"their* Dear Johns" before he received his. In veterans' lore, Dear Johns are regularly introduced in just this way, preceded by either a possessive pronoun or the definite article. Here's Homer Holbrook, who served as an infantryman in North Africa and Europe during World War II, talking in 2013: "Well, it happened a lot. I weren't the only one. I got the Dear John letter, telling me she'd found someone else"; James Allen, an African American veteran of the Korean war: "But like most men, after a while you get the Dear John letter. I got one." And Terry Engelhardt, an artilleryman in Vietnam: "After I got my Dear John, I didn't do much letter-writing."[15] This form of words – "my," "his," "their," "the" – recurs in veterans' testimony from World War II to the present, underscoring the ubiquity of romantic rejection.

Although talk of "the Dear John" suggests a rote format, veterans' testimony doesn't converge in a common definition of the term. Nor does it give this letter a standard form of words. On the advice of his Texan informant, Duncan supplied *American Speech* with a narrow version. A Dear John was a letter from a wife that announced her desire for a divorce. Many GIs might have corrected the professor, however, pointing out that girlfriends and fiancées also sent Dear Johns. An unsatisfactory marriage wasn't a prerequisite.

In oral history interviews, veterans of successive wars offer their own definitions of the Dear John, whether because they anticipate that their younger interlocutor (or another listener) mightn't be familiar with this slang phrase, or because they're paused and asked to clarify. As these examples show, there's more elasticity in the term and its explanation than Duncan appreciated:

> So many men in the service were getting letters after six months or a year in the service, saying "Dear John, I'm breaking up with you. I have a new boyfriend." So those were called Dear John letters and everyone was getting them. (Archie Kelley, veteran of World War II)

> The Dear John letter was "I don't want you any more," you know? (Ben Greene, veteran of World War II)

> Dear John letters are when a wife or a girlfriend or whatever writes you a letter and says, "uh, hey, somebody else has come along, and they're here and you're not, so bye bye." That's what that amounts to. (Fred Lamp, veteran of World War II)

> "Dear John, I'm married, I couldn't wait for you." (John Chervenko, veteran of World War II)

> "Dear Bill, We're done. We're through. Kaput. I found somebody else." (William Welby, veteran of World War II)

> A Dear John letter is a letter you get from some woman telling you your engagement is broken off. (Wayne White, veteran of World War II)

> A "Dear John" letter was when the girlfriend that you had before you went into the service told you, "Forget about it, Charlie." (Michael Ruggiero, veteran of World War II)

Suppose you're married, you're thousands of miles away from home and your wife writes you and calls you Turon, let's say that's your name. "Well, I've meet this so and so and everything . . . and I can't put up with you being gone all the time because it never ends" . . . And so . . . those were the Dear Johns. (Richard Butters, veteran of the Korean war)

Back then, a Dear John letter was when your girlfriend, or your fiancée or your wife, would write you and tell you she was breaking up with you. (Doyle Causey, veteran of the Vietnam war)

It's when somebody's girlfriend writes them and says, "Dear John, I've found somebody else." That's what's called a Dear John letter. "I can't wait for you any longer, I've fell in love with so and so." Yeah, your best friend sometimes. (James Rockwell, veteran of the Vietnam war)

A Dear John is when your girlfriend writes you a letter and says she doesn't want to be with you any more, doesn't want to see you or whatever . . . (Pastor Toro, veteran of the Vietnam war)[16]

The irreducible bottom line is that a Dear John letter calls time on a relationship. But as veterans construct the Ur-type, there's almost always more to it than that. Many of these definitions stress that the Dear John doesn't merely sever an old tie. Simultaneously revealing the existence of a *new* love, the sender compounds the trauma of abandonment with the blunt force of betrayal. The woman who "wouldn't wait" is the archetypal sender of a Dear John. As some men saw it, *all* women were liable to fall into that category. Leonard Newton, who served as a corporal in the army air force in World War II, makes this point jokingly: "mom used to say 'distance makes the heart grow fonder – of someone else.'"[17] Many of the definitions duly refer to, or hint at, "someone else." Women who write to break up relationships, as these definitions construe them, haven't simply fallen out of love or found it too difficult to sustain intimacy through the slow-moving, semi-public channels available to partners separated by war. They've become impatient and, in their distraction, fallen for another man. In veterans' testimony, women never left men for other *women*, though some did in fact enter into lesbian relationships.[18]

Disloyalty lies at the heart of the Dear John tradition, whether lurking between the lines or written in bold. Both the fact of a rival's existence and his identity are common motifs in veterans' Dear John stories, sometimes supplying their punchline. The new lover's generic qualities often inspire bitterness. Crucially, he is *there* (back home), not *here* (at war). In the era of the draft, the fact that this man had managed to evade Uncle Sam's clutches was an automatic mark of demerit, suggesting the new boyfriend was either evading the draft or unfit for service, a "4F-er" in GI slang.[19] In some self-serving veterans' accounts, geographic proximity alone – his "there-ness" – makes the interloper more desirable to the soldier's erstwhile girlfriend/fiancée/wife, not any superior personal attributes. Frequently, though, there's a more enraging form of proximity in play. The new boyfriend, physically near the fickle woman, is someone *personally* close to the recipient of the Dear John. He might be a best friend, as in Rockwell's definition, or a relative: a brother, say, or the brother of a brother-in-law.

One Dear John story tops that. Gerard Streelman, who served as an infantryman in the Pacific theater during World War II, related it like this in conversation with his son in 2007: "Another story I could tell you about that Dear John stuff happened later. This guy got a letter, a Dear John. Said, 'It's been a long time since we've seen you. In the meantime, I got acquainted with your dad. And I've been going out with him once in a while, and – we got married!' And she signed the letter, 'Your Mother.'"[20] Streelman delivers the punchline with the perfect timing and delighted glee of a seasoned raconteur, nimbly pivoting from a tragic story of a heartbroken soldier's suicide to this anecdote as a form of comic relief. After Streelman and his son stop chuckling, he adds a coda: "That's of course a joke. I don't think that happened. But funny things *did* happen in the war." The same yarn is told as a true story by another veteran, David Dennis, interviewed for the National World War II Museum. Identical with Streelman's anecdote – except that Dennis has the woman sign her Dear John, "Love, Mother" – the duplication hints at how effectively the GI grapevine spread tall tales of female treachery.[21]

In other veterans' recollections, the Dear John is an absent presence – a notification of severance never sent. Some men at war intuited that their wife's or girlfriend's feelings had altered by a tapering off in the frequency of her letters or a pronounced cooling of rhetorical ardor. Sgt. Malvin Wald anticipated this pattern when he set out "The Timetable for a Brush-Off" for readers of *Yank* in November 1942. Wald's ten-month life-cycle of a long-distance relationship begins with "long and tender" missives in the initial weeks, dwindling to shorter letters in the third and fourth months that make excuses about the female writer's busy-ness. By the sixth month, her tone is more aloof, though the letters are still signed "love," until finally in month ten "you get a square white envelope. It's her engagement announcement."[22] Veterans' stories suggest that some women did indeed write to convey word of a marriage that would already have happened by the time her Dear John arrived. Arthur H. Taylor had this experience while serving in World War II. Another army veteran, Harry Rives, recalls trying to console a fellow enlistee whose wife informed him by mail that she'd been dating someone else in his absence and was going to have this man's baby.[23]

Other men discovered they'd been rejected more indirectly. Chester Matyjasik, a veteran of World War II, recalls that his former girlfriend couldn't bring herself to write a Dear John, enlisting her sister to write and tell him their relationship was over.[24] Two decades later, Arthur Wiknik set off on an R&R trip to Hawai'i during his tour in Vietnam. Having planned to meet his girlfriend there, he was surprised to be greeted by his sister instead. "I love my sister, too, geez, you know I don't love her *that* much!," Wiknik jokes with his interviewer, Kelly Crager. When Wiknik tried to reach his girlfriend by phone, things only got worse. Her mother answered, and called out to her daughter, "It's him. It's *him.*" She misheard this as "It's Jim! It's Jim!," greeting Arthur with effusive endearments meant for her new boyfriend.[25]

Some men found out they'd been supplanted when a "helpful" friend or relative sent a clipping from their hometown paper with an engagement notice or wedding write-up. Theodore Cummings, who served with the Marine Corps in World War II, was sent a clipping about his girlfriend's marriage by his mother, who "thought [he] should see it." He was in New Zealand at the time, en route to the Solomon Islands and Guadalcanal.[26] John Newsom, a Marine Corps sergeant in Korea, remembers getting a letter from a friend who'd seen his girlfriend – "a sweet little thing" – pushing a stroller.[27] Needless to say, rumor mongers got things wrong on occasion. That a woman had been spotted "running around" or seen "about town" with another man didn't necessarily mean what the gossipy author of a "thought-you-should-know" letter assumed.

Malicious relatives who didn't care for "their" soldier's girlfriend or wife weren't above fabricating reports, or insinuations, of faithlessness. During World War II, GIs overseas bombarded Red Cross field workers with requests that the stateside organization investigate whether rumors about their wives' disloyalty were true. After some internal debate, the Red Cross made it organizational policy to decline all petitions made "for the purpose of assisting the service man to get a divorce," as Charlotte Johnson (National Director of the ARC Home Service) put it. "In considering marital or divorce problems particular care should be taken not to become personally involved, and not to involve the Red Cross by attempting to give advice which might be regarded as legal," warned a memorandum circulated in January 1943.[28]

Some soldiers, hearing word of a partner's infidelity, took suspicion to be as good as proof and severed ties – as their meddling informants had surely hoped they would.[29] Other veterans returned from war only to discover altered affections at closer range. Family members who fielded calls from newly demobilized soldiers, looking to get ahold of their girlfriends, sometimes had to divulge unwelcome news over the phone. When Charles McDougall was demobilized in July 1946, his girlfriend's mother picked up the telephone and informed him briskly, "Marion got married a month ago." (Before Charles shipped overseas, she'd pushed for a hasty marriage, while he demurred.)[30] Some parents answered an unexpected knock on the door from a returning serviceman and had to tell him that their daughter, the GI's beloved, was now living with another man. James Wayne found out in this way that his girlfriend had left him when he came back from his thirteen-month tour as a marine corporal in Vietnam. He'd been nineteen when he volunteered, right out of high school. His girlfriend's father, the first Black police officer hired in the town of Lafayette, Indiana, told Wayne that she'd moved out and was now married. Looking back decades later, he felt it was better that she hadn't sent him a Dear John. It would've been too distracting while he was in Vietnam, and too tempting to entertain fantasies of retribution.[31]

As these stories make clear, there was no single blueprint to compose a Dear John. Nor was composition mandatory. Relationships ended in as many ways as romances began.

RESPONDING TO THE DEAR JOHN

The specific contents and register of Dear John letters – not just what, but *how*, she wrote – generally receive rather short shrift in veterans' recollections. The brief one-liners quoted above often mark the full extent of what men have to say about women's letters. The parallel coinage "that's all she wrote" seems fittingly twinned with the Dear John, expressive of its flat insufficiency – a shrugged "So there you have it." As veterans construe them, these letters simultaneously convey too much and not enough. In tone, they're either cloyingly apologetic or maddeningly curt. Dear John letters are, by definition, an anticlimactic epistolary genre. After all, they mark the conclusion, not culmination, of an intimate relationship.[32]

The fact that breakup notes are bound to deflate the reader hasn't prevented some soldiers from feeling that their authors somehow *ought* to pay eloquent tribute to the romances they end, eulogizing lost love by giving it a respectful send-off. Vietnam veteran Peter Smith writes in his memoir *A Cavalcade of Lesser Horrors* of receiving a Dear John in Germany, as he waited to be sent to southeast Asia. The note was, he recalls, a "disappointing specimen, in sub-par handwriting penned on sub-par stationery, the kind of young woman's stationery they sold in flat boxes in drugstores." Smith's younger self wallowed in fanciful literary embitterment: "If you were going to write a goddamned Dear John letter, at least write it in an elegant hand. I wanted something you might expect from an F. Scott Fitzgerald heroine – something in fountain pen that looked like it had been written thoughtfully at a desk in the lobby of the Ritz in the failing afternoon light – not this." In hindsight, he arrives at a more sober verdict. "It was two pages of the regular Dear John stuff, not especially deep and for damned sure, not elegant. Then again, we hadn't been an especially deep or elegant couple. She ended it, 'Hope you understand.'"[33]

Some men *did*. Alva Smith, an Army Air Forces veteran of World War II, appreciated that his girlfriend was going off to college and wanted to enjoy life. "I wasn't there," he matter-of-factly points out. Looking back, other veterans are similarly sanguine about how long-distance and long-term separation scrambled wartime romance. Despite finding out about his girlfriend's marriage from a press clipping his mother sent, Theodore

Cummings muses that he "rationalized that pretty well. I said 'what the hell? Pretty girl. Liked to make love. Wanted to be – wanted to be wanted. Wanted to be looked after. Wanted company. Liked to laugh. What the hell?'"[34]

Recollection of being Dear Johned provides veterans with more than an opportunity to summarize or satirize "all she said." Often, the content of a letter is less central to veterans' story-telling than what happened next. One sub-set of stories takes romantic rebuff as an opportunity to mull over the mysterious ways in which destiny, or divinity, moves – ultimately all to the good. In these accounts, the Dear John letter serves the welcome function of canceling a misbegotten relationship. Whether the veteran knew it at the time or only in retrospect, he's thankful that the woman who broke things off freed him to meet someone else – someone better – sometimes hailed in oral testimony as the woman for whom he was *truly* intended.[35]

This "praise be" motif is especially common in the recollections of World War II veterans, distant from the events in question, and often after decades-long marriages to "other" women. Occasionally, the veteran's wife is a witness to the interview, present alongside her husband and the interviewer. This set-up might explain, at least in part, why lost loves are rarely recalled with great feeling. Cecil Waite, a naval machinist's mate in World War II, received a Dear John from his girlfriend, still in high school, who broke things off so she'd have a date for her prom. When Waite came home from the war, this young woman tried to cajole him into resuming their courtship, but he refused. "No, I'm sorry," he recalls having told her. "If you did this once, you might do it again." "But I married the one that was *given* for me," he continues, gesturing toward his wife of sixty-seven years.[36]

Delivered in a different register from sentimental "happily-ever-after" stories are humorous yarns about the ingenious forms of payback soldiers devised for the women who'd sent them Dear Johns. Counterintuitively, perhaps, a rich seam of comedy runs through veterans' story-telling about romantic breakdown. In jocular anecdotes, jilted GIs not only enjoy the last laugh, but sometimes also the final word. Arthur Taylor, a first lieutenant with the Third Army in World War II, mischievously relates how he guilt tripped the woman who'd sent him a Dear John – "By the time you get this, I will be Mrs. Puffpuffnick" – during the Battle of the Bulge. Crumpling up a piece of note-paper, Taylor wrote to tell her that thoughts of their love were the only thing that kept him going through great danger, pretending that her breakup note had never reached him. He concluded by telling her that he would pass this note to a courier who was "going to make a run for it," risking his life to get the letter to Taylor's girlfriend.[37]

A story with the stale flavor of urban legend involves a different form of revenge. Here's a version told by World War II veteran Claude Orville Bryant:

> I had a friend who got a Dear John letter from this girl that he was in love with back home. It hurt him, boy, it hurt him. We were in Hawaii when he got it so he went out – went out and picked up every picture he could get of [women] black, white, green, purple, what have you. Put in a thing and sent it back to her and said, 'I haven't seen you in a long time I forget what you look like.' He was letting her know he was through here.[38]

This tale did the rounds so thoroughly that it surfaced in *Time* in August 1944. The magazine had a jilted marine gathering up "pictures of Australian girls, native women with nothing above the waist, movie actresses, pin-up girls," and sending his ex a note that said: "I don't remember exactly who you are, but if your picture is among these, please pick it out and send the rest back to me."[39] Vietnam veterans tell versions of the same story, as do men who served more recently in Iraq and Afghanistan.[40]

Tellingly, this tale isn't just about vengeance. It's about male solidarity. A bunch of guys rally round and pool their resources to support a dejected buddy. Some altruistically relinquish photos of their own girlfriends to help punish a faithless woman with an impressive display of insouciance, showing just how little the "Dear Johned" soldier ever cared for her. Men in uniform devised other uses for photographs of wives and girlfriends who'd betrayed them. *Yank*'s first Brush-Off Club story showed men paying homage to a young woman's black-bordered photograph. Their mock solemnity suggested this was a funeral portrait, though only the relationship was dead. In New Guinea, Army Air Force engineers pinned pictures of women who'd sent them Dear Johns on an

4.2. The "Wall of Shame," detailed in Anthony Swofford's memoir, was dramatized in Sam Mendes's cinematic adaptation of *Jarhead* (2005). (Courtesy of Universal Pictures.)

"operations board" labeled "Casualties Sustained on the Home Front."[41] In later wars, the parodic semblance of mourning gave way to more overt forms of misogyny. Men posted faithless women's pictures in rogues' galleries to publicly shame them. In *Jarhead*, Anthony Swofford describes a "Wall of Shame" – a six-foot pole, plastered with more than forty photos – that provided grunts encamped in Saudi Arabia with an opportunity to verbally defame and literally deface unfaithful women back home. On the duct tape used to fasten photographs to the pole, jarheads scribbled venomous notes about their betrayal, "proudly display[ing] the narrative of their cuckoldry." Swofford does likewise when his girlfriend dumps him, and is rumored to be seeing someone new. "It is not necessarily a bad thing to be able to tell the story of your woman's betrayal," he concludes.[42]

Dear John stories commonly celebrate camaraderie. Indeed, extolling the brotherly bonds that unite men at war often appears the primary function of these reminiscences. Some tales of male ranks solidified by female fickleness recount the tender care comrades-in-arms showed for fellow men in distress. Veterans frequently evoke the receipt of a Dear John as a moment of raw vulnerability: perhaps the *only* occasion when men in uniform give one another tacit permission to break down in tears.[43] Many recollections center on the supportive actions of comrades rallying around, offering a supportive shoulder or sufficient alcohol to thoroughly drown sorrows. Robert Willis, a veteran of World War II, remembers being consoled when he was crying over a Dear John by a compassionate officer, a devoted family man, who was killed in action just a few days later. He felt distressed by this injustice: a man loved by a wife and two children had lost his life while Willis, with "nothing to live for," remained alive.[44] In Vietnam, grunts comforted one another with repetition of the stock phrase, "Don't mean nothin'." As glossed by veteran Stephen Dant, this was "a way of everybody trying to say you know, you're alive and you're going to get through this and it was a way to try to tell somebody ... a whole mixed bag of things but look at the big picture, I guess. This don't mean nothing."[45]

In veterans' lore, male bonds drew strength from broken vows between men and women. The apostrophized ties between men who rely on – and would give their lives for – other men seemingly require unreliable women as their foil. Soldiers' brotherly love, as some veterans memorialize it, far exceeds romantic love in its depth and durability. "Unlike marriage," male camaraderie is a "bond that cannot be broken by a word, by boredom or divorce, or by anything other than death," Philip Caputo proposes in *A Rumor of War*, a memoir documenting his service in Vietnam.[46] Eternally faithful, men in uniform do not send one another Dear Johns. But this alchemy works only if front-line troops are *men*. As political scientist Megan MacKenzie notes, the "Band of Brothers" myth both excoriates and excludes women. The mystical notion that men are bound together in wartime by unbreakable cords of devotion was long used to lock women out of combat roles. A female presence at the front would (according to this logic) dissolve unit cohesion by adding a volatile element into the mix.[47]

In 2013, the Department of Defense lifted a decades-old prohibition against female soldiers' participation in combat: a ban that had long been circumvented in practice.[48] Women have, however, always been present in war zones: not merely "over there," but performing various sorts of labor with – and for – male troops. Emotional care-taking is one form of feminized work, routinely overlooked and accordingly uncompensated, that women have undertaken for men in uniform.[49] Male veterans rarely (if ever) reminisce about women's role in their recuperation from emotional injury. Perhaps this invisible service has long been forgotten. Maybe it remains too embarrassingly expressive of dependency to recount. But female nurses, Red Cross staff, and USO workers recall quite vividly how disconsolate men in uniform have turned to women to re-inflate their punctured self-esteem.[50] And where some wanted verbal assurances of desirability, others sought more practical demonstrations. Mary Sargent, a Red Cross "Donut Dolly" stationed at an American airfield in India during World War II, recollects that it wasn't always enough to tell a man who'd gotten a Dear John that he'd find someone else. "The only thing to do was let him . . . walk home with you after the club closed at night . . . and then maybe kiss him good night and tell him that any girl who'd let such a nice guy get away must be pretty stupid."[51]

Servicemen in Vietnam also turned to women for reassurance that, if their wives no longer loved them, some other woman would. After a while, air steward Helen Hegelheimer could no longer bear to read the letters that young men flying out to, or home from, Vietnam anxiously pressed on her, desperate for confirmation that they were, or would be, loved.[52] Ironically, given male soldiers' widespread reluctance to entertain a uniformed female presence in their midst, women soldiers have also been called on to lend a sympathetic ear to their male comrades' Dear John stories. Specialist Katherine Daronche, who served in Iraq in 2005, found that men sought her out to share their emotional problems because she was "easier to talk to than the male soldiers."[53]

In contrast with the poignance of women's recollections of male vulnerability, a whiff of misogyny hangs over many Dear John stories told by men, especially those that involve individual or collective punishment of unfaithful women. Anecdotes in which the veteran wins back a woman who'd rejected him sometimes fall into this category. He cajoles her to fall in love again, sleeps with her, and then promptly dumps her. Here, seduction is a stratagem of degradation – like a ploy devised by the sadistic Vicomte de Valmont in *Les liaisons dangereuses*.[54] Or take this story of emotions toyed with, told as a comedy by a veteran of World War II:

> And like one time, I got a "Dear John" letter from a girl who apparently thought that I was serious. [Laughs] So I read it to all of the guys and they said, "Well, why don't we answer her?" So we made up an answer. All of us composed an answer to this "Dear John" letter in which we explained how heartbroken I was and this, that, and the other thing, and we mailed it to

her. And about two months later I got a letter saying she broke the engagement with the other guy. [Laughs] So then I write another one saying I didn't really mean it. So, you know, life goes on and your amusements come in different ways then.[55]

Animosity toward women is a staple ingredient of the Dear John tradition. Not surprisingly, it's the dominant element of a whole slew of stories about women who failed to return property, keeping engagement rings, for instance; or who sold off the guy's possessions, squandered shared savings, or ran up huge debts on joint accounts. But, in some stories, bitterness toward women in general is occasioned by the fact of rejection alone.

Consider this Vietnam veteran's anecdote, delivered with the slick precision of a comic skit, but with a decidedly sour after-taste. It details an "insurance strategy" devised by a young man who volunteered in 1968 to serve with the special forces in Vietnam:

> When I first went to Vietnam I thought I had planned ahead. There was a young lady in Alpena who knew that I cared deeply for her, and she expressed deep affection for me, so I knew she'd be writing. There was a young lady in Buffalo, New York, who I cared deeply for and she had expressed that for me, and finally there was one in Puerto Rico ... So I thought, "Good. I'm covered. I'll be alright." But within six months, I'd received Dear Johns from all three of them. Every one of them in writing their Dear Johns expressed sympathy. They understood that they were breaking my heart, yet they had to move on with their life ... So I'm like "*Wow!* You can't trust women." And that was quite a lesson for me.[56]

Whether the girlfriends could trust *him* – a man stringing three women along – is, of course, not part of the calculus. Donald McLennan wraps up this recollection with a statistic: empirical proof of his point's validity. By the end of their tours in Vietnam, six of eight men in his hootch had had divorces filed by wives back home. He speculates that, "dollars to donuts," even more guys serving in Iraq confronted broken marriages, though "it's hard to see how it could be worse that two thirds getting divorced."[57]

Contempt for women also ripples through stories about how men buoyed one another with reminders that girlfriends are thoroughly replaceable commodities. This theme is decades old, appearing in Sgt. Wald's "Timetable for a Brush-Off," in which a seasoned veteran yawns in the next bunk, "They're like street cars, chum." Arnold Garza, who served in the 1991 Persian Gulf War, offers an updated variation. He remembers trying to shake teenage soldiers out of their despondency when they got Dear Johns from high school sweethearts they'd "lusted for their whole lives." Garza would tell them: "'It's almost like a telephone pole. Every 40 yards you got another one there . . . So just march on. Don't worry. When you get back to Germany we'll get you another one, simple as that.'" Yet, in the same interview, Garza acknowledges that getting over the end of his own relationship wasn't so easy, attributing the start of his problems with alcohol to a Dear John.[58]

Occasionally, veterans ruminate more self-consciously on how men at war have used Dear John letters as a license for both woman-hating and women-hunting. In retrospect, some regard military service as an incubator for toxic masculinity. Patrick Vellucci, a Vietnam veteran, asked in an oral history interview about the frequency of Dear John letters, responds: "All the time. Yes, you wind up hating women because of that, and you hear a lot of military people are women haters, and it's true." "Bad-mouthing" women, Vellucci concludes, was how men got over Dear Johns. "That's what we did, we bad mouthed women." But the grunts he recollects didn't just talk contemptuously of women, they found other women for sexual gratification. "We went to Australia, and this [is] a beautiful country. All we did was look for people that we could have sex with . . . We went to Taiwan, we bought women, because in Taiwan that's what you did. I didn't realize till later on, you're contributing to a slave trade." "It was," he muses, "a different time, a completely different time."[59]

Vellucci's candor is rare. But the pattern he describes – men justifying pick-ups and brothel visits with reference to wives' and girlfriends' infidelity – follows a very well-trodden path. Needless to say, this behavior wasn't always provoked by a female partner's sexual disloyalty. The poet W. D. Snodgrass, looking back on his service in the navy during World War II, recalls being shocked "when friends whose wives' or girlfriends' chastity was so crucial to them felt no constancy incumbent on themselves." "The fact of facing possible death or injury," he continues, "made many feel driven to, and justified in, sexual inconstancies."[60] Men also rationalized their pursuit of sex by invoking the certainty that women would betray them, because that's what women *did*. That being so, a preemptive "first strike" was surely warranted. This righteous conviction, stoked by "Jody" calls, was corroborated by Dear John stories. Historian Andrew Huebner notes that women had greater reason to suspect that men in uniform would find other sexual partners while overseas than men had cause to fear betrayal by wives and girlfriends back home. Some women readily (others perhaps more grudgingly) endorsed the notion that men in uniform both needed and deserved sex as a reward for service. Anne Gudis, for instance, assured Sam Kramer that she had "no objections to men being unfaithful, if they must." She propped up this double standard with the buttress of essentialized female "nature." "It is easier for a woman, no matter how emotional she may be, to control herself."[61]

Other women, during World War II and subsequent conflicts, weren't so willing to accept a sexual status quo weighted so heavily in men's favor. But, unlike the soldiers who loudly decried women who sent Dear Johns, female anxieties and anger about male infidelity barely gained a public hearing.[62]

"DEAR JANE"

Gendered double standards come into sharper focus when we consider the Dear John's latter-day counterpart: the Dear Jane letter. This phrase debuted in a US national newspaper in 1959, not in a news column but in a review of Erskine Caldwell's novel *Claudelle Inglish* in the *Washington Post*. Illustrating the old adage "Hell hath no fury like a woman scorned," Caldwell has his eponymous protagonist wreak havoc on her Southern backwoods community after she receives a "Dear Jane" from her soldier boyfriend. Caldwell's set-up up-ends a familiar trope. When Claudelle's beau goes off to an army camp 1,200 miles from home, his letters soon "became briefer, less personal, and more hastily scrawled." They appear "less and less frequently" after his first six months of absence until, finally, a short note arrives. It reads "like a letter from a stranger that she had received by mistake": "In less than a dozen lines he said in unmistakable words that he had been very lonely at the army camp so far from home and that he had met a girl in the town nearby who had been kind and understanding and that he was going to marry her." Enraged by this rejection, Claudelle sets out to seduce every man in sight – including the store-keeper and preacher – by sun-up the following day, leaving a tsunami of emotional debris in her wake. "She is as decisive as Electra," the *Washington Post*'s reviewer admiringly noted, imputing the sophistication of Sophoclean tragedy to pulp Southern gothic. (Warner Bros. moved swiftly to buy the rights, and the studio's screen adaptation premiered in 1961.)[63]

Both the belatedness of the coinage and Caldwell's particular mode of emplotment are revealing about why the Dear Jane isn't, and couldn't be, simply an inversion of the Dear John. Why? Because socially constructed gender norms don't permit straightforward role reversals. Men and women are held to, and judged by, divergent standards. Not equal and opposite, but antithetical and hierarchical. As a result, while Dear Jane and Dear John letters might *say* the same things, their meaning reverberates differently depending on the author's sex. Socially acceptable responses to receipt of a breakup note are likewise conditioned by gender, as *Claudelle Inglish* makes clear. Although Caldwell has Claudelle's boyfriend behave – and write – just like a GI's flighty girlfriend, his Dear Jane elicits a hyperbolic (and unmistakably) *female* response. As we've seen, some men newly "Dear Johned" sought revenge by seduction of other women, or of the sender herself. Commanding officers and civilian society alike tended to tolerate, or even encourage, such behavior. However, no reader could come away from *Claudelle Inglish* feeling that the heroine's response to romantic rebuff is either appropriate or proportionate. The plot culminates in murder and suicide, as the men Claudelle has seduced and jettisoned turn on one another and, ultimately, on her. Moments after she dies from a gunshot wound, the beau who sent the "Dear Jane" reappears. He'd changed his mind, and rushed home on furlough to renew his promise to marry Claudelle. But too late.

Caldwell's novel exemplifies a larger pattern. Where men's receipt of a Dear John generates social solicitude – along with latitude to act out, exact revenge, or seek sexual compensation – the same situation ethics

4.3. The devastating consequences of a "Dear Jane" letter for a southern backwoods community were taken to extremes in Gordon Douglas's 1961 adaptation of Erskine Caldwell's novel. (Courtesy of Warner Bros.)

don't apply to women in possession of a Dear Jane. Women who retaliate, like Claudelle, confirm men's worst fears about the dangerously irrational excess of "female kind." A woman who's been served a Dear

Jane doesn't deserve a sympathetic hearing. She requires a straightjacket. (Or, in Caldwell's view, a shot-gun.)

Women had, of course, received Dear Janes long before Caldwell wrote one into popular fiction. Oral histories conducted with women looking back on World War II supply several examples. Dorothy Zmuda, a native of Stevens Point, Wisconsin, was in her early twenties during the war. In a long interview undertaken in 1992, she recalls the pressures young couples felt – and generated – to marry in haste. Dorothy turned down one suitor, newly drafted, who was desperate to find a girl, *any* girl, to wear his ring when he went off to war, even though the pair hardly knew one another: "They just had to be engaged to somebody before they left ... and then these marriages broke up or they met someone else. That's where the 'Dear Johns' came in you know, 'Dear John' letters." But Zmuda stresses that ending a relationship was far from an exclusively female prerogative. Her whole office got drawn into a wealthy female co-worker's elaborate wedding plans, complete with "place settings, silver, dishes," a "hope chest," and bridal shower. At the eleventh hour a letter from the bride-to-be's fiancé, stationed across the country, punctured this bubbly froth of preparation. Zmuda paraphrases the Dear Jane thus: "'Sorry, I was with a girl in California, and she's pregnant, and I feel that I have to marry her. She's carrying my baby.'" As Zmuda recollects this scene, it was "shattering" for all concerned, redoubling Dorothy's own aversion to wartime romance. "So that was why I didn't get connected to anybody ... If they got a little romantic, I was done with that."[64]

Needless to say, men ditched women for other reasons besides their having found – and sometimes also impregnated – someone new. Some men ended relationships because they feared their girlfriends or wives were, or might be, unfaithful. Women's enlistment sometimes fueled such fears, and female soldiers have faced particular challenges in sustaining romantic relationships. Where servicemen's female partners have been conditioned to silently tolerate the prospect (or fact) of male infidelity, the same imperative to remain chastely faithful hasn't been instilled in the husbands and boyfriends of women in uniform. Some men preferred to end relationships with women in uniform rather than manage feelings of insecurity, rage, or jealousy.[65]

During World War II, the first conflict in which American women enlisted en masse, some husbands "pre-emptively" threatened to divorce their wives if they joined the Women's Army Corps: an organization that sections of the press, energized by a vigorous GI slander campaign, depicted as a hotbed of vice and "perversion." Salacious rumor held that only lesbians, attracted by an all-female environment, and sexual profiteers, eager to sell favors to male officers, would willingly enlist in its ranks.[66] The WAC's official history written in 1953 by Mattie E. Treadwell (a former lieutenant colonel) makes appalled reference to pervasive prejudice against servicewomen that seriously dented recruitment in 1942 and 1943. "I'll not have my wife to be meat for the boys," one soldier-husband says. "Never thought my wife would double-cross me by joining the WACs or the Army," protests a second, treating enlistment itself as an act of disloyalty. "My heart is broken," chimes a third. And with more brutal finality, another husband-in-uniform announces: "Get that damn divorce. I don't want no damn WAC for a wife."[67]

Oral histories furnish further evidence of men who severed ties with women in uniform. For instance, Toby Newman, who enlisted in the WAC, recalls that her boyfriend at the time was pushing her to get married. When she tried to take things more slowly, he responded with a Dear Jane. Unlike most soldiers who received Dear Johns, she kept the letter, showing it to an interviewer decades later and offering a précis: "He says, 'You wanted to be free, now you're free.'"[68] Combat nurse June Wandrey, serving in Europe in 1944, was stunned to receive a letter from her officer boyfriend stationed in the United States, telling her that his friendship with another woman had "turned to love." Mailing his note back to her family, she told them she'd "joined the legion of soldiers in ETO who received a Dear John letter. 'Love postponed on account of war' became my battle cry."[69]

Two decades later, some nurses serving in Vietnam who became romantically involved with doctors found out only after the latter returned home that they'd been married all along, news broken in Dear Jane letters.[70]

Women's reminiscences of being rejected by male partners pepper archival collections. These are tales retrospectively told. Women did, however, try to draw public attention to the hypocrisy that held men and women to divergent standards of emotional and sexual fidelity *during* World War II. GI romances and marriages to women they'd met overseas were a sore spot for some American women: a depletion of the pool of eligible bachelors that was also indicative of rampant male infidelity. In late 1942, some 200,000 women signed a petition asking the War Department to prohibit marriages between American soldiers and foreign nationals, protesting that, unless the authorities stepped in, "American girls must face barren lives of spinsterhood after the war." When *Yank* reported on the petition, it took the opportunity to turn the tables: "The gals wouldn't need to worry about spinsterhood if they wrote us often that the sweet things they said before we left still count, and that they're waiting for the day when we'll be home again."[71]

Undeterred, American women continued to point out that these foreign girlfriends must, in some cases, have engaged in the very behavior that GIs constantly pilloried. "True enough, some girls back home have given you the brush," wrote "A WAC" to *Stars and Stripes*, "but did you ever stop to consider that the girl you married overseas might possibly have brushed off a former British boy friend in order to marry you?" Pity the poor Tommy who returned home to find his girl married to a GI Joe.[72]

Female dereliction of emotional duty wasn't solely responsible for high rates of male desertion, despite the insinuation routinely made by male reporters that women were the authors of their own romantic misfortunes. Twenty-one-year-old Louise Cozine of Santa Monica, a WAC, was so indignant over AP correspondent Hal Boyle's reportage on the Brush-Off Club in Algiers – headlined "GI Joe Goes Into Decline If Babe at Home Forgets" – that she penned him a note of protest. Boyle's column jocularly referred to officers whose "true loves absent-mindedly walked up the aisle while they were over here," ending with a sergeant's rhetorical question: "Is it a natural deceitful characteristic once dormant now back to the fore?"[73] Cozine didn't find this funny. She'd recently been jilted by an army officer, who informed her soon after ending their engagement of his marriage to another woman. She wanted to set the record straight. Men switched allegiances too, and women's "love, loyalty and letters" weren't always enough to prevent their boyfriends upping and marrying somebody else. Cozine proposed practical action, setting up a Women's Auxiliary Brush-Off Club "for the benefit of gals who'd been jilted." She also informed *Stars and Stripes* that WABOC (pronounced WAY-bok) branches existed in nearly every state in the Union. "One of the most popular features of our local group is our 'Rogues Gallery,'" she let GIs know, "consisting of a snapshot or portrait of the men who made each of our members eligible . . . each tagged with a long, prison-like number." By one account, the WABOC was the "fastest growing organization of lovelorn in the world."[74]

The WABOC clubs touted a principle of reciprocity: men and women in uniform would console one another for their mutual losses by embarking on new romances. In a more competitive spirit, some civilian women publicly announced *their* desire to help mend soldiers' broken hearts – desperate to pass the loyalty test other sisters had so miserably failed. GIs eagerly extended opportunities to do so, like the three waggish soldiers who shared their plight with the *Los Angeles Times* in March 1945: "[H]aving been jilted by the girls back home and being financially short," they sought "wealthy women to share our postwar plans."[75] That same month, sixteen GIs in the Pacific theater wrote to the *Chicago Daily Tribune*, lamenting that only two members of their eighteen-man unit still had "lady loves" waiting for them back home. Their appeal for letters from women generated a "tornadic response" from readers. "Those boys must have a lot of faith in human nature to want to hear from any girls, after such consistent disappointments," gushed one respondent, "but if cheerful, slaphappy letters will boost their morale, I'd love to write." The *Tribune* printed several excerpts from women's replies in the same vein. But it also aired the views of more disgruntled female readers, like the anonymous woman who wrote: "I was one of those gals who 'could wait forever if necessary,' and did for three years! Yes, he went away a sweet, wonderful boy, but came home a conceited hero who could conquer anything in a bar . . . and his old girlfriend (that's me) was left holding the bag."[76]

These snapshots from World War II may appear faded relics of a bygone era. But the notion that a soldier's broken heart might jolt "lonely hearts" into compensatory action isn't a thing of the past. As recently as 2012, military psychologist Michael Russell floated the idea that the best way to help shake men out of "irrational thinking" – the morbid conviction that they couldn't live without the women who'd sent them Dear Johns – would be for the armed forces to broker new romantic connections:

> While running the [naval] suicide prevention office, I once even proposed to the military the concept of a Web site called something like "dearjohn. com," which would be free to any service member with an overseas deployed address and open to any woman in America who would like to become a pen pal and keep a dumped and potentially despairing deployed soldier company. I think it would have done wonders to lower the suicide rate. Unfortunately I could not interest the military in operating a dating site.[77]

Tellingly, this proposal made no mention of female soldiers who'd been dumped and were in despair. Nor, a year after the repeal of "Don't Ask, Don't Tell," did it countenance the existence of same-sex romantic relationships.[78]

"SHE'LL CATCH ON, IN TIME"

"There really is no such thing as a 'Dear Jane' letter," opined columnist Linda Lee in the *New York Times* in 2002. "A man just goes, leaving no note."[79] A sweeping generalization, Lee's claim nevertheless helps explain why the Dear Jane is, and always has been, a much less visible feature of America's emotional topography than the Dear John. Dissatisfied with intimate relationships, many servicemen opted to fade, wordlessly, from the picture.

Today, we refer to this stealth exit strategy as "ghosting." But the practice isn't unique to the digital age, nor has it been uniformly condemned by women. In June 1918, a few months before the armistice, a doughboy wrote from France for guidance from the *New York Tribune*'s advice columnist. He was in a quandary, having fallen in love with a French girl. He had a sweetheart at home, however, and didn't know how to break this news to her. "Don't break it to her," the aptly named "Miss Information" snapped back. "Just quit writing. She'll catch on, in time. They all do."[80]

This advice, or more subtle social cues that disappearance was an acceptable way to extricate oneself from a romantic double-bind, could have been issued to servicemen in any decade since 1918. The same women who critiqued gendered hypocrisy in World War II sometimes despaired that their soldier-boyfriends had just stopped writing. And though women who sent Dear Johns were routinely accused of "cowardice," stabbing soldiers in the back while they served overseas because they were too timid to voice their feelings in person, the same charge could be leveled at men who hoped that silence would convey the intended message. When servicemen were deployed in dangerous circumstances, this tactic could appear less cowardly than calculatedly cruel. A sudden cessation of letters *might* mean that the soldier had simply given up the ghost on an unwanted relationship. But it could also mean that he'd been killed in action.

Silence is always susceptible to more than one interpretation, contrary to the old adage that it "speaks for itself." "Miss Information" endorsed this cliché with her blithe assertion that all women would, sooner or later, "catch on." But women who got the message didn't necessarily tolerate this treatment any more gladly – or meekly – than the male soldiers who loudly protested when girlfriends' letters melted into thin air. In 1919, Miss Wanda Drewes filed a $25,000 breach of promise suit when her erstwhile fiancé returned home from war with a French wife. He'd breathed not a word of this new relationship to her, leaving that task to his mother. Drewes reportedly shared with her lawyer 468 "burning love letters" from her fiancé. His epistles were not only inflamed with ardor for Wanda, but smouldered with disdain for French women and the doughboys who fell for them.[81]

This man's mother wasn't the only one to be left carrying the can. Indeed, it commonly fell to mothers to remedy their offspring's failure to undertake difficult emotional work, and not just in World War I. In 1942, one woman was so confounded by her son's romantic delinquency that she wrote to the OWI's radio character, "Chaplain Jim," in search of counsel. Mrs. Signy Fisher outlined her family's situation at some length: the sickness and misfortune that meant they were "extremely poor," her son's having "started to keep company" with a girl from a "well to do" family since they were both in high school, and his having been sent off to

Mobile with the army air corps. Since then, he had not only stopped communicating with the girlfriend to whom he'd become engaged before leaving home, but had ceased making the $4 monthly payments for her engagement ring. "I have," Mrs. Fisher continued, "tryed my best to coax him to tell me what was wrong but he simply ignores my letters." She included $1 for Chaplain Jim's trouble in responding. It took a month for an army assistant chaplain to reply with the admonishment that Fisher should contact her son's unit chaplain in Mobile, and also keep writing cheerfully to him, "to bear him up to the Throne of Grace upon the arms of prayer." We can only speculate whether Fisher found this advice useful. What transpired with her son, his fiancée, and the sentimental down-payment in which he no longer wished to invest, or perhaps simply couldn't afford, remains unknown.[82]

Of course, as we've seen, some women also simply quit writing. They, too, sometimes left a parent or sibling to convey news of a broken relationship. However, this behavior was never a *prescribed* path of action for women. Indeed, in the opinion of certain GIs, "ghosting" was even worse than sending a Dear John. A breakup letter at least let a man know where he stood. And being decisively cast aside caused less emotional stress than being kept dangling.

The obligation to write – something rather than nothing – fell exclusively to women. During World War II, as in subsequent conflicts, advice columnists instructed female readers that they should keep sending letters to soldiers no matter what. If a man in uniform didn't respond, the woman should presume that he was merely too busy, focused, or exhausted to correspond. Bill Mauldin, *Stars and Stripes*' beloved cartoonist, cautioned women in 1945 that "It's very hard [for GIs] to compose a letter that will pass the censors when you are tired and scared and disgusted with everything that's happening." Civilians enjoying comfortable lives back home had no excuse for easing up on mail, Mauldin chided.[83]

Since women were required to write while men were permitted to be silent, it must have been hard for some wives and girlfriends to appreciate when a prolonged lapse in correspondence signaled that they'd been wordlessly "let go" by their partners in uniform. What was acceptable behavior in men was commonly deemed intolerable, or even

pathological, in women. The psychopathologies of soldiers' female partners started to attract the attention of military psychiatrists in World War
II. This would become a growth field during the Vietnam years, as experts
tried to explain why (as they perceived it) women were sending more –
and more vicious – Dear Johns than ever before.

CHAPTER 5

"The Modern Penelope": Analyzing the Waiting Wife

O N MARCH 17, 1973, Associated Press photographer Slava (Sal) Veder was one of about forty journalists corralled in a pen at Travis Air Force base in Solano County, California. Together they were awaiting the arrival of planes carrying released American prisoners of war (POWs) back from southeast Asia to be reunited with their families. Operation Homecoming, as the Pentagon codenamed this choreographed repatriation exercise, was front-page news. Hostilities in Vietnam had finally ended in February with a cease-fire signed in Paris. But for months before this diplomatic breakthrough, negotiations had stalled over Washington's concerns about several hundred American POWs and a contested number of servicemen missing in action (MIA) in Vietnam, the majority of whom had been captured between 1965 and 1968. Most were airmen (predominantly officers) who'd been shot down or crash-landed in enemy territory. Nixon's administration demanded to know who they were, where they were, and when they, or their remains, would be repatriated. For the White House, Operation Homecoming represented an opportunity to append an uplifting coda to the war in Vietnam. With the ink barely dry on the Paris accords, soldiers and airmen who'd endured unprecedentedly long periods in captivity would come home lionized as the only heroes to emerge from America's most divisive yet least decisive conflict to date. Their safe return was intended to corroborate Nixon's claim that he had extricated the nation from Vietnam "with honor." Operation Homecoming was "a victory parade snatched from the jaws of defeat," in the words of *Washington Post* reporter Kathy Sawyer.[1]

When a jet liner finally touched down at Travis on the afternoon of March 17, a surge of excitement electrified the crowd. As family members jumped from parked cars, sharp-elbowed photographers jostled to document the dramatic finale to this extended saga.[2] Veder leapt into action. With lightning fast reflexes and some judicious shoving, he managed to capture the precise instant when fifteen-year-old Lorrie Stirm got airborne as she galloped – arms outstretched – toward the father, Lt. Colonel Robert L. Stirm, she hadn't seen for six years. As soon as Veder developed the negative half an hour later (the women's bathroom at Travis serving as a makeshift dark room), he knew just what to call his photograph. "Burst of Joy."[3] The following year, he won a Pulitzer prize for this instantly iconic image.[4] Then as now, Americans regarded "Burst of Joy" as a distillation of rapture that condensed and concluded multiple plot-lines: a freed prisoner brought home, a family reunited, a war finally ended.

Veder's photograph certainly stands in stark contrast with the Vietnam war's other emblematic images: a monk burning himself to death; a naked little girl (arms similarly outstretched) running from a napalm attack; the corpses of slain peasants lying in a ditch; a helicopter straining to lift evacuees from the roof of an apartment building as Vietnamese forces closed in on the last outpost of American power in Saigon. In reality, though, the family saga that Veder froze at its climax was not one of unalloyed delight. Had the photographer been facing the men who stepped off the plane onto the tarmac rather than toward their waiting family members, the result might have been quite different. Pictured with his back to the camera at the left edge of the frame, Robert Stirm serves as a uniformed stand-in for all returning prisoners of war, stoic and slightly stiff. Unable to see his face, viewers imagine the father's expression mirroring his daughter's ecstasy. But as the shutters clicked, Bob Stirm's face probably registered more somber emotions. Three days before landing at Travis, as he underwent medical checks, counseling, and debriefing at Clark Air Force Base in the Philippines, he'd been handed a Dear John letter by a chaplain. It was from his wife Loretta. She wanted a divorce.[5] Loretta appears at the right

5.1. "Burst of Joy," Slava (Sal) Veder's Pulitzer-winning photograph, depicts Lt. Col. Robert L. Stirm's homecoming from Vietnam on March 17, 1973. We see, from left to right, Robert L. Stirm, Lorrie Stirm, Bo Stirm, Cindy Stirm, Loretta Stirm, and Roger Stirm. (© Slava Veder/Associated Press.)

margin of Veder's image, smiling but hanging back as her four children dash toward their father.

By the end of 1973, newspapers reported that the couple had divorced in acrimony, with the decree finalized almost a year to the day after Veder pictured this homecoming scene. Stirm complained that he'd been "taken to the cleaners" by California's Family Law Act that presumed both partners "shared in a community" up to the date of their formal separation. Loretta won custody of two of the couple's children. She also acquired ownership of their suburban home and was permitted to keep the $136,000 in pay and allotments she'd received from the government during her husband's imprisonment. "All those dreams I had in prison were nothing but dust," Stirm told reporters.[6] He'd tried to persuade the judge that Loretta forfeited any entitlement to federal largesse on the grounds of infidelity. Legal failure left the former prisoner embittered toward both his wife and the federal government. "My service was honorable; hers was not," he vituperated. Years later, he told an interviewer that he kept a framed copy of Veder's photograph hidden in a drawer. "Burst of Joy" evoked too painful memories of a family sundered at its moment of apparent reunion. Worse yet, the spotlight Veder unwittingly shone on the Stirms's marriage had made its public dissolution even harder to endure. The picture, he protested, was a lie: one that replicated the glossy veneer his ex-wife had lacquered over her duplicitous life in his absence. Without coming clean to their children, Loretta had abandoned the marriage after just a year of his captivity, or so Bob claimed. "This picture does not show the realities that she had accepted proposals of marriage from three different men ... It portrays (that) every-body there was happy to see me."[7]

The tensions of homecoming after anguishing years of separation – relief commingled with apprehension, sometimes laced with recrimination – hover at the edges of Veder's image, perceptible only to those who scrutinize the scene with an informed eye. The fraught dynamics of return were not what many Americans wanted to see as 591 prisoners came back from Vietnam in 1973. Yet darker shadings did seep into public story-telling about returned prisoners of war. Consumers of American news media knew that Bob Stirm wasn't alone in receiving a Dear John. A few fellow prisoners had been divorced while in captivity, while others discovered on return that their (now former) wives had given up hope of seeing husbands deemed MIA years earlier, moving on with their lives and remarrying. Other former prisoners came home to their spouses, but found it impossible to resume married life. Within a year of their arrival back home, about 30 percent of the Operation Homecoming repatriates had divorced. In December 1975, one former prisoner reckoned "the 'Dear John' mortality rate" among his former camp mates at around 60 percent. Many commentators recounted these statistics, prodding the swollen numbers for larger trends and possible lessons about men, women, marriage, and war.[8]

In August 1968, at the height of US involvement in Vietnam, military psychiatrist Houston MacIntosh noted that he and his colleagues were encountering an increasing number of "modern Penelopes who [were] unsuccessful in adapting to their husbands' absence." Hitherto, psychiatric research had failed, MacIntosh noted, to focus on this "important clinical problem."[9] The Vietnam war remedied this deficit. The broken marriages of men seemingly unbroken by their North Vietnamese captors became a focus of national commentary – professional and popular – in the 1970s and 1980s. A steady flow of press stories and magazine features held up the behavior of wives of POWs and MIAs for public scrutiny. Former prisoners, capitalizing on their celebrity status, soon offered their own spin in a spate of memoirs that documented how North Vietnamese captivity had impacted American matrimony. Movies and teleplays inspired by these autobiographical writings followed suit. At the same time, "waiting wives" – along with women who had signally failed to wait for absent husbands – received sustained attention from psychologists and psychiatrists working for the armed forces.[10]

Many Americans had something to say on the subject of female fidelity and the Vietnam war, whether about the purportedly greater number of Dear Johns sent during this conflict, the fate of marriage under threat from second wave feminism, or about "disloyalty" more generally at a time when the personal and political seemed ever more inextricably entangled. To disgruntled veterans and disenchanted others, the "modern Penelope" appeared a travesty of Homer's unerringly faithful archetype.

MAIL, MARRIAGE, AND MISSING MEN

Sustaining a wartime romantic relationship by mail has always required patience, dedication and self-discipline. Under conditions of censorship that prevailed during World War II and Korea, civilians and soldiers alike had to accept that an array of third parties intruded into ostensibly private relationships, whether letter-writers could visualize these censorious specters peering over their shoulders or tried to suppress this knowledge. For most Americans, these strictures no longer applied during the Vietnam war. Mail wasn't censored. Nor were the tapes that many GIs increasingly relied on to remain in touch with home. But for several thousand Americans – the loved ones of POWs and MIAs in Vietnam –

this relative freedom of wartime expression did not pertain. For them, mail was as precious a commodity as it was scarce.

Typically, next-of-kin – wives or parents of a downed airman or serviceman missing in action – first learned of their loved one's disappearance by telegram.[11] A frustratingly terse few lines, perhaps accompanied by a visit from a casualty assistance officer, ushered spouses and parents into a wrenching new reality: the man they loved had vanished into an uncharted void. Beyond the bald fact of his plane having crashed, or of his failure to return safely from a mission, other details initially remained murky in most cases. Was the missing man alive or dead? Injured or healthy? Languishing in a North Vietnamese prison camp or shifting for survival in enemy territory? For many POW/MIA wives and families these questions remained unanswered for months or even years. For some, they remain unresolved. (After Operation Homecoming, about 2,500 American personnel remained unaccounted for – a figure far smaller than the number of servicemen whose fate was unknown after World War II and the Korean war.) If they were lucky, though, next of kin eventually received confirmation that the missing man was – or very recently had been – alive in captivity.[12]

Even without tangible proof of their loved one's existence, let alone any clue as to their location, POWs' and MIAs' spouses attempted to reach missing servicemen by mail. These efforts began as soon as the first American prisoners were captured in 1964. Establishing and sustaining contact wasn't easy, however. Mailing a letter to Hanoi was one thing; confirmation that the note had reached its addressee was quite another. The Republic of North Vietnam refused to accept that the Geneva Conventions of 1949 relative to the treatment of Prisoners of War applied to American military personnel. Since President Johnson had not *formally* declared war on North Vietnam, Hanoi maintained that captured US personnel were war criminals not prisoners of war. No internationally agreed statutes have ever established rights to which incarcerated war criminals are entitled. POWs, on the other hand, are permitted to send and receive mail, with the International Committee of the Red Cross (ICRC) serving as a conduit for communication between POWs and their families. The ICRC played the role of intermediary in this unorthodox conflict, too, despite uncertainty as to the success of its efforts. In 1967, at a time when approximately 600 American POWs were imprisoned in North Vietnam, local branches of the American Red Cross (ARC) forwarded 500 letters to the ICRC for onward transmission to Hanoi. However, the director of the ARC's International Service noted in an internal memo (dated September 1967) that the ICRC lacked proof that North Vietnamese authorities actually delivered these letters to their intended prisoner-recipients. The previous year, Hanoi returned parcels from prisoners' families containing books and food that had been mailed at the exorbitant cost of $100 per package.[13]

Over time, the volume of mail flowing in both directions increased, particularly from the US to North Vietnam. Between February 1970 and March 1973, when the majority of POWs were released, the ICRC transmitted 17,769 letters from American family members to prisoners.[14] But mail remained an intensely contested phenomenon throughout the war. For the North Vietnamese, letters – like newspapers and magazines arriving from the United States – were a currency that could be manipulated to influence prisoners' moods and attitudes. Rather than isolating prisoners altogether from the world beyond confinement, Vietnamese camp guards extracted items from the press, periodicals, and personal letters likely to dent POWs' morale and make them more receptive to the captors' worldview. POWs duly learnt quite a bit about the antiwar demonstrations roiling American cities and campuses. They also heard about the fitful progress of peace negotiations in Paris.[15]

With their diet of information strategically rationed, prisoners became convinced that they were more likely to hear bad news from home than good.[16] Sometimes this included information about their intimate relationships. One POW, Commander Raymond Vohden, found out about the end of his marriage when another prisoner came into his cell in the Hanoi Hilton (the ironic nickname Americans bestowed on the Hoa Lo prison), announcing, "Ray, I've got some bad news for you." The bad news had been clipped from *Stars and Stripes*. Posted by the North Vietnamese guards on a bulletin board, the item was headlined "POW's Wife Seeks Divorce." The wife in question, Vohden soon discovered, was his own.[17] Others received distressing communications from their wives in a less roundabout way. American POWs in

Vietnam echoed the stories told by an earlier generation of prisoners of the German Wehrmacht, who noted that the Nazis reliably delivered Dear John letters even as they withheld or destroyed other mail from home.[18]

How many POWs received Dear John letters remained a matter of speculation during their captivity. One prisoner's wife, Valerie Kushner, guessed that "a lot" had divorced their husbands. Others estimated very few. For its part, the DoD refused to dignify journalists' curiosity on the subject. The Pentagon did not wish, its spokesmen announced, to have a depressant effect on prisoners' morale. Defense officials anticipated that any reports about divorce proceedings initiated by POW/MIA wives would hastily be relayed by Hanoi to the captives themselves. The DoD insisted, rather disingenuously, that it was not gathering data on prisoners' marriages.[19]

The tight oversight exercised by the DoD over outgoing letters and the scrutiny to which the North Vietnamese subjected incoming correspondence, coupled with strong social prohibitions against ending relationships with men at war, make it unlikely that many spouses announced the initiation of divorce proceedings by mail. The DoD insisted that next of kin retain a file copy of all communications sent to POWs and MIAs in Vietnam. In some cases, US intelligence officials attempted to persuade prisoners' wives, like Sybil Stockdale, to include coded messages in letters to their husbands: a stratagem that risked more than simply the letters' destruction if the ruse were discovered.[20] Girlfriends and fiancées were not officially permitted to write at all. This privilege was reserved for recognized next of kin (NOK). As far as the DoD was concerned, wives, parents, and children counted as NOK; unmarried intimate partners did not.[21]

Next of kin's correspondence was hemmed in by restrictions on all sides. North Vietnam imposed an annual numerical cap on pieces of mail it would accept from the United States. And in their intermediary role, the Red Cross established that family members could send prisoners no more than three letters per month. Meanwhile, the US armed forces issued strong recommendations as to what family members should and shouldn't say to their missing or imprisoned loved ones. Major

A. W. Gratch, of the USAF's Directorate of Personnel Services, circulated the following guidelines:

> We recommend that letters be of a cheerful nature and be confined to personal and family matters. Write about activities of family and friends, such as vacations, visits, schooling, and other events and comments of interest. Suggest that no mention be made regarding the current status or pros and cons of the Vietnam conflict, victories or losses of our military forces, other service personnel who are missing or captured, etc. In short, comments either closely or remotely connected with the current political or military situation should be avoided. Letters should be directed at bracing the prisoner's morale and should not contain information which can be used by his captors. Please retain a copy of every letter you forward as it may become nec for us to refer to them at a later date.[22]

Since the pro forma note-paper that next of kin were required to use shrank from fifteen to seven lines at Hanoi's behest, few spouses probably needed to be told not to devote their paltry allowance of space to disquisitions on the rights and wrongs of the war or recitations of the latest body count broadcast nightly on American television news.[23]

Outside the sanctioned ICRC route, wives lacked options other than entrusting letters intended for prisoner-spouses to activists, like Cora Weiss, who traveled to North Vietnam to initiate informal peace talks and serve as a bridge between prisoners' families and Hanoi. Weiss's organization, the Committee of Liaison with Families of Servicemen Detained in North Vietnam (COLIAFAM), provided an alternate back channel for the exchange of mail between prisoners and their families, with activists transporting 300 letters back and forth on a monthly basis from the group's founding in December 1969 until the end of the war. Although this service tripled the volume of POW mail, the DoD discouraged families from working with COLIAFAM, disapproving of its leftist, antiwar character.[24]

Prisoners faced even tighter control over their correspondence – if they were permitted to write letters at all. In 1967, the Red Cross estimated that just forty American prisoners had secured permission to send mail home. Rightly or wrongly, ARC personnel detected "a high positive correlation between those who have been granted letter-writing

5.2. In this photograph, originally published in *Life* magazine in January 1969, Mrs. Arthur Mearns is seen mailing her weekly letter to her POW husband in Vietnam. She had heard nothing from him in three years. (Photo by Vernon Merritt III/The LIFE Picture Collection via Getty Images.)

privileges and those who are ready to criticize our government."[25] Mrs. Lindsay Miller agreed with that assessment, attributing the larger number of letters she received from her prisoner husband, Edison, to his antiwar broadcasts – of which she strenuously disapproved.[26] As time went by, more prisoners were able to write home, though many wives found that the arrival of letters from North Vietnam remained sporadic. Eileen Cormier annually received about five or six letters from her husband, Arthur, taken prisoner in 1965. By July 1972, she'd amassed thirty altogether. Many other wives and next of kin reported receiving far fewer pieces of mail. But if delivery was erratic, the length of these messages was more predictable. Like mail sent to prisoners, the letters they could send home were typically limited to just six lines.[27]

Six heavily surveilled lines every few months was a slender basis on which to sustain an intimate relationship. Some wives coped with separation by writing far more letters than they were permitted to send, turning this one-sided correspondence into a kind of diary that might one day be shared with their returned husband. Libby Hill, married just twelve days before her husband deployed to Indochina, remained hopeful six years after USAF Captain Howard Hill was shot down in December 1967. Her optimism that their brief marriage could be happily resumed rested on the "seventeen beautiful letters" she'd received from him in captivity.[28] Less fortunate wives had no word at all. And with only dimming memories of a husband to rely on, some spouses' hopes for a successful return to married life faded – along with expectations that the missing man would ever come home. "I loved my husband dearly. I think I still do. But how can I be sure I love a man I haven't seen or heard of in five years?," Mrs. Jo Ann Flora rhetorically asked *New York Times* reporter Nan Robertson in December 1972. By then, the imminent ceasefire had brought the prospect of the POWs' return, or their perpetual disappearance, achingly close. The Floras had been married less than three years when her Green Beret husband tumbled from a helicopter near the DMZ, vanishing into an evidentiary black hole.[29]

RIP VAN WINKLE REAWAKENS

Even before Operation Homecoming, the marriages – and prospective divorces – of Americans missing or imprisoned in Vietnam had sparked a good deal of interest from journalists and cultural producers. In December 1972, Iris Powers, an advocate for POW/MIA families whose own son was missing in action, estimated that about fourteen wives of missing servicemen had remarried or were poised to do so. "No Penelopes," she called them.[30] With the estimated number of POWs/ MIAs then standing at around 2,000, the intimate lives of MIA wives and girlfriends who'd "moved on" arguably received a disproportionate amount of attention. That was certainly the view of Mrs. George S. Patton. In a letter to the *Washington Post*, she complained that women who planned to abandon, or had already left, their marriages to men in captivity had become such a "popular topic." These unfaithful women had, she proposed, captivated the national imagination at the expense of the far greater number of stalwart spouses who remained true to their husbands in captivity, dutifully adhering to the military wife's "Semper Fi" credo.[31]

Since monogamy spelled monotony to journalists enticed by more dramatic material, it's not hard to see why the wrenching dilemmas of women who'd spent years separated from men who might never come home should have captured attention. Numerous news stories and magazine features probed the agonizing state of suspended animation endured by MIA wives and girlfriends as they waited (or did not wait) for the return of loved ones about whom little, or nothing, had been known with certainty for years. Hollywood also elbowed in on the act. Most cinematic histories of the Vietnam-themed production *The Green Berets* (1968) credit John Wayne's flag-waver as the *only* film to have been made about the war while it was in progress. But that well-worn claim neglects Mark Robson's *Limbo* (1972), based on a "torn-from-the-headlines" novel by Joan Silver and Linda Gottlieb. Drawing on extensive interviews, *Limbo* explored the choices of three women who responded in divergent ways to their common existential conundrum. Were they wives or widows?[32]

The marriages of men missing in Vietnam, whether known to be imprisoned or still unaccounted for, invited speculative story-telling. Commentators in the 1970s frequently invoked archetypal tales of absence and homecoming to frame their narratives. Homer's *The Odyssey* supplied the most obvious literary coordinates for aligning contemporary experience with classical antiquity. The challenges confronting modern military wives, though "usually less tangible than a courtyard of boozing suitors," were "just as real" as those that had confronted Odysseus's serially tested spouse, two psychologists proposed.[33] But since Penelope *had* remained faithful to Odysseus – in Homer's telling of the myth at any rate – other templates were required.

Alfred Lord Tennyson's *Enoch Arden* supplied a different scenario. Published in 1864, the Englishman's narrative ballad had bequeathed a name ("Enoch Arden decrees") to statutes some states adopted governing how soon women could remarry if their husbands remained unaccountably absent for protracted periods.[34] Tennyson's eponymous protagonist, shipwrecked and missing for many years, returns home to find his wife living with a new husband. Believing Enoch dead, she has settled into companionable marriage with his brother. As a result, the mariner must decide whether to make his presence known, destroying the idyll of domestic harmony he witnesses from afar, or to let it be. Selflessly, Enoch chooses to vanish again unannounced.[35] As Operation Homecoming approached, several press stories aired the comparable predicament of women who'd requested that the Pentagon reclassify their MIA husbands as dead in order to clear the way for their remarriage. The possibility that at least some of these men might, in fact, return from Vietnam was a melodramatic prospect as troubling to the women in question as it was enticing to journalists.

By early 1973, it was public knowledge that a number of wives had divorced men *known* to be alive and imprisoned in Vietnam. Some had remarried. Prominently documented by the media, Tangee Alvarez, wife of the longest-serving POW, Everett Alvarez, obtained a divorce and remarried in 1971. Everett learnt this news from his mother. A handful of other prisoners, such as Lieutenant Wayne Goodermote and Captain Charlie Plumb, similarly learnt of their wives' divorce plans from their mothers.[36]

Operation Homecoming didn't create a hitherto non-existent appetite for juicy morsels from the private lives of returning prisoners. But the fanfare accorded lionized heroes ensured that their marriages remained under the media spotlight, and the Klieg lights shone with particular intensity on these couples' dissolutions. This wasn't what the Pentagon had intended in long-range planning for an eventuality that remained distant in 1971. Operation Egress Recap was the first, fittingly opaque, title for homecoming arrangements that were envisioned as largely hidden from public view. DoD planners were fearful that returning prisoners would come back in woeful mental and physical shape, liable to spout unhelpful views about the war – and the Nixon administration – if not carefully chaperoned and "re-conditioned" prior to going home. To improve the optics of re-entry and to accelerate the returning men's restoration to good health, Egress Recap proposed that repatriated POWs would be hospitalized for their first few weeks in the "free world."[37]

When Hanoi began to release prisoners, a few returning well in advance of the Paris peace accords, American officials were taken aback by their surprisingly good health and apparent mental equilibrium. Operation Homecoming, as Egress Recap was more catchily recast, required RPWs to spend only a brief stint in military-mandated purgatory before going home. Weeks shrank to a mere three days.[38]

During this hiatus at Clark Air Force Base, returned prisoners were brought up to speed on what had changed during the years they'd spent in captivity: personal and political, social and cultural, national and global. Military chaplains played an important role in facilitating re-entry, filling in the many blanks left by prisoners' patchy (or nonexistent) mail service. As the declassified After Action Report on Operation Homecoming blandly put it, chaplains had to convey "sensitive information concerning changes in their family situation during captivity."[39] More bluntly put, they had to inform some returning men about deaths, illnesses, and accidents that had befallen parents or other loved ones while they were away. And, as Robert Stirm could attest, chaplains faced the daunting task of conveying news of divorce and remarriage, whether delivering explanations that wives had written or translating these developments into their own language. But none of this pressing, and often depressing, information was conveyed right away. Military Intelligence debriefers insisted on interrogating returnees *before* chaplains relayed "sensitive information" and prior to their permitted next-of-kin phone call. They feared that distraught men would yield less valuable intelligence about their captivity. So, news from home would have to wait. Returnees were required to speak before they could listen.[40]

Sometimes what they heard from chaplains was misleading or plain wrong. The Pentagon's domestic intelligence-gathering was by no means flawless. The After Action Report documented one especially regrettable instance in which a returnee's wife had borne two children while her husband was in captivity. Since nothing about this substantial change of family situation was included in the chaplain's background dossier, the man in question "received this information only when he met his wife."[41]

Operating at a more generic level, DoD personnel compiled a 219-page digest of important events and trends the returnees had missed, from the rise of Black Power to the assassinations of MLK and RFK, the Apollo 11 moonlanding to miniskirts, like the fuchsia, button-through number worn by Lorrie Stirm to greet her father.[42] That the returnees had been imprisoned for so long – and at a time of such seismic social change – made a third parable especially well suited to stories of home-coming from Vietnam. Journalists quickly dubbed repatriated former prisoners "modern-day Rip Van Winkles," invoking Washington Irving's famous Catskills tale in which the protagonist manages to miss the War of Independence by taking a twenty-year nap. This literary borrowing gave writers an opportunity to appraise society through the former prisoners' alienated eyes: a handy device to critique features of America's altered domestic landscape that returnees (or writers ventriloquizing their views) found hardest to navigate.[43]

In the press, humorous riffs abounded on former prisoners' appalled reactions to Americans' adjusted fashion sense. Why did men wear their hair so long, while women wore their skirts so short? And since when was it sartorially acceptable for men to sport loud checkered pants, luxuriant side burns, and shoulder-grazing lapels? The latter-day Van Winkles seemed especially prone to lambast the looser cut of sexual mores effected by Women's Lib. While their namesake had hibernated through the American Revolution, the former prisoners had missed not only fashion's "peacock revolution" but an even more world-shaking sexual revolution. Several former prisoners lamented that women had, as they saw it, emerged from this gender-quake on top.[44]

Several RPW marriages reportedly foundered on the rocks of women's emancipation. Some men struggled to adjust to the independence and authority women had enjoyed exercising in their absence, and were loath to relinquish on their husbands' return. While a number of prominent activist wives announced themselves eager to "snap back," as Sybil Stockdale put it, into the subordinate role decreed by marital hierarchy before their husband's long absence, other women resisted men's attempts to restore the spousal status quo ante. Although partners often experienced their years apart as a paralyzing limbo – a protracted depression of the pause button – time, unlike a halted cassette tape, kept moving. Inevitably, both husband and wife had changed during, and been altered by, long years of separation.[45] Many wives expressed surprise about how *little* their husbands' personalities had changed as a result of incarceration, while husbands often seemed shocked at how *much* their wives had altered.[46]

When homecoming revealed the chasm that separated spouses-turned-strangers, the consequences could be fatal. Captain Edward A. Brudno found the psychological recalibrations required by reunion impossible. In captivity, he'd written letters to his wife, Deborah, that oscillated between self-recrimination over his shortcomings as a spouse (in June 1970), entreaties that she forget him and move on (in February 1972), and fantasies of a blissful marital future ahead (in November 1972).[47] Absence, solitary confinement, and prolonged silence left plenty of scope for a prisoner's thoughts of home to bounce wildly between extremes of despair and delirium. Four months after his release from seven years in captivity, on the day before his thirty-third birthday, Brudno asphyxiated himself in a bedroom at his parents-in-law's home. He left behind a two-line note, written in the French language that he'd acquired as a prisoner. In it, he announced that life was "not worth living." Press coverage of Brudno's death – the first suicide of a RPW – offered readers an array of speculative hunches about what had caused a brilliant MIT graduate to plunge into a lethal tailspin. Might depression have resulted from Brudno's dashed dreams of becoming an astronaut or bitterness toward the antiwar movement? Brudno's brother proposed that Edward had developed chronic "inflexibility" as a result of incarceration. This sclerosis had left him unable to cope with the predictable stresses of rehabilitation. But the rabbi who officiated at Brudno's funeral gave a different interpretation of what had precipitated Edward's suicide. Rabbi David Jacobs stressed marital problems stemming from the personality changes Brudno had observed, and failed to accept, in his wife. "She had developed into a very strong person," Jacobs told mourners. "He wanted to be her strength and she became his strength, and he couldn't stand it." By this the Rabbi intended no criticism of the man being buried. Brudno's upended marriage was, Jacobs insisted, "a burden a hero cannot bear easily."[48]

Other returnees who found they couldn't live with the strong women their wives had become ended their misery not in death but divorce. Some of these stories also received considerable play in the press. The dissolution of Navy Commander Raymond Vohden's marriage was among them. Peter Arnett supplied readers of the *Los Angeles Times* with the anecdote about Vohden's discovery in captivity that his wife, Bonnye, intended to divorce him from a *Stars and Stripes* clipping. But a more complicated picture of betrayal and violated trust emerged from other reports. Like Brudno, Vohden had written to his wife from the Hanoi Hilton, urging her to "make a new life" after six years apart. Whether this gesture attested selfless devotion or was better understood as a loyalty test, it was retracted when Vohden returned from Vietnam. Back home again, he wanted to reconcile, offering to "forgive and forget." Although Bonnye insisted the relationships she'd entered into during his absence weren't sins requiring spousal absolution, she agreed to attempt a reconciliation. But Raymond found it hard to adjust to unfamiliar domestic dynamics. "Most shocking to me is the sexual revolution," he confided to a *New York Times* reporter, adding that he was "not a prude." The couple agreed to divorce amicably – until Vohden rooted through Bonnye's personal possessions and unearthed letters from other men. "I yelled at her some terrible things," Vohden told Arnett. Any chance of reconciliation, along with any pretence of amicability, evaporated in a cloud of white-hot rage.[49]

The seam of misogyny that ran through reports of returnees undone by "women's lib" befitted the Rip Van Winkle frame. Irving's protagonist left home because he couldn't abide his "termagant wife," who remains unnamed throughout. "A tart temper never mellows with age, and a sharp tongue is the only edged tool that grows keener with constant use," noted Irving, in sympathy with his endlessly scolded protagonist. Waking from his epic slumber, Rip Van Winkle was discombobulated by the many changes all around. He wasn't dismayed, however, to discover that the "terrible virago" who'd driven him away had died during his absence. As a *Life* magazine feature on the RPWs reminded readers, Rip had been "relieved" by this one "drop of comfort."[50] Dame Van Winkle, RIP.

5.3. Bonnye Vohden, one of several POW wives whose marriages foundered during years of separation, listens to President Nixon announce the withdrawal of American troops from Vietnam in 1972. By then, her husband, Navy Lt. Commander Raymond Vohden, had been imprisoned in North Vietnam for eight years. (Photo by Underwood Archives/Getty Images.)

PSYCHOLOGIZING THE "WAITING WIFE"

Throughout the 1970s, POW/MIA wives found themselves under various microscopes, all of which magnified their private lives, making personal thoughts, feelings, and choices more accessible to public dissection. Journalists had a particular profit-driven incentive to feed public curiosity about released prisoners and the women who waited loyally for their return – or did not. That the balance of this reportage tipped against wives who failed to embrace Penelope's example is suggested by a confidential DoD report, written in January 1972, which noted strong public disapproval for POW/MIA wives who contemplated remarrying.[51]

Not all of those who scrutinized the wives of POW/MIAs were looking either to monetize or moralize their misfortunes, however. In the late 1960s, psychiatrists and psychologists working with different branches of the armed forces began to publish scholarly studies of military wives. Harold MacIntosh's observation in 1968 about the dearth of attention paid by fellow psychiatrists to the "modern Penelope" was well made. Despite the military's longstanding conviction that a wife was "pivotal" to her spouse's professional success – "she may aid her husband in withstanding military pressures or encourage him to succumb to those pressures," one psychiatrist noted in 1973 – psy-professionals had largely ignored servicemen's spouses prior to the Vietnam war. In the late 1960s, anyone interested in this subject could count the relevant scholarly articles on the fingers of one hand – with digits to spare.[52]

American participation in World War II spurred the growth of both psychiatry and psychology as fields of intellectual inquiry with vital practical applications for the armed forces. Psychiatrists and psychologists played key roles in testing the aptitude of potential draftees for military service and theorizing the vectors of combat stress, as well as treating those mentally injured by war.[53] But wartime conditions stimulated only a modest amount of research into the emotional and psychological stresses suffered by soldiers' loved ones. Most of these pioneering studies, like Reuben Hill's *Families under Stress* (1949), were aimed at assessing separation-induced tensions between spouses and fatherless children's maladies. Taking the male bread-winner nuclear family as the American norm, these investigations foregrounded the dysfunctions that arose when women suddenly became solo parents and heads-of-household during their husbands' deployments. Researchers also documented the Oedipal complications of demobilized fathers' return home. Child psychology and parent–infant relations thus loomed large in research undertaken during and shortly after World War II.[54]

Wives remained neglected. With a handful of exceptions, such as Helene Deutsch, Evelyn Millis Duvall, and Edward and Louise McDonagh, few American clinicians, marriage experts, sociologists, or social workers probed the challenges experienced by women married or engaged to men at war.[55] The few pages these experts devoted to the topic accentuated "loneliness" as the defining test posed by separation, along with anxieties over wrinkles, gray hair, and fluctuating weight. Many women apparently feared they wouldn't pass muster on "second appraisal" by homecoming husbands. The McDonaghs faulted a "pathetic eagerness on the part of many war wives to 'keep things exactly as they are.'" But they neglected to note the substantial pressures women faced – whether from magazine advice columnists or their spouses' letters – to maintain the fiction of home as a place immune from flux.[56]

In the 1950s, military-funded psychiatrists and psychologists committed unprecedented resources to analyzing American POWs when they returned from North Korean camps in 1953. These returnees became the most intensively studied human subjects in US history as researchers attempted to understand how communist "brainwashing" techniques worked, or whether this much-feared Pavlovian practice existed at all.[57] About prisoners' wives, however, psy-professionals had precisely nothing to say. When clinicians redirected their attention to servicemen's romantic partners again in the 1960s they did so under the influence of new psychological models, particularly John Bowlby's attachment theory with its key concept of "separation anxiety."[58]

Pioneering studies of military wives in the Vietnam era offered more complex accounts of the symptomatology of separation, its psychic origins, and its possible therapeutic treatment. Richard Isay, Chester Pearlman, Constantine Cretekos, Douglas Bey, and Jean Lange (all psychiatrists who analyzed military spouses, with the exception of Lange, a self-described former "waiting wife") wrote about wives whose primary preoccupations were not visible signs of aging or feelings of loneliness, unlike their 1940s predecessors. These women were full of inexpressible rage turned inward. They were angry with the husbands who'd "abandoned" them for active duty, and enraged by an institution that required wives to satisfy their husbands' emotional needs while endlessly stifling their own. Repressed feelings surfaced in psychosomatic form: depression, headaches, crying fits, insomnia. Some wives attempted to have their husbands called back, manufacturing crises at home that might necessitate their extrication from front-line duty. A number of wives studied by these researchers had attempted suicide.[59] Others embarked on extramarital affairs as a form of retaliatory "acting out" against absent husbands. That, at any rate, was the thesis advanced by Isay in his widely cited analysis of what he dubbed the "Submariners' Wives Syndrome" published in 1968.[60] Writing six years later, Bey and Lange noted that many wives who entered into sexual relationships during their husbands' absence felt guilty for having engaged in behavior that society condemned, even as it condoned "soldiers visiting prostitutes." Guilt sometimes expressed itself in heightened fear that their absent husband would come to harm, as though battlefield injury were a form of karmic payback for female infidelity – an anxiety that mirrored servicemen's superstitious dread of Dear Johns as harbingers of death.[61]

Research on military spouses developed apace in the 1970s as the "waiting wife" archetype was tested by Vietnam. The unique stresses of POW/MIA wives – indefinitely prolonged separation, erratic (or zero) communication, existential uncertainty, social placelessness in communities organized around married couples – formed key foci of investigation. To help prepare for the prisoners' eventual return, the Navy established a Family Studies Branch of its Center for Prisoner of War Studies in San Diego under the leadership of Dr. John Plag in 1972.[62] Plag and his colleagues were frequently cited in press reports on POW/MIA wives and families, lending their evaluations of spouses a semi-public character. Tasked with studying "processes of adjustment involved in family reunions after prolonged separation," Plag and his team amassed a vast database of variables that might prove conjugally consequential. As reported in the *New York Times*, the Center's computer banks not only hoarded "minutiae" relating to each prisoner's idiosyncratic interests and foibles, they also carefully monitored fluctuations in his spouse's appearance and attitudes. According to reporter Everett R. Holles, "If his wife has changed the color of her hair or gained weight since he last saw her, it is recorded. Everything, in fact, that might pose a problem for the returned man's physical recovery and psychological readjustment is grist for Operation Egress Recap."[63] This attempt to develop an algorithm for marital functioning after separation yielded the "T-Double ABCX Model for adjustment and adaptation."[64]

Complex though this formula sounded, the San Diego researchers' key findings were quite straightforward. First, strong marriages generally survived a husband's extended absence. Relationships that had been precarious beforehand did not. Where marriages had been brief, or partners temperamentally mismatched, the relationship could be expected to founder – during the husband's captivity or soon after his return.[65] Second, "wives were in control of the reintegration process." Or so one of the Center's earlier studies announced in 1975. During the years of separation, McCubbin and his co-authors observed, women typically engaged in conjugal cost–benefit analyses as they deliberated whether they wanted to pick up the pieces when (or if) their husband returned. "[S]ome, after weighing their personal feelings about the quality of their marriage before separation and considering their personal aspirations as well as the hardships they endured during separation, had determined in advance of their husbands' return that they had no recourse but to terminate the marriage and begin a life for themselves."[66]

Following social scientific protocol, this report didn't mention any specific women by name. Loretta Stirm seemingly exemplified this pattern, however. Her Dear John letter, which a chaplain handed Bob at Clark AFB, expressed irremediable dissatisfaction with their marriage from long before his captivity in Vietnam. Married at nineteen, she'd shouldered the burden of raising four infants largely alone. Her note insisted that she loved Bob; that she'd kept his memory alive for their children, saying nightly prayers for his safe return. "But you must remember how very unhappy we were together," she entreated. "It wasn't your fault – we are extremely unsuited and managed to make each other miserable . . ."[67]

Loretta had not waited faithfully for her husband to return. But she *had* waited to divulge her decision. Was this deferred revelation anomalous? Confounding? Some Americans apparently thought so. Dr. Edna J. Hunter, who succeeded Plag as head of the Navy's Family Studies Branch in San Diego, told an audience in 1979 that "persons not too informed" about the POW situation had often asked her "incredulously why some wives waited so long, only to announce to their husbands so quickly on return that the marriage was over." Hunter herself did not find this surprising. Socialized to prioritize their husbands' professional performance above all else, career officers' wives understood very well how distressing word of divorce would be to men in captivity. "Thus, they would be reluctant to write him a 'Dear John' letter while he was sitting in prison," Hunter opined. Most POW wives, like Loretta Stirm, conscientiously chose to wait until their husbands returned from Vietnam to communicate their desire to divorce. In the meantime, they carried the weight of this momentous decision alone, its gravity accumulating as years went by. Yet as their fellow citizens' consternation suggests, women who observed the cardinal tenet that a breakup be delayed until the soldier's return weren't spared social censure. In some Americans' eyes, ending a relationship with a man in uniform remained unconscionable at any time.[68]

THE POLITICS OF LOSS

The San Diego psychologists made another striking claim based on personal interviews with more than half of all POW/MIA families and questionnaires submitted by many others. Although prisoner-husbands were "basically excluded from the decision-making process," most returnees "tacitly accepted a decision that had previously been determined" by their wives about whether, and under what terms, their marriages would resume.[69] Acquiescence may indeed have been the norm. However, husbands who did *not* accept their wife's decision to seek a divorce tended to speak out loudly about their aggrieved feelings. And because returned POWs enjoyed ready access to journalistic amplifiers, accounts of betrayal and abandonment hogged far more air-time and column inches than stories of marriages either dissolved by mutual consent or carefully resuscitated after reunion.[70]

If women were, as McCubbin et al. insisted, "in control" of the decision to divorce, they rarely exercised authority over publicly circulated narratives about their marriages. It's telling that the contents of Loretta Stirm's letter ending her marriage are common knowledge only because Bob Stirm chose to share them with a reporter some twenty years after his return from Vietnam. Like many other Dear Johns, hers was served up second-hand – in pre-digested nuggets – for consumers she'd not intended. Loretta declined to be interviewed for the ensuing *Los Angeles Times* story, which appeared in 1993: a lengthy recitation of Bob's abiding bitterness about their divorce and the Pulitzer-winning photograph that had made his family famous. Two decades on, Bob continued to contrast his honorable service with Loretta's disloyalty.[71]

5.4. At the time of this photograph's first publication in 1964, Tangee Alvarez, seen receiving news of her husband Everett's capture in North Vietnam, was depicted as an exemplary "waiting wife." Her decision to divorce him during his absence changed public perceptions. (Photo by Jon Brenneis/The LIFE Images Collection via Getty Images.)

The treacherous wife motif, which was first apparent in "Operation Homecoming" reportage, became more pronounced as former POWs started to produce memoirs. A trickle of life-writing soon turned into a torrent. Larry Chesley, author of the inaugural contribution to the genre, *Seven Years in Hanoi* (1973), related that he'd received a six-line letter from his wife, Jo Dean, informing him of their divorce. Following standard prisoner procedure, in which all mail from home was committed to memory for sharing with fellow POWs, Larry memorized her words before handing the missive back to his Vietnamese captors.[72] Despite this valiant performance of stoicism, he felt punched in the stomach, continuing to register emotional anguish in somatic ways for weeks after receiving this unwelcome news. As historian Natasha Zaretsky points out, in Chesley's account and several others, wives appear as de facto "enemy collaborators," handing the North Vietnamese a weapon they wielded with malicious skill.[73] Embellishing this theme, Everett Alvarez's memoir, *Chained Eagle* (1989), reported that his captors "gleefully" chose Christmas day to hand over the letter in which his mother conveyed the bitter news that Everett's former wife, Tangee, had obtained a "Mexican divorce" and remarried.[74] Searching for a metaphor equal to his pain, Alvarez described his mother's implosive revelation – "*Tangee has decided not to wait*" – as "like dynamite," before depicting himself "impaled" by words that seemed to thrust from the page. Tangee had "uncoupled" him, leaving Alvarez (the engineless carriage?) "stranded and bewildered in a godforsaken land far from home." After this passage, readers hardly needed Alvarez's moral spelled out. There was no crime darker than a woman's betrayal.[75]

For some former prisoners, the most damning evidence against their former wives was that these faithless women had reduced courageous men to tears. Ernest Brace and Steve Long discovered en route home that their wives had left them: "Through all the years of harassment, the leg irons, the beatings with bamboo rods, the rope burns, and the efforts they [the Vietnamese] had made to demoralize us, neither of us could remember crying. Steve and I cried in front of each other in that small room." The memoir's title, *A Code to Keep*, alluded to the twin pledges that Brace and other steadfast married prisoners had observed: the POW Code of Conduct (divulge no more than name, rank, serial number, and date of birth) and their conjugal vows. If, under severe duress, men managed to observe both, why couldn't women – under no duress at all – maintain their marital commitments?[76] Brace floated this as a rhetorical question. Dialling up the invective, Charlie Plumb ended his tribulation-filled account of captivity with a blunt accusation aimed at his former wife: "You broke your vow." Calling his memoir (in humble lower case) *i'm no hero*, Plumb more than implied his spouse's villainy.[77] Ex-wives appeared in these accounts more viciously wounding than sadistic North Vietnamese prison guards.

Like the press stories that preceded them, POW memoirs recounted former wives' betrayals at length and with feeling. Neither temporal distance nor remarriage sufficed to tamp down these men's rage. Several former prisoners remained mad at their exes for draining their psychological stamina in captivity, and for depleting their bank balances and pension funds in absentia. In some returnees' narratives of marital breakdown, including Robert Stirm's and Everett Alvarez's, exes appear as embezzlers or thieves. Whether troubled by wives' new-found independence, their spendthrift habits, or extramarital affairs – or some combination of these complaints – several returnees swiftly initiated divorce proceedings. Just four months after Operation Homecoming, returnee Fred Cherry alleged "adultery, desertion and abandonment" in divorce proceedings against his wife. (Years later, he sued the USAF to recover $147,184 in salary and allowances paid to his by-then ex-wife while he was imprisoned.)[78] Some RPWs ended their marriages for different reasons. Carol Shepp McCain, who'd suffered a near-fatal car wreck while her husband John was held prisoner for five and a half years in Hanoi, was reportedly taken aback to hear in 1980 that he was divorcing her. He'd recently met a "glamorous young heiress," Cindy Lou Hensley. Carol blamed this development on neither her accident nor his captivity in Vietnam. "I attribute it more to John turning 40 and wanting to be 25 again than to anything else," she told reporter Paul Farhi.[79]

Contrary to the projections of the San Diego psychologists, wives were not always the marital "deciders" or arbiters of reintegration. Some women who earnestly hoped to reconstruct married life found that their partners remained both emotionally and physically AWOL on return. Some returnees were so eager to discharge their patriotic duty as homecoming hero that they neglected more personal affirmations. Overheard by a journalist, one returnee who'd just disembarked at Travis shooed his wife away as she rushed to embrace him. After years of separation, his first words to his spouse – issued in a stern whisper – were, "I have to salute the flag, don't bother me."[80] Paradoxically, the hoopla that engulfed former POWs during and for months after Operation Homecoming – civic pageants, gala dinners, speaking engagements, product endorsement opportunities – encouraged some men to bask in the public limelight rather than settling down to the emotionally arduous work of reforging marital bonds.[81]

Of all the alterations that returning prisoners encountered in their wives, antiwar politicization apparently proved the least tolerable. This theme surfaced in several memoirs as well as some clinical studies. In their husbands' absence, certain wives had become "strongly antiwar," in the words of military psychiatrist Dr. Robert S. Andersen, who'd worked with returnees at Scott Air Force Base in Illinois. Since the POWs (almost all career officers) tended to be "conservative in their political beliefs and hawkish on the war issue," political differences opened an unbridgeable chasm in some marriages.[82] Some men broadened an accusation of abandonment leveled at particular spouses into an ideological critique of home front treachery writ large. Antiwar wives had done more (and worse) than hand the North Vietnamese a figurative weapon in the form of a Dear John letter. They'd wilfully made common cause with the enemy, failing to keep faith not only with their husbands but with their nation's military mission in southeast Asia.[83]

Accounts of marital breakdown framed in this way resonated with ascendant right-wing revisionism during the late 1970s and 1980s. Increasingly, the "silent majority" – never inaudible even during the war – pronounced the war in Vietnam to have been a "noble cause," ignobly lost. American purposes in Indochina had been betrayed by a fickle home front, traduced by an oppositional press, and sold down the river by Nixon's White House. The latter had insisted the military fight with "one hand tied behind its back," and then turned its back on hundreds of MIAs abandoned in Vietnam at the war's end. Traitorous women became a lightning rod for conservative ire. Jane Fonda was a particularly useful hate-figure, branded with the pejorative nickname "Hanoi Jane." But antiwar POW spouses – along with "unwaiting" wives – also readily fit the bill.[84]

It's perhaps ironic, then, that the most prominent POW activist wives weren't countercultural peaceniks but, like their imprisoned husbands, "conservative" and "hawkish." Sybil Stockdale and the other spouses who formed the National League of Families of American Prisoners and Missing in Southeast Asia devoted their formidable organizational energies toward – and increasingly against – the Nixon administration, lobbying to secure a full account of all POW/MIAs in southeast Vietnam. Where antiwar groups like Women Strike for Peace and COLIAFAM sought to end the war swiftly by linking the removal of US forces from Vietnam with the repatriation of prisoners, the League was willing to protract hostilities. Their insistence that Hanoi was dissembling on the POW/MIA issue, and that Nixon and Kissinger shouldn't tolerate a less than complete account of the fate of all American servicemen still unaccounted for in Vietnam, did nothing to accelerate diplomatic negotiations to end the war. Judging from their memoirs, however, former prisoners didn't object to wives' activism with the League or with Voices in Vital America (VIVA), the for-profit advocacy organization responsible for remembrance bracelets inscribed with POW/MIA names. Some returnees announced themselves proud of their wives' achievements. For their part, several conservative women activists, like Sybil Stockdale and Dorothy McDaniel, hailed the end of their public lives with loud expressions of relief. With the prisoners safely home, domesticity and deference to male authority could happily prevail once again.[85]

In just one publicly recorded case did a wife's POW/MIA activism push in the opposite direction: toward a divorce she initiated against a husband whose leftist politics she found intolerable. Mrs. Lindsay Marie Miller had been married for twenty years to the highest ranking Marine Corps prisoner, Lt. Col. Edison Wainwright Miller, when he was accused by James Stockdale of mutiny and aiding the enemy on return home in 1973. The same *Washington Post* story that related this news also reported that his wife was seeking to terminate a long marriage that had produced five sons.[86] Pronouncing herself "ashamed" by her husband's "cowardice" in captivity, Lindsay sued for divorce. While Edison had apparently thrown his lot in with the North Vietnamese in captivity, she had thrown hers in with VIVA, and regarded his antiwar statements as a "betrayal" of American loyalists.[87]

POLITICIZING THE PERSONAL

The theme of betrayal so pointedly underscored in POW memoirs both reflected and perpetuated an increasingly pervasive interpretation of why, and by whom, the war in Vietnam had been lost. The military had been stabbed in the back by the press, antiwar protestors, and a political establishment too craven to fight for every last man in Vietnam, selling out the MIAs in the interest of extricating the nation from a war Nixon had chosen to end rather than win. In this narrative, spousal treachery was readily conflated with the administration's larger disloyalty to men who'd served in Vietnam. This motif also runs through several POW movies that appeared in the 1980s, as President Ronald Reagan encouraged the rescripting of Vietnam as lost cause that not only could have been won, but could yet be redeemed by keeping faith with the POW/

MIAs. In *The Hanoi Hilton* (1987), a feature promoted on the back of its alleged fidelity to POWs' lived experiences, one steadfast prisoner receives a "Dear John" just minutes before the film ends with the prisoners' triumphant release. In anguish, the betrayed POW exclaims: "Son of a bitch! She waited till *now*?" (More improbably, the same batch of mail yields a notice about another prisoner's overdue *Playboy* subscription, a piece of mail the ICRC would surely never have forwarded.)[88]

In uncanny mimicry of the feminist proposition that the "personal is political," conservative POW memoirists – and cultural producers inspired by them – stamped wives' intimate choices with an indelibly ideological meaning. The ending of marriages was woven into a larger national tapestry of loss: a lost war, lost respect for traditional values, lost male authority, lost national valor all tied together by allegations of individual and institutional disloyalty. Postwar POW narratives duly reinforced propositions asserted *during* the war about Dear John letters.

By the late 1960s, several commentators had decried both the quantities and qualities of breakup notes sent to men serving in Vietnam. We've already encountered Dr. Emanuel Tanay's assertion that Dear Johns were vaster in number, and more vicious in nature, than in any prior conflict. Other military psychiatrists chimed in with corroborative evidence of the especially gratuitous character of women's rejection notes sent to men in Vietnam. Far from trying to anticipate and assuage the recipient's hurt feelings as a more prototypical letter-writer might have in the past, these women wrote letters that could only *exacerbate* the recipient's distress. Dr. Stephen Howard noted that some young women sent their GI boyfriends ostensibly contrite confessions of infidelity. But their letters brimmed with such explicit and expansive details of their new sexual encounters that Howard concluded their senders were motivated by (usually unconscious) rage. Tanay and Howard understood these women to be suffering from an intense form of separation anxiety. Angry with boyfriends who'd "abandoned" them to go to war, they lashed out in letters, rupturing romantic relationships – behavior that appeared simultaneously pre-emptive and retaliatory.[89] Fearing they'd be left alone after their boyfriends or husbands returned from war, or failed to return, these young women turned their anger and anxiety into a self-fulfilling prophesy.

Several psychiatrists concurred that servicemen's wives and girlfriends were particularly susceptible to the "Dear John Syndrome" (Tanay's coinage) because of the Vietnam war's unpopularity. Bey and Lange ventured that the "civilian social milieu," in which the war was commonly held to be "futile and stupid," made it hard for women to justify their partners' participation. Lacking the social support and community validation that had buoyed up "waiting women" in previous wars, wives and girlfriends struggled to maintain commitments to men in Vietnam.[90]

Some veteran memoirists and novelists lent the imprimatur of in-country experience to this proposition. John M. Del Vecchio's best seller *The Thirteenth Valley* (1982) posited a correlation between the war's lack of support and women's lack of emotional staying power with splenetic sarcasm:

> The war was unpopular. Could any soldier really expect something more from his woman? The war was immoral, wasn't it?, with all the indiscriminate killing, the bombings, the napalm, the defoliants. By extension then, were not the soldiers immoral too? Could anyone expect any righteous woman to stand by a barbaric man? By 1970 it had almost become the patriotic duty of a wife or girl friend to leave her man if he went to Vietnam.[91]

Other authors went further, attributing the Dear John letters they or their fictional avatars received to more woundingly personal enactments of political sentiments. These women didn't just fail to stand by their men in Vietnam, they took up with new lovers encountered at protest meetings. Winston Groom, who served with the Fourth Infantry Division and later achieved celebrity with his creation *Forrest Gump*, began his literary career with *Better Times Than These* (1978). In this novel, an officer and a private are betrayed by girlfriends who've been mesmerized by the same Svengali antiwar agitator. Professor Widenfield subverts their personal allegiances with seductive sloganeering about a war that neither he nor his gullible dupes properly understand.[92]

Veteran poet and memoirist W. D. Ehrhart drips similar scorn on his contemptible rival, Niles Mancini, the rich kid who steals Ehrhart's fiancée, Jenny, while the teenage Marine is miserably serving his country. Ehrhart flags this betrayal in the opening paragraphs of *Vietnam–Perkasie*

(1983), cueing readers to anticipate a Dear John letter that winds the author's trusting younger self like a sucker punch. On page 2, Ehrhart transposes first-hand sentiments into the musings of a second-person nineteen-year-old everyman, wondering whether "the high school sweetheart you'd gotten a Dear John letter from five months ago was wearing [a miniskirt] while every filthy bearded hippie in Trenton fucked her eyeballs out, and her loving every minute of it with flowers in her hair." The memoir's subsequent reveries about sweet, chaste, devoted Jenny reek of this bile, her ostensible virtues underscored only to accentuate her true duplicity. When her Dear John arrives, it comes out of the blue for Bill, but not for readers primed to expect this betrayal from the start. "I don't get it," Ehrhart recalls telling a buddy. "She wrote to me every day. Every fuckin' day right up to the end of July. Not even a hint." When the friend tries to calm Bill by suggesting that Jenny's just "confused" – "Ain't like everybody's plantin' Victory Gardens back home" – Ehrhart will have none of it. If an unpopular war helped explain female faithlessness, altered public attitudes still didn't excuse altered private affections. The exchange concludes with Bill swearing he'll "fuckin' kill 'em both" when he gets home.[93]

In a second volume of memoirs, *Passing Time*, Ehrhart revisits Jenny's Dear John letter, this time emphasizing that it appeared after a month's silence which he'd filled with dire imaginings: car wrecks, cancer, leukemia, "knives and threats in dark alleys on moonless nights." Having projected himself into the role of Jenny's steadfast carer – spending his life with a wheelchair-bound invalid, blinded, missing a leg – he's all the more appalled by her perfunctorily apologetic half-page letter: "brief, alien, and distant." Though Jenny's Dear John concludes with a plea that Bill forgive her, two chapters in successive memoirs suggest he could not.[94]

Strikingly, dozens of oral histories by Vietnam veterans say nothing whatsoever about girlfriends having rejected them for antiwar motives or activist men; nor does their testimony suggest that the Dear John letters they received were unusually cruel or explicit. Some women undoubtedly did reappraise the war while their boyfriends or husbands undertook tours in Vietnam, while others doubtless disapproved of American warmaking in southeast Asia all along. But did girlfriends and wives sever romantic relationships for that reason? The thesis that Dear Johns were singularly expressive of home front disapproval is much more easily proposed than proved. Conceivably, it tells us more about the politics of those making the claim than about the motives of women who broke off relationships with men serving in Vietnam.

Many commentators drew a stark comparison between the supportive home front of World War II and Americans' disaffection during the Vietnam years. "The national belief in the righteousness of that war helped a woman to see her husband's contribution as necessary and heroic, and the moral support of the country made her feel a part of the cause for which he was fighting," argued Jane Whitbread, writing in the women's magazine *Redbook* in 1969.[95] All relationships, including intimate partnerships, assuredly do have social dimensions: nested within concentric circles of family, peer group, local and national community that subtly, or more intrusively, signal approval or disapproval of a couple's commitment. Concerted social disapproval can indeed make it hard to sustain a romantic relationship. Yet what authors like Whitbread were apt to forget – as were Vietnam-era soldiers, veterans, and their psychiatrists – was that an earlier generation of servicemen had railed just as vehemently against female infidelity in the 1940s. The longer World War II went on, the louder GIs' denunciations of fickle women grew, and the higher their projections of postwar divorce rates. Veterans of the "good war," like those of the "bad war" in Vietnam, filled their memoirs, novels, and oral testimony with stories of the Dear John letters they and their buddies had received. They did not, however, attribute romantic rejection to either individual or collective antiwar sentiment or pro-Axis sympathies.

What, then, might we conclude from the continuities and discrepancies marking these two wars? First, it's clear that American women didn't experience World War II as a moral straightjacket that constrained them from ending relationships with men at war. As we've seen, severing ties with soldiers has never been a socially sanctioned wartime practice, but unknown numbers of women nevertheless terminated ties with men in uniform during World II, as they have in every other conflict. The reasons why women sent Dear Johns to men at war, whether in the 1940s or during the Vietnam era, were no doubt often tangled and sometimes inchoate. Whether Vietnam generated an unprecedented volume of breakup letters is impossible to verify; the evidence is entirely anecdotal. The contents of women's letters, like the circumstances and feelings that inspired them, are also largely unknowable. But these blank sheets have been imprinted with unmistakably bold messages, written by male recipients and their allies. The Vietnam-era Dear John came to symbolize feelings of abandonment, betrayal, rejection – an emblem of home-front treachery as potent and pervasive as the figure of the spat-upon veteran. For the women who wrote these letters, the personal may or may not have been political. But it was certainly politicized.

CHAPTER 6

Emotional Injury: Causes and Consequences

66 IF AN ARMY COULD BE CONSCRIPTED OF NO ONE BUT JILTED MEN, there wouldn't be a force on earth that could beat them, because they would be the meanest sonsofbitches in the world." So proposed Winston Groom in *Better Times Than These*, a novel in which soldiers serving in Vietnam are betrayed by girlfriends who've simultaneously turned against the war and against the men fighting it. As orchestrator of his characters' actions, Groom could ensure this utterance rang true in the universe of his fiction. Unencumbered by attachments to the worthless women who sent them Dear Johns, his soldiers gain ruthless determination from the experience of romantic rejection, their aggression honed on a whetstone of righteous ire. Although Groom traded on his first-hand authority as an infantryman who'd served in Vietnam, which reviewers of *Better Times* approvingly noted, few military psychiatrists would have concurred with his proposition about the martial prowess of jilted men.[1] Nor would some other combat veterans.

Consider this episode recounted by Dennis Nicks, who served as an army captain in Vietnam in 1969:

> Not too long after we arrived, one of our soldiers got a Dear John letter and he really took it to heart ... It really bothered him. I think he got drunk. And since he was a door gunner, he had access to guns ... so he went down and got his machine gun and this is in the evening, and he's by the flight line and he's carrying his machine gun with the belt of ammunition. Starts

shooting it over the barracks . . . No one was hurt, but I believe there were some holes in some of the barracks walls. That got everybody's attention. Everybody's hitting the floor, trying to figure out what's going on – whether we're being attacked.

The crisis was defused by one of the distraught soldier's friends who came forward to talk his buddy into putting down the machine gun, while other men stood nervously aside, "ready to shoot him if they had to do it." The moral of Nicks's story was clear: "when you mix firearms, and alcohol and somebody who's emotionally unstable that's the kind of thing you can get some times."[2]

Veterans of World War II and Korea told versions of the same story. Or they recollected, as another Vietnam veteran, George Rostron did, incidents when men who'd just received Dear John letters endangered other members of their units as they stumbled blindly out on patrol. Too distracted or too despondent to obey orders, they courted death – sometimes wilfully, but sometimes unthinkingly. In the episode remembered by Rostron, a soldier fixated on a distressing letter from his wife neglected to place trip flares in an area frequented by enemy personnel at night. He also failed to move his men to secondary positions after dark, as his sergeant had instructed. Five or six men died as a result, horrifically blown apart by satchel charges (dynamite or C4 explosives transported in canvas bags).[3]

Medics, Red Cross workers, and chaplains in Vietnam served as first-responders to soldiers in the throes of despair and self-destructive rage who'd just received news that their wives or girlfriends no longer wished to sustain relationships. Like their predecessors who'd served in these capacities in earlier conflicts, medical personnel and padres fretted about men who went absent without leave (AWOL) on receipt of devastating news from home – one form of desertion begetting another. They treated soldiers who drank themselves into oblivion or dissolved into uncontrollable crying jags. Like the courageous GI in Nicks's recollected scene, they attempted to talk down men whose furious rage, often intensified by alcohol, found expression in life-endangering volatility, as jilted soldiers brandished loaded firearms and threatened to take their buddies' lives – or their own. They tended to the bodily and psychic wounds of men whose response to rejection was self-mutilation. And they dealt with front-line soldiers whose retaliatory impulses were enacted on the battlefield, but who hardly resembled the lethally efficient, hardened "sonsofbitches" envisioned by Groom. "I lost track of the number of times that I had to counsel a young man, 10,000 miles from home, who had received the infamous 'Dear John' letter from his girlfriend, or yes, even from his wife," recalls Raymond Scurfield, a psychiatric social worker who served in Vietnam. As for the range of reactions these communications elicited, Scurfield listed: "Shock. Dismay. Rage. Disillusionment. Betrayal. Depression. Abandonment. And perhaps worst of all – helplessness."[4]

During the Vietnam war, military psychiatrists and psychologists "discovered" military wives as objects of scientific investigation. The couple was a "dynamic dyad," as psychiatrist Constantine Cretekos put it, in which the soldier-spouse's ability to discharge his military responsibilities efficiently depended on his female partner's equilibrium.[5] If wives became unbalanced during separations – experienced depression, started drinking heavily, embarked on affairs, broached divorce – then husbands were liable to topple into dysfunction. America's long war in southeast Asia, marked by escalating levels of troop demoralization, gave rise to new psychological theories about men under stress. Military psychiatrists didn't simply catalog the many ways in which recipients of Dear John letters acted out, they evaluated the relationship between romantic breakup and psychological breakdown. Negative reactions to distressing news from home were to be expected, but why was some men's behavior so extreme, putting themselves and others at risk? What *kind* of injury did emotional rejection inflict? And what constituted a "normal" reaction to heartbreak (if the condition was best termed as such), as opposed to a neurotic or pathological response? As psy-professionals contemplated these issues, the military judicial system weighed up what indisciplined or unlawful behavior a Dear John letter excused.

NOSTALGIA

These questions assumed particularly pointed form in Vietnam. But the proposition that some soldiers' psychological maladies originated at home – not on the battlefield – had a long pedigree. Physicians treating men in both the Union and Confederate armies during the Civil War noted a common affliction among soldiers who seemed so undone by longing for home that they sank into dangerous lassitude: unable to sleep, bereft of appetite, and devoid of willpower. For some, homesickness proved lethal. One soldier serving with the 15th Iowa Infantry, Cyrus Boyd, observed in 1863: "More men *die* of homesickness than of all other diseases – and when a man gives up and lies down he is a *goner*."[6] Physicians termed this debilitating state of despondency "nostalgia," numbering sufferers in the thousands. In the war's first year alone, Union physicians counted 572 cases among white troops, an annual total that peaked at 2,000 cases in 1863. Doctors separately tallied the number of Black soldiers who succumbed to, and sometimes died from, a condition to which they were seen as especially susceptible.[7] So, too, were prisoners of war, idly marooned in squalid encampments, where clean water, adequate sanitation, and nourishing food tended to be in equally short supply. Union soldiers attributed thousands of fatalities suffered by their comrades at the notorious Andersonville prison in Georgia to nostalgia – "merely the medical term for homesickness," one man from Maine explained in a letter to his mother that recounted 8,000 deaths there in a two-month period during 1864.[8]

Some scholars regard Civil War physicians' clinical category of nostalgia as a primitive attempt to diagnose Post Traumatic Stress Disorder (PTSD). But to project contemporary understandings back into the past – with the teleological assumption that PTSD, the "correct" diagnosis, merely awaited discovery with superior scientific knowledge – obscures more than it clarifies about how historical actors experienced and understood the psychological perils of war.[9] A fundamental distinction separates late-nineteenth-century appreciations of *why* service members succumbed to emotional distress from insights originating in the 1970s, when PTSD first emerged from psychiatrists' work with Vietnam veterans. The diagnosis of PTSD enshrined in the third edition of the American Psychiatric Association's *Diagnostic and Statistical Manual of Mental Disorders* (DSM III) in 1980, centered on psychological distress arising from traumatic events. Psychiatrists understood trauma to originate in the extreme, norm-violating violence that soldiers had witnessed or perpetrated.[10] The gruesome business of fighting and killing – with injuring consequences for all in the orbit of maimed humanity – lay at the heart of this diagnosis. By contrast, physicians who treated distraught soldiers in the Civil War did *not* understand battle as the precipitant of emotional injury. Rather, it was absence from home – the anguishing experience of being far from loved ones, and chronic yearning to get back to them – that rattled some men so profoundly.

Neither the symptoms nor the sources of "nostalgia" precisely anticipate PTSD. One distinguishing feature of PTSD, often noted by clinicians working with Vietnam veterans, is the disorder's delayed onset. Symptoms commonly appear only months or years after the precipitating trauma, surfacing in oblique ways indicative of repressed, unassimilable experience. Nightmares, hallucinatory visions, and flashbacks are PTSD's hallmarks. "Nostalgia" made its imprint much more immediately palpable. As described by one contemporary witness, the debility "fastens upon the breast of its prey, and sucks, vampyre-like, the breath of his nostrils."[11]

That Americans considered nostalgia such a pervasive and perilous affliction tells us a good deal about nineteenth-century sentimental culture, with its sacralization of "home" and the loving ties constitutive of domestic life. Middle- and upper-class American men were *meant* to feel, express, and exhibit emotion when the occasion merited such displays. Sentimentality was a lauded attribute of refined masculinity – until, that is, emotionalism collided with martial duty. Bonds with loved ones *could* sustain a soldier's esprit, hence repeated injunctions to women during the Civil War to send cheering missives to men at the front.[12] But excessive craving for domesticity could dissipate commitment to duty: a conundrum concerning "home"'s double-edged character as a source of both danger and succor that continued to bedevil military thinking about morale in later wars. What changed over successive decades was the *locus* of both professional interest in, and popular constructions of, soldier's affective ties. As "mother love" gradually lost its cultural cachet, psychiatrists shifted their attention from maternal relationships toward romantic intimacy as the pre-eminent source of soldiers' psychological maladies.[13]

During the Civil War, however, mothers reigned supreme in sentimental constructions of "home." Historian Alice Fahs notes "the virtual absence of representations of fathers" in Civil War popular culture.[14] Ignoring bonds between fathers and sons and the ties that bound brothers to one another, poets, musicians, and painters poured forth endless paeans – in verse, song, and portraiture – to mothers' sustaining love for their sons. Although the median age of Union soldiers was 23.5 years, they were commonly construed as "boys" not men. Some physicians believed young soldiers were especially prone to nostalgia, suffering detachment from home all the more acutely on account of their youth.[15]

MOTHER'S DAY 1918

6.1. At a time when "Mother Love" reigned supreme in sentimental wartime culture, doughboys in France were encouraged to take time out to celebrate Mother's Day in 1918, a scene conjured by Clifford Berryman. (Courtesy of National Archives and Records Administration.)

"Mother love" continued to be a pervasive trope of patriotic culture in World War I. In part because so many soldiers serving with the AEF overseas were young and unmarried, mothers – rather than wives or "sweethearts" – dominated depictions of who and what connected men in uniform with home. Propaganda posters, popular songs, and the fledgling medium of motion pictures lauded "patriotic mothers" who parted willingly with their sons, prompting them to enlist with edifying homilies about where duty to nation and family lay, and waving them cheerily off as they marched into war. Official valorization of maternalism peaked on Mother's Day in 1918, when General Pershing required all men serving overseas with the AEF to take time out from their martial duties to attend to an equally important maternal obligation – penning appreciative sentiments for expedited dispatch back from France to the home front.[16]

SOLDIER'S HEART

The Great War, with its monumental toll of dead, maimed, and psychologically wounded soldiers, invigorated physicians' efforts to understand why some men broke down mentally under the strain of war. Nostalgia fell from the diagnostic lexicon, giving way to new conceptions of stress with more organic sources, or so some physicians initially believed. Medical researchers speculated that "shell shock" – the war's most distinctive new coinage – arose from exposure to the percussive blast of exploding ordnance, or perhaps from imperceptible fragments of shell casing embedded in the patient's brain. These hypotheses failed, however, to account for men who exhibited symptoms of shell shock without ever having been near the front or under prolonged fire.[17]

Shell shock manifested itself in distinctive symptoms still associated with that term a century later: mutism or stuttering speech, temporary paralysis or a halting gait, and a hollow-eyed stare. But mentally altered soldiers of the Great War also commonly complained about the peculiar behavior of their hearts, as had their forebears during the Civil War. While nostalgia faded as a clinical category in the twentieth century, "Soldier's Heart" or "Irritable Heart" – a phrase first employed by Dr. Jacob Mendez Da Costa in 1871 – survived as catch-all terms for the myriad cardiac irregularities that men in uniform presented to military physicians. In his treatment of Civil War veterans in Philadelphia, Da Costa encountered many men with symptoms of "cardiac muscular exhaustion, palpitation of the heart, the feebleness of the pulse while the patient is at rest and the great acceleration of the heart movement on the slightest exertion." Nineteenth-century hypotheses about the root cause of this disorder proposed that constricting garments or over-exertion might be responsible. However, by 1916, tight-fitting apparel had been ruled out and thyroid malfunction ruled in to explanations of cardiac arrhythmia that didn't bear any apparent relationship with excessive exertion.[18]

During World War II, American psychiatrists working in field hospitals overseas continued to find that disturbed soldiers – now termed psycho-neurotic or neuro-psychiatric (NP) cases – routinely presented cardiac symptoms. Dr. Merrill Moore, who served in the South Pacific, noted that not only were complaints of pain and discomfort in the heart very common, they were "usually spoken of with special dread." Typically, patients related their heartbeat's peculiarities to the accompaniment of "grimacing," in sharp contrast to the more jocular ways in which service-men grumbled about back pain. (Hence the ubiquitous – and humor-ous – GI catchphrase "oh my achin' back!") The soldiers whose cases Moore documented, few of whom had participated directly in combat, were minutely attuned to the skipped beats, worrisome trills, and arpeg-gios performed unbidden by this most vital organ. In Moore's view, while men might be good at describing their heartbeat's idiosyncracies, they lacked insight into the *origins* of these peculiarities, tending to take the symptoms literally as indicative of heart disease.[19]

Not so the clinicians who treated chronically distressed GIs. A quarter of the entire American psychiatric profession served in uniform during the war. And by the early 1940s most clinicians had come to regard soldiers' heart complaints as more psychosomatic than organic in nature. Steeped in Freudian precepts – which held that blocked emotion would surface in symbolically suggestive somatic form – military psychiatrists readily discerned an association between dysfunctional mother–son relationships and cardiac conditions. That neurosis would surface in *heart* complaints stood to reason. But this interpretation didn't incline all members of the military medical community toward sympathy for "psycho-neurotic" soldiers. Twin prejudices still lingered: against malingers suspected of feigning such complaints, and against men seen as too pathetically immature to elicit compassion.[20]

Listen to Dr. Louis Bishop of New York's Bellevue Hospital expounding on the subject of "Soldier's Heart" in a professional journal in 1942. Noting that in England the condition was termed "disordered action of the heart" or DAH, he pointed out that this acronym had a sardonic alternative version – "Desperate Affection for Home." Bishop took a dim view of such desperation:

> In general it would seem that the sudden change to war after the first twenty years of a life of peace is not easily borne by some boys. Then too, may not "mother's heart" be responsible here and there for a case of "soldiers' heart"? In America, mothers, teachers, and public-spirited citizens have invariably discouraged boy fights or dog fights, the carrying of toy pistols, the brandishing of pen-knives, the display of fireworks, and the joy of using dangerous firecrackers.[21]

Bishop's jaundiced analysis of the nation's enfeebling matriarchy reflects ascendant anti-maternalism in American thought in the interwar period: a backlash against decades of sentimentality regarding mothers in general and more recent veneration of Gold Star Mothers in particular. In the 1930s, the federal government had financed trips for several hundred women who'd lost their sons in the Great War to visit their graves in France – a move that attracted considerable criticism, not least from senior military figures (like General George S. Patton) who felt many mothers had shown more interest in shopping than mourning. Disdain for "mom" and her child-rearing practices reached its fullest flowering in Philip Wylie's *Generation of Vipers* (1942). In the eyes of at least some prominent opinion leaders, "mother love" should be regarded not as a sustaining force, but as a pillow that stifled sons' healthy emotional development.[22]

Even men who eschewed the extravagant misogyny that was Wylie's stock in trade, found much awry with American mothering and the passive, dependent young men it had seemingly produced. Merrill

Moore's case histories – boxes of which are housed at the Library of Congress – almost all trace soldiers' neuroses back to early infancy, commonly to mothers who were "worriers." Such women regularly bemoaned their malfunctioning hearts and, though rarely hospitalized for cardiac complaints, quickly "went to pieces" under stress. Mothers who cultivated their sons' excessive dependency were responsible for the parlous state of "morale of the mass" of GIs overseas. These soldiers' gestalt, as Moore perceived it, "could be expressed in these terms: 'Home to mama.'"[23] "It might even be said," Moore and his colleague J. L. Henderson ventured in 1944, "that war neuroses are 'made in America' and only come to light or are labeled in combat."[24]

While "mama" received the lion's share of blame from military psychiatrists for young men's psychological vulnerability, soldiers' romantic partners didn't escape professional notice or judgment either. Wives' emergence as a source of psychic malady in the psychiatric literature of World War II reflects the greater proportion of married men in uniform in this conflict. But spouses weren't simply edging mothers aside. The two dominant female influences in soldiers' lives were frequently twinned in psychiatric evaluations of "NP" cases. Psychiatrists regarded men with "difficult" mothers as more likely to make injudicious marital choices. These damaged young men selected spouses who in some unconscious way or other resembled their mothers, thus replicating in their marriages the unhealthy co-dependency they'd experienced growing up.[25] Psychiatrist Eli Ginzberg found that young men who married early had the highest rate of incapacitation for further service. He speculated that they'd entered wedlock prematurely, seeking to address unconscious "special needs." When military service forced them to leave the wives on whom they were emotionally dependent, they found separation "very upsetting."[26]

As Susan J. Matt notes in her history of homesickness, intense attachments to home, seen as a source of emotional strength in the Civil War, were widely regarded as detrimental to men serving in World War II.[27] Rather than representing a source of loving sustenance – dangerous to soldiers only if they yearned too ferociously for return – "home" oozed toxicity by the 1940s. Its dysfunctions were a dangerous poison to men whose psychological development had been stunted by unhealthy parenting. Drawing on their casework with servicemen in North Africa, psychiatrists Roy Grinker and

John Spiegel noted that: "The thought of home intrudes itself disagreeably on the soldier's mind, when there are special causes for worry which increase his preoccupation with the subject and decrease his fighting efficiency. Lack of mail, worrisome letters, suspicion of wives' unfaithfulness, broken engagements, financial troubles."[28]

Monthly psychiatric reports on the state of morale, produced in the many theaters in which men served overseas, sought to gauge how much soldiers worried about home, predicated on the belief that "worrying a lot" or "pretty much" signified lower esprit.[29] Tellingly, these questionnaires didn't ask men to qualify the ways in which they *thought* of home, only to quantify their fearfulness, as though home were synonymous with anxiety. Among GIs' domestic concerns, fear of infidelity topped the bill. "Drifting wives" – in Moore's nautically inflected phrase, common among psychiatrists who favored metaphors of anchorage – recurrently appeared in psychiatrists' wartime case notes.[30] In March 1945, Major Theodore Lidz drew on observations made in the Southwest Pacific area to conclude starkly that "men who are 30 and over with children have too many worries to become good soldiers. Early in the war another great factor was the infidelity of wives and sweethearts, which was evident even in combat neurosis." It was not coincidental that, in Lidz's estimation, as many as 80 percent of NP cases came from broken homes. A "shadowed homelife" loomed ominously over many service personnel at war. Scarred in infancy by parents' estrangement, separation, and divorce, these men feared the replication of unwelcome patterns in their own marriages.[31]

Military psychiatrists stationed elsewhere noted that marital anxieties, far from abating as the war progressed, metastasized the longer men were away from home. If "home" became less concrete in the imagination as months went by, rumor and gossip – arriving by mail or kindled by alarming items about female treachery in *Stars and Stripes* – kept men's suspicions stoked high.[32]

Amid worries that wives would become untethered from marital moorings and give husbands the slip, the Dear John served as a totem of soldiers' anxieties about love and loyalty. Psychiatrists warned that such letters could trigger psycho-neurosis if servicemen didn't build superior psychological defenses. *Nervous in the Service*, a mimeographed booklet written by Captain Robert E. Peek (of the 21st General Hospital in France) to explain neurosis and its sly *modus operandi* in lay terms, made this point in pictorial form with cartoons drawn by a former patient, John Dalrymple. "The things that help break down a soldier's resistance to fear or anxiety, are spoken of as 'precipitating factors' in causing neurosis," Peek explained. "Poor morale" was one such precondition, and spirits could sink perilously for various reasons. Dalrymple chose to depict his demoralized GI as a tearful sad sack, slumped in front of two beer barrels with loosened taps dripping toward emptiness. A free-floating page of the letter he clutched was visible in the foreground. "And while I like you very much I don't love you, and etc.," it read, conforming to the standard formula for a tritely apologetic Dear John. Peek entreated his readers to snap out of their funk: to stop obsessing about combat, quit picking their feet, and start taking an interest in other people. "A neurosis is like getting bed bugs," the pamphlet concluded. "It can happen to anyone, but how long you keep it, depends on YOU!"[33]

6.2. In a pamphlet written by Capt. Robert E. Peek and illustrated by John Dalrymple, a former patient at the 21st General Hospital in France, GIs received tips on how to avoid becoming "Nervous in the Service." Not getting in a funk over Dear John letters was strongly recommended. (Courtesy of National Archives and Records Administration.)

NARCISSISTIC INJURY

Military psychiatrists serving in World War II debated, as their predecessors had, how best to treat casualties whose neuroses were triggered by longing for home or frantic desire to restore a severed romantic relationship. Should distraught men be allowed to go home on furlough in the hope that face-to-face communication might enable a husband to resolve marital difficulties? This was one possible implication of Eli Ginzberg's insight that "Many a soldier broke under the double blow of losing a loved one and not being able to fight to keep her – because he was thousands of miles from home."[34] According to this logic, Dear John letters were devastating not only because of their contents, unwelcome under any circumstances, but because recipients could rarely do anything other than reel from the blow before absorbing the shock. Unwanted and unloved, soldiers felt acutely powerless as they confronted rejection. While stationed abroad, all the serviceman could do was to "philosophize, rationalize and simply bide his time," noted the sociologists McDonagh and McDonagh.[35] Men in this situation could pen an angry riposte or a plaintive letter begging for reconsideration, entrusting their replies to the Army postal service. But they couldn't plead their case in person – not unless provision for emergency home leave were granted. For servicemen stationed on small Pacific Islands or in far corners of the China–Burma–India theater this prospect was about as remote as their geographic location. Even if an emergency furlough *were* granted, the slow passage home made it all the more unlikely that a broken relationship could be fixed by reunion weeks after the bad news had been conveyed.

During World War II, Red Cross field workers received innumerable requests for leave on compassionate grounds from soldiers desperate to resuscitate their hypoxic marriages. Some petitions succeeded.[36] But Ginzberg's case studies also illuminated the dangers of emergency furlough. His study *The Ineffective Soldier* recounted the case of "H.H.V." who, after three months' silence from his hitherto clinging wife, heard from her that she wanted a divorce. Granted compassionate leave, H.H.V. went home only to find that his wife had taken an apartment with a female friend: "She had been unfaithful to him, had spent all their savings, and had even sold most of their household effects and furnishings. When he arrived at her apartment, she was not there although he had notified her of his coming. Much later that night she arrived home from a date with another man. H.H.V. went back to camp in far worse condition than he had been before his furlough."[37] Where H.H.V. turned his rage inward, other men in similar situations lashed out violently against their wives or the men they'd taken up with. This possibility was perhaps another reason why, quite apart from formidable logistical obstacles, emergency furlough requests were more often declined than approved.

The psychopathology of rejection formed a substratum of World War II's psychiatric literature. Grinker and Spiegel noted that a substantial element of projection might be involved in cases where betrayed men adopted a particularly "unforgiving attitude toward their erring wives." Sometimes excess ire flowed from a guilty conscience that latched appreciatively onto a misplaced target. Married men who "themselves have been unfaithful overseas" were apt to judge wives most harshly, Grinker and Spiegel proposed.[38] A different spin on the theme of displacement was given by Captain Samuel Futterman, MC, of the VA Mental Hygiene Clinic in Los Angeles. Writing in 1946, he noted a tendency among combat soldiers whose superior officers had deserted or otherwise let down their men under fire to project anxiety over anticipated acts of desertion onto civilians, "including former fiancées." "The men seem to find in [these women], indications that they also might desert at some hour of great need as they felt they were deserted on the battlefields in a crucial life and death struggle," Futterman continued. "Several engagements were regrettably broken because of such thinking."[39]

Developing these Freudian analytic insights, Grinker and Spiegel introduced the term "narcissistic injury" to capture the kind of blow experienced by some soldiers who responded to romantic rejection or infidelity with pathological excess. This characterization suggested that unhealthy *self*-regard – rather than mourning the loss of a cherished love object – was responsible for some men's neurotic symptoms or violent rage on receipt of a Dear John. According to this diagnosis, rather than buckling from a figurative blow to the heart, narcissists recoiled from blunt trauma to the *ego*. "The narcissistic injury is more than they can endure in view of the already existing injuries to self-esteem caused by combat," ventured Grinker and Spiegel.[40]

Narcissism and associated personality disorders assumed even greater prominence in military psychiatrists' diagnoses of disordered servicemen in Vietnam. Having initially remarked on the "phenomenally low incidence" of psychiatric casualties in Vietnam compared with World War II and Korea, military medical staff began to revise this verdict in the late 1960s.[41] In particular, they documented pervasive "disorders of loneliness." Psychiatrists who treated disordered men in Vietnam understood this condition as distinct from "homesickness," and they regarded excessive alcohol intake, drug use, and the contraction of sexually transmitted diseases as outgrowths of loneliness. Soldiers' attempts to escape into an altered state of consciousness – by getting drunk, getting high, or getting laid – were likely to be exacerbated by the arrival of Dear Johns. Lonely young men read these letters as confirmation that they'd not only been cut off from, but abandoned by, "The World" and its fickle inhabitants. "We should remember," cautioned Dr. Stephen Howard, a former Marine battalion surgeon in South Vietnam, "that the war is fought more by boys, by teenagers, than by men, and so the girl at home is not unlikely simply to find someone else. The effect of a 'Dear John' letter can be devastating."[42]

Psychiatrists attributed "maladaptation to loneliness" in part to the youthfulness of GIs in Vietnam, whose median age was just nineteen. But other situational factors compounded the acute feelings of alienation and isolation that seemed to beset soldiers serving in Vietnam. The nature of this frustrating war against an oftentimes elusive enemy provided few opportunities for heroic self-assertion on the battlefield. Young men looking to prove their masculinity in ways promoted by John Wayne movies and pulp adventure magazines would be disappointed by this war's infrequent and inconclusive firefights.[43] Many never participated in direct engagements with the enemy. With only 14 percent of uniformed personnel serving in active combat, most rear echelon troops spent their tours in relative comfort and security.[44] The one-year rotation system – with draftees being parachuted into and then extricated from units – meant there was little esprit de corps of the sort that had bonded "primary groups" in World War II, when recruits had trained together, deployed together, and served side by side, sometimes for years.[45] With eyes focused on a fixed personal horizon, grunts tended to think about the war in highly individualistic terms: as a contest to survive until their date of separation rather than any loftier collective enterprise.[46]

Several military sociologists, doctors, and psychologists also commented on the absence of genuine friendships between soldiers in Vietnam. This counterintuitive phenomenon was first noted by eminent military sociologist Charles Moskos in a long story for the *New York Times* Sunday magazine in September 1967. Under conditions of impermanence – built into the very terms of a twelve-month tour – many men judged it too emotionally hazardous to forge close bonds with their fellow GIs. Instead, a "powerful pseudo intimacy" sometimes sprang up. The superficial character of these attachments was evidenced by the fact that, when men left their units to return to "The World," they virtually never kept in touch. These professional findings stand in stark contrast to the way in which many Vietnam veterans have romanticized the transcendent love that bound men together in combat and thereafter.[47]

Military psychiatrists also took note of how GIs responded to the deaths of their buddies. Many seemingly mourned only briefly for lost comrades-at-arms. But a few responded with pathological excess, using grief to rationalize atrocities perpetrated on the battlefield and off. Dr. Richard Fox, in a widely cited article published in 1974, attributed vengeful combat aggression to "narcissistic rage." The study of narcissism had developed apace in the American psychiatric profession during the 1960s, with "narcissistic personality disorder" a new entry into the second edition of the DSM issued in 1968. Atomization within combat units – and the dwindling level of popular support the war enjoyed, resulting in less public affirmation of servicemen – seemed to exacerbate some men's narcissistic tendencies. Fox noted that such soldiers exhibited "little of the typical pattern of mourning." Instead, the death of a friend triggered murderous rage and an all-consuming desire for revenge. "It gradually became apparent that these patients had reacted to the death of their buddy as though it were a narcissistic injury rather than an object loss," Fox remarked, drawing psychoanalytic insights from Heinz Kohut. Buddy relationships in combat – "almost instantaneous in origin and without history" – kindled a mirror form of narcissism, "in which the individual sees himself in the buddy and at the same time sees the buddy as an extension of himself."[48] This explained why the death of a fellow GI registered more as "an injury to the self rather than as a loss of a clearly perceived, separate other."

Back home again, some veterans continued to exhibit signs of narcissistic rage, experiencing homicidal impulses that, on occasion, were directed toward their spouses. As other psychiatrists noted, men with this personality disorder were likely to respond to Dear John letters and to partners' infidelity – actual or imagined – with violence, unable to absorb the blow to their self-esteem caused by a severed emotional attachment.[49]

DESERTION

As soon as GIs started talking about Dear Johns in 1942, they associated these letters with an array of wayward – but, in many men's eyes, thoroughly warranted – behaviors. Of these, getting blind drunk was the commonest, closely followed by going AWOL. Sometimes these two phenomena went hand-in-hand. Finding something to drink, or enough alcohol to thoroughly souse their sorrows, might involve deserting one's post. (The beer served to GIs by the army during World War II was only 3.2 percent ABV, to many soldiers' chagrin.[50]) It's perhaps not surprising, then, that when Corporal Sam Kramer's NCO, 1st Sergeant Albert Martin, wrote to Anne Gudis to rebuke her for the "Go to Hell!" V-mail she'd sent her boyfriend, he stressed that Kramer had gone AWOL after reading her vicious note. "IN ALL MY 20 YEARS IN THE ARMY I'VE NEVER SEEN A MAN'S MORALE FALL TO PIECES AS QUICKLY AS HIS DID TODAY," Martin typed, in emphatic upper-case letters. Sam's whereabouts remained unknown. "HE NEITHER SMILED NOR SPOKE BUT JUST MUMBLED AND TOOK OFF," Martin informed Gudis. Then he tried to make Anne feel even more guilty by telling her that Sam had "LEFT A LETTER TO BE OPENED IN CASE HE DOESN'T RETURN." Martin left Anne hanging with this insinuation that Sam intended to commit suicide, distraught by her angry brush-off.[51]

Martin directed his ire toward Anne alone. He seemingly condoned Sam's errant behavior as an understandable response to her outrageous

V-mail, even though absence without leave was an offense that could result in a court-martial. Veterans of World War II tell other stories in which their commanding officer either turned a blind eye toward temporary desertion – or actively encouraged them to go AWOL – as they reeled from the arrival of a Dear John letter.

The most elaborate anecdote in this vein is told by Kenneth Brown, who served as a Marine Corps corporal in the Pacific theater. In both written and oral testimony, Brown recounts how he sought the counsel of a chaplain after receiving a Dear John, but found himself instead at the General's desk at Division Headquarters:

> Well, I told him the whole story about how this girl I thought so much of had gone and married another fellow. He listened sympathetically. When I was through he said, "Pvt. Brown, that's the saddest story I have ever heard." Then he surprised me by asking how much money I had. I pulled out my billfold and counted out a dollar and twenty-eight cents which was all I had.
>
> "Oh, that's not enough," he said. He then reached into his pocket and pulled out a ten and a five dollar bill and shoved them across the shiny desk toward me. I still didn't get it and asked him what I was supposed to do with that.
>
> "Private Brown," he said, "There's only one thing that's going to get you feeling better and that's to get this worry completely off your mind. You've got to do something to dull the pain and I'm told the best thing is alcohol. You can't get drunk on a dollar twenty-eight and so I'm giving you fifteen. Don't worry about getting it back to me."
>
> I picked up the money and started for the door when it dawned on me that I didn't know how to get drunk. Also I didn't know how to get out of the situation but I knew I had to. I turned around and told the Commander that I surely appreciated his offer but that I couldn't get off the base. Our outfit was on standby and no leaves were given for any reason. He laughed and said, "Don't worry about that. When the MPs pick you up in a day or two and throw you in the brig, just have them call me and I'll come and bail you out."

Hesitantly, Brown explained that he was a Mormon and didn't drink. In response to the General's follow-up inquiries about the precepts of

Mormonism, Brown informed him that Mormons also don't gamble and don't use profanity – clean-living attributes which led to Brown being assigned to the Division Chaplain as his assistant. In that capacity, Brown avoided the mass slaughter of Iwo Jima that eliminated most of his unit, making his story unique. A Dear John circuitously saved his life.[52]

GIs in later wars shared a common intuition that the brass might extend a good deal of latitude toward heartbroken servicemen suffering at the hands of faithless wives and girlfriends back home. They foresaw a gendered closing of the ranks as men turned on the women who'd turned against them. But just how far could the Dear John card be played? And was it invariably an ace capable of transforming a run of misfortune into a winning hand?

The expectation that romantic rejection might – just possibly – function that way moved one soldier who served in Korea to test his luck in a very public way. Corporal Ed Dickenson spent most of his ill-starred military service in a POW camp, captured by North Korean and Chinese forces in November 1950, just six weeks after he was sent into action in Korea. In captivity, he wrote articles for the communist publication *Towards Truth and Peace*, along with letters to *China Monthly* and the New York *Daily Worker*. These essays and letters condemned American war-mongering, corroborating the Chinese line that US forces had employed bacteriological weapons in Korea. Dickenson earned further notoriety back home when he refused repatriation to the United States in the major prisoner exchange, "Operation Big Switch," that brought the Korean war to an end in July 1953. Dickenson was one of twenty-three American servicemen to announce that he wouldn't be coming home. The astonishing preference for "Red China" shown by these "turncoat GIs," as press headlines styled them, helped convince many Americans that rumors of communist brainwashing must be true. How else to explain why American citizens would abandon the wealthiest nation on earth in favor of the People's Republic?[53]

Dickenson underwent an eleventh-hour change of heart. Under pressure from US military authorities to reverse his decision, as were all the American POWs who refused repatriation, Dickenson announced in October 1953 that he'd return after all. He was one of just two from the group of twenty-three to accept the army's promise that all would be forgiven if these men accepted repatriation and came back home. With the "turncoat" POWs front-page news, Dickenson's story attracted a good deal of publicity. Eisenhower himself entreated citizens to refamiliarize themselves with the parable told in Luke 15:11–32, while *Life* ran an illustrated feature, "A Prodigal and His Kin," about the errant corporal's return to his Appalachian home in Cracker's Neck, where he was reunited with his voluble mother, laconic father, and twelve siblings.[54] Other news magazines followed suit. Most newspapers published several installments of Ed's odyssey from North Korean camp to West Virginian cabin.

Needless to say, journalists were eager to learn why the twenty-three-year-old had initially elected China over Cracker's Neck. Ed, somewhat coyly, invoked an old sweetheart from back home. *New York Times* reporter, Robert Alden, related that Dickenson – during his first media appearance at Panmunjom, Korea – had told the press pack of a girlfriend who'd "found someone new" while he was a prisoner. "She sent a 'Dear John' letter, if you know what that is," Ed confided. Confident that readers knew exactly what Dickenson meant, Alden provided no gloss of the term.[55] Even if Americans hadn't encountered this phrase during World War II, they might well have seen newspaper reports on "Dear Johns" being sent to GIs in Korea. "My buddy just got a Dear John letter," one corporal wrote to the *Chicago Daily Tribune* in August 1952, imploring someone – "preferably some girl" – to send the heartbroken nineteen-year-old mail so that he'd once again be the "sparkplug of our unit."[56]

A more prominent sign of the Dear John's arrival as a cultural reference shared by soldiers and civilians was the release of Jean Shepard's and Ferlin Husky's single, "A Dear John Letter," just as the Korean war ended in July 1953.[57] While it's unlikely that Dickenson would've heard this hit record in captivity in Panmunjom, Korea, he nevertheless intuited enough about popular sympathy for emotionally bereft GIs to float the idea that romantic rejection had impelled him to flirt with defection. A Dear John might excuse quite a bit of temporarily disordered thinking, or so Dickenson must've hoped.

Journalists eagerly trailed the young woman who'd "jilted" Ed in the "land of the Lonesome Pine" from which they both hailed. What they

found there sheds different light on wartime epistolary romances –
a salutary reminder that men and women sometimes harbored incom-
patible understandings of the commitment implied by an exchange of
letters. First, reporters discovered from locals that Ed had been writing to
"several girls" while in Korea. Fifteen-year-old Joyce Begley "wasn't gro-
wed up yet," as she put it, when Ed went away. (She'd have been twelve.)
She "hardly knew him" until he wrote her from a North Korean prison
camp, having been shown her photo by a friend. Joyce announced that
she would be glad to "further their acquaintance" when he got home,
wanting him to come back "real bad." Thus far, however, they'd only
exchanged two letters.[58]

Mrs. Pete Morris, Cracker's Neck storekeeper and custodian of local
gossip, helpfully told reporters that Ed had been writing to another local
girl, twenty-year-old Kate Laney. (The United Press stringer whose story

6.3. "Cpl. Edward Dickenson's girlfriend writes a letter to him in Korea, October, 1, 1953,"
ran the original caption. Caught up in the saga of Dickenson's defection to "Red China"
and his subsequent change of heart, Kate Laney didn't see herself as his girlfriend. She'd
just written so he'd "get mail and hear from home." (Photo by Hank Walker/The Life
Picture Collection/Getty Images.)

was carried by several national newspapers included estimates of both young women's weight, as well as their hair- and eye-color, and relative attractiveness.) For her part, Laney denied she'd ever dated Ed, but had simply responded to his mother's request that she correspond with her son. "I wrote him like most girls wrote to fellows over there, so they would get mail and hear from home," Laney told nosy reporters. In her mind, this hadn't been a romantic attachment; more a civic obligation owed by young women to men from their community who'd been sent off to war. When Ed had responded with a marriage proposal, she hadn't turned him down flat, but "suggested they discuss it when he came home" – scrupulously following advice columnists' guidance on how to dial down amorous GIs' expectations.[59] That she then accepted his proposal on their first date, and married within days of Dickenson's return, hints at the social pressure Laney may have felt to formalize a now very public relationship. Knowledge of her alleged "Dear John" was so widespread that it even featured on a radio news quiz show for high school students.[60]

After this flurry of interest in Dickenson's love life, subsequent public accounts of his short-lived choice in favor of China made only one further mention of a Dear John letter. In late November 1953, he told reporters that the "Dear John" wasn't what had made him initially stay with the Chinese. "I tried to observe everything they did so I could expose it when I went back," he claimed, referring to the machinations of his communist captors.[61] Dickenson spent the intervening month between his change of heart about defection and his return home confined in Tokyo, where he was intensively debriefed by US army counterintelligence corps officers. In Dickenson's lengthy written state-ments and in transcripts of these interrogations, the former POW said nothing about being in a state of heartbroken despondency, never even mentioning a girlfriend or -friends. Instead, he underscored how he'd been bribed by the Chinese with promises of "money, prestige and a wife of [his] choice" if he defected to the People's Republic. When these material and marital rewards failed to entice him, the Chinese changed tack from bribery to blackmail, threatening to hand over to the CIA all the propaganda articles and letters Dickenson had written in favor of the PRC. Under questioning from American officers, Dickenson also ventured the explanation that he'd surreptitiously been working as an undercover agent on his own initiative: the same tale of clandestine cloak-and-dagger heroism he would later offer reporters.[62]

Dickenson's case wasn't closed with these debriefings in Tokyo. Two months after returning to West Virginia, he was arrested on charges of "unlawful intercourse" with the enemy, despite the army's apparent promises that he could expect leniency.[63] At his court-martial in April 1954, Dickenson's defense team made no reference to a Dear John letter as a mitigating factor, building their case on the proposition that the plaintiff – a "basically emotionally unstable" and "easily intimidated" character – had been "brainwashed" in captivity. Browbeaten into submission by his communist captors, Dickenson was thus incapable of exercising sound judgment when he refused repatriation. This marked the first test of a brainwashing defense in a military court. Novel, but futile. The prosecution successfully argued that no matter how coercive the Chinese had been, American soldiers ought to remain capable of withstanding psychological duress. Dickenson was duly found guilty. Sentenced to ten years confinement at hard labor and dishonorably discharged, he spent three and a half years in disciplinary barracks. As cooperative with his American captors as he'd been with the Chinese – "a confirmed US government witness," according to military intelligence officers – Dickenson was paroled early.[64]

By the time Dickenson was released in November 1957 – embittered, divorced, but "saved" and headed for Baptist seminary – public interest in his convoluted tale of double-crossings and altered allegiances, both intimate and ideological, had long since ebbed. The *New York Times* buried its item, "Korea Turncoat Ends Jail Term," on page 21.[65]

What didn't fade over time, however, was the connection between soldiers' romantic rejection and desertion. The war in Vietnam reanimated this issue. Absence Without Leave was a command problem that increasingly vexed MACV as morale and discipline corroded in the late 1960s. One of the most prominently spotlit defectors, Specialist 4 Mark Shapiro, who absconded to Sweden with a number of other antiwar GIs in 1968, was believed by his officers to have turned a personal problem into a grand political gesture. In December 1967, Shapiro apparently tried to coax his girlfriend into agreeing to marry him. She declined.

Undeterred, he insisted that she must continue to tell him that she loved him, "even if she did not." Things deteriorated from there: a history of emotional need, coercion, and resistance compressed into a cable relayed from Vietnam to the Pentagon: "In Feb 68, [Shapiro] received a letter from the girlfriend that she could no longer tell him she loved him because it was untrue. Wrote no more letters to her. His CO in RVN reported to Mrs. Shapiro that he remained awake a few times all night and cried."[66]

Shapiro's defection made the headlines and attracted the attention of documentary filmmakers.[67] More privately, however, commanders in Vietnam worried that the larger phenomenon of AWOL – provoked by romantic rejection – was widespread, even if most deserters didn't make it nearly as far as Sweden. A memo on "Methods to Reduce AWOL and Desertion Rates" submitted to the Commanding General, II Field Forces Vietnam by Headquarters 26th Infantry Division on December 28, 1969, ranked "Dear John letters" in second place as a "catalyst." The author deemed "shyness, inability to mix with other members of the unit" the

6.4. Vietnam war defector Mark Shapiro addresses the press in Uppsala, Sweden, on July 11, 1968, while US military personnel pondered whether his actions owed more to a severed romance than to political convictions. (Photo by Leif Skoogfors/Corbis via Getty Images.)

most reliable warning sign that a soldier might go AWOL, but Dear Johns featured above "excessive drinking or use of drugs," problems with authority, and restrictive leave policies among the many vectors of desertion. The solution? According to the anonymous author of this memo, junior officers and NCOs needed to become better listeners, more attuned to enlisted men's personal problems. "[A] man's real or imagined problem often becomes insignificant to him if he can find someone who takes time to hear it. The failure to communicate with the individual when counseling is needed can relay a sense of indifference and lead to AWOL."[68]

ATROCITY

Desertion was not, however, the most serious offense linked with Dear John letters in Vietnam. One unusually public court-martial highlighted the role that a terminated relationship might also play in the commission of atrocities. The horrific episode in question came to light in the stateside press in August 1968, when newspapers reported that courts-martial had been ordered for seven marines who had killed five unarmed Vietnamese civilians in cold blood at Van Duong bridge near Hue over the course of two days in May 1968. Two of the Vietnamese had been executed by an impromptu firing squad, one was hanged before having his throat slit, and two other men were taken behind a building and shot at point blank range. The marines then dumped the bodies in a ditch, covering them with straw. "You didn't see nothing," the patrol leader allegedly told his subordinates. But this intimidatory injunction didn't stop some men in the unit from reporting what had gone on. When the first courts-martial convened in Da Nang in September, the *Los Angeles Times* headlined its coverage, "The Worst U.S. Atrocity in Vietnam:" a badge of shame that would later be fixed on the My Lai massacre.[69] Although the slaughter of about 500 villagers in two hamlets of Son My village occurred in March 1968, two months *before* the Van Duong bridge murders, this earlier atrocity didn't become public knowledge in the United States until November 1969, when Seymour Hersh broke the story.[70] By then the events at Van Duong bridge had sunk below the horizon of American newsworthiness.

The courts-martial of seven marines for the murder of five Vietnamese, aged from thirty-two to sixty-five, garnered only modest press attention in the United States. Anticipating the line of defense adopted by supporters of Lt. William Calley, court-martialed and convicted in 1970 for the murder of twenty-two Vietnamese at My Lai, family members of the defendants decried military hypocrisy. The Marine Corps trained boys as killers, then turned around to indict them "for a mistake made when making the gravest decision of all: taking a human life." So said Joe Allen. His brother Lance Corporal Denzil Allen, the highest ranking defendant, was found guilty on five counts of unpremeditated murder.[71]

Allen's defense counsel, Captain Sandy McMath, asserted that the defendant had developed "very serious complexes," exhibiting a "split personality." However, he told journalists that he doubted an insanity defense would wash in Vietnam. And instead of testing this hypothesis in the courtroom, he encouraged his client to plead guilty on all counts in return for a twenty-year sentence.[72] But in one court-martial an insanity defense *was* endorsed: that of Private Mark Gonzalez. His trial, held in January 1969, was the final one associated with the Van Duong bridge murders. Twenty-year-old Gonzalez, the only defendant to plead innocent, was also the sole defendant to be found not guilty. A "Dear John" letter was apparently instrumental in securing this outcome.[73]

In November 1968, Gonzalez, having already been examined by several military psychiatrists, American and Vietnamese, was flown back to his hometown of Detroit for further psychiatric evaluations while his case was still pending. During this time, Gonzalez spent four hours under examination by Dr. Emanuel Tanay, the Wayne State clinical professor of psychiatry who famously diagnosed a "Dear John Syndrome" in Vietnam. Indeed, it was involvement in Gonzalez's defense that led Tanay to his discovery of the "syndrome."[74] The professional paper in which he anatomized this pathology opened with a brief account of the author's sojourn in South Vietnam at "the Invitational Order of the President" to testify at a general court-martial in January 1969. Without naming the defendant, Tanay outlined his case. In May 1968, the young marine private had been hospitalized for two weeks, running an inexplicably high fever of 106 degrees. On the day of his discharge from the hospital to rejoin his unit, he received a Dear John letter from his girlfriend, "informing him that she was getting married." Two weeks later, "he killed four Vietnamese whom he considered Viet Cong suspects." Tanay was categorical about the connection between these two events: "The extensive evaluations of this young soldier established clearly that the rage precipitated by the 'Dear John' letter was the causative factor in the homicides." Appropriately, in Tanay's professional estimation, the defendant was deemed "not guilty by virtue of insanity" and permitted to return home to complete his education.[75]

Tanay may personally have been convinced that the Dear John letter inflicted such a profound "blow to his self-esteem" – or narcissistic injury – that Gonzalez murdered four Vietnamese in a state of temporary insanity.[76] But that was not a conclusion unanimously shared by other psychiatrists who analyzed the young marine both in Vietnam and in the United States. Nor did Tanay's confidential clinical appraisal of Gonzalez assert the connection as forcefully as did his later published account.

Psychiatric evaluations of the defendant, gathered among Tanay's private papers at Wayne State University, offer diverse insights into Gonzalez's state of mind in May 1968. All those who examined him agreed that Gonzalez, a withdrawn and taciturn young man, displayed a passive-aggressive personality. Médécin Capitain Nguyen-Khoa-Lai proffered a more severe diagnosis of "psychosis with manic-depressive tendencies."[77] The product of a broken home, with an alcoholic, womanizing father who beat him and his mother, Gonzalez lacked self-confidence to an acute degree. He was convinced that peers found him somehow risible and unworthy of respect. Enlisting for service with the Marine Corps in Vietnam – then re-enlisting for a second term – was a way to prove his toughness. Gonzalez self-consciously presented an "exaggerated masculinity," and was correspondingly insecure about his sexuality, noted Dr. Hermann Steinmetz. Raised in the Catholic faith, Gonzalez struggled to develop a healthy attitude toward sex. Mark and the fiancée whom he'd dated in, and after, high school had forsworn sex before marriage. He felt that pre-marital intercourse, like masturbation, was "sinful" and "improper." Nevertheless, eager to prove his virility to peers, he'd visited a brothel while on R&R in Hong Kong, and boasted to the psychiatrists that he "rather enjoyed it."[78] As for Mark's romantic relationship, it appeared to have been waning before a Dear John letter confirmed its severance. His girlfriend (unnamed in all the reports) had written daily during Gonzalez's first thirteen-month tour, but her letters tapered off when he returned for a second year in Vietnam. Perhaps she felt that *he* had effectively terminated their relationship, choosing to volunteer for further active duty when he could have remained stateside.[79] With no discernible trace of irony, military medical personnel regarded the decision to re-enlist for a second tour as a reliable indicator of mental instability, often connected with trouble at home.

Several of Tanay's colleagues made reference to the letter Gonzalez's fiancée sent him while he was in hospital, breaking off their engagement. Strikingly, however, neither the Vietnamese military psychiatrist, Nguyen-Khoa-Lai, nor Lieutenant A. S. Halpern (Division Psychologist of the 1st Marine Division) mentioned the breakup in their psychological evaluations of Gonzalez conducted in July 1968. Halpern, like the civilian psychiatrists, noted Gonzalez's "strong passive streak," "extreme depend-ence," and repressed aggression toward both parental figures. All the psychiatric evaluations pointed to other factors that jolted Gonzalez's already unstable state of mind before he participated in the killings. A friend had been wounded in combat; his unit had incurred several fatalities; and Gonzalez was enraged that the American military fought "with restraint," while the North Vietnamese Army showed an "absence of human values." Dr. Bruce Danto felt it noteworthy that Gonzalez had read William Lederer's and Eugene Burdick's best-selling novel *The Ugly American* during his stay in hospital. The patient announced himself distressed by the "bad image" of Americans in southeast Asia that it conveyed.[80] (Whether Gonzalez was perturbed because the unflattering portrait of his fellow countrymen rang true or because it struck him as unfair Danto didn't elaborate.)

The civilian psychiatrists agreed that Gonzalez exhibited an "acute, severe anxiety reaction" when he killed four Vietnamese civilians. For his part, Halpern found "no evidence of psychosis or indications of a pathological loss of control." He believed that Gonzalez's "repressed hostility" – directed primarily toward his parents – had been "stimulated and acted upon under continual stress." Whether Gonzalez had been temporarily insane, and thus incapable of exercising moral judgment when he murdered four Vietnamese, was more obliquely called into question by Danto. He observed that, nearly six months after the episode, Gonzalez still revealed a "major defect in his thinking about the issue of right and wrong as it relates to the event of murder." Steinmetz likewise found Gonzalez certain he'd be acquitted because his belief that he'd done nothing wrong – or nothing "so bad" – remained strong. But in one regard, Mark's thinking *had* evolved. In October 1968, he was sufficiently recovered from romantic disappointment as to ask Steinmetz whether it would be appropriate to send his ex-girlfriend birthday greetings. Although she wanted to marry someone else, there was, Mark queried, "no reason why they could not remain friends." Tellingly, he worried less about whether *she* would welcome such an overture than about the possibility that this gesture might upset her new fiancé.[81]

Together, these professional evaluations paint a complicated picture of Gonzalez's underlying psychic vulnerabilities and local circumstances conducive to indiscriminate murder, unconstrained by laws of war that both sides routinely disregarded. Multiple factors – individual and collective, psychological and environmental – contributed to the commission of atrocities in Vietnam: killings which were far more commonplace than American civilians appreciated at the time.[82]

As the other courts-martial made clear, it didn't require a Dear John letter to provoke the mental state in which murder was possible. To insist that romantic rejection was *the* precipitant for Gonzalez's murderous rage was to tease a single thread from a tangle of underlying susceptibilities and situational stresses the young marine experienced in a context where killing "Viet Cong suspects" at point-blank range was a routine occurrence.[83] "Some soldiers take, so to speak, the law into their own hands," Gonzalez approvingly told Tanay during his psychiatric evaluation. "[T]hey execute those who they believe to be Viet Cong, since this way they are saving lives of American boys." The "college boys" who interrogated VC suspects – purporting to be able to distinguish Viet Cong from Vietnamese civilians on the basis of superior book learning – often let prisoners go, with lethal consequences. Better to take no hostages, Gonzalez felt. Having rationalized his part in shooting dead four "smiling" Vietnamese at point blank range on two successive days, Gonzalez haltingly informed Tanay, "I haven't killed anybody ...

I mean I haven't murdered anybody, I just did my duty." The other defendants may have similarly believed they were merely waging war in the way war had to be waged in Vietnam: with military necessity collapsing the ethical distinction between "killing" and "murder." Perhaps, like Allen's defense counsel, their lawyers believed an insanity defense "would not carry much weight in Vietnam." But Gonzalez's case proved otherwise.[84]

This outcome owed a good deal to a Dear John letter, or rather to what Tanay made of it in the Da Nang courtroom. The note Gonzalez received from his fiancée figured not only in his defense but also in American press reports of the proceedings.[85] Tanay subsequently elevated this notorious missive to an even greater position of responsibility for Gonzalez's state of mind when he introduced the "Dear John Syndrome," first to a professional association meeting in April 1969, and then in a scholarly journal. Trading on his appearance as a witness in this court-martial, Tanay established his bona fides as an authoritative expert on the devastating consequences of breakup notes for soldiers in Vietnam – and, though Tanay showed less sympathy for them, Vietnamese civilians with whom they crossed paths.

After a jubilant exchange of congratulatory notes with Gonzalez's defense lawyer, First Lieutenant Thomas A. King, Tanay's file on the case closed with a sharp note to Gonzalez. The latter had an unpaid account of $85, and Tanay threatened "some other action" if the balance remained unsettled. Gonzalez had gone AWOL, much to the annoyance of the psychiatrist who'd turned his Dear John into a get-out-of-jail-free card.[86]

A Dear John helped Gonzalez return from Da Nang to Detroit a free man. But judge advocates general certainly did not consider temporary insanity – instigated by romantic rejection – to be grounds for exoneration in every instance of homicide perpetrated by American servicemen in Vietnam. Murder cases weren't restricted to killings of Vietnamese. One alarming novelty of the Vietnam war was "fragging": the name given to episodes in which soldiers attempted to intimidate or murder fellow men in uniform by detonating fragmentation grenades. In most cases, the perpetrators were enlisted men; their victims, officers. Fraggings became increasingly common in 1968, reaching a peak in 1971, with 222 "actual assaults" and 111 other episodes listed as "possible assaults."[87]

In a number of cases, investigating officers found that marital breakdown contributed to unhinging the perpetrator prior to the attack. Three of the fraggers profiled by George Lepre, in an exhaustive study of the phenomenon, were attempting to obtain emergency leave – thereby hoping to mend spousal relations – when they clashed with superiors whom they believed wilfully obstructive. One fragging occurred because the offender was enraged that he'd been denied emergency leave, even though his wife had just given birth to another man's child. He threw a grenade at the officer "in hopes that this would shock his superiors enough to give him leave."[88] Another enlisted man, Specialist Five John Wheat, received a letter from his wife requesting a divorce shortly before the couple's first wedding anniversary. Unlike the other distraught soldier, nineteen-year-old Wheat was granted compassionate leave to travel home and see his estranged wife. But by then he'd fallen out with his staff sergeant. High on tranquillizers, Wheat booby-trapped the company's ammunition bunker, intent on blowing up his nemesis. When the grenade exploded, it killed an officer, Captain John C. Seel, who was not the intended target. Wheat was apprehended at Honolulu airport, en route home, and returned to Vietnam to face a general court-martial in July 1970.[89]

Wheat did not go free. In his case, a Dear John letter was not considered sufficient cause to render the recipient temporarily insane, obliterating his moral capacity. Wheat was found guilty, dishonorably discharged with the forfeiture of all pay and allowances, and sentenced to confinement at hard labor for twenty years.[90] He subsequently served nine years.

The military judicial system apparently weighed the life of an American officer on a different scale than the one used for Vietnamese peasants. The racialized animosity many Americans felt toward *all* Vietnamese – whether ARVN or adversary, civilian or combatant – surely contributed to making Asian lives less "grievable," in Judith Butler's term. Vietnamese deaths could also be rationalized along the lines Gonzalez articulated: casualties necessary to safeguard American lives. In the lethal Catch-22 logic of Vietnam, "VC suspects" were transformed into confirmed "enemy casualties" by the very fact of having been killed by US forces. Pre-emptive strikes thus found posthumous vindication. By contrast, the killing of American officers and NCOs by American enlisted men – or of enlistees by fellow enlistees – couldn't be taken lightly. Without respect for the hierarchy that rank represented, what would become of military discipline? Fragging posed such a frontal assault to the military's most basic principles that arraigned fraggers could expect, and generally received, stringent sentences.[91]

It's perhaps not surprising, then, that a Dear John's perceived gravity differed according to circumstance. These circumstances included another form of lethal violence: American soldiers who took their *own* lives in the wake of relationship breakdown.

CHAPTER 7

Severed Ties and Suicide

OVER THE LONG YEARS OF AMERICAN MILITARY INVOLVEMENT in Iraq and Afghanistan, sometimes dubbed the "forever wars," the Department of Defense has wrestled with twin crises: a soaring number of suicides committed by active duty personnel and veterans alongside a skyrocketing rate of divorce in the armed forces. In many military and academic analyses, these aren't conceived as parallel problems. They're conjoined phenomena, one not only preceding but *provoking* the other. Numerous studies have asserted a connection between intimate relationship breakdown and suicidality. And some military psychiatrists have identified the most likely trigger for suicide with even greater precision. At the American Psychiatric Association meeting in 2008, Colonel Elspeth Cameron Ritchie (then Psychiatry Consultant to the Army Surgeon General) addressed attendees about the alarming escalation of lethal self-harm in the military. By then, the rate had risen from its baseline of 10 to 12 suicides per 100,000 troops per year to almost 20 per 100,000 per year: "[T]he most common precipitant for a suicide in our population is a Dear John or Dear Jane letter or e-mail," Ritchie bluntly informed her professional colleagues. Recipients "become upset or distressed but don't tell anybody. They go into the porta-potty and shoot themselves."[1]

Ritchie's matter-of-fact sketch of the conditions under which deployed soldiers take their own lives is anguishing in the extreme. It's hard to imagine a more miserable setting than a portable toilet, baking in

100 degree heat, on a base somewhere in Iraq or Afghanistan. There's no redeeming grace to be extracted from an anguished soldier, an automatic weapon, and a pungent plastic cubicle. War-lore of the past tended to wrap soldiers' suicide in a gauzy shroud of heroism, casting it as defiant bravado that was not, perhaps, primarily intended to end a life at all, but rather aimed to advance the cause of victory "under a hail of enemy bullets."[2] Ritchie's scenario defies romantic re-reading of the sort that would transmute suicide into self-sacrificial valor. Her soldiers clearly want only to extinguish their pain, doing so in the most expedient fashion possible and in the most secluded – but also most squalid – setting to hand.

Ritchie reprised a well-worn association between Dear John letters and suicide. Ever since the term's coinage, notes breaking off relationships have been linked to soldiers' foreshortened lives, whether ended through distracted negligence or fateful deliberation. In the 1940s, advice columnists invoked the specter of suicide to warn women from ending relationships. Having advised one conflicted young woman not to break off her engagement with a serviceman until he returned home, Mary Haworth printed a supportive letter from a veteran who underscored the wisdom of her advice by stating that many soldiers were in hospital as a result of Dear John letters: "And many others are known to have committed suicide as a result of being jilted by a girl back home."[3] As we've seen, Corporal Sam Kramer's NCO did more than hint to Anne Gudis that her V-mail might have goaded its recipient to take his own life.[4] Veterans of World War II offered numerous accounts – in memoirs, oral testimony, and novels – of anguished soldiers killing themselves as a result of Dear John letters. This plot motif recurs in several of the war's blockbuster works of fiction. *Battle Cry*, written by Marine Corps veteran Leon Uris, contains a scene in which a distraught Marine overdoses on sleeping pills after receiving a Dear John.[5]

A nexus between severed intimacy and lethal self-harm can be traced both back and forward in time from the 1940s. Although it's anachronistic to refer to Dear John letters in a Civil War context, one recent study of military suicide references Union soldier Angelo Crapsey, who fatally shot himself in 1865. As recollected in family history, a note from his fiancée – in which she announced her impending marriage to another man – may have been the precipitant.[6]

A century later, men serving in Vietnam found that Dear John letters could have devastating consequences. For Rick Salde, who served as an army sergeant, a suicide instigated by a Dear John letter offered his first brush with death at the very moment he arrived in country. Getting off the chopper, he spotted medics throwing a body bag on board and asked what had happened: "They said he'd got a Dear John from his wife that day and had taken an M-16 and blown his brains out." Looking back, Salde contextualized this event as a tragic occurrence common to all wars, but still not well enough appreciated by American civilians. "[T]his is a big thing that history needs to know about too, because they forget about this."[7]

Decades of soldier story-telling, along with a plethora of recent military investigations into suicide, suggest Salde may have overstated the case. "History" has not forgotten the lethal sting imputed to Dear John letters. Nor has the contemporary defense establishment. For a decade after 2003, not a year went by without military sources and media outlets re-soldering the link between Dear John letters and soldiers' deaths at their own hands. Whether the dateline was Fort Bragg, Baghdad, or Bagram, the copy ran along increasingly well-worn lines. Many stories resembled this one. "The young Marine had just gotten a Dear John letter from a woman he had described as 'my everything,'" *Los Angeles Times* reporter, Tony Perry, wrote from Helmand Province, Afghanistan, in 2010. "Days later, he killed himself while on guard duty."[8] Three years later, testifying before the House Committee on Appropriations, Subcommittee on Defense, General James F. Amos, Commandant of the Marine Corps, accentuated the gravity of Dear Johns in making the case for resilience training, nodding to committee members that these letters were "a big deal with regards to suicide."[9]

Given the regularity with which Dear John letters and suicide have been yoked together, we might do better to ask whether causality has been *over*stated rather than underplayed. Caution, as well as sensitivity, is required in any attempt to fathom why people take their own lives. Sometimes those who commit suicide leave notes that offer explanations: accounts that may simultaneously be accusations or apologetic pleas for posthumous absolution for pain inflicted on loved ones left behind. But final words don't necessarily supply a definitive last word on what led the writer into life-ending despair. The forces that impel people to take their own lives are often many and inchoate. Scholars of suicide sometimes refer to it as an "enigma" – or "black box" – that's near impossible to unlock from the outside.[10] These metaphors of encryption suggest that the key to the riddle belongs with the person who has taken his or her own life, a secret carried to the grave. But even if the dead could speak, they mightn't be able to disaggregate variables and correlates – stressors, precipitants, and root causes – that those who conduct psychological autopsies on soldiers who commit suicide are in the business of tabulating and categorizing.

Rather than treating military suicide as a puzzle to be solved, this chapter reconsiders the commonly asserted connection between Dear John letters and lethal self-harm. What does it tell us that one particular mode in which the end of a relationship is communicated is so often invoked in accounts of military suicide? What does singling out Dear John letters – and, by implication, the women who write them – obscure about the corrosive impact of war on intimate relationships? And what consequences does this accusatory gesture risk?

HEARTBREAK AND SUICIDE IN SOLDIERS' STORY-TELLING

At the age of 102, Sam Sachs still vividly recollected his service as a lieutenant colonel with the 82nd Airborne Division in World War II. In 2017, Sachs recorded a lengthy oral history interview for the Library of Congress Veterans' History Project. Asked whether he remembered any soldiers taking their own lives, a topical issue at the time of the exchange, Sachs summoned up a wrenching scene:

> I did have suicides. And I can tell you the story of one suicide that happened in Italy ... He was a truck driver in my unit. He got a Dear John letter. Do you know what a Dear John letter is? ... And he was a nice looking young fellow. Well, anyway. What he did. He took his rifle, tied a piece of twine to the trigger and then the other end to his big toe. And he

positioned that thing ... Amazing how he did it. And he put that thing on a chair, and the rifle was pointing right at his heart ... I don't know if he practiced it. But when he pulled that trigger with his toe, the bullet went right through his heart ... [They] only found one bullet hole.[11]

Sachs recalls with striking precision this story of a distraught GI who took his own life with strikingly purposeful precision. Most veterans' accounts of suicide in which Dear John letters played a role are less sharp in their detail. They conjure scenes of lives ended in messier ways, with semi-automatic weapons fired off wildly, a gun barrel placed in a soldier's mouth or pointed at his brains – leaving nothing so clean, nor as figuratively apt, as a hole seared through the heart.[12]

Veterans of all the United States' twentieth- and twenty-first-century wars have tragic tales of this kind to recount. It's no surprise that guns feature prominently in servicemen's suicide stories, whether from World War II and Korea in the middle of the twentieth century or Iraq and Afghanistan at the start of another millennium. As Dr. Theodore Ning, who served as an army medic in Vietnam, points out, "You live with your weapon that's right next to you, you're prepared to fight at any time. But you're also given a huge allotment for alcohol, and other drugs were really readily available, so you could go off the deep end very easily." During his time in country, Ning, then a newly qualified doctor with a young family at home, became an expert in defusing potentially fatal volatility. "My job was kind of to separate the man from the weapon and it happened enough times I got pretty good at it ... because I could pass myself off as a draftee ... [I could] get close to the guy, and once I was close I could take the weapon away from him. So that was a common phenomenon I saw."[13] As many military disquisitions on suicide have subsequently acknowledged, the ready access that active duty personnel have to weapons and live ammunition makes it easier for men and women who experience suicidal ideation to enact life-ending fantasies. About 70 percent of army suicides in the twenty-first century have been committed with a firearm.[14]

Soldiers have, however, found numerous ways to kill themselves. Guns are not a prerequisite. Veterans' testimony includes instances of pilots who intentionally self-destructed in mid-air; men who threw themselves from water towers; and ship-bound soldiers and sailors who hurled themselves off vessels at sea. Richard Blair, who served in the Navy in the Korean war, recollects that one boy, having received a Dear John letter while docked at Pearl Harbor, jumped overboard on the final leg of the journey home. After three days spent searching, his comrades concluded that this young man must have drowned – as, they suspected, was his intention. His corpse was not recovered.[15] Other veterans of World War II and Korea attest that naval transports were particularly dire places in which to digest unwelcome news. On land there were opportunities for distraction and camaraderie. At sea, not only was alcohol often in short supply, the consoling company of women was non-existent. Mailing a reply to the sender of a Dear John had to await return to dry land, and making a telephone call was out of the question. Infernally hot and noisy, with bunks tiered from floor to ceiling and atrocious sanitary arrangements, life on board was hard to endure at the best of times. World War II veteran Paul Charest, who served with the Merchant Marine, recalls a fellow GI killing himself in his bunk on the voyage home: an awful discovery made by the man sleeping below. His corpse was stowed in the freezer until the vessel docked at San Francisco. "He was the first man off the ship," Charest remembers. Under any other circumstances, this privilege would've invited other men's envy.[16]

The most distinctive mode of transport used by the US military in Vietnam, the Huey helicopter, offered another lethal possibility to suicidal men. Walking into the tail rotor had only one possible outcome, as Vietnam veteran Lester Elam recalled, chopping and splicing sentences in distressed recollection of a serviceman in his unit:

There was several stories of guys, you know, naturally getting Dear John letters and stuff. One particular time – you know, you love to get letters from home, and this fellow got his Dear John letter, and I worked nights, 6 in the evening to 6 in the morning. Well, this happened during the morning. He went onto the flight line, and they fired up the helicopter, and they got a main rotor blade on top when – which, you know, a tail rotor, small one on the back, and the Dear John letter, he walked into the tail rotor, and it just crushed everybody. You know, because of the Dear John letter. People don't realize how that is a lifeline to back home, you know.[17]

Less catastrophic methods could go awry. And some gestures were perhaps subconsciously intended to fail. Ilsa Hansen Cooper, who served with the Army Nurse Corps in Vietnam, recalled patients whose suicide bids had not succeeded. Two men tried to slash their wrists after getting breakup notes from their spouses. Cooper remembers, "we had quite a few guys who got Dear John letters from their wives or girlfriends while they were over there, saying, um, 'I don't want to be married to a cripple.' That happened more than once ... women just couldn't handle the thought of having a less than perfect or less than whole husband or boyfriend ..." These women defied longstanding prescriptions that assigned wives and girlfriends a pre-eminent place in the physical and psychological rehabilitation of injured veterans: variously help-meets, carers, comforters, and lovers. These roles were valorized by Hollywood's most enduringly popular, and weepily sentimental, depiction of homecoming servicemen after World War II, *The Best Years of Our Lives* (1946).[18]

As Dr. Ning's testimony hints, excessive alcohol consumption could loosen inhibitions and provide dutch courage to men in despair. Sometimes, however, resolve was acquired at the expense of manual dexterity. Suicidal soldiers whose coordination or weaponry (or both) failed them at the crucial moment received a second chance at life, whether they wanted it or not. Dr. Calvin Chapman, Flight Surgeon and Commander of the 3rd Tactical Dispensary at Bien Hoa Air Base, described one such incident in a letter home to his family written on October 14, 1965:

Wednesday we had the first suicide attempt since I have been here. A 25 year old white male airman, married 7 years, received a Dear John letter from his wife a week ago. It really tore him up, and all week he has been brooding, despondent and drinking. He has seen the chaplain twice and has tried to figure out the situation but to no avail. Yesterday morning, after quite a few beers, he made the decision he had been pondering all week. He decided to take his own life – He told his companions it was a nice day to die, grabbed his automatic pistol, shoved in the clip, and as his buddies wrestled with him to take the gun away, he pulled the trigger twice but the gun misfired. In his drunk and distraught condition, it took 5 medics to get him onto a litter and restrained … Then, after complete sedation, we choppered him to Saigon.[19]

How this story concluded, Chapman didn't recount. Perhaps he heard nothing more from colleagues in Saigon about his former patient's fate. But in other recollections the ending is more definitive, especially in one sub-genre of soldiers' story-telling that runs along these lines. A distressed GI goes out on patrol and acts with such cavalier recklessness that his buddies conclude he's aiming to get killed. Or "shot-by-Charlie," as Vietnam veteran John Nugent puts it.[20]

Episodes of this kind are scattered through veterans' oral testimony. Unadorned and stark, they feature men who no longer want to live and find a way to achieve that aim without pills, a razor blade, rope, or a gun. When these soldiers court death at the enemy's hands, their motives appear purely and unmistakably nihilistic – suicide by an alternate route. Their deaths, as recalled by fellow soldiers, lack any trace of suicidal *heroism*. This trope recurs in classical depictions of battle, such as the Spartans' defense of Thermopylae, as well as more recent accounts of combat. In 1916, for instance, the writer Robert Graves characterized his friend Siegfried Sassoon's actions on the battlefield in France as "suicidal feats of bravery." Second Lieutenant Sassoon continued to bring in the bodies of dead and wounded fellow Royal Welch Fusiliers, despite (or perhaps because of) ferocious enemy fire. For this "conspicuous gallantry" Sassoon was later awarded the Military Cross.[21] Stamped in the heroic mold, ancient or modern, such soldiers' actions – volunteering for, or leading, intensely dangerous missions – look *purposeful*. They advance a larger mission than ending one man's misery. And they may even, as in Sassoon's case, have saved others' lives: hence sociologist Émile Durkheim's categorization of such suicides as "altruistic." Since death-courting despair and death-defying courage look identical to external observers, the possibility remains open that getting killed was *not* the stupendously courageous soldier's intent.[22]

When veterans tell stories of suicide, they generally foreclose heroic interpretations by emphasizing the unmitigated futility of these unnecessary deaths. This observation applies with particular force to the recollections of Vietnam veterans. Chuck Gross's memoir, *Rattler One-Seven*, mentions a young lieutenant who, after getting a Dear John letter from his wife, "started volunteering for every dangerous mission that came along. It looked to me like he was trying to get himself killed in combat," Gross concludes, refusing to put any spin of gallantry on this man's death-wish.[23] In Dan Evans's *Doc: Platoon Medic*, soldiers who try to get themselves killed receive even shorter shrift. After Evans responds badly to a Dear John letter, the battalion surgeon under whom he works sternly warns him off any misplaced heroics: "Don't you dare go out there and commit suicide by being foolish. Most Medal of Honor winners receive their medals posthumously."[24] Adopting a different approach, James T. Lawrence's *Reflections on LZ Albany* depicts a suicidal Vietnam grunt, newly in receipt of a Dear John, standing up under enemy fire. Lawrence pictures this man at the moment of death, with arms outstretched – his suicide a crucifixion scene. Making the Christian iconography explicit, Lawrence imagines "nail holes in his hands," as he dies mouthing the words, "Forgive her, Father, for she knows not what she does."[25]

Oral testimony tends to be yet more bleak. Perhaps this stems from the greater spontaneity with which veterans talk of other soldiers' suicides to interviewers. Whereas memoirists may be tempted, like Lawrence, to find redemptive meaning in tragic episodes they commit to paper, the veterans quoted in this chapter generally retrieve memories of suicide in response to neutral inquiries from interviewers. Sam Sachs's interviewer broke with convention in posing a direct question about suicide. More often, these recollections surface in response to queries about ostensibly safer topics. Asked about the importance of mail to servicemen away from home, some veterans recall the arrival of Dear John letters. Or they relate a fellow soldier's suicide in reply to the "any-other-business" question that oral historians typically pose toward the end of an interview, extending a last opportunity to share something memorable. It's not surprising that these especially distressing deaths, inverting most soldiers' fundamental fear of being killed by the enemy, should remain imprinted on veterans' memories decades later.

Some men and women, revisiting tragic events from a temporal distance, evidently still feel troubled about personal failure to forestall suicide bids or to show sufficient compassion in their aftermath. More diffusely, some veterans exhibit guilt for having survived when others did not.[26] Elsie Hamaker, who served as a junior lieutenant in the Army

Nurse Corps in the Pacific theater, still remembered one of her corps-men receiving a Dear John sixty years earlier: "and it happened his name was John too. And he attempted suicide, and had to be put in a locked ward. Well, John had talked to me so much, and when it came to . . . when he went into the ward, I thought is it going to embarrass him if I go and see him, and I ended up not going. I have regretted it ever since."[27] Whether John survived his self-inflicted injuries, Hamaker didn't divulge in this interview recorded in 2005.

For some men, telling suicide stories affords an opportunity not for self-recrimination but to vituperate against the women they regard as responsible for the deaths of fellow men at war. Few veterans exhibit as much empathy as Sam Sachs, who prefaces his story of a suicidal soldier by ruminating that young women in wartime America could hardly be blamed for wanting fun and passion in their lives while their soldier boyfriends were away. "The girls back home . . . Listen, they're young people, you know. The blood is running. They need excite-ment. They need somebody in their lives. And the guy's overseas and he's not doing her any good and some people just can't take it . . ."[28] Whether Sachs arrived at this equanimity in old age, decades after the events in question, or had always appreciated that the thirst for adven-ture and sexual pleasure wasn't confined to men in uniform is impos-sible to say.

Others tend to be less understanding. Their suicide stories are told with a sense of amazement – or fury – that women would send Dear John letters to men deployed in combat zones. Sometimes they express aston-ishment that soldiers would crumple so readily, their world caving in, when the relationships in question were so fragile: marriages mere months in duration, or flings too fleeting to have led to an engagement let alone a wedding. Bryant Mitchell, who served as a military policeman in Vietnam, told his interviewer: "Oh, we [MPs] had to take care of the guys, man. Some of the kids would get a 'Dear John' letter from home, go to a secluded place, 'Boom,' blow their heads off, I mean, *from a girlfriend.* It was the saddest thing you'd ever want to see because this wasn't your wife, the mother of your children even." Similarly, Vietnam veteran Carl Banks, recalling a soldier from the First Cavalry who'd "emptied a damn M-16 right through the top of his head because he got a Dear John letter," pauses to stress that this man had been married just four months before going over to Vietnam. "I mean *think* about that."[29]

Some veterans tell these stories with the forceful insistence of a cautionary tale: an implicit (sometimes more explicit) warning to women who might be minded to write Dear John letters to servicemen away fighting present-day wars. "The women that do that," fumes Ronald Pica, whose friend had killed himself in mid-air after receiving a Dear John letter in Vietnam, "I don't know what they're thinking. You *know?*" Pica had served in Vietnam with the Air Force from 1967 to 1968. In an oral history interview thirty-five years later, two months into the United States' latest war in Afghanistan, the veteran offered blunt advice to any women who might think about severing ties with a serviceman while he was away: "Lie to the guy till he gets back on home ground and then deal with it . . . 'coz you can't divorce the guy while he's overseas. You can do nothing 'til he hits back to the States. Only thing you can do is destroy him mentally."[30] Decades of letter-writing advice to women reiterated this same sentiment, alluding to the direst possible response to a Dear John to make any woman dissatisfied with an intimate relationship think twice about ending it.

LINES OF INQUIRY

Soldiers have found ways to end their own lives in all wars. Only quite recently, however, has the Pentagon made suicide an object of systematic study.[31] Before the "forever wars," the armed forces prided themselves on having a suicide rate lower than that of the general civilian population.[32] Another common nostrum in the military was that troops deployed in war zones were even less likely than stateside personnel to take their own lives. David Orman, a psychiatrist who served as a consultant to the Army Surgeon General on suicide prevention, told the *Washington Post* in July 2003 that military suicides typically dropped during combat because troops were "very preoccupied with staying alive."[33]

Although the Department of Defense didn't begin actively tracking suicides until 2001, military psychiatrists and commanders had, of course, been aware that some soldiers took their own lives in earlier conflicts. During World War II, psychiatrists Roy Grinker and John

Spiegel noted a number of cases of men whose zeal for the most danger-ous assignments appeared expressive of suicidal intent. While suicide is not a major focus of their published study, *Men under Stress*, it hovers as a possible explanation for some of their most disturbed subjects' actions.[34] Other psychiatrists, like John Milne Murray (chief psychiatrist of the Army Air Forces), focused on certain servicemen's ruinously self-destructive alcoholism – or "suicide on the installment plan," as Colonel Paul Eggertsen, a senior Air Force psychiatrist, later put it.[35]

In Vietnam, MACV tabulated statistics on soldiers who took their own lives or were suspected of having done so. Suicide occupied a hazily bordered place in the larger matrix of demoralization along with drug and alcohol abuse and other "disorders of loneliness" that increasingly vexed the military psychiatric community. Then as now, it could be hard to distinguish between inadvertent deaths – in drunken car wrecks, for instance, or from mishandled weapons – and lives ended with calculated premeditation. Acknowledging this indeterminacy, military record-keepers devised a second category to sit alongside suicide, "accidental self-destruction."[36] One command, Headquarters II Field Force Vietnam, tallied thirty-one suicides between July 5, 1968 and November 13, 1969, listing the exit routes these soldiers had chosen: "24 resulted from gunshot wounds, five were due to an overdose of drugs; one individual killed himself with a hand grenade and one stabbed himself to death."[37] While some of these deaths might plausibly have been instances of "accidental self-destruction," others assuredly were not.

Categorizing modes of death presented less of a challenge than appraising motives or devising interventions that might reduce deaths by suicide. HQ II Field Force noted that suicide "is normally committed while an individual is deeply depressed," adding parenthetically that "the environment in Vietnam is conducive to anxiety." Bristling with edgy unease, this milieu also provided ready access to intoxicants that could both ease and exacerbate anxious soldiers' depressive symptoms. "Marijuana or other drugs," the report noted, removed "normal inhib-itions" and might "trigger a suicide." A commanders' conference in December 1969 reached an anodyne conclusion: "The problem on sui-cides is finding the person who is irrational and helping him."[38] In conditions rife with irrationalism, trickling down from above and welling

7.1. American Red Cross field director Frank Perkins helps a young trooper, PFC Birdell Starkes, with a family emergency, Dong Ha, South Vietnam, 1968. (Photo by Mark Stevens, courtesy of the National Archives and Records Administration.)

up from below, identifying those most at risk of lethal self-harm was no mean feat. All told, suicide claimed the lives of 379 US service members in Vietnam, the DoD revealed in 1973.[39]

As soon as psychiatrists began to conduct retrospective post-mortems into suicide among servicemen in Vietnam, they referenced Dear John letters among the catalysts. "I have seen more than one suicide precipitated by such an event," observed Dr. Stephen Howard, a former Marine Corps psychiatrist, in 1975.[40] A more extended inquiry into suicide among combat troops in Vietnam, published in 1998, announced that Dear John letters "sometimes produced tragic consequences." In support of this claim, the authors cited Emanuel Tanay, though the tragedy that inspired his diagnosis of the "Dear John syndrome" involved a multiple homicide, not lethal self-harm.[41]

The association between lost love and lives lost not only persisted into the twenty-first century, it became more entrenched as military researchers grappled with a crisis that continued to escalate over the decade following the launch of "Operation Iraqi Freedom" in March 2003. The number of military suicides spiked in 2012, with 323 fatalities in the army alone. Several prior years had been billed as the peak for suicide only to be surpassed by the next twelve months' tally. Over the course of a decade, the armed forces traveled past a grim succession of milestones. In 2008, the army's annual suicide rate, 20.2 deaths per 100,000 people, overtook the civilian rate for the first time since the Vietnam war.[42] This was also the first year in which more soldiers took their own lives than died in combat.[43]

In the midst of what the Pentagon had begun calling an "epidemic" of suicide, the armed forces had to reckon with another worrisome manifestation of emotional attrition. "These days the Army is fighting a problem as complex and unpredictable as any war: disintegrating marriages," Leslie Kaufman announced in the *New York Times* in April 2008.[44] The previous year had seen 8,700 divorces involving US military personnel, compared with 5,500 in 2001.[45] This figure also continued to rise annually over the next decade.

Never having compiled statistics on suicide among active-duty troops hitherto, the DoD began in 2003 to devote substantial resources to studying what gave rise to this alarming phenomenon and what might be done to prevent it. This endeavor required the accumulation and interpretation of mountains of data. The process of fathoming why so many men and women in uniform were killing themselves began with commanding officers. Every time a soldier took his or her own life, or was suspected of having done so, their CO had to complete a detailed questionnaire called the Army Suicide Event Report (ASER), colloquially referred to as a 37-Liner, "even though it contains only thirty-one lines of questions," journalist David Finkel pointed out. In addition to gathering demographic data about the age, ethnicity, and sex of soldiers who committed suicide, the ASER covered topics such as "marital status, financial status, alcohol use, drug use, suicide prevention training, behavioral health history, and 'Details of suspected suicide event, including suspected method of death (e.g. hanging, drowning, overdose).'"[46]

This information passed up the chain of command, finally landing on the desk of the Army Vice Chief of Staff. Commencing in 2009, General

Peter Chiarelli convened monthly review boards at the Pentagon to comb through the data, looking for statistically significant correlations from which lessons might be learned and future catastrophes averted. Colonels and generals in whose units recent suicides had occurred "sat at a massive conference table in high-backed leather chairs," psychoanalyst Nancy Sherman observed as an invited witness. Some commanding officers were video-conferenced in from bases in Iraq, Afghanistan, and elsewhere. "Each commander, flanked by a team, reviewed the known facts of the case, the risky behavior, the proximate causes – prescription painkillers, family disputes, troubles with mortgage payments, infidelities, a spouse's health problems, the death of an uncle, tensions with command, disappointment in being passed over for promotion, a parole – a raft of real-life issues, some with little to do with the war."[47]

That fatalities often had, as Sherman put it, "little to do with the war" became an increasingly pronounced theme of both closed-door military inquests into suicide and public pronouncements on this issue. Several studies emphasized that deployments had a negligible – or perhaps zero – bearing on the likelihood that a service member would take her

7.2. On January 12, 2012, General Peter Chiarelli addresses a Pentagon briefing on suicide, introducing findings from the Army's "Generating Health & Discipline in the Force" report. (Photo by Alex Wong/Getty Images.)

or his own life. Former Defense Secretary Leon Panetta went on record in 2012 with the assertion that more than half the active-duty soldiers who committed suicide had *no* history of deployment. Press reports reiterated the same claim.[48]

With deployment downplayed as a significant variable among the stressors pushing soldiers toward suicide, toxic and terminated intimate relationships came under closer scrutiny. Elspeth Ritchie's disturbing portrait of stricken soldiers shooting themselves in the Porta-potty took its cue from the fifth report of the army's Mental Health Advisory Team (MHAT V). Led by personnel from the Walter Reed Army Institute of Research, the team administered annual questionnaires in Iraq and Afghanistan about the state of soldiers' psychological wellbeing, supplementing statistical surveys with site visits.[49] In 2008, MHAT V announced, "As has been consistently true for reviews going back as far as 20 years, military suicide is most often precipitated by the loss of a relationship – either a spouse or an intimate partner." In support of this claim, the report cited a short review published by *Military Medicine* in 1988 and a Suicide Risk Management and Surveillance Office study that ascribed 68 percent of suicides in Iraq to intimate relationship failure. MHAT V concluded that "this highlights the importance of the 'Dear John' letter as a factor in the deployed setting." The researchers duly recommended that the army improve its programs for shoring up military couples.[50]

The army was already moving in this direction with ventures such as "Battlemind" and "Spouse Battlemind" that aimed to teach soldiers and their spouses approaches to good mental health and improved marital satisfaction derived from cognitive behavioral therapy. The precepts of positive psychology, training individuals and couples to "avoid thinking traps" and "hunt the good stuff," underpinned these programs. The goal of making uniformed personnel more psychologically robust received a major boost in 2009 when the army unveiled its Comprehensive Soldier Fitness (CSF) program, delivered through online surveys and in-person seminars. Devised by Dr. Martin Seligman, positive psychology's leading guru, CSF became the flagship of army efforts to engineer "resilience": a buzzword pervasive in all branches of the armed forces during the early 2000s. Underpinning CSF was the premise that traumatic experiences needn't result in PTSD diagnoses and long-term psychological debility. Instead, with the right mind-set, extreme stress could spur "post-traumatic growth." Seligman thus recast the perils and duress of wartime service as an opportunity for individuals to improve their capacity to "bounce back," thereby achieving their full human potential.[51]

In October 2012, CSF was rebranded CSF2, Comprehensive Soldier *and Family* Fitness, denoting the program's extension to spouses and children, with a nod to the then-modish concept of "Web 2.0." The "family skills component" was developed by psychologists John and Julie Gottman, drawing on John Gottman and Nan Silver's primer *The Seven Principles for Making Marriage Work* (1999). Writing in *The American Psychologist* in 2011, the Gottmans reiterated what they regarded as MHAT V's key finding. The "signature emotional injury" preceding suicide was commonly a failed relationship, hence "the importance of the 'Dear John' letter (or today the 'Dear John' video) in the deployed setting" – language they lifted almost verbatim from the 2008 report.[52] In addition to CSF2, the army also expanded programs like its chaplaincy-delivered "Strong Bonds," aimed at shoring up couples as the foundation of "ready families." Other branches of the services rolled out comparable projects.[53]

Over the past decade or more, army mental health initiatives have advanced along parallel tracks, designed in anticipation that a derailing on one might require diversion to the other. While projects like "Strong Bonds" and CSF2 strive to make intimate partnerships stronger, the goal of resilience training is also to help soldiers endure romantic breakdown with greater stoicism. The hazards of romantic coupledom – crystallized by the Dear John – form a common denominator of resilience training, couples' support programs, and suicide prevention measures. In relationship-building ventures, this letter's appearance is the eventuality to be forestalled by fortifying intimacy and toughening love. "[W]hen soldiers receive that 'Dear John' letter, they are at a far greater risk for suicide, so it is vital to help families and partners to stay together," announced Dr. Harold Wain (chief of the psychiatry consultation liaison service at Walter Reed) in 2008, making the case that more federal funding should be channeled into strengthening military couples.[54] Meanwhile, in suicide prevention training, the Dear John waves as a red flag. It's an ominous warning sign to which the recipient's "battle buddy" should respond promptly, operationalizing the army's "ACE" mantra, Ask, Care, Escort.[55]

This message has been drummed into soldiers using new digital tools, including an interactive video game rolled out in 2008, "Beyond the Front," that soon became compulsory for all active-duty army personnel to play. (The title was intended as a play on words, "front" also denoting the façade some struggling soldiers try to maintain rather than seeking psychiatric help they perceive as a badge of shame.[56]) In the game, players must decide on appropriate steps to take after its fictional avatar, Specialist Kyle Norton, receives a surprise email from his fiancée, announcing her pregnancy by another man. Soon thereafter, an IED kills his buddy. "Players who repeatedly choose to reach out to fellow soldiers and family members within the scenario get a happy ending," reporter Gordon Lubold informed readers of the *Christian Science Monitor.* "Players who opt – in their character – not to tell anyone about their problems will steer the game to a sad end."[57]

The army was cautious in lauding the success of its suicide prevention programs, not least while the annual rate of mortality continued to rise. However, one tacit vote of confidence in the army's more robust support system came from syndicated advice columnist Abigail Van Buren. "Dear Abby," like her fellow agony aunts, had long urged women not to send Dear John letters to men at war. At the height of Operation Iraqi Freedom, in October 2006, she cautioned a woman ("Feeling Guilty" from Tennessee) to wait until her fiancé returned from Iraq before breaking off their engagement: "Under no circumstances should you write him a 'Dear John' letter or tell him anything that could unnerve or depress him. If you feel guilty now, how do you think you would feel if he was injured or killed after you dumped that kind of news on him?" This advice drew a mixed bag of reviews from her readership. Some told Abby they felt honesty was always a superior policy. More supportive comments came from Vietnam veterans, recounting incidents of men who'd committed suicide after getting Dear John letters. They agreed that women should hold off on ending a relationship with a deployed soldier.[58] In 2015, however, Van Buren changed tack. In response to a letter from "John," a World War II veteran who'd received a Dear John many years ago and wanted to know Abby's opinion of such letters, she offered a revised opinion:

> A decade ago I would have said – and did tell someone – to wait until the service member came home. My thinking was the news might demoralize the recipient and distract the person enough to get him killed. I changed my mind after hearing from service members stationed in the Middle East who told me I was wrong – that it's better to get the word while there were buddies close by who can be emotionally supportive. They suggested that if the service member hears the news when he gets back – alone and possibly traumatized by what he has been through – that it could make the person more vulnerable to suicide.[59]

CORRELATIONS AND CAUSES

When a Naval Institute Press publication confidently asserted in 2012 that "the number-one precipitating event for active-duty suicide is defined as 'loss of love object,'" the author repeated a proposition that had by then achieved the status of common-sense: a claim whose self-evidence seemingly needed no further corroboration.[60] There is, however, a good deal more to be said about the correlation between suicide and ended relationships – and, more specifically, the letters that sometimes announce a couple's dissolution.

First, we should note a striking slippage in some military studies that treat "precipitants" as synonymous with "causes." The widely cited MHAT V report from 2008 that stressed the importance of the "Dear John factor" did exactly this when it critiqued current suicide prevention programs for "largely ignor[ing] the major cause of suicide in Iraq – relationship failure."[61] But establishing a chain of events, in which a Dear John letter might further destabilize a psychologically vulnerable soldier, is not the same as demonstrating *causality* in a more fundamental sense. The verb "precipitate," according to the *Oxford English Dictionary*, means "to hurry, urge on, (course of events, etc.); hasten occurrence of." Accelerants and causes need to be understood as analytically distinct. A precipitant might help us understand the *timing* of a suicide, but it doesn't fully explain *why* someone decided to take their own life. Military researcher Jacqueline Garrick points out that "suicide is rarely attributed to one root cause." It would be more apt, though, to propose that suicides oughtn't to be ascribed to one root cause. Several military studies have done just the opposite, elevating intimate relationships and their termination to explanatory pride of place.[62]

According to DoD data gathered since 2008, relationship breakdown had occurred in approximately half of the suicide cases surveyed (46–50 percent). In one-quarter of these cases, an intimate partnership had ended within a month prior to the soldier taking his or her own life. Similarly, in 2014, the National Center for Telehealth and Technology listed the risk factors most associated with military suicides as failed relationships (45–50 percent of the time), legal problems (30–40 percent of the time), and financial troubles. In 40–47 percent of cases, a suicide was preceded by the death of a family member.[63] These findings suggest the need for a more complex understanding of why so many service members have taken their own lives during the past two decades: an account that neither privileges relationship breakdown as the "number-one precipitant," nor disentangles ended partnerships from the multiple stresses that bear down on many service personnel and their partners. Though it provides a stark snapshot of despair – useful for focusing public attention and tapping federal funds for enhanced prevention programs – the frequently replayed scenario of a serviceman receiving a Dear John letter and killing himself does not suffice as an explanation for elevated levels of suicide in the armed forces.

We also need to ask *why* relationships involving service personnel – including dual military couples – have been more prone to failure than civilian partnerships. As Garrick points out, "very little research has been done beyond identifying a failed relationship issue prior to a suicide, but relationships rarely fail without contributing causes." Among these factors, she enumerates "domestic violence, infidelity, sexual dysfunction or impairment, resentments, parenting disagreements, or other distancing between the partners."[64] Both geographically and emotionally, "distance" is often widened by deployment: the single variable that military researchers and defense establishment figures have commonly minimized in explaining the "epidemic" of suicide since 2003.[65]

Not all recent studies concur, however, that deployment has played little role in rising rates of military suicide. One investigation completed in 2014, drawing on the National Institute of Mental Health/Army Study to Assess Risk and Resilience in Servicemembers (STARRS), found an elevated risk of suicide among currently and previously deployed soldiers, as well as among certain groups of service members who had never been sent overseas. The authors noted that increased susceptibility to self-harm was associated with a diverse array of factors. Being a young white man of junior enlisted rank, and within the first term of service, put an individual at heightened risk of suicide. So, too, did demotion within the previous two years and failure to graduate high school or acquire a GED. Black servicemen, these researchers hypothesized, had developed stronger social support networks as a result of adversity and discrimination they'd faced both before enlisting and within the ranks. But deployed female soldiers, this study noted, were more likely to take their own lives.[66]

Other scholars, such as anthropologist Kenneth MacLeish, who undertook sustained fieldwork at Fort Hood, point to the truncated way in which "deployment" figures as a variable in many military studies of suicide. The Department of Defense Suicide Event Report (DoDSER) itemizes whether a soldier who took his or her own life had been deployed and, if so, how often. Researchers duly use deployment as a proxy for whether a soldier was, or was not, exposed to severe danger before ending his or her life. Yet, as MacLeish points out, a young recruit needn't have been sent to Iraq or Afghanistan to have experienced the intense nervous energy of life inside an institution that, for more than a decade, was fighting (and failing to win) two wars at once.[67] Under conditions of perpetual "readiness," the specter of deployment was never far distant. Nor was the likelihood that a first deployment would quickly be followed by another and then another, and perhaps more after that. Meanwhile, what the military refers to as "dwell time" between deployments contracted as operations in Iraq and Afghanistan lengthened. As MacLeish notes: "ultimately the imperative that appears to be the main driver of soldiers' self-harm – the relentless operational tempo of indefinite war – turns out to be the very thing that must be protected from the fallout of increasing suicides."[68]

In short, it was (and still is) easier for some military commanders and psychiatrists to castigate failing relationships than to candidly reckon the psychological toll of prolonged war-waging in Iraq and Afghanistan on soldiers and their partners. Service members' minds and marriages have thus had to be made more "resilient" in the interest of sustaining ceaseless conflicts. MacLeish and other scholars have been highly critical of CSF and other projects aimed at increasing soldiers' and spouses' resilience. Indebted to the proposition that the psychological duress intrinsic to war represents an opportunity for personal growth, CSF2 announces that couples can – and *ought* to – "thrive" in the face of adversity. Indeed, viewed through the rose-tinted spectacles of positive psychology, adversity ceases to look so adverse. Rather, suffering represents a chance to expand the outer limits of personal or spousal endurance – without due recognition that, at a certain point, even elastic snaps. As MacLeish and others point out, the guiding precepts of resilience make service members responsible for their own good mental health, with dangerous consequences. If an incapacity to "grow" from traumatic experience marks an individual as psychologically deficient – the implicit message of CSF – then those in distress are even less likely to seek professional help for mental health problems, long a source of stigma in military communities.[69]

THE DEAR JOHN AS "SMOKING GUN"

Critics of "resilience" characterize programs like CSF as neoliberal exercises in the "responsibilization" of soldiers for their own wellbeing – monitored annually through an online questionnaire in check-box fashion – while funding for in-person mental health treatment is scaled back. Academic criticism reflects soldiers' own bitter verdict that the army is merely "throwing a survey" at its enormous mental health deficit.[70] Less widely remarked, though, is the fact that the ideology of resilience hasn't just "responsibilized" individual soldiers. It has also implicated their spouses. As the custodians of marital functionality, romantic partners shoulder primary responsibility for sustaining "Strong Bonds." And in military programs and pronouncements, the partners in question are almost invariably wives or girlfriends.

The substantial and ever-growing literature on suicide in the military focuses overwhelmingly on male soldiers and their female partners. One investigation of the "resilient spouse" (published in 2019) explicitly ruled *out* of its sample of 333 respondents the "nine males and one individual who did not answer the gender question" posed by the researchers.[71] Study after study has found that white, young, under-educated men in their first term of service constitute the most "at risk" group for suicide. Few military researchers have had much to say about female soldiers and suicide, although they have noted that a higher proportion of service-women's marriages break down than do those of men in uniform. Whether sexuality and gender identity play any role in suicidality also remains under-examined.[72] By implication, if not more explicit categor-ization, the soldier most likely to be suicidally inclined is young, white, enlisted and *straight*. When the military couple appears as a target of psychological intervention, this pair remains conceived as a soldier hus-band and female (usually civilian) wife. Although the couples' resources on Army OneSource and Strong Bonds employ a carefully gender-neutral language of "spouses," their visuals tell another story. Almost all the accompanying images depict men in uniform embracing or holding hands with women in civilian attire.[73]

That it's the job of women to preserve "their" soldier's mental health by ensuring a stable marriage is hardly a new message. What's different is the packaging. In the past, military wives were encouraged to elevate their husband's emotional needs over their own. Her reward was his, and the institution's, superior professional efficiency: gratification achieved by self-denial. In the era of resilience, female partners are promised self-realization and fulfillment derived from "hunting the good stuff," build-ing "love maps," and achieving "dreams." Martyrdom is no longer mod-ish. But the bottom line remains unchanged. Wives and girlfriends are still expected to undertake a disproportionate share of emotional work in military couples. It falls to women to make relationships work, to persist even if they don't, and accept sole responsibility for the consequences should they choose to terminate a faulty romantic connection.

The prominence of Dear John letters in recent military messaging on suicide works to validate a widespread pre-existing assumption that whatever goes awry in military couples is the exclusive fault of women.

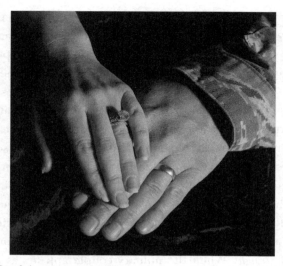

7.3. "Strong Bonds is a commander driven program led by the unit chaplain corps which builds individual resiliency by strengthening the military family," announces the program's website. "The mission of the Strong Bonds program is to strengthen relationships." (Photo by Tech. Sgt. Oscar Sanchez courtesy of the Pentagon.)

Hearing about a soldier who killed himself soon after reading a breakup note, listeners may well feel that the wife or girlfriend who sent it did something callous at best, lethal at worst. The Dear John figures as a "smoking gun" – to borrow a favored George W. Bush administration metaphor – in this scenario: a loaded weapon handed to a vulnerable man by his romantic partner. In military lore, a "no-fault" Dear John is an oxymoronic conceit. A letter that severs intimacy constitutes an *ipso facto* admission of guilt on the part of the female sender. One way or another, she has wronged her partner, whether that wrong takes the form of betrayal (sleeping with someone else) or abandonment (withdrawing her love at an especially precarious time). And she compounds the original sin by the indirect *manner* in which she notifies her partner that their relationship is over, choosing a letter rather than a face-to-face communication. Implicit in the invocation of lethal Dear John letters is the assumption that, had a partnership ended more directly, the severance of intimacy would be easier for the male partner to endure. But whether that hypothesis is warranted remains unclear.

When military leaders identify Dear Johns as common precipitants of suicide or, more directly, the *reason* why many men in uniform take their own lives, they tend to link only the letter and the death. This closed loop of implied causation – a breakup note, a distraught soldier, an ended life – leaves no room to ponder what *preceded* the unwelcome message. What prompted one partner to want out of a relationship, and why announce this desire in writing? Researchers into suicide rarely examine the contextual factors that make sustaining intimacy challenging for military couples. This is hardly surprising. Their interest, after all, lies in why lives end in self-murder, not in why relationships fail. Yet this orientation means that dysfunctional or terminated partnerships often appear as "independent variables" in military research on suicide: as though the couple were a solitary Petri dish in which toxic cultures bloom, isolated from any poisonous elements floating in the external environment.

In reality, of course, couples are *not* hermetically sealed from larger social and institutional surroundings. And these surroundings, particularly in wartime, can make it hard to make love work. The business of being at war – and preparing for war – exerts profound pressure on couples. As we've seen, the approach of armed conflict has often pushed people to formalize relationships sooner rather than later in search of emotional, and sometimes also economic, security. In the era of the draft, some young men married in haste, hoping (but failing) to avoid military service. More recently, in the All-Volunteer age after Vietnam, some couples have rushed to marry, looking to capitalize on the incentives the armed forces offer to married personnel. The physical and psychological hazards of military service may encourage unhealthy dependency on the part of one or both romantic partners. Longstanding advice offered to soldiers' romantic partners has promoted emotional asymmetry in intimate relationships. Women have been socialized to subordinate their own needs, if necessary, to sustain the performance of affection no longer actually felt.

Third parties haven't been alone in proffering such prescriptive advice. Men deployed overseas have also sometimes manipulated romantic partners into sustaining frayed connections with the threat of suicide. One veteran of World War II, University of Chicago literature professor Wayne C. Booth, looking back on a distant epistolary wartime romance, marveled that his then-teenaged girlfriend had stuck with him. She continued to write letters even after he berated her for a fourteen-day silence, cruelly insinuating that he might end his life as a result of her negligence. A corpsman serving in Vietnam was even more manipulative, telling his nineteen-year-old wife that he was "going to kill himself" and was volunteering for every dangerous mission because she didn't love him – a claim predicated on her failure to write more than once a day.[74]

When military researchers and commanders draw attention to the injurious properties of Dear Johns, they focus narrowly on the moment of notification, without clarifying the causes of breakdown. Drawing attention to the senders of these letters, they obscure what male partners may have contributed to the disintegration of a romantic relationship. Historic, but persistent, double standards have extended wide latitude to men in uniform to sleep with partners other than their wives or girlfriends without the vilification commonly heaped on women who "cheat" on men in uniform. Women have been expected to tolerate infidelity as a male prerogative. Not all do so, however. Some Dear John letters are instigated by betrayal on the part of the writer's husband or boyfriend. Iraq war veteran Thomas Stefanko acknowledged this in an oral history interview. Asked whether there were "very many Dear John letters" among the men under his command, he replied, "Yes, yeah." "And some of that was self-imposed, I guess, because, in a situation like that, relationships happen," he continued. Stefanko alluded to sexual liaisons between male and female soldiers whose presence in combat zones has fueled some military wives' anxieties about their husbands' fidelity during long separations. Ready access to pornography in the digital era has also exacerbated some women's feelings of emotional abandonment, thus corroding trust in deployed husbands and causing "attachment injuries."[75]

There are, in short, numerous reasons why military couples split up and why partnerships strained by deployment, and endless preparations for further deployments, are particularly liable to end in divorce. And there may also be *particular* reasons why some spouses and girlfriends elect to end things by letter or email rather than in person.

Soldiers who've received Dear John letters, or supported buddies whose relationships ended with a breakup note, often brand the women who send them "cowardly": a turbo-charged insult in a professional world where cowardice is both especially reviled and un-erringly feminized. But female "cowardice" looks rather different if we factor another destabilizing element into the mix of twenty-first-century military life. The rising incidence of intimate partner violence (IPV), or domestic abuse in older parlance, has been well documented. Over the past decade, researchers have found a strong correlation between the extremely high incidence of PTSD among veterans of OIF/OEF and heightened levels (and forms) of violence suffered by their romantic partners or former partners.[76] Sometimes, this violence is lethal.

Very occasionally, a soldier commits homicide and then kills himself: a phenomenon known as "murder-suicide."[77] More often than not, the murder victim in this scenario is the killer's estranged wife or girlfriend. Sometimes, it's her new boyfriend, or a man presumed by the perpetrator to be such. Over the course of a single six-week period in 2002, three Special Forces sergeants came home from Afghanistan to Fort Bragg, North Carolina, and murdered their wives – shooting or strangling them. Two of the perpetrators then turned their guns on themselves, while the third hanged himself. A fourth soldier also killed his wife at the same base during this period, stabbing her fifty times before setting her trailer ablaze. (He did not subsequently commit suicide.) More recently, Fort Hood, near Killeen, Texas, has been roiled by an unprecedented spate of homicides and suicides, including some murder-suicides, with national press attention focused by the horrific killing and dismemberment of Private Vanessa Guillén in 2020.[78]

Repeated linkage of Dear Johns and suicides may solidify the sup-position that women alone bear responsibility for the breakdown of intimate relationships with men in uniform. In this truncated narrative, there's only a letter and an ended life. Without any clues as to what caused the relationship to break down, all we have are female finger-prints on the figurative smoking gun. As we've seen before, some outside observers quickly leap to the conclusion that women who sever ties by letter are guilty of something akin to manslaughter, and as such deserve retaliatory pay-back. This is a well-worn proposition in the military lexicon of emotional injury: the claim that breaking an intimate bond with a man at war is treacherous at best, murderous at worst.

Anne Gudis experienced the sharp end of this sentiment after *Yank* published her V-mail in September 1943. Two months later, she told Sam Kramer how violated she felt by his betrayal of her privacy, pointing to the vicious responses and heated gossip around Newark that publication had provoked. "The people could not have had more to say if I had murdered someone," she explained in a hesitant attempt to reconnect. One of the strangers-in-uniform who wrote to rebuke her entertained a sadistic fantasy of avenging the wrong Anne had done her boyfriend: "Now if I should have the privilege of meeting you just now, I'd proceed to spank you in a place not to be mentioned here, and darned good too for sending such a saucy note to a fellow in the Service. If I should ever meet you, I shall do just that, and laugh at your pain. Remember that will you." Rather superfluously, the author of this note signed himself "One who detests women."[79]

More prominent men than this anonymous misogynist have also conjured visions of the painful fate they believe faithless women should endure. Some male cravings for retaliatory violence have exceeded spanking and verbal tongue-lashings. General George S. Patton's irate injunction that women who sent Dear John letters "should be shot" ripples through veteran-authored fiction and memoirs.[80] It's not a view exclusively held by Americans. British infantryman R. M. Wingfield, a veteran of World War II's culminating campaign in North-West Europe, speculated in his 1955 memoir that "there must be scores of women who in their 'Let's be sensible about this, dear ...' vanity were guilty of murder. These were our private letter-writing Fifth Column who knocked the guts out of the fighting men." "People who write the 'Dear John' type letter to any soldier should be punished," Wingfield continued, "but there is no punishment fit for those who write them to an Infantryman."[81]

Penned decades ago, these sentiments still reverberate through today's online echo chambers. On discussion boards where veterans share stories of betrayals past and other users post replies, some continue to read Dear John letters as death warrants that merit punishment in kind. More regrettably yet, some men have enacted that lethal verdict.

Conclusion

NOT ALL DEAR JOHN STORIES TERMINATE IN TRAGEDY. SOME even yield proverbially happy endings. Take, for instance, the tale of Anne Gudis and Sam Kramer that's been threaded through this book. After Anne sent her "Go to Hell!" V-mail to Sam in September 1943 and he submitted it to *Yank*, their relationship entered a hiatus. A few months of testy silence ensued, during which Anne's aunt attempted to broker a truce via Sam's chaplain, Lieutenant Leonard Paul. Before too long Sam forgave Anne's irreverent outburst. She, in turn, pardoned him for having publicized it. After some hesitancy, attested by the rough drafts Anne kept of her first attempts to re-engage, the pair resumed their correspondence. Perhaps because Anne anticipated that her V-mail hadn't delivered a death-blow to their relationship, she kept all the letters – by turns hostile, humorous, and amorous – that unknown readers of *Yank* sent her. She imagined sharing this cache with Sam one day, maybe to alleviate the sting of shame she'd felt when her V-mail appeared in print, or to induce a twinge of remorse in him. Over the remainder of the war years, the pair maintained a steady flow of letters back and forth across the Atlantic until Sam re-entered civilian life in the fall of 1945. Like Odysseus, he eventually returned to his hometown of Ithaca – not in the Ionian Sea, but upstate New York. His Penelope, though sorely tested, had waited faithfully. The couple wed soon after Sam's demobilization and remained married for more than fifty years. Following Sam's death in 2013, aged ninety-six, they now lie buried together under a single headstone in Ithaca.[1]

Anne's notorious V-mail – billed as the only bona fide specimen of a Dear John letter in Bryant University's extensive collection of women's World War II correspondence – turned out not to be a definitive breakup note after all. That this V-mail wasn't a "real" Dear John, however, doesn't diminish its utility as historical evidence. Idiosyncratic though Anne and Sam's story may have been, it was far from unique. Some other veterans of World War II and subsequent conflicts also reported that on return home, if not before, they managed to patch things up with the women who had rebuffed them while they were gone. One Vietnam veteran, who'd attempted to get himself killed by sitting "for hours on end" on his tank "making a silhouette," subsequently married the woman whose breakup note triggered this suicidal behavior.[2] What a Dear John meant – to its writer, to its recipient, and for their relationship – was subject to mutation over time and according to individual perspective. This mutability complicates the categorization of letters. As Anne Gudis's V-mail illustrates, not all notes that bear the appearance – and, seemingly, the intent – of a Dear John letter decisively ruptured the relationships in question. How, then, should we label such letters? Or would we do better to avoid neat categories altogether, acknowledging that the authentic specimen is largely chimerical. Dear Johns, after all, owe their public existence to urban legend, rumor, and story-telling – almost always initiated by the letters' recipients, not their senders.

If it's unwise to try to pigeonhole particular types of letter, it's also dangerous to assume that the meaning of other people's intimate correspondence can be read with confidence at a remove. Many of the GIs who wrote to Anne Gudis intuited this. They'd noted the curious discrepancy between her V-mail's barbed injunction and the affectionate sign-off, "Love, Anne." Evidently, a lengthy backstory lay behind the "shortest V-mail letter in ETO," and dozens of soldiers pestered Anne to divulge it. Contrary to some historians' suggestions, far more of her mail came from curious than censorious readers of *Yank*.[3] Although these young men appreciated that wartime letter-writing was a rule-bound activity, many seemed more eager to hear Anne's story than to observe appropriate etiquette. Those who hoped for a new pen-pal – along with the possibility of postwar in-person romance – must have known that the War Department forbade correspondence between soldiers and women unknown to them. Yet official proscription was no impediment to flirtation.

Sam and Anne's obstacle-strewn romance, and the energy that swirled around it, condenses many of this book's themes. Their wayward courtship highlights the difficulties of maintaining a connection over time and across distance for couples separated by war. And it underscores how many third parties aspired to correct young people's emotional comportment in wartime: the press, the military, civic and religious authorities, as well as random strangers – in uniform and out. Then as now, observing and commenting on other people's intimate relations had a voyeuristic allure, often tinged with a moralizing impetus. In times of war, moralizers tend to favor a language of "morale," insisting that what's good for soldiers' esprit will serve the cause of victory. Typically, they assign women primary responsibility for ensuring that "boys in uniform" remain suitably buoyant.

Although American opinion leaders and institutions busily devised rules about who should or shouldn't love soldiers, and how feeling should be expressed or suppressed, the history of wartime intimacy has always involved prescription and transgression in equal measure. In successive wars, the military has treated romantic love as a strategic commodity – something to be pressed into service and mustered into shape – only to find (and then rediscover) that it's much harder to ration, restrict, and route the flow of intimate feeling than to marshal war's more tangible *materiel.* Young people rushed to marry even when sonorous voices of authority – like Eleanor Roosevelt's – told them them to wait; or when presidents like LBJ reworked draft procedures overnight to ensure that wedding vows weren't exchanged to dodge service in Vietnam. Soldiers and their partners haven't just married in defiance of military regulations. They've also grown apart, quarrelled, split up, and sought divorces despite reminders – written, spoken, or merely insinuated – that ending relationships with servicemen constituted an unacceptable breach of wartime's terms of engagement. Despite relentless entreaties to "write right!," the wives, fiancées, and girlfriends of men in uniform haven't always stayed on message. Intimacy's instability was made manifest by the Dear John letter's emergence during World War II, and has been reaffirmed by its persistence ever since.

Considering how much has changed in American civic and military life since that term's coinage in 1942, the durability of the Dear John as a precise locution and larger cultural motif might seem remarkable. In today's All-Volunteer Forces, more women, more people of color, and more LGBT individuals serve their country in uniform than in the past. Deployed overseas, uniformed personnel enjoy access to devices that permit them to talk to – and see! – their loved ones in real-time and round the clock: a development that would've struck many mid-century Americans as more akin to sci-fi fantasy than a plausible future their children and grandchildren would inhabit. But obituaries announcing the Dear John's obsolescence in the digital age, buried alongside the handwritten letter, have proven premature. What, then, does this phenomenon's durability tell us about love, letters, and loyalty in wartime America over successive decades that span two transformative centuries?

One answer to this question points to the Dear John's potency as an emblem of home-front disloyalty. Servicemen and veterans recount instances of women's abandonment and infidelity to broadcast private feelings of hurt, rage, or bitterness. Individuals may experience catharsis in publicly sharing a Dear John experience. Collectively, though, the airing of these tales – their recycling and repetition by successive generations of men in uniform – serves larger functions. Most obviously, the Dear John has provided a reliable vehicle for service members' sense of alienation from, and sometimes outright contempt for, civilians and domestic American life. Tapping into deep-rooted fears of betrayal, latent and actual, the profundity of this feeling is hard to understate. The conviction that folks back home are ignorant and indolent, frivolous and faithless – neither attuned to nor appreciative of servicemen's exertions, sacrifices and suffering – has formed a core element of martial self-understandings from World War II to the present. This perception of an unbridgeable chasm between the home front and those doing the fighting on their behalf seemingly has little to do with any particular war being "popular" or "unpopular." Americans often assign these tags schematically to wars past, regardless of other ways in which they're collectively remembered: "good" (World War II), "bad" (Vietnam), "forgotten"

(Korea), and "forever" (Iraq and Afghanistan). Yet through all of these conflicts, regardless of how much or how little popular support they've garnered, men in uniform have frequently felt neglected, ill-used, and wronged – while on active duty and as demobilized veterans.

Although Americans have grown accustomed to thinking of World War II as a "good" and, by extension, popular war that enjoyed unanimous domestic consent, the moral stakes didn't seem nearly so clear-cut to many Americans at the time as they've come to appear in hindsight.[4] But even if they had, servicemen would likely still have groused about the injustice of the draft system, bemoaning the multiple tribulations of military life. Many GIs noted, and bristled at, the unfairness of a system that required *some* American men to put their lives on the line, while others did not. Whole categories of citizens were exempt. Women served in uniform only by choice: a choice many GIs, wedded to traditional gender roles (if not to tradition-loving wives), felt they oughtn't to make. Meanwhile, draft boards found legions of men ineligible on grounds of ill-health, illiteracy, insanity, or other forms of psychological unfitness. On "neuro-psychiatric" grounds alone, 1,846,000 men were rejected.[5] Early on, marriage also excused some men from service, as did employment in vital war industries. Not all men in uniform shared the wartime state's estimation of which jobs were essential. They certainly didn't approve of factory workers, dockers, and teamsters taking industrial action while millions of American servicemen remained at war overseas. With legions of their peers apparently let off the hook, it's hardly surprising that many men in uniform expressed withering contempt for civilians back home: 4-Fs, slackers, strikers, and, above all, Frank Sinatra.[6]

GIs commonly felt that the military had stolen their time and, with it, opportunities for more rewarding professional futures after the war. Men perceived as belonging to the categories enumerated above were reviled for another reason: they stole, or threatened to steal, servicemen's girlfriends and wives. That unworthy males back home were diverting "their" women's affections was a particular bone of contention with men in uniform. The Dear John letter crystalized fears and resentments inspired by the prospect – or fact – of emotional abandonment and sexual infidelity. Folded into this envelope were servicemen's deep-seated grievances about who was where, doing what, and with whom, in their absence.

A sense of fundamental inequity galvanized this bitterness. Those on the home front monopolized all the pleasure; men in uniform endured all the privations. "We don't enjoy being in the army. It ain't fun," one anonymous GI told the *Chicago Daily Tribune* in May 1944, "but when those gals back home give us the gate for some 4-F or defense worker – that burns our hides."[7]

In the opinion of many GIs, women who let men down were guilty of multiple wartime offenses, national as well as personal. Wartime's gendered division of labor, promoted from on high and widely endorsed from below, assigned women not just the passive role of waiting, but the active obligation of *writing* – loving notes full of unwavering affection and assurances of home's unchanging stability. Those who failed to discharge one or other of these duties were objects of soldierly scorn. Women who wrote to announce that they'd neither be waiting nor writing any more were particularly reviled. A girlfriend's or wife's decision to sever ties by mail appeared all the more damaging if the serviceman was on active duty overseas. Dear John letters announced news that was wrenching in its own right. Rejection stings. But it often hurt all the more acutely under circumstances in which loving ties with home, and the assurance of constancy, were at a premium.

Dear John letters didn't simply announce a man's rejection. They did so in a way that offered little opportunity to respond, whether by negotiation or retaliation – or not with sufficient speed, at any rate. Many soldiers experienced being "Dear Johned" as a form of emasculation: an offense against the natural order of romantic things in which men enjoyed the primary power of decision. Dear John letters were distressing and distracting for multiple reasons, augmented by superstitious convictions that bound love, letters, and loyalty to soldiers' very survival. The conviction that a man who'd lost a woman's love was less likely to return home was widely shared. A Dear John could thus appear akin to a death warrant. And some soldiers responded to rejection in ways that turned the belief that "female infidelity predestined male fatality" into self-fulfilling prophesy.[8] As literary scholar Helena Goscilo notes, "'Dear John' letters or the deaths of sexually betrayed combatants were empirical markers of the consequence-laden distinction between 'the ones who waited, and the ones who didn't'" – an allusion to the schematic division of women into two camps made by the narrator of Leon Uris's novel *Battle Cry*.[9]

Men in uniform carried similar fears, animosities, and magical beliefs into subsequent wars in Korea and Vietnam. Servicemen's bitterness toward folks back home was especially pronounced in Vietnam, a war that had become indisputably unpopular by 1968. Though it may not have been the case that American women sent more breakup notes in this war than in any other, the fixed place this assertion soon achieved in Vietnam war-lore is revealing. The Dear John symbolized home-front betrayal. The callous breakup note surfaced, and has kept resurfacing, in veterans' oral story-telling, former POWs' memoirs, military psychiatric studies, pop songs, and Hollywood movies. Nearly fifty years after the last American troops left Vietnam, the image of the heartbroken, disconsolate GI continues to resonate. Shoppers on eBay can purchase a Verlinden figurine of a crestfallen grunt slumped over a Dear John letter that currently retails for $26.34 – with "100% buyer satisfaction."[10]

More recently, servicemen continued to lament the arrival of Dear Johns during Operation Desert Shield and Desert Storm (1990–1991), despite the Gulf War's comparative brevity. Thereafter, the prolonged engagements in Iraq and Afghanistan produced a steady stream of Dear John letters, emails, and texts. Often linked in military analyses with a sharp rise in suicide among active-duty personnel and veterans, the Dear John's darkest shadowings have been foregrounded in the twenty-first century. Certain critics of the endless wars in Iraq and Afghanistan have construed suicide as a troubling manifestation of the military's lack of care for its own.[11] For some soldiers, however, the Dear John epitomizes civilian America's detachment from these conflicts and those who serve in them. Veterans' memoirs, documentary films, and journalistic accounts of the "forever wars" supply numerous examples of soldiers' anger at being forgotten, or discarded, by civilians at home. Mindless repetition of the mantra "Thank You for Your Service" registers as a hollow gesture, thinly papering the chasm of civilians' indifference to what men and women in uniform have been doing, seeing, and suffering on behalf of a country that would rather not know. Lip service is no service at all.[12] In the All-Volunteer era, only a thin sliver of the population serves in uniform. In this sense, today's more diverse military is also *less* representative of the populace in geographic and socioeconomic terms. Recruits are drawn heavily from military families and from particular regions, leaving the vast majority of American civilians more disengaged from the armed services than ever before.[13]

Dear John stories powerfully encapsulate soldiers' feelings of abandonment – by individual women, and by society at large. Seen through soldiers' disenchanted eyes, romantic rejection is one manifestation, albeit a particularly hurtful one, of their expendability: mere cogs in a war machine financed and fueled by civilians who prefer not to inspect the attrition suffered by the machinery's moving parts too closely.

But if Dear John story-telling is expressive of soldiers' disaffection with civilian society writ large, this oral tradition has also often served as a carrier for rage against women more particularly. Sharing tales about cavalier or more calculatedly cruel brush-offs by fickle women provides men at war with a reminder not only of the rejection suffered by their comrades in the past, but of the betrayals that lie ahead for soldiers who naively believe *their* women will wait faithfully. The Dear John lurks as a figurative spear-filled pit waiting to trap the unwary.

It's a curious paradox of twentieth-century military life that male recruits should have been trained – from almost the very moment of their induction – to expect the worst of women, even as many soldiers took women's love to be an essential prerequisite of battlefield survival. Jody calls, first introduced by African American drill sergeant Willie Duckworth in 1944, helped instil the belief that female sexual disloyalty was an inescapable concomitant of military service. Jody, the unerringly successful "back door man," would find a way to part the recruit from his home, his car, and his girl.[14] As soldiers and marines marched in formation around the parade-ground or grinder, they chanted cadences that not only affirmed Jody's predatory prowess but also attested women's readiness to be seduced:

> Jody this and Jody that,
> Jody is a real cool cat.
> Ain't no use in calling home,
> Jody's on your telephone.

Ain't no use in going home,
Jody's got your girl and gone.
Ain't no use in feeling blue,
Jody's got your sister too.[15]

As this cadence suggests, Jody's wiles were both reviled and slyly admired.

That soldiers and marines should have been encouraged by their drill sergeants to expect women's betrayal is all the more striking when we recall that Nazi psychological warfare efforts were dedicated to stoking the same anxieties. Air-dropped flyers warned GIs that, behind their backs, the "girls they left behind" were being seduced by their slimy bosses and other oleaginous war-profiteers, seducers often given stereotypically "Semitic" features.[16] Whether these luridly anti-Semitic posters, often explicitly pornographic in their imagery, aroused the intended feelings can only be guessed. During Operation Desert Shield, Saddam Hussein's psy-warriors were said to be operating along similar lines, but without the necessary cultural savoir-faire to know that trying to rile up American servicemen by telling them their girlfriends were being seduced by Bart Simpson, among other iconic males, was likely to elicit more mirth than mistrust.[17]

Female infidelity, the stimulus that most powerfully animates Dear John story-telling, has thus figured as both a problem and a resource for the military. A cause of individual attrition, women's disloyalty is simultaneously a source of collective male adhesion: solvent and glue. Individual men may fall apart when an intimate relationship ends – especially (it's often claimed) if given notice of romantic severance by letter. Yet seven decades of Jody calls and Dear John stories suggest that men in uniform have continued to endow the *specter* of female disloyalty with potent integrative properties. Since World War II, generations of new recruits have been indoctrinated into the inevitability of romantic rejection: a fate that binds men together in shared anticipation of intimate injuries inflicted by women. Jody calls promise to salve these wounds through male camaraderie. Conceivably, these toxic chants do more to heighten aggrieved feelings than to soften the blow of romantic rejection, should it arrive. The twenty-first-century military has sought to discourage marching cadences whose lyrics rely on obscenity, including

C.1. Nazi propaganda leaflets deployed anti-Semitic tropes to promote American servicemen's fears that wealthy men were seducing their girlfriends and wives back home. (Courtesy of Alamy.)

the many things "Jody" might be getting up to with the soldier's girl, his sister, or his mother.[18] Yet this initiative has failed, along with other attempts to outlaw behaviors in which woman-hating finds expression. To feminist critics, these failures are hardly surprising, given how pervasive the disparagement of women has been in the armed forces. For decades, men in uniform made exclusionary arguments against women's front-line service based on the cohesion of brotherly bonds which a female presence would purportedly destroy. Whether martial masculinity *can* dispense with misogyny remains a matter of debate.[19]

For the military, Dear John letters can serve, and have served, usefully deflective functions. As we've seen, on at least one occasion it was more palatable for a court-martial to decide that a breakup note from a girlfriend explained why a marine would kill Vietnamese peasants in cold blood rather than reckoning directly with the perpetration of war crimes in a context that made such atrocities endemic. Over the past decade, some military commanders and researchers have more readily endorsed the hypothesis that Dear John notes were the "number one precipitant" of soldier suicides rather than connecting lethal self-harm with the prospect, or experience, of deployment. Similarly, they've more often stressed the harm romantic partners inflict on one another than the damage war-making does to intimate relationships.

These elisions and silences aren't the result of a wilful cover-up. Rather, establishments have built-in blindspots, like those found in car mirrors, that block particular areas from unobstructed view. In the case of the armed forces, the spot that can't easily be seen by those dedicated to the profession of arms is the many forms of psychological violence – some felt instantaneously, others slow to surface – that war inflicts on uniformed participants and those in their orbit. Military commanders and psychiatrists have thus been (and still are) more likely to ascribe soldiers' mental health crises and marital difficulties to sources they regard as *extrinsic* to the military – personality disorders, bad mothers, unreliable wives, mountainous debt, chronic addictions – rather than to the business of making war and preparing for armed conflict. Soldiers' psychic injuries are not, however, all the products of infantile trauma or troubled intimate relationships "outside" the military. Soldiers' romantic lives don't, in any case, exist at a remove from the professional world in which they unfold.

From an outsiders' perspective, injury appears an inescapable fact of wartime military service. Bodily harm, emotional suffering, and psychological damage are all intrinsic features of waging war. "To cast any unwanted excesses of war's violence as second order, peripheral, or 'collateral' to its 'necessary' violence is not only to misunderstand war but also to conspire in a confusion of its ends and means," proposes anthropologist Kenneth MacLeish.[20] That being so, intimate relationships will always number among conflict's casualties. Yet this proposition is hard to acknowledge – perhaps difficult even to perceive – for those with a vested stake in institutional self-preservation. Not surprisingly, the military, in the present as in the past, prefers to conceive itself as an inherently *improving* institution that takes malleable human material, subjects it to pressure, and thereby makes it stronger.

A final, more literal, answer to the question about the Dear John's persistence would point out that men keep telling Dear John stories because women have kept writing these letters. This is true. But so, too, is the fact that men send "Dear Janes" to women in uniform, and that male soldiers terminate relationships with civilian female partners, sometimes doing so by letter, email, or text. The Dear John alone, though, continues to occupy significant cultural bandwidth in the contemporary United States.

Over the past fifteen years, the military has expressed alarm at the escalation of relationship breakdown in an institution that had prided itself on having a stronger ethos of commitment – martial and marital – than that which prevailed in individualistic and hedonistic civilian America. If romantic partnerships involving uniformed personnel fail at higher rates than ever before, this volatility isn't unconnected with larger trends beyond the services. Fewer Americans now expect to spend their entire adult life with the same partner than was the case in the middle of the twentieth century. Twenty-first-century existence is typified by impermanence – in employment, living arrangements, and intimate connections. How far social media, internet porn, and dating apps are to blame for destabilizing monogamous coupledom remains a matter of conjecture. A causal link between the internet and romantic instability is easily hypothesized, harder to prove. Certainly, though, many soldiers and their partners now *suspect* that adulterous liaisons are more readily found than ever. But since the digital age facilitates both cheating and snooping, affairs may also be more readily found out. And this helix spiral of mistrust circling around untrustworthiness does nothing to boost the durability of romantic bonds. Rumors of infidelity – a constant background hum in military communities in the past – have arguably grown louder in the present. As a lightning-rod for fears of betrayal, the Dear John looms accordingly large over contemporary military life.[21]

In the twenty-first century, many active duty personnel believe that sustaining intimate relationships is harder now than it was during previous conflicts – and not only because the internet and smart phones make both connecting and disconnecting easier. America's twenty-first-century conflicts have lasted longer than any previous military campaigns. As a result, serial deployments became commonplace, while the "dwell time" between them contracted, leaving little opportunity for service personnel and their partners to resume domestic life together before they confronted another separation. PTSD, Traumatic Brain Injury, and severe depression – the "signature injuries" of the forever wars, as a RAND report put it – afflict an estimated third of all personnel who've served in Iraq and Afghanistan.[22] These conditions can make it hard for service members and veterans to live with themselves – and with anyone else. Today's uniformed personnel also survive more catastrophic injuries than did severely wounded men and women in the past. As medical anthropologist Zoë Wool has shown, rehabilitative efforts are heavily invested in "fixing" soldiers so they can resume married life, including a "normal" sex life. To that end, physicians arm male patients with drugs to overcome erectile dysfunction, along with anti-depressants, sleeping pills, and pain killers. Needless to say, though, whatever positive effects these pharmacological fixes may produce, broken relationships can't be remedied by prescription.[23]

Intimacy is always precarious and evanescent. Love takes work, and love's work can be especially fraught when war separates partners, injecting radical uncertainty into prospects of reunion and a shared life's restoration. Viewed from a certain perspective, it's not surprising that romantic relationships should figure heavily among war's fatalities. Nor is it peculiar that women, despite prompts warning them not to, should have written (and still write) Dear John letters to men at war. Perhaps the couple rushed into a relationship, prompted by the looming prospect of separation and its attendant dangers. Perhaps she struggled to sustain regular communication as pleasurable activity turned into burdensome duty, or as connection itself dwindled. Perhaps two partners' expectations for the relationship's exclusivity and longevity diverged. Perhaps the relationship was always, or had become, unhealthily possessive or abusive . . .

With empathy, we can appreciate numerous pressures that contribute to the disintegration of military couples. But we shouldn't presume to know why any particular woman wrote a letter that we can't read. This book hasn't unearthed a "secret history" of why women write Dear John letters. Such an exposé can't be written. Private motives remain largely inaccessible, along with the original letters. Instead, *Dear John* has explored the public properties of private lives in wartime, showing how – and suggesting why – images and interpretations of women's breakup letters have percolated so persistently through civilian society, within specialized professional communities, and among bands of brothers. The Dear John letter has helped make women, not war, the culprit for love's breakdown under pressure. It's time other stories – and other voices – were heard.

Acknowledgments

The seed of this book first germinated while I lived in Newark, New Jersey. The story of Anne Gudis's epistolary romance with Sam Kramer reverberated with particular force because her hometown was, for a decade, my own. Like several of the young GIs who wrote to Anne after her V-mail appeared in *Yank*, I felt a vicarious connection with this spirited young woman due to our shared place of residence. Her family home on Hobson Street in Newark's Weequahic section still stands, having narrowly avoided the bulldozers that cut a swathe through the neighborhood to construct the I-78 Express. Friends from my fifteen years' teaching history at Rutgers University-Newark were among the first to hear talk of a "Dear John book." Some students, veterans of the wars in Iraq and Afghanistan, volunteered personal experiences of the emotional toll of deployment. Despite relocation across the Atlantic, I continue to appreciate the friendship of Fran Bartkowski, Andy Buchanan, Mary Nell Bockman, Karen Caplan, Eva Giloi, Gary Roth, Matt Shurtleff, and Christina Strasburger. I miss the sage counsel and warm companionship of Marilyn Young, who befriended me on the evening after my interview at Rutgers in 2001, and who lost her vigorous battle against cancer shortly before I departed for Warwick in 2017.

Historians are always deeply indebted to archivists and librarians for access to raw material. I'm appreciative of all those who answered my inquiries, sent scanned materials, and assisted me during on-site visits. One person stands out for her exceptionally generous and unfailingly cheerful assistance: Megan Harris, Senior Reference Specialist for the Veterans History Project of the Library of Congress. Without Megan's assistance, I could never have tracked down the many oral histories featuring Dear John stories in the VHP's vast collection. I'm immensely grateful for the hours of work that Megan devoted to helping locate material, and for making my visits to the American Folklife Center so enjoyable.

Eric Van Slander was a very knowledgeable and genial guide to the War Department's decimal filing system at the National Archives in College Park, Maryland. Thanks are also due to: Sheon Montgomery, Reference Archivist, Vietnam Center and Sam Johnson Vietnam Archive, Texas Tech University; Eisha Neely and her colleagues in the Division of Rare and Manuscript Collections, Carl A. Kroch Library, Cornell University; Sarah Lebovitz at the Walter P. Reuther Library, Archives of Labor and Urban Affairs, Wayne State University; Bruce Kirby, Reference Librarian, Manuscript Division, Library of Congress; David Sager, Recorded Sound Research Center, Library of Congress; Elizabeth Dunn and Jennifer Baker at the David M. Rubenstein Rare Book & Manuscript Library, Duke University; Jessie Mrock at the Institute on World War II and the Human Experience, Florida State University; Andrew Harman, Archivist, Center for American War Letters Archives, California's Gold Exhibit and Huell Howser Archives, Leatherby Libraries, Chapman University; Matt Messbarger, Arizona State University Archives; Lisa Caprino, Huntington Library, San Marino; Nikolai Kendziorski, Archives Manager, Fort Lewis College; and Jennifer Barth, Reference Assistant, Wisconsin Historical Society.

Several colleagues supplied "Dear John" stories, snippets, and suggestions. I'm particularly thankful for the archival materials sent by Kurt Piehler of Florida State University. Others extended invitations to speak at their institutions, duly providing opportunities to test out material and ideas on live audiences. I appreciate the solicitousness with which Beth Bailey and Kara Vuic encouraged me to make a long trip from the British Midlands to the American heartland to participate in a workshop at the University of Kansas in February 2018. This lively gathering more than rewarded the journey. Adam Seipp and Jason Parker proved wonderfully convivial hosts for a talk at Texas A&M in April 2018. I was energized by the input of students and colleagues in the audience on that occasion. Brian McAllister Linn deserves special thanks for his kind words of encouragement, and his astute observations on suicidal heroism. In 2019, Tarak Barkawi, Shane Brighton, and Gavin Rand gave me an opportunity to share more "Dear John" material at the London School of Economics. Gary Gerstle's invitation to deliver a paper at the Cambridge American History Seminar in March 2019 was fortuitous in many ways. Not only did the audience respond warmly to the story of Anne Gudis and Sam Kramer, Gary's choice of discussant was also inspired.

Andrew Preston's thoughtful engagement with that paper provided the impetus to take my book proposal to Cambridge University Press for consideration in the series Andrew edits with Beth Bailey, another early champion of the "Dear John" project. I'm delighted that Beth's and Andrew's interest was matched by that of editor Deborah Gershenowitz. Her successor, Cecelia Cancellaro, exhibited yet more enthusiasm, adding a family story of her own to my store of anecdotal evidence. I'm deeply grateful for Beth's, Andrew's, and Cecelia's combined investment in, and excitement over, this project, and for their comments on the manuscript in draft form. At CUP, Victoria Inci Phillips showed incredible diligence in tracking down permissions for the images that enliven this book. Lisa Carter did a sterling job of keeping the production process ticking over smoothly, and Steven Holt deserves special praise for copy-editing the manuscript with an exceptionally attentive eye.

At the University of Warwick, my home since July 2017, colleagues have provided both intellectual input and friendship: especially Richard Aldrich, Roberta Bivins, Dan Branch, Jonathan Davies, Rebecca Earle, Roger Fagge, Anne Gerritsen, Sacha Hepburn, Tony King, Tim Lockley, Lydia Plath, and Claire Shaw. Students who took my modules on war, sex, and gender in the United States during the academic years 2019/2020 and 2020/2021 proved highly receptive to the book's larger themes, perhaps learning more about Dear John letters than they'd bargained for.

The last and deepest thanks go to my family. Among the Carruthers and Morrison families, John is, aptly enough, *the* default male name. My father, John Hardie Carruthers, died after a brief illness in

September 2017. His gentleness, patience, and grace continue to serve as an inspiration and model. The other Johns also deserve thanks, notably my brother-in-law John J. Morrison and my "favorite nephew," John P. Morrison. So, too, do my equally favorite nieces, Maura and Julia, and my sister Siobhán, my earliest co-author and illustrator. My mother, Patricia Carruthers, taught me to read and write, including tutoring in epistolary etiquette. She has also been my longest standing champion. To her, I owe my life-long love of prose, and much else besides.

Above all, I'm grateful to my husband, Joe Romano. Over more than a decade, we have shared innumerable adventures, epic and everyday. He gave up a rewarding career to move with me to Warwickshire, and has made our Elizabethan cottage into a place of comfort and joy. His love sustains me. In addition, he's given me another extended family in Vermont. Joe's organizational skills and persistence have ensured that I possess a delightful place in which to study, write, and (more recently) teach. For turning a dilapidated Victorian shed into a beautiful study, thanks are owed, too, to the hard work and practical skills of Jeff and David Nelms. My tiny teahouse proved all the more welcome a sanctuary during the long months of lockdown in which most of this book was written. Unexpectedly, the onset of a pandemic helped clear my schedule in the spring and summer of 2020, though one hesitates to give Covid-19 too much credit for anything positive. Writing was a welcome distraction amid so much distress.

Finally, I'm thankful for all those men and women who, whether unwittingly or deliberately, left behind traces of wartime love and loss. This book would have been inconceivable without them.

Notes

INTRODUCTION

1. President Barack Obama signed legislation leading to the end of "Don't Ask, Don't Tell" on December 22, 2010, with the policy change taking effect in September 2011. On this legislative history, see US Department of Defense, "Don't Ask, Don't Tell Is Repealed," https://archive.defense.gov/home/features/2010/0610_dadt/. There is an extensive literature on "Don't Ask, Don't Tell," the controversies that surrounded it and arguments over its repeal. For the perspectives of LGB service personnel, see Steve Estes, *Ask and Tell: Gay and Lesbian Veterans Speak Out* (Chapel Hill, NC: University of North Carolina Press, 2009), 185–209. On the debate over rescinding DADT, Beth Bailey, "The Politics of Dancing: 'Don't Ask, Don't Tell' and the Role of Moral Claims," *Journal of Policy History* 25, 1 (2013): 89–113; Aaron Belkin and Melissa S. Embser-Herbert, "A Modest Proposal: Privacy as a Flawed Rationale for the Exclusion of Gays and Lesbians from the US Military," *International Security* 27, 2 (Fall 2002): 178–197.
2. Anon., "First-Ever Gay 'Dear John' Letters Begin Reaching U.S. Troops Overseas," *The Onion*, September 21, 2011, www.theonion.com/first-ever-gay-dear-john-letters-begin-reaching-u-s-tr-1819572970.
3. Ibid.
4. *American Heritage Dictionary of the English Language*, 5th edition, https://ahdictionary.com; J. E. Lighter (ed.), *Random House Historical Dictionary of American Slang* (New York: Random House, 1994); Paul Dickson, *War Slang: American Fighting Words and Phrases since the Civil War* (Mineola, NY: Dover Publications, 2011), 147; "Dear John Letter," Grammarist, https://grammarist.com/idiom/dear-john-letter/; "Dear John Letter," World Wide Words, www.worldwidewords.org/qa/qa-dea5.htm; "Dear John (The Irene Rich Show)," Old Time Radio Catalog, www.otrcat.com/p/dear-john-the-irene-rich-show.
5. Milton Bracker, "What to Write the Soldier Overseas," *New York Times Magazine*, October 3, 1943, 14. For biographical information on Bracker, see the finding aid to his private papers at the Wisconsin Historical Society, http://digicoll.library.wisc.edu/cgi/f/findaid/findaid-idx?c=wiarchives;view=reslist;subview=standard;didno=uw-whs-micr0611;focusrgn=bioghist;cc=wiarchives;byte=122584374.
6. Sgt. Ed Cunningham, "Jilted G.I.s in India Organize First Brush-Off Club," *Yank* (China–Burma–India edition), January 13, 1943, 5.

257

7. Howard Whitman, "Jilt in the Mail Gets Yank Down: 'Dear John' Letters Are Not Ones He Wants," *Chicago Daily Tribune,* May 31, 1944, 1.

8. Whitman, "Jilt in the Mail." On military psychiatry and "nerves" in World War II, see Ben Shepherd, *A War of Nerves: Soldiers and Psychiatrists* (London: Pimlico, 2002), 205–227; Paul Wanke, "American Military Psychiatry and Its Role among Ground Forces in World War II," *Journal of Military History* 63 (January 1999): 127–146; Hans Pols, "War Neurosis, Adjustment Problems in Veterans and an Ill Nation: The Disciplinary Project of American Psychiatry during and after World War II," *Osiris* 22, 1 (2007): 72–92.

9. Mary Haworth response to "R.S." "Mary Haworth's Mail," *Washington Post,* July 12, 1944, 10.

10. Prominent advice columnists Dorothy Dix and Kathleen Norris adopted the same line. See, for instance, Dorothy Dix, "Unfaithful Mate Seeking Divorce," *Daily Boston Globe,* December 17, 1945, 9; Kathleen Norris, "Cruel Notes Hit Boys' Morale," *Arizona Magazine of the Greater Arizona Republic* (Phoenix), July 22, 1945.

11. On women and World War II, Karen Anderson, *Wartime Women: Sex Roles, Family Relations, and the Status of Women during World War II* (Westport, CT: Greenwood Press, 1981); D'Ann Campbell, *Women at War with America: Private Lives in a Patriotic Era* (Cambridge, MA: Harvard University Press, 1984); Susan M. Hartmann, *The Home Front and Beyond: American Women in the 1940s* (Boston, MA: Twayne Publishers, 1982); Maureen Honey (ed.), *Bitter Fruit: African American Women in World War II* (Columbia, MO: University of Missouri Press, 1990); Emily Yellin, *Our Mothers' War: American Women at Home and at the Front during World War II* (New York: Free Press, 2004).

12. On this belief in a Civil War context, see Frances Clarke, "So Lonesome I Could Die: Nostalgia and Debates over Emotional Control in the Civil War North," *Journal of Social History* 41, 2 (Winter 2007): 269. On soldiers and mail in World War II, Gerald F. Linderman, *The World within War: America's Combat Experience in World War II* (New York: Free Press, 1997), 301–304.

13. W. D. Snodgrass, "Love and/or War," *Georgia Review* 46, 1 (1992): 99–100.

14. Michael Charles McQuiston, interview with Dale Revelli, n.d., AFC/2001/001/88486, Veterans History Project, American Folklife Center, Library of Congress [hereafter VHP].

15. Homer, *The Odyssey,* translated by Robert Fitzgerald (London: Vintage Books, 2007 [1961]). On the revisionist version in which Penelope sleeps with her suitors, thereby conceiving Pan, Robert Bell, *Women of Classical Mythology* (New York: Oxford University Press, 1991), 348–351.

16. "A Civil War Era 'Dear John' Letter," *Hammond Gazette,* September 15, 1863, www.rarenewspapers.com/view/605219.

17. See, for example, William L. Richter, "'It Is Best to Go In Strong-Handed: Army Occupation of Texas, 1865–1866," *Arizona and the West* 27, 2 (Summer 1985): 125; John Sickles, "'Nothing Gives Me More Pleasure Than to Hear From You': The Civil

War Letters of Sgt. Samuel B. Seely," *Indiana Magazine of History* 104, 3 (September 2008): 279.

18. Ken Ringle, "The Woman behind Hemingway's 'Farewell': In a Long-Lost Diary, Details of a One-Sided Romance," *Washington Post*, September 17, 1989, F1.

19. Agnes von Kurowsky to Ernest Hemingway, March 7, 1919, reproduced in Mandy Kirkby (ed.), *Love Letters of the Great War* (London: Macmillan, 2014), 180–181.

20. Henry Serrano Villard and James Nagel, *Hemingway in Love and War: The Lost Diary of Agnes von Kurowsky, Her Letters, and Correspondence of Ernest Hemingway* (Boston, MA: Northeastern University Press, 1989); Linda Wagner-Martin, *Hemingway's Wars: Public and Private Battles* (Columbia, MO: University of Missouri Press, 2017), 19–20. "A Very Short Story" first appeared in Ernest Hemingway, *In Our Time* (Paris: Three Mountains, 1924), with a slightly altered version published six years later; *In Our Time*, rev. ed. (New York: Scribner's, 1930). For a brief discussion of "Dear John" letters in the Great War, see Sebastian Hubert Lukasik, "Military Service, Combat, and American Identity in the Progressive Era," PhD dissertation, Duke University, 2008, 277–278; and on wartime letter-writing and soldiers' fears of spousal infidelity, Andrew J. Huebner, *Love and Death in the Great War* (New York: Oxford University Press, 2018).

21. "U.S. Military by the Numbers," National World War II Museum, New Orleans, www.nationalww2museum.org/students-teachers/student-resources/research-starters/research-starters-us-military-numbers. On occupation soldiering, see Susan L. Carruthers, *The Good Occupation: American Soldiers and the Hazards of Peace* (Cambridge, MA: Harvard University Press, 2016).

22. Roderick Phillips, *Untying the Knot: A Short History of Divorce* (Cambridge: Cambridge University Press, 1991), 185–197.

23. Anon., "'I'm Jealous,' Writes Lass to Her Soldier Lad in France," *San Francisco Chronicle*, September 21, 1917, 9.

24. On "Mother Love" in World War I, Susan Zeiger, "She Didn't Raise Her Boy to Be a Slacker: Motherhood, Conscription, and the Culture of the First World War," *Feminist Studies* 22, 1 (Spring 1996): 6–39. On the interwar shift in thinking about mothers and motherhood, Rebecca Jo Plant, *Mom: The Transformation of Motherhood in Modern America* (Chicago, IL: The University of Chicago Press, 2010); Rebecca Jo Plant, "The Veteran, His Wife, and Their Mothers: Prescriptions for Psychological Rehabilitation after World War II," in *Tales of the Great American Victory: World War II in Politics and Poetics*, eds. Diederik Oostdijk and Markha Valenta (Amsterdam: Amsterdam University Press, 2006), 95–105. On the centrality of images of women and romantic love to conceptions of wartime obligation in the 1940s, Robert B. Westbrook, "'I Want a Girl, Just Like the Girl That Married Harry James': American Women and the Problem of Political Obligation in World War II," *American Quarterly* 42, 4 (December 1990): 587–614.

25. "A Dear John Letter," written by Johnny Grimes, owned by Lewis Talley and Fuzzy Owen, and performed by Jean Shepard and Ferlin Husky, Capitol Records, May 1953.

On this song and its sequel "Forgive Me John," see Ivan M. Tribe, "Purple Hearts, Heartbreak Ridge, and Korean Mud: Pain, Patriotism, and Faith in the 1950–53 'Police Action,'" in Charles K. Wolfe and James E. Akenson, eds., *Country Music Goes to War* (Lexington, KY: University Press of Kentucky, 2005), 135–136. Apparently, some radio stations had balked at playing Shepard and Husky's hit during the Korean war for the same reason that it caused quivers during subsequent conflicts. See Boris Weintraub, "Music: Change and Continuity in the Country Genre," *The Sunday Star* (Washington, DC), February 9, 1969, D-4. On its banning during the Gulf War, Ken White, "War Songs Popular with Radio Listeners," *Las Vegas Review*, February 20, 1991, 1f.

26. Emanuel Tanay, "The Dear John Syndrome during the Vietnam War," *Diseases of the Nervous System* 37, 3 (March 1976): 165–167; "Weary of the Army, GIs in Vietnam Marching to a Different Drummer," *Newsday*, January 13, 1971. Tanay, born in Poland in 1928, survived the Holocaust in hiding before finding refuge in the United States; Emanuel Tanay interview, United States Holocaust Memorial Museum, www .ushmm.org/exhibition/personal-history/media_oi.php?MediaId=1128&th=ghettos. By the time of his death in 2014, he had achieved recognition as one of the country's leading forensic psychiatrists, the author of both scholarly and popular works on the subject. See Emanuel Tanay, *American Legal Injustice: Behind the Scenes with an Expert Witness* (Lanham, MD: Jason Aronson, 2010).

27. Tom Nawrocki served with the Marine Corps in Vietnam; interview with Jessica VanGorder, November 30, 2010, AFC/2001/001/76363, VHP.

28. On the disloyal girlfriend as traitor, see Kalí Tal, "The Mind at War: Images of Women in Vietnam Novels by Combat Veterans," *Contemporary Literature* 31, 1 (Spring 1990): 76–96; and on disloyal wives and Dear Johns in war films more generally, Donald Ralph and Karen MacDonald, *Women in War Films: From Helpless Heroine to G.I. Jane* (Lanham, MD: Rowman and Littlefield, 2014), 103–108. On antiwar protestors' alleged spitting, see Jerry Lembcke, *The Spitting Image: Myth, Memory, and the Legacy of Vietnam* (New York: New York University Press, 1998).

29. *Hamburger Hill*, dir. John Irvin, RKO Pictures, 1987; *Platoon*, dir. Oliver Stone, Orion Pictures, 1986; *Love and War*, dir. Paul Aaron, NBC, 1987; Norman Mailer, *The Naked and the Dead* (New York: Modern Library, 1948); *The Naked and the Dead*, dir. Raoul Walsh, RKO/Warner Bros., 1958; Leon Uris, *Battle Cry* (New York: Putnam, 1953); *Battle Cry*, dir. Raoul Walsh, Warner Bros., 1955; James Jones, *The Thin Red Line* (New York: Scribner, 1962); *The Thin Red Line*, dir. Terrence Malick, 20th Century Fox, 1998.

30. Anthony Swofford, *Jarhead: A Marine's Chronicle of the Gulf War and Other Battles* (New York: Scribner, 2003); *Jarhead*, dir. Sam Mendes, Universal Pictures, 2005. For a contemporary press report, corroborating the frequency of Dear Johns in the Gulf, see Associated Press, "Desert Bloom: Love, Lust, Emptiness, Heartbreak – and War," April 4, 1991.

31. Nicholas Sparks, *Dear John* (New York: Warner Books, 2006); *Dear John*, dir. Lasse Hallström, Sony Pictures Entertainment, 2010.

32. Lisa Schencker, "LDS Missionaries Recall Dreaded 'Dear John' Letter," *Salt Lake Tribune*, April 5, 2012.

33. Samantha Majic, "Sending a Dear John Letter: Public Information Campaigns and the Movement to 'End Demand' for Prostitution in Atlanta, GA," *Social Sciences* 6, 138 (2017): 1–22; Valencia J. Milton, "'Dear John' Letter Fights Prostitution," *Telegram & Gazette* (Worcester, MA), January 9, 2006, A1.

34. "Love Story," *M*A*S*H*, season 1, episode 14, first broadcast January 7, 1973; "Sergeant Carter Gets a 'Dear John' Letter," *Gomer Pyle: USMC*, season 1, episode 20, first broadcast February 5, 1965.

35. Bill Mauldin, *Up Front* (New York: H. Holt and Company, 1945), 24.

36. *Los Angeles Times*, July 6, 2012; "Is USS Hornet Haunted?," https://uss-hornet.org/tours/mystery-tour. It's worth noting the recent popularity of the "Museum of Broken Relationships," with the original Zagreb, Croatia, institution followed by a second site in Los Angeles, and traveling exhibits in other countries, including York Castle in the UK. See https://brokenships.com//; on the traveling exhibit in York from March 2019–March 2020, www.yorkcastlemuseum.org.uk/exhibition/museum-of-broken-relationships/.

37. Anthologies include David H. Lowenherz (ed.), *The 50 Greatest Letters from America's Wars* (New York: Crown Publishers, 2002); Andrew Carroll, *Behind the Lines: Powerful and Revealing American and Foreign War Letters – and One Man's Search to Find Them* (New York: Scribner, 2005); Susan Besze Wallace, *Love & War: 250 Years of Wartime Love Letters* (Arlington, TX: Summit Publishing Group, 1997). For Civil War letters, see Annette Tapert, *The Brothers' War: Civil War Letters to Their Loved Ones from the Blue and Gray* (New York: Times Books, 1988); Jakie L. Pruett and Scott Black (eds.), *Civil War Letters, 1861–1865: A Glimpse of the War between the States* (Austin, TX: Eakin Press, 1985); Bob Blaisdell (ed.), *Civil War Letters: From Home, Camp and Battlefield* (Mineola, NY: Dover Publications, 2012). For World War II letters, see Mina Curtiss (ed.), *Letters Home* (Boston, MA: Little, Brown and Company, 1944); Howard H. Peckham and Shirley A. Snyder (eds.), *Letters from the Greatest Generation: Writing Home in WWII* (Bloomington, IN: Indiana University Press, 2016). For anthologies of Vietnam war letters, Bill Adler (ed.), *Letters from Vietnam* (New York: Presidio Press, 2003); Bernard Edelman (ed.), *Dear America: Letters Home from Vietnam* (New York: W. W. Norton: 1985). For letters from the wars in Iraq and Afghanistan, see John McCain, foreword, *Last Letters Home: Voices of Americans from the Battlefields of Iraq* (New York: CDS, 2004); Lisa Moses and Alice Yeager (eds.), *God bless Y'all All –: Letters to Soldiers from the Children of Alabama* (Florence, AL: Lambert Book House, 2004).

38. Letter from Sullivan Ballou to "My very dear Sarah," July 14, 1861, www.pbs.org/kenburns/civil-war/war/historical-documents/sullivan-ballou-letter/; *The Civil War*, Ken Burns, PBS, episode 1, first broadcast September 23, 1990. On the emotional impact of this letter, Christopher Hager, *I Remain Yours: Common Lives in Civil War Letters* (Cambridge, MA: Harvard University Press, 2018), 1–2.

39. United States Postal Service, *Letters from the Sand: The Letters of Desert Storm and Other Wars* (Washington, DC: USPS, 1991); *Dear America*, dir. Bill Couturié, HBO, 1987; Edelman, *Dear America*.

40. Smithsonian National Postal Museum, "Mail Call," https://postalmuseum.si.edu/mail call/index.html.

41. Edelman, *Dear America*, dust jacket; David Burnett, "American Soldier Reads a 'Dear John' Letter from Home," March 1971, Salt Lake Community College, Digital Archive Collection.

42. Sp-4 Roger Hicks, letter to the editor, *Los Angeles Sentinel*, January 21, 1971, A6. On disposal of Dear Johns, Andrew Carroll references sailors ritually burning Dear Johns and dumping the ashes at sea, *War Letters: Extraordinary Correspondence from American Wars* (New York: Washington Square Press, 2011), 215; on Dear Johns being used as "bumf" and returned to sender, Gregory V. Short, *Ground Pounder: A Marine's Journey through South Vietnam, 1968–1969* (Denton, TX: University of North Texas Press, 2012).

43. Judy Barrett Litoff and David C. Smith, *Since You Went Away: World War II Letters from American Women on the Home Front* (Lawrence, KS: University Press of Kansas, 1991); "U.S. Women and World War II Letter Writing Project," Bryant University, https://digitalcommons.bryant.edu/ww2letters/.

44. "Mail Call: V-Mail," National World War II Museum, www.nationalww2museum.org/war/articles/mail-call-v-mail.

45. "The Importance of Being Terse," Mail Call, *Yank*, September 26, 1943, 29; Litoff and Smith discuss this correspondence, *Since You Went Away*, 53–63. The correspondence Anne Gudis received is contained in the Kramer Family Papers, collection 3970, Division of Rare and Manuscript Collections, Cornell University Library [hereafter KFP].

46. Paul Fussell, *Wartime: Understanding and Behavior in the Second World War* (New York: Oxford University Press, 1989), 253.

47. "An Elucidation," letter from Sgt. Chan Burke and Pfc. Richard P. Bibergall to Mail Call, *Yank*, October 10, 1943, 19.

48. David Howard, "A Kriege Log: Wartime Experiences 1941–1945," unpublished ms., General Arnold Collection, SMS 329, Series 4, Folder 3, Box 8, United States Air Force Academy, with thanks to Kurt Piehler for sending me this item.

49. James Salter, "Dear John, and Other Epistles," *Civilization* 5, 6 (December 1998/January 1999): 69; "Laugh, Clown, Laugh Motif Hit Show Mends Broken Hearts on Okinawa," *Variety*, July 17, 1946, 32.

50. Anon. to "Johnny Smack-O," printed in Anna Holmes (ed.), *Hell Hath No Fury: Women's Letters from the End of the Affair* (New York: Ballantine Books, 2002): 177–182; Maria Popova, "Rare Recording of a Vietnam War Soldier Reading a Breakup Letter from Home," Brain Pickings, www.brainpickings.org/2013/02/22/dear-john-hell-hath-no-fury/.

51. For instance, Conrad Wogrin, a World War II army veteran, refers to another GI's spouse as "one of those Dear John ones"; oral history interview with Susan Tracy, February 3, 2016, Conrad Anthony Wogrin collection, AFC/2001/001/104144, VHP.

52. VHP, www.loc.gov/vets/; National WWII Museum, New Orleans, www.ww2online.org/; the Rutgers Oral History Archives, https://oralhistory.rutgers.edu/ [hereafter ROHA], and Texas Tech University's Vietnam Center and Sam Johnson Vietnam Archive, www.vietnam.ttu.edu/ [hereafter TTU].

53. See, for example, Denham Clements, a Marine Corps officer, who recalls having felt during his tour in Vietnam that "too many young marines" had come to him, "whimpering, clutching a Dear John." But to his great surprise, he received one himself shortly after returning; "Remembrances from members of the Basic Officers Class 4–67 from the Basic School at Marine Corps Base Quantico, VA," n.d. p.14, Item 21240101001, TTU.

54. Betty H. Carter Women Veterans Historical Project at the University of North Carolina-Glassboro, http://libcdm1.uncg.edu/cdm/landingpage/collection/WVHP/. See also the Samuel Proctor Oral History Program, "American Women and Military Service," University of Florida, https://oral.history.ufl.edu/projects/vhp/american-women-and-military-service/; The Women's Memorial, Oral History Archive, Arlington, VA, http://beta.womensmemorial.org/oral-history/category/?cat=type/oral-history/archive/.

55. Tim O'Brien, *The Things They Carried* (Boston, MA: Houghton Mifflin, 1990).

56. Vicky Raab, "Send Us Your Dear John Letters," *New Yorker*, February 5, 2010.

57. On gay, lesbian, and bisexual relationships in the armed forces, see Allan Bérubé, *Coming Out under Fire: The History of Gay Men and Lesbian Women in World War II* (Chapel Hill, NC: University of North Carolina Press, 2010 [1990]); Randy Shilts, *Conduct Unbecoming: Gays and Lesbians in the U.S. Military* (New York: St. Martin's Griffin, 2005); Margot Canaday, *The Straight State: Sexuality and Citizenship in Twentieth-Century America* (Princeton, NJ: Princeton University Press, 2009); Estes, *Ask and Tell.*

58. Elizabeth Lutes Hillman, *Defending America: Military Culture and the Cold War Court-Martial* (Princeton, NJ: Princeton University Press, 2005); Kellie Wilson-Buford, *Policing Sex and Marriage in the American Military: The Court-Martial and the Construction of Gender and Sexual Deviance, 1950–2000* (Lincoln, NE: University of Nebraska Press, 2018); on adultery, Deborah L. Rhode, *Adultery: Infidelity and the Law* (Cambridge, MA: Harvard University Press, 2016), chapter 3, "Sex in the Military."

59. Hal Boyle, "GI Joe Goes into Decline If Babe at Home Forgets," *Austin Statesman*, November 5, 1943.

60. Dorothy Dix, "Soldiers Should Never Waste Regrets over Fickle Girls," *Daily Boston Globe*, August 8, 1943, B40.

61. For a discussion of the way in which heterosexual romantic love is (and long has been) configured as a "battle of the sexes" and how this paradigm naturalizes domestic violence, see Tom Digby, *Love and War: How Militarism Shapes Sexuality and Romance* (New York: Columbia University Press, 2014). For a celebration of homosocial bonds between men at war by a Vietnam veteran and writer, William Broyles, Jr., "Why Men Love War," *Esquire*, May 23, 2014 [November 1984], www.esquire.com/news-politics/news/a28718/why-men-love-war/.

CHAPTER 1

1. The backstory of this relationship is set out in a letter from a family friend to Sam's chaplain. Mrs. Pauline Dubin to Lt. Leonard S. Paul, n.d., folder 3, box 2, KFP. A different version of their courtship story, in which Sam and Anne *had* met prior to his embarkation for Europe, is offered by historians Judy Barrett Litoff and David C. Smith, *Since You Went Away: World War II Letters from American Women on the Home Front* (Lawrence, KS: University Press of Kansas, 1991), 53.
2. "The Importance of Being Terse," Mail Call, *Yank*, September 26, 1943, 29.
3. On letter-writing and courtship in the nineteenth century, William M. Decker, *Epistolary Practices: Letter Writing in America before Telecommunications* (Chapel Hill, NC: University of North Carolina Press, 1998); William Kuby, *Conjugal Misconduct: Defying Marriage Law in the Twentieth-Century United States* (New York: Cambridge University Press, 2018), chapter 1. Etiquette manuals provided women with templates for composition of letters parrying a man's romantic interest or "confessing a change of feeling"; see, for instance, Emily Thornwell, *The Lady's Guide to Perfect Gentility in Manners, Dress and Conversation* ... (New York: Derby & Jackson, 1857), 168–169, www.loc.gov/item/3503 8368/; G. A. Gaskell, *Gaskell's Compendium of Form, Educational, Social, Legal and Commercial* ... (Chicago: W. M. Farrar, 1881), 224. I discuss the discouragement of "unknown females" writing to soldiers further in Chapter 2. For a more positive take on "mail romances" that led to wartime marriages, see John H. Mariano, *The Veteran and His Marriage* (New York: Council on Marriage Relations, Inc., 1945), 229.
4. Letter from Kramer to Gudis, July 5, 1942, folder 4, box 1, KFP.
5. Letter from Kramer to Gudis, July 21, 1942, folder 5, box 1, KFP.
6. Letter from Kramer to Gudis, July 21, 1942. On dating mores in the 1940s, Beth L. Bailey, *From Front Porch to Back Seat: Courtship in Twentieth-Century America* (Baltimore, MD: Johns Hopkins University Press, 1989). On the social construction of the "bad girl" and "sex delinquent" in World War II, Amanda H. Littauer, *Bad Girls: Young Women, Sex and Rebellion before the Sixties* (Chapel Hill, NC: University of North Carolina Press, 2015), chapter 1; Karen Anderson, *Wartime Women: Sex Roles, Family Relations, and the Status of Women during World War II* (Westport, CT: Greenwood Press, 182), 103–111; Marilyn E. Hegarty, *Victory Girls, Khaki-Wackies, and Patriotutes: The Regulation of Female Sexuality during World War II* (New York: NYU Press, 2008). Emily Post offered girls advice about whether to say goodbye to beaux before they shipped off: *War-Time Supplement to Etiquette* (New York: Funk & Wagnalls Company, 1942).
7. Letter from Kramer to Gudis, August 19, 1942, folder 5, box 1, KFP.
8. Letter from Kramer to Gudis, June 17, 1942, folder 2, box 1, KFP.
9. On the contemporary military's family orientation, see Jennifer Mittelstadt, *The Rise of the Military Welfare State* (Cambridge, MA: Harvard University Press, 2015); Kenneth T. MacLeish, *Making War at Fort Hood: Life and Uncertainty in a Military Community* (Princeton, NJ: Princeton University Press, 2013); John Worsencroft, "'We Recruit Individuals but Retain Families': Managing Marriage and Family in the All-Volunteer Era, 1973–2001," in *Managing Sex in the US Military*, eds.

Beth L. Bailey, Kara Dixon Vuic, Alesha Doan, and Shannon Portillo (Lincoln, NE: University of Nebraska Press, forthcoming).

10. Gretta Palmer, "Marriage and War," *Ladies' Home Journal* 59, 3 (March 1942): 110. For historical background on the military's attitude to marriage, Kellie Wilson-Buford, *Policing Sex and Marriage in the American Military: The Court-Martial and the Construction of Gender and Sexual Deviance, 1950–2000* (Lincoln, NE: University of Nebraska Press, 2018), 47–77.

11. On women as "camp followers," see Cynthia Enloe, *Does Khaki Become You? The Militarization of Women's Lives* (Boston, MA: South End Press, 1983); Betty Sowers Alt and Bonnie Domrose Stone, *Campfollowing: A History of the Military Wife* (New York: Praeger, 1991).

12. Palmer, "Marriage and War."

13. Richard B. Johns, "The Right to Marry: Infringement by the Armed Forces," *Family Law Quarterly*, 10 (1977): 360–361; Capt. Ross W. Branstetter, "Military Constraints upon Marriages of Service Members Overseas, Or, If the Army Had Wanted You to Have A Wife . . .," *Military Law Review* 102, 5 (1983): 8.

14. Office of the Chief of Chaplains, "Marriage and Related Subjects," n.d. (1943), Section X, The Marriage of Enlisted Personnel, box 198, 291.1 Marriages, Records of the Office of the Chief of Chaplains, RG 247, NARA. On government "allotments" issued to the wives of servicemen, see note 36.

15. On the gender politics of war mobilization, see Susan Zeiger, "She Didn't Raise Her Boy to Be a Slacker: Motherhood, Conscription, and the Culture of the First World War," *Feminist Studies* 22, 1 (Spring 1996): 6–39; Susan A. Brewer, *Why America Fights: Patriotism and War Propaganda from the Philippines to Iraq* (New York: Oxford University Press, 2011), chapter 2. On gendered divisions of labor during the Great War, see Susan Zeiger, *In Uncle Sam's Service: Women Workers with the American Expeditionary Force, 1917–1919* (Philadelphia, PA: University of Pennsylvania Press, 1999); Kimberly Jensen, *Mobilizing Minerva: American Women in the First World War* (Champaign, IL: University of Illinois Press, 2008); Lynn Dumenil, *The Second Line of Defense: American Women and World War I* (Chapel Hill, NC: University of North Carolina Press, 2017).

16. Jennifer Keene, *Doughboys, the Great War, and the Remaking of America* (Baltimore, MD: Johns Hopkins University Press, 2001), 18.

17. Keene, *Doughboys*, 18–19; Andrew J. Huebner, *Love and Death in the Great War* (New York: Oxford University Press, 2018), 59–60.

18. "Men of Draft Age Rushing to Wed in D.C.," *Washington Post*, August 28, 1940, 12.

19. "'Martial' Spelled 'Marital,'" *LAT*, August 15, 1940, A4.

20. Associated Press, "First Lady Opposes Calling Married Men, Says Nation Needs Uniform Draft Rules," *NYT*, January 14, 1941, 27.

21. "Divorce Case Charging Man Wed to Avoid Army Deferred," *LAT*, June 13, 1941, 14.

22. William Fielding Ogburn, "Marriages, Births, and Divorces," *Annals of the American Academy of Political and Social Science* 229 (September 1943): 20–29.

23. Evelyn Millis Duvall, "Marriage in War Time," *Marriage and Family Living* 4, 4 (November 1942): 73–76. On the youthfulness of those marrying, see also Constantine Panunzio, "War and Marriage," *Social Forces* 21, 4 (May 1943): 445. On young wives not regarding marriage as entailing a commitment to monogamy, see Littauer, *Bad Girls*, chapter 1.

24. On *Chaplain Jim*, see Ronit Stahl, *Enlisting Faith: How the Military Chaplaincy Shaped Religion and State in Modern America* (Cambridge, MA: Harvard University Press, 2017), 108–117; *Chaplain Jim* script #86, "The Case of the Soldier, the Ring and the Girl," August 4, 1942, box 24, Office Management Division. Decimal File, 1920–45, 000.77, Records of the Office of the Chief of Chaplains, RG 247, National Archives and Records Administration, College Park, MD [hereafter NARA].

25. Palmer, "Marriage and War"; Clifford Kirkpatrick, EM 30, *Can War Marriages Be Made to Work?* (Washington, DC: American Historical Association, 1944), www.historians.org/about-aha-and-membership/aha-history-and-archives/gi-roundtable-series/pamphlets/em-30-can-war-marriages-be-made-to-work-(1944). See also Kathleen Norris, "Don't Wed Him Until He Comes Home from War," *Daily Boston Globe*, March 28, 1943, D3.

26. Stanley Frank, "To Wed in Haste?," *Redbook* 96, 2 (December 1950): 25.

27. Muriel Nissen, "Is This Your Problem? Sweethearts of G.I.s Are Advised to Wed After Man Is Discharged," *Hartford Courant*, June 7, 1953, D13. For the same advice issued during the Vietnam war, Sylvie Reice, "Uncle Sam Fails as Cupid – Love Gets Caught in Draft," *LAT*, July 19, 1966, C6.

28. John H. Burma, "Attitudes of College Youth on War Marriage," *Social Forces* 24, 1 (October 1945): 97. On fears of "war widowhood," see also "The War Marriage. University of Missouri versus University of Kansas," *University Debaters' Annual, vol. 1942–43*, ed. E. M. Phelps, 159–191.

29. John F. Cuber, "Changing Courtship and Marriage Customs," *Annals of the American Academy of Political and Social Science* 229 (September 1943): 32; Edward C. McDonagh, "The Discharged Serviceman and His Family," *American Journal of Sociology* 51, 5 (1946): 452.

30. Samuel Tenenbaum, "The Fate of Wartime Marriages," *American Mercury* 61 (November 1945): 530–536.

31. Seabury quoted in Tenenbaum, "Fate of Wartime Marriages," 530.

32. Willard Waller cited by Tenenbaum, "Fate of Wartime Marriages," 530. See also Willard Waller, *The Veteran Comes Back* (New York: Dryden Press, 1944); Hornell Hart and Henrietta Bowne, "Divorce, Depression and War," *Social Forces* 22, 2 (December 1943): 191–194. On marriage guidance counseling and the war, Kristin Celello, *Making Marriage Work: A History of Marriage and Divorce in the Twentieth-Century* (Chapel Hill, NC: University of North Carolina Press, 2009), chapter 2; Rebecca L. Davis, *More Perfect Unions: The American Search for Marital Bliss* (Cambridge, MA: Harvard University Press, 2010), chapter 2.

33. Grace Sloan Overton, *Marriage in War and Peace: A Book for Parents and Counselors of Youth* (Nashville, TN: Abingdon-Cokesbury Press, 1945), 64.

34. Tenenbaum, "Fate of Wartime Marriages," 532. See also Cuber, "Changing Courtship and Marriage Customs," 33.

35. Hegarty, *Victory Girls*, chapter 4; Littauer, *Bad Girls*, chapter 1.
36. The government's monthly contribution to an enlisted man's family and the "allotment" that came out of the husband's pay totalled $50. This sum was paid to the wife, together with $30 for a single child, and $20 apiece for any additional offspring. Nell Giles, "That Army–Navy Pay Check," *Ladies Home Journal* 61, 3 (March 1944), 4; Ann Pfau, "Allotment Annies and Other Wayward Wives: Wartime Concerns about Female Disloyalty and the Problem of the Returned Veteran," in *The United States and the Second World War: New Perspectives on Diplomacy, War and the Home Front*, ed. G. Kurt Piehler and Sidney Pash (New York: Fordham University Press, 2010), 101–102.
37. Office of the Chief of Chaplains, "Marriage and Related Subjects," Section IV, "Prohibited Mixtures of Race." See also United States Army Forces Western Pacific, Chaplains' Division, Chaplain James C. Bean (Col.), Monthly Circular Letter, December 28, 1945, box 403, RG 247.
38. Chaplain E. C. Noury, Fort Ord, CA to Right Rev. Msgr. William R. Arnold, Chief of Chaplains, War Department, November 6, 1942, box 197, RG 247.
39. William R. Arnold to Adjutant General, January 31, 1942, box 197, RG 247. For one case of a chaplain pressurizing a reluctant officer to wed the woman he'd impregnated "for the sake of the baby," see Letter from Capt. William McKinney (HQ Army Air Forces Redistribution Station No. 1, Atlantic City) to Chaplain Fraser, Office of the Chief of Chaplains, December 3, 1943, 291.1 Marriages, vol. 3, box 198, RG 247.
40. Minutes of Meeting on Absentee-Proxy Marriage, September 17, 1942, folder 618.31, Marriage, Absentee, box 984, Group 3, 1935–46, Records of the American National Red Cross, RG 200, NARA.
41. See correspondence on proxy marriage in box 197, RG 247. On legal aspects of proxy marriage, see Lillian M. Gordon, "Marriage by Proxy: The Need for Certainty and Equality in the Laws of the American States," *Social Service Review* 20, 1 (March 1946): 29–48.
42. Mr. Day, Assistant Counsel, to Horace Sprage, "Absentee Marriages – Conference with Bishop O'Hara," January 12, 1943, box 984, RG 200.
43. Mrs. August Belmont to Miss Charlotte Johnson, December 16, 1942, box 984, RG 200.
44. Sgt. James O'Neill, "Most-Married Man in America," *Yank*, October 1945, 5.
45. John Modell and Duane Steffey, "Waging War and Marriage: Military Service and Family Formation, 1940–1950," *Journal of Family History* 13, 2 (January 1988): 200–201.
46. On the oscillation "between two extremes" of public opinion on war marriage, see Svend Riemer, "War Marriages Are Different," *Marriage and Family Living* 5, 4 (November 1943): 84. Letter from Kramer to Gudis, July 19, 1942, folder 5, box 1, KFP.
47. Susan L. Carruthers, *The Good Occupation: American Soldiers and the Hazards of Peace* (Cambridge, MA: Harvard University Press, 2016), chapter 4.
48. Beth Bailey and David Farber, *The First Strange Place: Race and Sex in World War II Hawaii* (Baltimore, MD: Johns Hopkins University Press, 1992); Mary Louise Roberts, *What Soldiers Do: Sex and the American GI in World War II France* (Chicago, IL: University of Chicago Press, 2013); Sarah Kovner, *Occupying Power: Sex Workers and Servicemen in Postwar Japan* (Stanford, CA: Stanford University Press, 2012); Maria Höhn and

Seungsook Moon (eds.), *Over There: Living with the U.S. Military Empire from World War Two to the Present* (Durham, NC: Duke University Press, 2010). Patton's widely repeated dictum, "if they don't fuck, they don't fight," is quoted by Roberts, *What Soldiers Do*, 160. On the May Act, Hegarty, *Victory Girls*, 14–41. On sex and soldiers in World War I, Nancy K. Bristow, *Making Men Moral: Social Engineering during the Great War* (New York: New York University Press, 1996); Kimberley A. Reilly, "'A Perilous Venture for Democracy': Soldiers, Sexual Purity, and American Citizenship in the First World War," *Journal of the Gilded Age and Progressive Era* 13, 2 (April 2014): 223–255; Andrew Byers, *The Sexual Economy of War: Discipline and Desire in the U.S. Army* (Ithaca, NY: Cornell University Press, 2019).

49. Allan M. Brandt, *No Magic Bullet: A Social History of Venereal Disease in the United States since 1880* (New York: Oxford University Press, 2020 [1985]); Robert Kramm, *Sanitized Sex: Regulating Prostitution, Venereal Disease, and Intimacy in Occupied Japan, 1945–1952* (Berkeley, CA: University of California Press, 2017).

50. On the "fraternization ban" in Germany and its counterpart in Japan, see Carruthers, *Good Occupation*, 111–128, 135–136, 274–280. On German and Japanese "war brides," Susan Zeiger, *Entangling Alliances: Foreign War Brides and American Soldiers in the Twentieth Century* (New York: New York University Press, 2010), 71–118.

51. Lt. Col. Albert B. Kellogg, "Marriages of Soldiers," July 1942, 291.1 Births to Marriages Vol. 1 to 2, box 197, RG 247; Zeiger, *Entangling Alliances*, chapter 1.

52. Zeiger, *Entangling Alliances*, 86–87.

53. Carruthers, *Good Occupation*, 295–297; Oliver Frederiksen, *The American Military Occupation of Germany, 1945–1953* (Darmstadt: Historical Division, Headquarters, United States Army, Europe, 1953), 136–137.

54. Carruthers, *Good Occupation*, 146–148; Zeiger, *Entangling Alliances*, 181–182. HQ Japan Logistical Command, Office of the Commanding General, APO 343, "Marriage to Japanese Nationals," September 24, 1950, folder 290.1, box 461, Records of the Eighth Army RG 338, NARA.

55. On hostility to US servicemen's sexual relationships with German women, see David Brion Davis, "The Americanized Mannheim of 1945–1946," in *American Places: Encounters with History*, ed. William Leuchtenberg (New York: Oxford University Press, 2002); Maria Höhn and Martin Klimke, *A Breath of Freedom: The Civil Rights Struggle, African American GIs, and Germany* (New York: Palgrave Macmillan, 2010); Timothy L. Schroer, *Recasting Race after World War II: Germans and African Americans in American-Occupied Germany* (Boulder, CO: University Press of Colorado, 2007); and on local men's responses to sexual relationships between US personnel and Asian women, Yasuhiro Okada, "Race, Masculinity, and Military Occupation: African American Soldiers' Encounters with the Japanese at Camp Gifu, 1947–51," *Journal of African American History* 96 (2011): 179–203; Michael Cullen Green, *Black Yanks in the Pacific: Race in the Making of American Military Empire after World War II* (Ithaca, NY: Cornell University Press, 2010).

56. Memo, September 11, 1951, file 291.1, box 491, General Correspondence, 1951. 248–291.1. Records of the Eighth U.S. Army, 1944–56, RG 338.

57. On suspicion of foreign women, see Zeiger, *Entangling Alliances,* passim.

58. On "camp towns" around US bases in Asia and American perceptions of servicemen's Asian partners, Katharine H. S. Moon, *Sex among Allies: Military Prostitution in U.S.–Korea Relations* (New York: Columbia University Press, 1997); Sealing Cheng, *On the Move for Love: Migrant Entertainers and the U.S. Military in South Korea* (Philadelphia, PA: University of Pennsylvania Press, 2010); Rebecca Forgash, *Intimacy across the Fencelines: Sex, Marriage, and the U.S. Military in Okinawa* (Ithaca, NY: Cornell University Press, 2020).

59. Telegram from CINCEUR Heidelberg, to Department of the Army, Washington, DC, May 2, 1952, box 513, RG 247.

60. Chaplain Gomer Rees, Study of 183 Marriages of Americans to Japanese Women, September 11, 1952, Administrative Office. Decimal File, 1951–53, Vol. XV, box 513, RG 247. Despite its more positive appreciation of these marriages, Rees's report wasn't free from racialized stereotypes. He considered Japanese wives more submissive than American women, and ascribed the success of these bi-national marriages in part to Asian women's greater willingness to placate their US husbands. The idea that foreign women were more submissive than their "aggressive" American counterparts was seemingly widespread; Capt. Richard G. Druss, "Foreign Marriages in the Military," *Psychiatric Quarterly* 39, 1–4 (December 1965): 223.

61. Ruben Salazar, "GI Romances Create Added Vietnam Worry," *LAT,* October 28, 1965, 16.

62. "Interracial Marriages Said Major Problem," *Washington Post,* December 4, 1965, E17. For an account of Vietnamese "war brides" and that construct's demise during the Vietnam war, see Zeiger, *Entangling Alliances,* 214–235.

63. See materials in USARV Chaplain Section/Administration and Management Division, Entry P 1332, Daily Journals, 1965–73, box 1, December 1965–March/April 1967, Records of U.S. Forces in Southeast Asia, 1950–1975, RG 472, NARA.

64. Anon., "Study Depicts GI Who Marries in Vietnam as a Troubled Man," *NYT,* February 26, 1967, 7.

65. HQ MACV Dir 608–1, Personal Affairs. Marriages in Command, 1971, box 1, Entry P 70, MACV, Adjutant General Military Personnel Division. Special Actions Branch. Records relating to Marriage Applications, 1971–72, RG 472. Gloria Emerson, "More Americans Are Marrying Vietnamese Despite the Obstacles," *NYT,* September 12, 1970, 3; UPI, "Increase Seen in U.S.–Viet Marriages," *LAT,* January 1, 1970, A12; Judy Klemesrud, "Vietnamese War Brides: Happiness Mixed with Pain," *NYT,* September 13, 1971, 42; Ivan B. Goldman, "GI Fights U.S., Vietnam to Bring His Wife Here," *Washington Post,* September 23, 1971, B1.

66. Fred J. Cook, "Who Should Be Drafted? Who Should Be Exempt? The Draft Boards Escalate," *NYT Magazine,* September 12, 1965, SM54.

67. Jack Raymond, "The Draft Is Unfair," *NYT Magazine,* January 2, 1966, SM163.

68. Steve Hendrix, "A Rush to Avoid the Vietnam Draft: The Day LBJ Eliminated the Marriage Exemption," *Washington Post,* September 23, 2017.

69. Jerry Buck, "Young Couples Dash to the Altar as Deadline to Avoid Draft Nears," *Washington Post,* August 28, 1965, A6.

70. Drew Pearson, "Avoiding the Draft Is Becoming the Favorite Sport among Youth," *LAT*, September 27, 1965, A6; Richard Eder, "Hasty Marriages No Bar to Draft," *NYT*, September 1, 1965, 17; Nan Robertson, "Husbands' Status in Draft Outlined," *NYT*, September 5, 1965, 39.

71. Nancy F. Cott, *Public Vows: A History of Marriage and the Nation* (Cambridge, MA: Harvard University Press, 2000), 201.

72. Scholarly literature on the subject of military service, marriage, and divorce is sizeable and divided between researchers who find war (or combat, more narrowly) to have negatively impacted servicemen's and veterans' marriages, and others who find no correlation between military service and marital instability. For an overview of the literature, William Ruger, Sven E. Wilson, and Shawn L. Waddoups, "Warfare and Welfare: Military Service, Combat, and Marital Dissolution," *Armed Forces & Society* 29, 1 (Fall 2002): 85–107. Important contributions to the debate include William I. Anderson and Derek W. Little, "All's Fair: War and Other Causes of Divorce from a Beckerian Perspective," *American Journal of Economics and Sociology* 58, 1 (October 1999): 901–922; Eliza K. Pavalko and Glen H. Elder, "World War II and Divorce: A Life-Course Perspective," *American Journal of Sociology* 95, 5 (March 1990): 1215; John Modell and Duane Steffey, "Waging War and Marriage: Military Service and Family Formation, 1940–1950," *Journal of Family History* 13, 2 (January 1988): 195–218; Cynthia Gimbel and Alan Booth, "Why Does Military Combat Experience Adversely Affect Marital Relations?," *Journal of Marriage and the Family* 56, 3 (August 1994): 691–703. For a more recent study, Benjamin R. Carney and John S. Crown, *Families under Stress: An Assessment of the Data, Theory, and Research on Marriage and Divorce in the Military* (Santa Barbara, CA: RAND Corporation, 2007).

73. On Vietnam and divorce, Jere Cohen and Mady Wechsler, "Veterans, the Vietnam Era, and Marital Dissolution," *Armed Forces and Society* 36, 1 (October 2009): 19–37; E. James Lieberman, "American Families and the Vietnam War," *Journal of Marriage and Family* 33, 4 (November 1971): 709–721.

74. On the turn to an All-Volunteer Force, Beth Bailey, *America's Army: Making the All-Volunteer Force* (Cambridge, MA: Harvard University Press, 2009); and on family policy, Worsencroft, "'We Recruit Individuals but Retain Families.'"

75. Mady Wechsler Segal, "The Military and the Family as Greedy Institutions," *Armed Forces & Society* 13, 1 (Fall 1986): 25.

76. Worsencroft, "'We Recruit Individuals but Retain Families;'" Mittelstadt, *Rise of the Military Welfare State*, chapter 5; Sondra Alabano, "Military Recognition of Family Concerns: Revolutionary War to 1993," *Armed Forces & Society* 20, 2 (Winter 1994): 283–302.

77. Kara Dixon Vuic, "Mobilizing Marriage and Motherhood: Military Families and Family Planning since World War II," in *Integrating the US Military: Race, Gender, and Sexual Orientation since World War II*, ed. Walter Bristol, Jr. and Heather Marie Stur (Baltimore, MD: Johns Hopkins University Press, 2017), 142–166.

78. Directive quoted by Clifford Krauss, "The Marines Want Singles Only, But They Are Quickly Overruled," *NYT*, August 12, 1993, A1.

79. Boomer quoted by Bill McAllister and Barton Gellman, "Aspin Reverses Ban on Married Marines," *Washington Post*, August 12, 1993, A1.

80. LCDR Michael E. Foskett, "The Impact of Divorce among Marines, E-5 and Below, on Unit Operational Readiness," Masters of Military Studies thesis, Marine Corps University, Quantico, VA, 2013, 16. Salary figures from Clifford Krauss, "Marine Leader Contritely Admits He Erred on 'Singles Only' Order," *NYT*, August 13, 1993, A1.

81. Schroeder quoted by Krauss, "Marines Want Singles Only." For a skeptical take on the success of these ventures, see E. T. Gomulka, "Until Death Do Us Part?," *United States Naval Institute Proceedings*, 124, 11 (November 1998): 49–51. For the USMC's "Prevention and Relationship Enhancement Program" (PREP), see www.quantico.usmc-mccs.org/marine-family/family-readiness/marine-corps-family-team-building-mcftb/prevention-and-relationship-enhancement-program-prep/?mobileFormat=false.

82. Mary V. Stremlow, *A History of the Women Marines, 1946–1977* (Washington, DC: US Government Printing Office, 1986), 151.

83. Vuic, "Mobilizing Marriage," 175.

84. "Marriage Policy," The Women's Memorial, https://www.womensmemorial.org/marriage-policy.

85. "Playthings," Leisa D. Meyer, *Creating GI Jane: Sexuality and Power in the Women's Army Corps during World War II* (New York: Columbia University Press, 1996), 39. On the slander campaign, Mattie E. Treadwell, *The Women's Army Corps* (1954), chapter 11, https://history.army.mil/books/wwii/Wac/index.htm; M. Michaela Hampf, "'Dykes' or "Whores": Sexuality and the Women's Army Corps in the United States during World War II," *Women's Studies International Forum* 27 (2004): 13–30; Ann Pfau, *Miss Yourlovin: GIs, Gender and Domesticity during World War II* (New York: Columbia University Press, 2008), chapter 2, e-book www.gutenberg-e.org/pfau/chapter2.html.

86. Bettie J. Morden, *The Women's Army Corps, 1945–1978* (Washington, DC: US Army Center of Military History, 1990), 15.

87. On demobilization and the WAC, https://history.army.mil/books/wwii/Wac/ch36.htm. On gender and the Army Nurse Corps, see Charissa Threat, *Nursing Civil Rights: Gender and Race in the Army Nurse Corps* (Urbana, IL: University of Illinois Press, 2015); Kara Dixon Vuic, *Officer, Nurse, Woman: The Army Nurse Corps in the Vietnam War* (Baltimore, MD: Johns Hopkins University Press, 2011), 115–116.

88. Council on Foreign Relations, "Demographics of the U.S. Military," July 13, 2020; www.cfr.org/backgrounder/demographics-us-military.

89. Segal, "The Military and the Family," 26. The 2010 DoD statistics are derived from Eileen Patten and Kim Parker, "Women in the U.S. Military: Growing Share, Distinctive Profile," Pew Social & Demographic Trends, 2011, p. 6; www.pewresearch.org.

90. On women soldiers' elevated likelihood of divorce, Brighita Negrusa and Sebastian Negrusa, "Home Front: Post-deployment Mental Health and Divorces," *Demography* 51 (2014): 895–916; S. Negrusa, B. Negrusa, and J. R. Hosek, "Gone to War: Have Deployments Increased Divorces?," *Journal of Population Economics* 27 (2014):

473–496; Kenona H. Southwell and Shelley M. MacDermid Wadsworth, "The Many Faces of Military Families: Unique Features of the Lives of Female Service Members," *Military Medicine* 181, 1 (January 2016): 70–79.

91. I develop these points further in chapter 7. The image galleries of various military marriage programs almost invariably depict men in uniform embracing, or holding hands with, women in civilian attire. See, for example, the marriage resources on Military OneSource, a DoD online resource for military personnel and their families: www.militaryonesource.mil/family-relationships/relationships/military-relationships-support/; likewise the army's Strong Bonds program, www.strongbonds.org.

92. Ester Wier, *Army Social Customs* (Harrisburg, PA: Military Service Publishing, 1958), 79, quoted by Wilson-Buford, *Policing Sex and Marriage*, 31.

93. *I Was a Male War Bride*, dir. Howard Hawks, 20th Century Fox, 1949. Kenneth MacLeish notes that the "male Army spouse" is an "obscure and slippery category" that leaves some husbands of servicemen feeling "feminized by their peripheral or proxy attachment" to the institution; Kenneth T. MacLeish, *Making War at Fort Hood: Life and Uncertainty in a Military Community* (Princeton, NJ: Princeton University Press, 2013), 19–20.

94. James Reston, "More Than Weapons," *NYT*, August 19, 1965, 2.

95. On the R&R program, Meredith H. Lair, *Armed with Abundance: Consumerism and Soldiering in the Vietnam War* (Chapel Hill, NC: University of North Carolina Press, 2011), 109–116. For contemporary accounts that, unusually, included wives' perspectives on R&R, Julie Byrne, "Bit of GI Heaven Away from War's Hell," *LAT*, May 26, 1968, 11; Julie Byrne, "Hawaii Reunions Muster Up Courage for GIs and Wives," *LAT*, May 27, 1968, C1.

96. Military History Branch, Headquarters Military Assistance Command, Vietnam [MACV], *Command History*, 1967, vol. II, p. 897, box 6, Entry A1 32, RG 472.

97. Riemer, "War Marriages Are Different," 87.

98. Randy Shilts, *Conduct Unbecoming: Gays and Lesbians in the U.S. Military, Vietnam to the Persian Gulf* (New York: Penguin Books, 1993), 67–68; Francine Banner, "'It's Not All Flowers and Daisies': Masculinity, Heteronormativity and the Obscuring of Lesbian Identity in the Repeal of 'Don't Ask, Don't Tell,'" *Yale Journal of Law and Feminism* 24, 1 (2012): 61–117.

99. On a lesbian Marine corporal who married her best male friend to give her an alibi, see Eric Schmitt, "Gay Soldiers See Hope and Fear in Ban's End," *NYT*, November 16, 1992, A10. On the fake Dear John ending a fake romance, Helen Gerhardt, "Back from the Front, with Honor, A Warrior's Truth," *NYT*, February 13, 2005, J9.

CHAPTER 2

1. The online galleries of the Smithsonian National Postal Museum's "Mail Call" exhibit showcase many such iconic images; "Mail Call," https://postalmuseum.si.edu/mailcall/index.html. For discussions of the significance of mail to front-line troops, see Gerald F. Linderman, *The World within War: America's Combat Experience in World War II*

(New York: Free Press, 1997), 302–304; Peter S. Kindsvatter, *American Soldiers: Ground Combat in the World Wars, Korea, and Vietnam* (Lawrence, KS: University Press of Kansas, 2003), 109–110; and for a poetic tribute, capturing the sentiments of men in uniform, see Randall Jarrell, "Mail Call," in *Little Friend, Little Friend* (New York: Dial, 1945).

2. Editorial, "Soldiers' Letters," *LAT*, June 9, 1917, II4.

3. Anon, "What to Write in Letters to Soldiers," *Detroit Free Press*, April 7, 1918, E2.

4. Anon., "Write the Right Letter," *Vogue* 103, 11, June 1, 1944, 148.

5. On mail and mailing privileges in World War II, Judy Barrett Litoff and David C. Smith, "'Will He Get My Letter?' Popular Portrayals of Mail and Morale During World War II," *Journal of Popular Culture* (Spring 1990): 23. On service personnel serving in the Korean war, Anon., "Free Mail Voted for Troops in Korea; GI Bill Rights Asked," *Washington Post*, July 11, 1950, 3. Military personnel in Vietnam were granted this privilege in 1965; Associated Press, "Free Mail Rights for G.I.'s," *NYT*, September 1, 1965, 34; on reduced rates for civilians mailing packages to service personnel in Vietnam, "Special Rate in Effect for Vietnam Mail," *Washington Post*, December 25, 1965, 1. The declassified annual Command Histories produced by Military History Branch, Headquarters Military Assistance Command, Vietnam [MACV] contain many references to problems with mail, in the first instance, and attempts to remedy them: *Command History 1966*, box 3; *Command History 1967*, box 5; *Command History 1968*, box 6; *Command History 1969*, box 7; *Command History 1971*, box 9, Entry A1 32, RG 472, Records of US Forces in Southeast Asia, NARA.

6. Editorial, "Mail From Home," *NYT*, May 21, 1951, 26; letter from Sgt. Wilbur Radeline, "Sergeant's Plea for Mail," *LAT*, March 15, 1951, A4. These complaints did not abate as the war continued in a protracted stalemate. See, for instance, letter by Cpl. Robert R. Kubick, August 19, 1952, "Letters to The Times," *NYT*, September 1, 1952, 16; letter by Pvt. James M. Henry, "Letters to The Times," *NYT Sunday Magazine*, December 14, 1952, SM4.

7. Robert Alden, "Mail Call in Korea is Ritual to G.I.'s," *NYT*, January 23, 1953, 2.

8. "Why Not Become a Sammy Backer If You Really Desire to Help?," *Indianapolis Star*, August 5, 1917, 1. For the song's music and lyrics, Herbert W. Willett, "Be A Sammy Backer," September 1917, Library of Congress, https://loc.gov/item/ihas.200211680.

9. "Orphan Soldiers Get First Call from Sammy Backers," *Indianapolis Star*, August 8, 1917, 10; "Sammy Backer Is A Man's Job," *Indianapolis Star*, August 10, 1917, 15; "Girl Asks Right to Back Sammy," *Indianapolis Star*, August 24, 1917, 16; "Work of the 'Sammy Backer' About to Begin: How to Become a Pal of a Boy in France," *Arizona Republican*, September 3, 1917, 10; "Sammy Backing for Men Only," *Indianapolis Star*, October 15, 1917, 8.

10. William Kuby, *Conjugal Misconduct: Defying Marriage Law in the Twentieth-Century United States* (New York: Cambridge University Press, 2018), 25–67. On Civil War personal ads and correspondence between women and soldiers, see Nancy L. Rhoades and Lucy E. Bailey (eds.), *Wanted – Correspondence: Women's Letters to a Union Soldier* (Athens, OH: Ohio University Press, 2009).

11. Chaplain H. L. Winter, First Infantry, "Letters from Home What Sammy Wants," *Indianapolis Star*, October 1, 1917, 6.

12. Thomas Dinsmore, Assistant National Director, Military and Naval Welfare Service [American Red Cross], to Field Directors, Insular and Foreign, "Organizing Correspondence between Civilians and Men in Service," June 11, 1942, folder 618.9, box 988, Group 3, Records of the American National Red Cross, RG 200 NARA; Marion May Dilts, *Army Guide for Women* (New York: Longmans, Green and Co., 1942), 205; Frank Henry, "Troubles of the Meade Mailman," *The Sun*, February 8, 1942, M1.

13. Letter from Sam Kramer to Anne Gudis, May 11, 1942, folder 1, box 1, KFP.

14. Letter from Sam Kramer to Anne Gudis, May 25, 1942, folder 1, box 1, KFP.

15. Associated Press, "American Women Asked Not to 'Adopt' Soldiers Overseas, *St. Louis Post Dispatch*, December 26, 1917, 1; "Please Don't Adopt a Soldier," *LAT*, December 27, 1917, 12.

16. Litoff and Smith, "'Will He Get My Letter?,'" 23–24.

17. V-mail from S/Sgt J. to Anne Gudis, September 25, 1943, folder 13, box 2, KFP.

18. V-mail from Pvt. Francis Trefz to Anne Gudis, November 1943, folder 13, box 2, KFP.

19. See various letters to Anne Gudis, folder 13, box 2, KFP.

20. Letter from "Phil" [Seriffignano] to Anne Gudis, September 29, 1943; letter from "Phil" to Anne Gudis, November 24, 1943, folder 13, box 2, KFP.

21. *New Journal and Guide*, January 6, 1951; "Girl's Bid for Korea Letters Brings Deluge," *LAT*, June 25, 1951, 11.

22. On Korean war letter-writing drives, "Drive for Letters to GI's Launched," *LAT*, December 10, 1951, 35; "San Pedro Woman Sends 100 Letters Daily to GIs," *LAT*, June 14, 1953, 17; "Mail to Korea G.I.'s Held Top Need Now," *NYT*, August 8, 1953, 2. On "Operation Mail Call," Milt Brouhard, "Operation Mail Call Becomes Non-profit State Corporation," *LAT*, August 25, 1967, 42; Linda Mathews, "Operation Mail Call: 'Mom' Enlists 60,000 Pals for Lonely Men in Vietnam," *LAT*, November 12, 1967, B1, B3. On another letter-writing project developed by students at Villanova University, Associated Press, "Villanova Drive Plans Mail Deluge for GIs," *Washington Post*, October 19, 1969, F6.

23. "Emily Post Says: 'War Mother's Letter Explains Itself,'" *Daily Boston Globe*, December 4, 1943, 9.

24. Catherine Redmond, *Handbook for Army Wives & Mothers: And for Daughters, Sisters, Sweethearts, Grandmothers and All American Women Who Have a Soldier Away at War* (Washington, DC: Infantry Journal/Penguin Books, 1944); Dilts, *Army Guide for Women*, 199–205; G. A. Reeder, *Letter Writing in Wartime: "How and What to Write About"* (New York: Books, Inc., 1943); Ethel Gorham, *So Your Husband's Gone to War* (New York: Doubleday, Doran and Co., 1942).

25. Margaret Buell Wilder, *Since You Went Away . . . Letters to a Soldier from His Wife* (New York: McGraw-Hill, 1943); Margaret Halsey, *Some of My Best Friends Are Soldiers: A Kind of Novel* (New York: Simon and Schuster, 1944). On Hollywood's contribution to wartime mail

drives, see Thomas Doherty, *Projections of War: Hollywood, American Culture, and World War II* (New York: Columbia University Press, 1999), 180.

26. On *Chaplain Jim*, Ronit V. Stahl, *Enlisting Faith: How the Military Chaplaincy Shaped Religion and State in Modern America* (Cambridge, MA: Harvard University Press, 2018), 109. The script for "The Case of the Soldier Who Never Received Any Mail," *Chaplain Jim*, Episode 1, Number 1, April 6, 1942, can be found in box 23, Office Management Division, Decimal File 000.77, 1920–45, Records of the Office of the Chief of Chaplains, RG 247, NARA. Later *Chaplain Jim* scripts can be found in boxes 24–26 of the same series.

27. Frances Clarke, "So Lonesome I Could Die: Nostalgia and Debates over Emotional Control in the Civil War North," *Journal of Social History* 41, 2 (Winter 2007): 269. On women being urged not to write "gloomy" or "complaining" letters, Christopher Hager, *I Remain Yours: Common Lives in Civil War Letters* (Cambridge, MA: Harvard University Press, 2018), 147–149.

28. Corrine Hardesty, "Don't Worry a Soldier With Your Troubles," *Washington Post*, September 10, 1942, C3. Editorial, "Soldiers' Letters," *LAT*, June 9, 1917, II4; "'Girl-and-Dog' Photographs Go Big with Soldiers in France," *Boston Daily Globe*, June 29, 1918.

29. Reeder, *Letter Writing in Wartime*, 24. Betty Barit likewise encouraged women to use "screwy drawings" in their letters; "How to Write a Letter to a Soldier," *The American Magazine* 133 (April 1942): 142.

30. Violet Moore, "How to Write to a Soldier," *Atlanta Constitution*, May 16, 1943, 2D; "Soldier's Letter Box," *Call and Post* (Cleveland), March 14, 1942, 23.

31. "Ac-cent-tchu-ate the Positive," music by Harold Arlen, lyrics by Johnny Mercer, performed by Johnny Mercer and the Pied Pipers, Capitol Records, 1944. Gorham, *So Your Husband's Gone to War*, 187–188; Louise Paine Benjamin, "Safe Conduct: The Do's and Don'ts of Keeping Him Loving You Always," *Ladies' Home Journal* 60 (January 1943): 71. On the censorship of civilian mail, see Reeder, *Letter Writing in Wartime*, 191–197; Jonathan Wake, "The Censor Reads Your Letters," *Good Housekeeping* 115, 5 (November 1942): 117.

32. On women's war work and shifting gender roles, Karen Anderson, *Wartime Women: Sex Roles, Family Relations, and the Status of Women during World War II* (Westport, CT: Greenwood Press, 1981); D'Ann Campbell, *Women at War with America: Private Lives in a Patriotic Era* (Cambridge, MA: Harvard University Press, 1984); Susan M. Hartmann, *The Home Front and Beyond: American Women in the 1940s* (Boston, MA: Twayne Publishers, 1982); Emily Yellin, *Our Mothers' War: American Women at Home and at the Front during World War II* (New York: Free Press, 2004).

33. Frances Fenwick Hills, "Letters from Home," *Good Housekeeping* 114, 6 (June 1942): 69. For an example of this motif's persistence in the Korean war, "'Mail from States Kicked Us in the Pants,' Officers Says," *Washington Post*, June 20, 1951, 2. Wartime psychiatrists and sociologists were well aware of, and concerned by, GIs' tendency to develop idealized visions of home; see W. Edgar Gregor, "The Idealization of the Absent," *American Journal of Sociology* 50, 1 (July 1944): 53–54.

34. "Morale Report," APO 922, January 31, 1944, folder "Censorship Survey of Morale, 1943–45," box 24, Entry 553, G-2 Theater Censor. Summaries of Censorship Violations (Comments Sheets) 1942–44, Records of the GHQ Southwest Pacific Area and U.S. Army Forces, Pacific, RG 496, NARA.

35. On servicemen's attitudes toward war work, Louise Paine Benjamin, "Orders: For the Girls at Home," *Ladies' Home Journal* 60 (November 1943): 118; J. O. Reinemann, "Extra-marital Relations with Fellow Employes in War Industry as a Factor in Disruption of Family Life," *American Sociological Review* 10, 3 (June 1945): 399–404. For the "clinging vine" quote, Mona Gardner, "Has Your Husband Come Home to the Right Woman?," *Ladies' Home Journal* 62 (December 1945): 41.

36. On GIs' fears of, and anger about, female infidelity, see Ann Pfau, *Miss Yourlovin: GIs, Gender and Domesticity during World War II* (New York: Columbia University Press/ Gutenberg e-book, 2008), chapter 1; Andrew J. Huebner, *The Warrior Image: Soldiers in American Culture from the Second World War to the Vietnam Era* (Chapel Hill, NC: University of North Carolina Press, 2008), 86–89; Lee Kennett, *GI: The American Soldier in World War II* (New York: Charles Scribner's Sons, 1987), 76. For contemporary takes on this problem, Samuel Futterman, "Changing Sex Patterns and the War," *Marriage and Family Living* 8, ii (May 1946), 29; Edward C. McDonagh, "The Discharged Serviceman and His Family," *American Journal of Sociology* 51, 5 (March 1946): 452–454. Chronic anxiety about spousal fidelity was by no means confined to US troops. On British POWs, Alfred Torrie, "The Return of Odysseus: The Problem of Marital Infidelity for the Repatriate," *British Medical Journal* 2, 4414 (August 11, 1944): 192–193.

37. Ann Pfau, "Allotment Annies and Other Wayward Wives: Wartime Concerns about Female Disloyalty and the Problem of the Returned Veteran," in *The United States and the Second World War: New Perspectives on Diplomacy, War, and the Home Front*, eds. G. Kurt Piehler and Sidney Pash (New York: Fordham University Press, 2010), n. 8, 120.

38. Anonymous enlisted man quoted in "Report for Censorship Survey of Morale, Rumors. Propaganda. APO 501, February 1945," Folder Censorship Survey of Morale, 1943–45, box 24, RG 496. The engagement of nineteen-year-old Eva Caprari to an Italian POW attracted particular attention from both the stateside press and military newspapers. See, for example, "Eva Would Wed Italian PW, but Army OK Is Dubious," *Stars and Stripes* (London edition), January 13, 1945, 4. Dozens of American women, many of them of Italian heritage, petitioned the Provost Marshal General's Office for permission to marry Italian prisoners with whom they'd fallen in love and, in some cases, with whom they'd conceived babies. Permission was invariably denied, but some couples married surreptitiously in defiance of official prohibitions. Correspondence between women and the Provost Marshal General's Office can be found in box 1268, Entry 451, POW Operations Division, Operations Branch, Unclassified Decimal Index, 1942–45, Records of the Provost Marshal General, RG 389, NARA. On attempts to manage the sexuality and sex lives of Axis POWs in the United States, see Matthias Reiss, *Controlling Sex in Captivity: POWs and Sexual Desire in the United States during the Second World War* (London: Bloomsbury Academic, 2018).

39. Committee of the National Research Council, *Psychology for the Fighting Man: What You Should Know about Yourself and Others* (Washington, DC: Infantry Journal/Penguin Books, 1943), 278–279.

40. "Write Right!," *Vogue*; Will V. Neely, "What NOT to Write Your Soldier Boy Overseas," *Afro-American* (Baltimore), January 1, 1944, 2; Reeder, *Letter Writing in Wartime*, 60. On the same point, Louise Paine Benjamin, "Safe Conduct," 71.

41. Elsewhere, I discuss the correspondence between a wife in the United States and husband serving in occupied Italy during World War II, who responded to her nagging fears about his fidelity with the promise that he would tell her if he slept with another woman, "even though it might almost kill you." See Susan L. Carruthers, *The Good Occupation: American Soldiers and the Hazards of Peace* (Cambridge, MA: Harvard University Press, 2016), 149. The correspondence itself is contained in the Maurice F. Neufeld Papers, LOC.

42. Violet Moore, "How to Write to a Soldier," *Atlanta Constitution*, May 16, 1943, 2D. Letter from Mrs. Pauline Dubin to Lt. Leonard Paul, n.d., folder 3, box 2, KFP; V-mail from Sam Kramer to Anne Gudis, August 7, 1943 and August 16, 1943, folder 6, box 1, KFP.

43. V-mail from Lt. Leonard Paul to Anne Gudis, September 16, 1943, folder 12, box 2, KFP; Henry Elkin, "Aggressive and Erotic Tendencies in Army Life," *American Journal of Sociology* 51, 5 (March 1946): 410–411. On GIs' language more generally, Paul Fussell, *Wartime: Understanding and Behavior in the Second World War* (New York: Oxford University Press, 1989), chapter 17.

44. "Glossary of GI Slang," *American Speech* 16, 3 (October 1941): 169.

45. Milton Bracker, "What to Write the Soldier Overseas," *New York Times Magazine*, October 3, 1943, 14.

46. On the screening process, Ellen Herman, *The Romance of American Psychology: Political Culture in the Age of Experts* (Berkeley, CA: University of California Press, 1995), 88–90. For a contemporary discussion angled at mothers who should, the author suggested, take responsibility for this parlous state of affairs, J. C. Furnas, "Why Is He 4-F? Are You to Blame?," *Ladies' Home Journal* 61, 9 (September 1944): 26, 76, 78–79, 81, 83.

47. On Sinatra as "the most hated man in the armed services," James Kaplan, *Frank: The Voice* (New York: Doubleday, 2010), 206. On soldiers' responses, William Friedman Fagelson, "Fighting Films: The Everyday Tactics of World War II Soldiers," *Cinema Journal* 40, 3 (Spring 2001): 94–112. On Sinatra's screen performances as soldier and/or veteran, Colleen Glenn, "A Real Swinger of a Nightmare: Frank Sinatra and the Grim Side of the WWII Veteran's Story," *Quarterly Review of Film and Video* 36, 6 (2019): 470–497.

48. Enlisted man, 172nd Infantry, APO 43, quoted in "Censorship Survey of Morale, Rumors, Propaganda," April, July 1945, box 24, RG 496. Redmond quoted Milton Bracker's article in drawing up her list of "do's and don'ts" for women letter writers; *Army Handbook*, 216.

49. "Write the Right Letter," 148; Bracker, "What to Write the Soldier Overseas," 14; UPI, "'Dear John' Letters," X.

50. John Steinbeck, "Letters from Home Make or Break Soldiers," *Daily Boston Globe*, August 3, 1943, 20. "Mary Haworth's Mail," *Washington Post*, July 18, 1944, 7.

51. Maureen Daly, "Write Right!," *Chicago Daily Tribune*, April 4, 1943, D9. Barit, "How to Write a Letter to a Soldier," 142.

52. *Chaplain Jim*, Issue 128, February 14, 1943, box 25, RG 247.

53. Howard Whitman, "Jilt in the Mail Gets Yank Down: 'Dear John' Letters Are Not Ones He Wants," *Chicago Daily Tribune*, May 31, 1944, 1.

54. Elizabeth Woodward, "Column for Teens," *Daily Boston Globe*, March 17, 1952.

55. Kitte Turmell, "Teen Talk: Loving Care for Servicemen" *The Sun* (Baltimore), December 14, 1969, C13.

56. Jean Adams, "Teen Forum," *The Sun*, November 20, 1968, B7 .

57. Richard V. Oliver, "Say 'Dear John' Letters Bane of Fighting Men in Vietnam," *Afro-American*, November 4, 1967, 8; Abigail Van Buren, "Dear Abby," *LAT*, January 2, 1969, F3; Abigail Van Buren, "'Dear John' Huh? What About the 'Dear Mary'?," *Atlanta Constitution*, February 12, 1969, 21. For examples from later in the war, see letter from 1st Lieutenant Joseph S. Dolan, "Letters to the Editor," *NYT*, July 13, 1969, E13; "Weary of the Army, GIs in Vietnam Marching to a Different Drummer," *Newsday*, January 13, 1971, 5.

58. "Absence Makes the Heart Grow Fonder," *Tropic Topics*, October 1943.

59. "Write the Right Letter," *Vogue*, June 1, 1944, 148. Molly Mayfield, "Ask Mrs Mayfield," *The Sun*, June 10, 1969, B7.

60. UP, "Some Wives Hurt Soldiers' Morale: Letters Asking Divorces Upset Men Abroad – Red Cross Also Warns on Gossip," *NYT*, January 8, 1945, 20; Pfau, "'Allotment Annies,'" 104–105. For ARC internal debate on how to handle, or rebuff, the growing volume of servicemen's requests that Red Cross field workers investigate allegations of spousal infidelity, see Folder 618.3, "Family Problems and Disagreements," box 983, Group 3, 1935–46, Records of the American National Red Cross, RG 200, NARA.

61. Mike Davis, "Vietnam Conversation," *Afro-American*, July 22, 1967, A5.

62. "Soldier Slays Girl and Self," *Chicago Daily Tribune*, September 3, 1919. For a more extended contemporary discussion of the ethics of wife-killing, see Hall Caine, "Has a Man a Right to Kill His Wife?," *Washington Post*, March 17, 1918, ES12.

63. Enlisted man, 1st Infantry, APO 6, quoted in "Censorship Survey of Morale, Rumors, Propaganda," April, July 1945, box 24, RG 496.

64. Pvt. Leo Dykes letters to Lawyer Dykes, March 17, 1944, August 17, 1944 and January 31, 1945; John Hope Franklin Research Center for African and African American History, Rubenstein Library, Duke University. For biographical information on Dykes, see Will Hansen, "New Acquisitions: Family Letters from the Segregated Armed Forces," June 28, 2013, https://blogs.library.duke.edu/rubenstein/2013/06/28/new-acquisitions-family-letters-from-the-segregated-armed-forces/.

65. Will V. Neely, "Clean Up Your House, Warns GI Correspondent, to Our Erring, Lonely War Wives," *Pittsburgh Courier*, May 19, 1945, 9.

66. Huebner, *Warrior Image*, 89. For two Korean war cases, "Girl Shot Dead in Church: Soldier Uses Gun at Crowded Service, Then Kills Himself," *NYT*, December 31, 1951, 6; "Soldier Jilted Kills Sweetheart, Sister Then Poisons Self," *Philadelphia Tribune*, July 23, 1953, 2; on

Vietnam, Robert S. Laufer and M.S. Gallops, "Life-Course Effects of Vietnam Combat and Abusive Violence: Marital Patterns," *Journal of Marriage and the Family* 47, 4 (November 1985): 839–853. There's a growing literature on what the military now refers to as "intimate partner violence" perpetrated by veterans, particularly focusing on the role of PTSD; see Erin P. Finley et al., "Patterns and Perceptions of Intimate Partner Violence Committed by Returning Veterans with Post-traumatic Stress Disorder," *Journal of Family Violence* 25 (2010): 737–743; April A. Gerlock et al., "Comparing Intimately Violent to Non-violent Veterans in Treatment for Posttraumatic Stress Disorder," *Journal of Family Violence* 31 (2016): 667–678. For an example of a "Dear John defense," absent any Dear John letter, see Art Harris, "The Hero and the Cheatin' Heart: Desert Storm Is Still Claiming Victims. A Story of Love and Betrayal," *Washington Post*, August 11, 1991, F1.

67. "Grace Moore Assails Trifling Soldier Wives," *LAT*, July 28, 1945, 3.
68. On Pellecchia, "Soldiers' Unfaithful Wives Beware," *Stars and Stripes*, August 6, 1945; Pfau, "'Allotment Annies,'" 102.
69. On the punishment of women for "fraternization" in France and Germany, see Mary Louise Roberts, *What Soldiers Do: Sex and the American GI in World War II France* (Chicago, IL: University of Chicago Press, 2013), 78–83; Fabrice Virgili, *Shorn Women: Gender and Punishment in Liberation France* (Oxford: Berg Publishers, 2002); Perry Biddiscombe, "Dangerous Liaisons: The Anti-fraternization Movement in the U.S. Occupation Zones of Germany and Austria, 1945–1948," *Journal of Social History* 34, 3 (2001): 611–647. Patton quoted by Adela Rogers St.John, *The Honeycomb* (New York: Doubleday & Co., 1969), 89. That Dear John letters were murderous was a theme that reverberated in some British military circles too; Linderman, *World within War*, 311.

CHAPTER 3

1. On the perils of letter-writing as an asynchronous activity, Christopher Hager, *I Remain Yours: Common Lives in Civil War Letters* (Cambridge, MA: Harvard University Press, 2018), 137–138.
2. Susan L. Carruthers, *The Media at War: Communication and Conflict in the Twentieth Century* (Basingstoke: Palgrave Macmillan, 2010), 242–248; Susan L. Carruthers, "Communications Media, the U.S. Military, and the War Brought Home," in *At War: The Military and American Culture in the Twentieth Century and Beyond*, eds. David Kieran and Edwin A. Martini (New Brunswick, NJ: Rutgers University Press, 2018), 258–278.
3. "The Importance of Being Terse," Mail Call, *Yank*, September 26, 1943, 29.
4. Judy Barrett Litoff and David C. Smith , "'Will He Get My Letter?': Popular Portrayals of Mail and Morale during World War II," *Journal of Popular Culture* (Spring 1990): 21–43. "Kodak created, U.S. Government adopts 'V . . . -MAIL' . . . for communication with our men on distant fronts," advertisement for Kodak, *Redbook* 80, 1 (November 1942): 75.
5. "Using V-Mail," Mail Call exhibition, Smithsonian National Postal Museum, https://postalmuseum.si.edu/exhibition/victory-mail/using-v-mail; "V-Mail's Limitations," https://postalmuseum.si.edu/exhibition/victory-mail-using-v-mail/v-mails-limitations; "Report on sending mail to servicemen," courtesy of the Library of Congress, Marine Corps Combat Recordings RGA 8763 PNO 22–25.

6. "Sure it'd be easy with 'Scotch Tape,'" advertisement for Scotch Tape, *Ladies' Home Journal* 62, 6 (June 1945): 53; "Make your spare moments his big moments by V-mail," advertisement for Stanley Wessel & Company, *Good Housekeeping* 120, 5 (May 1945): 228; "Instead of marking time . . . I'm making love by V-mail," advertisement for Stanley Wessel & Company, *Good Housekeeping* 120, 6 (June 1945): 147; "'The problem that gave me V-Mail letter trouble – but doesn't any more," advertisement for Castoria, *Ladies' Home Journal* 62, 2 (February 1945): 136.

7. V-mail from Privates Matt Kornblowski, Bill Barnes, Fred Worcester, and Charles Gentry to Anne Gudis, September 25, 1943, folder 12, box 2, KFP.

8. V-mail from Cpl. J. Schlett and S/Sgt. W. Yource [?], 1028th Sig Co. [n.d] to Anne Gudis, folder 12, box 2, KFP.

9. V-mail from Lt. Leonard Paul to Anne Gudis, September 16, 1943, folder 12, box 2, KFP.

10. V-mail from Pfc T. D'enformanto [?] to Anne Gudis, September 26, 1943, folder 12, box 2, KFP.

11. On casualty notification by telegram, which might be delayed by a week to ten days while a body was identified, see Franc Shor, "Letters from Home," *LAT*, March 19, 1944, F4. On Anne Gudis and Sam Kramer's first missed connection, Judy Barrett Litoff and David C. Smith, *Since You Went Away: World War II Letters from American Women on the Home Front* (Lawrence, KS: University Press of Kansas, 1991), 53.

12. Letter from Sam Kramer to Anne Gudis, July 16, 1942; telegram from Sam Kramer to Anne Gudis, July 16, 1942, folder 5, box 1, KFP.

13. Frank Neill, "Soldiers on the Line," *The Sun* (Baltimore), December 13, 1942, MS7.

14. Memo from Robert S. Wilson, ARC National Headquarters, to Mr. DeWitt Smith, "Free Telephone Calls for Patients Returning from Overseas Theaters," October 23, 1944, folder 618.9, box 988, Group 3, 1935–46, Records of the American Red Cross, RG 200.

15. "Soldier Phones from Hawaii to Passaic, Hears Girl Say 'Yes,'" *New York Herald Tribune*, August 13, 1942, 19.

16. Tom Nawrocki interview with Jessica VanGorder, November 30, 2010, AFC/2001/001/76363, VHP; Dennis Brodkin interview with Shaun Illingworth and Mohammad Athar, April 29, 2015, transcript p. 49, Rutgers Oral History Archives, https://oralhistory.rutgers.edu/interviewees/1737-brodkin-dennis.

17. Morton G. Ender, "G.I. Phone Home: The Use of Telecommunications by the Soldiers of Operation Just Cause," *Armed Forces & Society* 21, 3 (Spring 1995): 435–453; Larry W. Applewhite and David R. Segal, "Telephone Use by Peacekeeping Troops in the Sinai," *Armed Forces and Society* 17, 1 (Fall 1990): 117–126; D. Bruce Bell et al., "The Desert Fax: A Research Note on Calling Home from Somalia," *Armed Forces & Society* 25, 3 (Spring 1999): 509–521.

18. For a rare recent article that *does* mention Dear John phone calls, see Sydney J. Freedberg Jr., "When the Troops Come Home," *National Journal*, September 18, 2010, 9.

19. Morris Finder, "That's All She Wrote," *American Speech* 32, 3 (November 1957): 238–239.

20. Eli Ginzberg, *The Ineffective Soldier: Lessons for Management and the Nation. Vol. III. Patterns of Performance* (New York: Columbia University Press, 1959), 41.

21. "Wax Letters Latest Fad for Soldiers," *Afro-American*, March 7, 1942, 13.

22. Associated Press, "Phonograph Messages for Overseas Prohibited," *New York Herald Tribune*, July 6, 1943, 24.

23. On "talking letters" in Korea, folder 618.9, box 1282, Group 4 (1947–1964), RG 200. On "Voices from Home," folder 618.9, box 45, Group 5 (1965–1979), RG 200.

24. "Vietnam War Audio Correspondence," Mail Call exhibition, Smithsonian National Postal Museum, www.si.edu/es/object/npm_2011.2020.1.

25. Robert Taylor, "Tapes: This War's Cherished Link between Home and Vietnam," *Boston Globe*, May 19, 1968, A3.

26. Taylor, "Tapes"; Meredith H. Lair, *Armed with Abundance: Consumerism and Soldiering in the Vietnam War* (Chapel Hill, NC: University of North Carolina Press, 2011); Ralph A. Henry, ARC HQ Far Eastern Area, to Jane Betterly, National Director, SMVH, August 15, 1966; Boyd Work to Pete Upton, February 23, 1971, both in folder 618.9, box 45, Group 5, RG 200.

27. Robert C. Paul, Director Office of Public Relations, to Pete Upton, National Director, Office of Public Relations, "Voices from Home Program," February 22, 1971, folder 618.9, box 45, Group 5, RG 200.

28. Marie Youngberg, National Director, Services for Military Families, to John Dugan, National Director, Service at Military Installations, April 19, 1965, folder 618.9, box 45, RG 200.

29. Ibid.

30. Edward A. Turville, Chairman, 1967 Committee on Resolutions, to Carter Kissell, Chairman, Greater Cleveland Chapter, May 16, 1967, folder 618.9, box 45, Group 5, RG 200.

31. "Love Story," *M*A*S*H*, season 1, episode 14, first broadcasted January 7, 1973.

32. AP, "More 'Dear John' Letters Blamed on War Backlash," *Austin Statesman*, April 29, 1969, 3; Dr. Joyce Brothers, "'Dear John' Syndrome Takes Its Bitter Toll in Vietnam," *Boston Globe*, June 6, 1969, 20; Emanuel Tanay, "The Dear John Syndrome during the Vietnam War," *Diseases of the Nervous System* 37, 3 (March 1976): 165.

33. AP, "More 'Dear John' Letters," 3; Tanay, "Dear John Syndrome," 165.

34. I encountered just one oral history in which the veteran interviewee recalled another man having received a Dear John accompanied by a photograph depicting the sender with her new boyfriend. The letter in question also announced that she was keeping the soldier's engagement ring. Theodore Charles Graziani interview with Eileen Hurst, August 18, 2015, AFC/2001/001/101967, VHP.

35. Anthony Swofford, *Jarhead: A Marine's Chronicle of the Gulf War and Other Battles* (New York: Scribner, 2003), 65; *Jarhead*, dir. Sam Mendes, Universal Pictures, 2005.

36. David Mikkelson, "Dear John Video," last updated April 26, 2005, www.snopes.com/fact-check/video-bye-bye/.

37. Andrew Husband, "Military Vet Catches Wife Cheating in Truly Depressing Viral Video," July 31, 2015, www.mediaite.com/online/military-vet-catches-wife-cheating-in-

truly-depressing-viral-video/. For readers' comments on Dear Johns, "Kaboom: A Soldier's War Journal," "Dear John," December 26, 2007, http://kaboomwarjourna larchive.blogspot.com/2007/12/dear-john.html; "Dear John Letters," A Minute Longer: A Soldier's Tale, July 8, 2003, rooba.net.

38. Ender, "G.I. Phone Home"; Carruthers, "Communications Media," 264; Pat Matthews-Juarez, Paul D. Juarez , and Roosevelt T. Faulkner, "Social Media and Military Families: A Perspective," *Journal of Human Behavior in the Social Environment* 23 (2013): 769–776; Hope Hodge Seck, "The End of MotoMail," *Marine Corps Times*, September 23, 2013, 3.

39. Lizette Alvarez, "An Internet Lifeline for Troops in Iraq and Loved Ones at Home," *NYT*, July 8, 2006, A1.

40. Lisa Silvestri, *Friended at the Front: Social Media in the American War Zone* (Lawrence, KS: University Press of Kansas, 2015); James Dao, "Military Announces New Social Media Policy," *NYT*, February 26, 2010. On ongoing oversight by officers, Staff Sgt. Patrick D. Ward, "Social Media Postings: Should Marine Leaders Monitor Their Marines?," *Marine Corps Gazette* 95 (November 2011): 81–83.

41. Andy J. Merolla, "Relational Maintenance during Military Deployment: Perspectives of Wives of Deployed US Soldiers," *Journal of Applied Communication Research* 38, 1 (February 2010): 4–26; Jennifer Rea et al., "The Role of Online Communication in the Lives of Military Spouses," *Contemporary Family Therapy* 37 (2015): 329–339; Sarah P. Carter and Keith D. Renshaw, "Spousal Communication during Military Deployment: A Review," *Journal of Family Issues* 37, 16 (2015): 2309–2332; Katheryn C. Maguire, Daria Heinemann-LaFave, and Erin Sahlstein, "'To Be So Connected, Yet Not At All': Relational Presence, Absence, and Maintenance in the Context of a Wartime Deployment," *Western Journal of Communication* 77, 3 (2013): 249–271.

42. Leonard Wong and Stephen Gerras, "CU @ The FOB: How the Forward Operating Base Is Changing the Life of Combat Soldiers," Strategic Studies Institute, US Army War College, Carlisle, PA, https://ssi.armywarcollege.edu/faculty-staff/author-bio-wong/. See also LTC Susan W. Durham, "In Their Own Words: Staying Connected in a Combat Environment," *Military Medicine* 175 (August 2010): 554–559.

43. Maureen Daly, "Write Right!," *Chicago Daily Tribune*, April 4, 1943, D9.

44. On the inhibiting sensation of having "nothing new to say," Ramon Hinojosa, Melanie Sberna Hinojosa, and Robin S. Högnäs, "Problems with Veteran–Family Communication during Operation Enduring Freedom/Operation Iraqi Freedom Military Deployment," *Military Medicine* 177 (February 2012): 192. On spouses' percep-tions of "withholding," Talya Greene et al., "How Communication with Families Can Both Help and Hinder Service Members' Mental Health and Occupational Effectiveness on Deployment,"*Military Medicine* 175 (October 2010): 747.

45. Durham, "In Their Own Words," 558.

46. Joseph Raimond Oltman, interview with Mary Kelley, member of Bend Chapter, Daughters of the American Revolution, September 15, 2014, AFC/2001/001/97996, VHP.

47. Col. Thomas S. Stefanko, interview with Eileen Hurst, n.d., AFC/2001/001/102712, VHP.

48. Hinojosa et al., "Problems with Veteran–Family Communication," 195.

49. *U.S. Army Deployment Cycle Readiness: Soldier's and Family Member's Handbook* (2008), 62–63, www.myarmy.onesource.com, Deployment_Cycle_Readiness_Handbook-1.pdf; Department of Defense, *Military Deployment Guide: Preparing You and Your Family for the Road Ahead* (February 2012), 131; *The Fleet and Family Support Center, Deployment Support Handbook* (Commander, Navy Installations Command, 2015), 25. For similarly worded advice about sitting on letters overnight issued during the Vietnam war, see Emily Post, *The Emily Post Book of Etiquette for Young People* (New York: Funk & Wagnalls, 1967), 81.

50. *U.S. Army Deployment Cycle Readiness: Soldier's and Family Member's Handbook*, 131.

51. Dan Harris, "Digital Heartbreak," ABC Nightline, March 30, 2015.

52. Alison Batdorff, "Home–Front Connection: A Blessing or a Burden? Technology Gives Some Soldiers Relief and Others Stress,"*Stars and Stripes*, October 9, 2007, www.stripes.com/news/home-front-connection-a-blessing-or-a-burden-1.69717.

53. Robin Gail Ault, interview with Rebecca Wiggenhorn, May 15, 2010, Clark State Community College, Greene Center, Beavercreek, Ohio, AFC/2001/001/76220, VHP. On dumping by Facebook chat, Silvestri, *Friended at the Front*, 49, 51. See also "Kaboom" blog, http://kaboomwarjournalarchive.blogspot.com/2007/12/dear-john.html.

54. Anonymous soldier quoted in "Morale Report, APO 922," January 31, 1944, folder "Censorship Survey of Morale, 1943–45," box 24, Entry 553, Records of the GHQ Southwest Pacific Area and U.S. Army Forces, Pacific, RG 496; Anonymous enlisted man, quoted in APO 6, box 9, Entry 551, G-2 Office of the Chief of Counter Intelligence; Theater Censor. Correspondence with Base Censors, 1944–45, RG 496.

55. "Censorship Survey of Morale – Rumors. Propaganda." APO 501, April 1945, box 24, RG 496. Ann Elizabeth Pfau, *Miss Yourlovin: GIs, Gender, and Domesticity during World War II* (New York: Columbia University Press/Gutenberg e-book, 2008), introduction, www.gutenberg-e.org/pfau/introduction.html. See also Ann Pfau, "Postal Censorship and Military Intelligence during World War II," unpublished paper delivered at the Winston M. Blount Postal History Symposium, Smithsonian National Postal Museum, September 27, 2008.

56. Military History Branch, Headquarters Military Assistance Command, Vietnam [MACV],*Command History*, 1966, "Postal Operations," box 5, Entry A1 32, RG 472.

57. MACV,*Command History*, 1967, vol. II, "Postal Operations," box 3, Entry A1 32, RG 472.

58. Carruthers, "Communications Media," 262–263.

59. "Have You Written a Soldier Today?,"*Afro-American*, September 11, 1943, 3.

60. On today's "false sense of connection," Jean Scandlyn and Sarah Hautzinger, *Beyond Post-traumatic Stress: Homefront Struggles with the Wars on Terror* (Walnut Creek, CA: Left Coast Press, 2014), 23–24.

CHAPTER 4

1. "Soldiers' 'Love Insurance' Now Has Heart Balm Clause," *LAT*, February 3, 1942, 8.

2. "'Lost Love' Dividend Won: Soldier's 'Insurance' Provides Him $15 and Date with Film Starlet," *LAT*, February 15, 1942; "Hollywood Night Club Tour Awaits Corporal," *LAT*, February 14, 1942; for the photo, "Lost 'Love Insurance' Nets Soldier Date with Actress," *LAT*, February 16, 1942, A1.

3. Sgt. Ed Cunningham, "Jilted G.I.s in India Organize First Brush-Off Club," *Yank* (China–Burma–India Edition), January 13, 1943, 5; "Here's How to Start a Brush-Off Club Branch," *Yank* (New York Edition), July 16, 1943.

4. Kenneth L. Dixon, "Business Is Booming for the Brushoff Club," *Washington Post*, October 10, 1943, B5; Associated Press, "Yanks' New Year's Eve in Naples Noisy, but Far from Cheerful," *Washington Post*, January 2, 1944, M19; Chris Cunningham, "Florida Girl Left Austin Newspaperman Eligible for Brush-Off Club in Algiers," *Austin Statesman*, November 5, 1943; Associated Press, "Brush-Off Club Is Formed for Jilted Servicemen," *Washington Post*, March 31, 1944, 5. The African American press also reported on this phenomenon; see, for example, Chequita Cynthia, "Service Men's Service," *New York Amsterdam News*, November 20, 1943, 16.

5. TSgt. Robert Kerr, Information Section, First Marine Division, "The Deep Six," *Leatherneck* (December 1954): 62–63.

6. LCpl. Tom Kidman, "A Common 'Enemy': Retaliation Is a Bummer," *Sea Tiger* (III Marine Amphibious Force) 5, 22 (May 30, 1969): 12.

7. On the "Good Hunting Committee," Cynthia, "Service Men's Service"; INS, "Film Queens Help Six Jilted Soldiers Forget Home Girls," *Washington Post*, April 4, 1942, 19.

8. Milton Bracker, "What to Write the Soldier Overseas," *NYT Magazine*, October 3, 1943, SM14.

9. J. E. Lightner (ed.), *Random House Historical Dictionary of American Slang* (New York: Random House, 1994), "Dear John"; John Costello, *Love, Sex and War: Changing Values, 1939–45* (London: William Collins, 1985), 273–274; Lee Kennett, *GI: The American Soldier in World War II* (New York: Charles Scribner's Sons, 1987), 75–76; Kenneth D. Rose, *Myth and the Greatest Generation: A Social History of Americans in World War II* (New York: Routledge, 2008), 109; Ann Pfau, *Miss Yourlovin* (New York: Columbia University Press, 2008), chapter 1, www.gutenberg-e.org/pfau. The longest discussion of Anne Gudis's relationship with Sam Kramer is provided by Judy Barrett Litoff and David C. Smith, *Since You Went Away: World War II Letters from American Women on the Home Front* (Lawrence, KS: University Press of Kansas, 1991), 53–63. A less scholarly collection of women's breakup notes also mentions Anne Gudis's V-mail, Anna Holmes, *Hell Hath No Fury: Women's Letters from the End of the Affair* (New York: Ballantine Books, 2002), 168.

10. Cunningham, "Jilted G.I.s"; letter from Ahmed S. to "Mail Bag," *Yank*, August 18, 1944, 16; "The Importance of Being Terse," *Yank*, September 26, 1943, 29.

11. Hal Boyle quoted in "American Soldiers Abroad," *American Speech* 19, 4 (December 1944), 310; Dixon, "Business is Booming for the Brushoff Club."

12. Letter from Anne Kramer to Professor David Smith, January 20, 1989, folder 48, box 2, KFP.

13. On the fluidity of veterans' memory and oral testimony, see Adam R. Seipp, "Buchenwald Stories: Testimony, Military History and the American Encounter with the Holocaust," *Journal of Military History* 79, 3 (July 2015): 721–744. Likewise, what historians deem significant in veterans' oral histories shifts in tandem with evolving interpretive paradigms: Philip F. Napoli et al., "Oral History, Moral Injury, and Vietnam Veterans," *Oral History Review* 46, 1 (2019): 71–103.

14. R. M. Duncan, "Dear John," *American Speech* 22, 3 (October 1947): 187.

15. Homer Holbrook, interview with Joe Brookner, August 16, 2013, AFC/2001/001/ 92159, VHP; James W. Allen, interview with Judith Kent, December 20, 2020, AFC/ 2001/001/03391, VHP; Terry O. Engelhardt, interview with Theodore Ekdahl, n.d., AFC/2001/001/66616, VHP.

16. Archie Parmelee Kelley, interview with Robert King, April 5, 2013, AFC/2001/001/ 8959, VHP; Ben Greene, interview with Margaret Castro, n.d., AFC/2001/001/89205, VHP; Fred Lamp, interview with Mary McCord, September 11, 2003, AFC/2001/001/ 27015, VHP; John Chervenko, interview with Paul Sinders, n.d., transcript, https:// memory.loc.gov/diglib/vhp/story/loc.natlib.afc2001001.00721/transcript?ID=sr0001, AFC/2001/001/00721, VHP; William Clifford Welby, interview with Carol Berg, September 19, 2005, AFC/2001/001/48475, VHP; Wayne A. White, interview with Samantha Richardson, n.d., AFC/2001/001/48342, VHP; Michael B. Ruggiero, interview with Shaun Illingworth, January 28, 2013, transcript p. 40, https://oralhistory.rut gers.edu/interviewees/1784-ruggiero-michael-b, Rutgers Oral History Archive [hereafter ROHA]; Richard K. Butters, interview with Branden Butters, September 9, 2012, AFC/2001/001/23823, VHP; Doyle W. Causey, interview with Mark Doud, April 30, 2002, AFC/2001/001/01257, VHP; James Williams Rockwell, interview with Joshua Shore, November 15, 2014, AFC/2001/001/98851, VHP; Pastor Toro, Jr., interview with Matthew Boccio, n.d., AFC/2001/001/69109, VHP.

17. Leonard Thomas Newton, interview with Gabe Newton, n.d., AFC//2001/001/98544, VHP.

18. Alison Lefkovitz, "'The Peculiar Anomaly': Same-Sex Infidelity in Postwar Divorce Courts," *Law and History Review* 33, 3 (August 2015): 665–701.

19. Hal Boyle, "GI Joe Goes Into Decline If Babe at Home Forgets," *Austin Statesman*, November 5, 1943, 19.

20. Gerard Arnold Streelman, interview with William Streelman, May 9, 2007, AFC/2001/ 001/105595, VHP. Stories like this didn't spring from imagination alone. For an account of a nineteen-year-old soldier whose wife had an affair with her father-in-law while her husband (his son) was at war, see Alton E. Carpenter and A. Anne Eiland, *Chappie: World War II Diary of a Combat Chaplain* (Mesa, AZ: Mead Publishing, 2007), 97.

21. Streelman interview; David A. Dennis, oral history interview, n.d., www.ww2online.org /view/david-dennis, National World War II Museum, New Orleans. Another common quip ran, "Dear John, I'm sorry, but I've decided to marry the mailman"; Wayne C. Booth, *My Many Selves: The Quest for a Plausible Harmony* (Logan, UT: Utah State University Press, 2006), 162.

22. Sgt. Malvin Wald, "The Timetable for a Brush-Off," *Yank*, November 4, 1942, 19.

23. Arthur H. Taylor, interview with Michael Willie, March 30, 2005, AFC/2001/001/ 32806, VHP; Harry Clayton Rives, interview with Mary Morris, March 30, 2007, AFC/ 2001/001/58583, VHP.

24. Chester Matyjasik, interview with Thomas Swope, June 3, 2003, transcript, https:// memory.loc.gov/diglib/vhp/story/loc.natlib.afc2001001.07705/transcript?ID=s r0001, AFC/2001/001/07705, VHP.

25. Arthur Wiknik, interview with Kelly Crager, November 11, 2008, OH0650, transcript pp. 90–91, the Vietnam Center and Sam Johnson Vietnam Archive, TTU.

26. Theodore R. Cummings, interview with Eileen Hurst, September 20, 2010, AFC/2001/ 001/78232, VHP.

27. John Newsom, interview with Da Vinci High School Veterans at War Project, November 20, 2013, AFC/2001/001/93450, VHP.

28. Charlotte Johnson, National Director, Home Service to Mr. Hepner, October 21, 1942; Memo from Mr. Bondy to Area Administrators, Services to Armed Forces, Re. "Policy on Requests for Assistance with Divorce Problems," January 30, 1943; both in folder 618.3, box 983, Group 3 (1935–46), RG 200.

29. The ARC issued public pleas that "busybodies" cease "passing on … unfounded gossip"; UP, "Some Wives Hurt Soldiers' Morale: Letters Asking Divorces Upset Men Abroad – Red Cross Also Warns on Gossip," *NYT*, January 8, 1945, 20; Ann Pfau, "Allotment Annies and Other Wayward Wives: Wartime Concerns about Female Disloyalty and the Problem of the Returned Veteran," in *The United States and the Second World War: New Perspectives on Diplomacy, War, and the Home Front*, eds. G. Kurt Piehler and Sidney Pash (New York: Fordham University Press, 2010), 104–105.

30. Charles W. McDougall, interview with G. Kurt Piehler and Pete Mele, November 9, 1996, transcript. p.32, https://oralhistory.rutgers.edu/interviewees/1107-mcdougall-charles-w, ROHA.

31. James Thomas Wayne, interview with Amanda Hopkins, n.d., AFC/2001/001/10433, VHP.

32. For instance, Vietnam veteran and poet W. D. Ehrhart complains that his girlfriend's Dear John was "brief, alien, and distant – less than half a page," ending, "'Please forgive me,'" W. D. Ehrhart, *Passing Time: Memoir of a Vietnam Veteran against the War* (Amherst, MA: University of Massachusetts Press, 1995 [1986]), 132.

33. Peter Smith, *A Cavalcade of Lesser Horrors* (Minneapolis, MN: University of Minnesota Press, 2011), 122–125.

34. Alva L. Smith, interview with George Bray, n.d., AFC/2001/001/104362, VHP; Theodore Cummings interview.

35. For a published example of this framing of a Dear John, see Andrew Carroll, *War Letters: Extraordinary Correspondence from American Wars* (New York: Scribner, 2001), 215.

36. Cecil E. Waite, interview with Paul Beckworth, May 6, 2016, AFC/2001/001/104916, VHP. For other veterans' Dear John stories that end in a happy marriage to someone other than the letter's sender, see also Bryce E. Erickson, interview with Jennifer J. Einspahr, May 23, 2005, AFC/2001/001/39327, VHP; Robert S. Ray, Jr., interview with Susan Few, February 9, 2012, AFC2001/001/82591, VHP; Tom S. Belovich,

interview with Thomas Swope, May 29, 2003, AFC/2001/001/07676, VHP; John M. Roberts, interview with Daniel Brightwell, September 16, 2010, AFC/2001/001/73743, VHP.

37. Arthur H. Taylor interview.

38. Claude Orville Bryant, interview with Brian M. Allen, n.d., AFC/2001/001/73462, VHP.

39. "The Nation: The Way Home," *Time*, August 7, 1944, 16, quoted by Rose, *Myth and the Greatest Generation*, 107.

40. See, for example, a version posted online by a Vietnam veteran, "Cherrieswriter," that purports to be from a Marine stationed in Afghanistan; "Mail Call in Vietnam – Dear John ...," https://cherrieswriter.com/2013/11/01/mail-call-in-vietnam-dear-john/. More recent versions of this story reference men mailing pornographic images – sent with breakup notes by former girlfriends, who depicted themselves with new boyfriends – back to the woman's parents.

41. "Operations Board," *Yank*, April 28, 1944, 7; see Pfau, *Miss Yourlovin*, chapter 1.

42. Anthony Swofford, *Jarhead: A Marine's Chronicle of the Gulf War and Other Battles* (New York: Scribner, 2003), 92.

43. On men crying and getting drunk, Eliseo Perez-Montalvo, interview with Richard Verrone, July 15/August 5, 2003, transcript, p. 53, OH0314, TTU.

44. Robert Bernard Willis, interview with Tabitha de Guzman, December 2, 2007, AFC/2001/001/58575, VHP.

45. Stephen W. Dant, interview with Richard Verrone, May 18, 2005, transcript, pp. 101–102, TTU.

46. Philip Caputo, *A Rumor of War* quoted by William Broyles, Jr., "Why Men Love War," *Esquire*, May 23, 2014 [November 1984], www.esquire.com/news-politics/news/a28718/why-men-love-war/.

47. Megan MacKenzie, *Beyond the Band of Brothers: The US Military and the Myth That Women Can't Fight* (Cambridge: Cambridge University Press, 2015), 19–41.

48. MacKenzie, *Beyond the Band of Brothers*, 42–72; Erin Solaro, *Women in the Line of Fire: What You Should Know about Women in the Military* (Emeryville, CA: Seal Press, 2006); G. L. A. Harris, *Living Legends and Full Agency: Implications of Repealing the Combat Exclusion Policy* (Boca Raton, FL: CRC Press/Taylor & Francis, 2015).

49. Stephanie McCurry, *Women's War: Fighting and Surviving the American Civil War* (Cambridge, MA: Harvard University Press, 2019), 2. Nurses commonly found themselves required to undertake this kind of recuperative work for men under their care. See Jane E. Schultz, "The Inhospitable Hospital: Gender and Professionalism in Civil War Medicine," *Signs: A Journal of Women in Culture and Society* 17, 2 (1992): 363–392; Kimberly Jensen, "'A Base Hospital Is Not a Coney Island Dance Hall': American Nurses, Hostile Work Environment, and Military Rank in the First World War," *Frontiers: A Journal of Women's Studies* 26, 2 (2005): 206–235; Charissa Threat, *Nursing Civil Rights: Gender and Race in the Army Nurse Corps* (Urbana, IL: University of Illinois Press, 2015); Kara Dixon Vuic, *Officer,*

Nurse, Woman: The Army Nurse Corps in Vietnam (Baltimore, MD: Johns Hopkins University Press, 2010).

50. On USO workers in World War II, Meghan K. Winchell, *Good Girls, Good Food, Good Fun: The Story of USO Hostesses during World War II* (Chapel Hill, NC: University of North Carolina Press, 2008); and for a more comprehensive history of women entertainers in war zones, Kara Dixon Vuic, *The Girls Next Door: Bringing the Home Front to the Front Lines* (Cambridge, MA: Harvard University Press, 2019).

51. Mary Thomas Sargent, *Runway towards Orion: The True Adventures of a Red Cross Girl on a B-20 Air Base in World War II India* (Grand Rapids, MI: The Triumph Press, 1984), 108–109, quoted by Vuic, *Girls Next Door*, 88.

52. Helen Hegelheimer, interview with Laura Calkins, June 15, 2004, transcript, p. 61, OH0367, TTU.

53. Juliet Macur, "In the Line of Fire," *NYT*, November 20, 2005, 16.

54. Bruce Rader, interview with Maria Jones, April 18, 2010, AFC/2001/001/94901,VHP. Chodleros de Laclos, *Dangerous Liaisons* (London: Penguin, 2007 [1782]), trans. Helen Constantine.

55. Edwin A. Kolodziej, interview with Neal A. Hammerschlag and Sandra Stewart Holyoak, February 16, 2001, transcript p. 13, https://oralhistory.rutgers.edu/interviewees/1041-kolodziej-edwin, ROHA.

56. Donald James McLennan, interview with Josef Buntic, n.d., AFC/2001/001/49271, VHP.

57. Ibid.

58. Wald, "Timetable for a Brush-Off"; Arnold Sias Garza, Jr., interview with Lauren Varga, n.d., AFC/2001/001/104186, VHP.

59. Patrick Vellucci, interview with Rebecca Schwarz and Sandra Stewart Holyoak, December 9, 2010, transcript p. 48, https://oralhistory.rutgers.edu/interviewees/137 9-vellucci-patrick, ROHA. On American men's attitudes toward American women in Vietnam, Heather Marie Stur, *Beyond Combat: Women and Gender in the Vietnam War Era* (Cambridge: Cambridge University Press, 2011), chapters 2 and 3.

60. W. D. Snodgrass, "Love and/or War," *Georgia Review* 46, 1 (Spring 1992): 97–112.

61. Letter from Anne Gudis to Sam Kramer, January 1944, KFP.

62. Andrew J. Huebner, *The Warrior Image: Soldiers in American Culture from the Second World War to the Vietnam Era* (Chapel Hill, NC: University of North Carolina Press, 2008), 89–90.

63. Erskine Caldwell, *Claudelle Inglish* (Boston, MA: Little, Brown, 1959); David Sanders, "Just Blame It All on Imperfect Love," *Washington Post*, March 29, 1959, E7; "*Claudelle* In Debut Run," *LAT*, October 7, 1961, B7. Not all reviewers were favorably impressed. For a negative take, see Robert Kirsch, "New Caldwell Novel Disappoints," *LAT*, March 17, 1959, B5.

64. Dorothy Zmuda, interview with Kathy Borkowski, June 16, 1992, "Wisconsin Women during World War II Oral History Project," Wisconsin Historical Society, Madison, WI. See also Violet Cowden, interview with Beth Carmichael, May 3, 2007, transcript, p. 7,

http://libcdm1.uncg.edu/cdm/singleitem/collection/WVHP/id/4298/rec/1, "Women Veterans Historical Project," UNC-Glassboro.

65. On military wives and infidelity, Cynthia Enloe, *Manuevers: The International Politics of Militarizing Women's Lives* (Berkeley, CA: University of California Press, 2000), chapter 5; Betty Alt and Bonnie Stone, *Uncle Sam's Brides: The World of Military Wives* (New York: Walker and Company, 1990), chapter 4. On higher rates of divorce among female personnel in the contemporary military, see Kenona H. Southwell, "The Many Faces of Military Families: Unique Features of the Lives of Female Service Members," *Military Medicine* 181, 1 (2016): 71; Benjamin R. Karney and John S. Crown, *Families under Stress: An Assessment of Data, Theory, and Research on Marriage and Divorce in the Military* (Santa Monica, CA: RAND Corporation, 2007).

66. Mattie E. Treadwell, *The Women's Army Corps* (Washington, DC: Government Printing Office, 1954), chapter 11, https://history.army.mil/books/wwii/Wac/ch11.htm; Leisa D. Meyer, *Creating GI Jane: Sexuality and Power in the Women's Army Corps during World War II* (New York: Columbia University Press, 1996), chapter 2; M. Michaela Hampf, "'Dykes' or 'Whores': Sexuality and the Women's Army Corps in the United States during World War II," *Women's Studies International Forum* 27 (2004): 13–30.

67. These comments were written by enlisted men and found by officers censoring their correspondence; Treadwell, *Women's Army Corps*, 211–212, and n. 89.

68. Toby Newman (née Kafka), interview with Frank Gradl, March 4, 2015, AFC/2001/001/100500, VHP.

69. Letter from "Del" to June Wandrey, n.d., and letter from June Wandrey to family, n.d., reproduced in Carroll, *War Letters*, 248–249. For other female veterans' recollections of Dear Janes sent during World War II, see WAC veteran Martha Kemper, interview with Richard Lugar, n.d., AFC/2001/001/29720, VHP; and WAVE veteran Marie Brand Voltzke, self-interview, n.d., AFC/2001/001/02884, VHP.

70. Joan Craigwell, former USAF nurse, quoted in *San Diego Tribune*, May 4, 1988.

71. "The Gals Back Home," *Yank* (British edition), January 3, 1943, 17.

72. Letter from "A WAC" to the B-Bag, May 20, 1945, *Stars and Stripes* (London edition), May 26, 1945, 2.

73. Boyle, "GI Joe Goes Into Decline If Babe at Home Forgets."

74. Hal Boyle, "Army Brush-Off Club Now Has Women's Auxiliary," *LAT*, December 5, 1943, 23; "Brush Off Club (Girls)," letter by Louise M. Cozine, President WABOC, *Stars and Stripes* (London edition), May 26, 1945, 2. For the "fastest growing" claim, see "American Soldiers Abroad," *American Speech*, 19, 4 (December 1944), 310.

75. Letter from Ralph W. Berry, Robert L. Johnson, and Derald D. Hageman, "Postwar Plans," *LAT*, March 5, 1945, A4.

76. Marcia Winn, "Front Views and Profiles," *Chicago Daily Tribune*, March 5, 1945, 12.

77. Michael Russell, "Suicide and Suicide Prevention," in *When The Warrior Returns: Making the Transition at Home*, eds. Nathan D. Ainspan and Walter E. Penk (Annapolis, MD: Naval Institute Press, 2012), 107.

78. Francine Banner, "'It's Not All Flowers and Daisies': Masculinity, Heteronormativity and the Obscuring of Lesbian Identity in the Repeal of 'Don't Ask, Don't Tell,'" *Yale Journal of Law and Feminism* 24, 1 (2012): 61–117.
79. Linda Lee, "A Night Out with 16 Angry Women: Hasta La Vista, Baby," *NYT*, October 27, 2002, H4.
80. Miss Information, "Free Advice for Lovelorn Lads," *New York Tribune*, June 23, 1918, E6.
81. "Jilted, Sues as Soldier Brings War Bride Home: Girl Scorned for Maid of France Shows 468 Love Notes," *CDT*, July 10, 1919, 19.
82. Letter from Mrs. Signy Fisher to Chaplain Jim, July 27, 1942; Chaplain Leighton E. Harrell to Mrs. Signy Fisher, August 27, 1942, Box 23, Entry 1, RG 247, NARA.
83. Bill Mauldin, *Up Front* (New York: Henry Holt, 1945), 24.

CHAPTER 5

1. On the politics of prisoner negotiation and homecoming, Michael J. Allen, *Until the Last Man Comes Home: POWs, MIAs, and the Unending Vietnam War* (Chapel Hill, NC: University of North Carolina Press, 2009). For the numbers and timing of prisoner-takings, 17–18; and the fact that 84 percent of the POWs were airmen, of whom 88 percent were officers, 41. Kathy Sawyer, "POWs: Picking Up the Pieces," *Washington Post*, December 4, 1975, E11.
2. On "Burst of Joy," Bill Beaumont-Thomas, interview with Sal Veder, "Sal Veder's Best Photograph: A Vietnam POW's Joyful Reunion with His Family," *The Guardian*, October 8, 2015, www.theguardian.com/artanddesign/2015/oct/08/sal-veder-best-photograph-vietnam-pow-joyful-reunion-with-family; Carolyn Kleiner Butler, "Coming Home," *Smithsonian Magazine* (January 2005), www.smithsonianmag.com/history/coming-home-10 6013338/.
3. Butler, "Coming Home."
4. Stephen Isaacs, "Nixon Probes Win Pulitzer Prizes," *Washington Post*, May 7, 1974, A3.
5. Ronit Y. Stahl, *Enlisting Faith: How the Military Chaplaincy Shaped Religion and State in Modern America* (Cambridge, MA: Harvard University Press, 2017), 225; Butler, "Coming Home."
6. "'It Has Taken Me to the Cleaners': State Divorce Law Costly to Former POW," *LAT*, December 18, 1973, A3; "Former P.O.W. Is Divorced," *NYT*, March 13, 1974, 15.
7. Nancy Faber, "A POW's Marriage Ends Bitterly," *People*, April 1, 1974; George Esper, "POW's Homecoming a Picture of Joy, But a Tapestry of Sadness," *LAT*, July 4, 1993, A1, A24.
8. The 60 percent "Dear John mortality rate" was estimated by Douglas Ramsay, the only diplomat to have been taken prisoner in Vietnam; quoted by Sawyer, "POWs: Picking Up the Pieces." In reality, the divorce rate among former POWs was around 30 percent. For a discussion of the meanings ascribed to POW marriages and their dissolution, see Natasha Zaretsky, *No Direction Home: The American Family and the Fear of National Decline, 1968–1980* (Chapel Hill, NC: University of North Carolina Press, 2007), chapter 1.

9. Houston MacIntosh, "Separation Problems in Military Wives," *American Journal of Psychiatry* 125, 2 (August 1968): 260–265.

10. Schilling Manor in Salina, Kansas, formerly Schilling Air Force Base, which was repurposed as a community for the wives and children of men serving in Vietnam, attracted particular attention, both during the war and thereafter, as a uniquely pertinent site in which to investigate the "waiting wife." See Dorothy Brockhoff, "The Colonel's Ladies," *Washington University Magazine* (Summer 1968): 2–9; "'Waiting Wives' of Ft. Riley Called Country's Most Unique," *Atlanta Daily World*, February 8, 1968, 3; LTC Harold E. Allen, "Schilling Manor: A Survey of a Military Community of Father Absent Families," PhD dissertation, Catholic University of America (1972); Donna Moreau, *Waiting Wives: The Story of Schilling Manor, Home Front to the Vietnam War* (New York: Atria Books, 2005).

11. On casualty notification telegrams, Megan Harris, "Beyond 'I Regret to Inform You,'" Veterans History Project blog post, February 23, 2015, https://blogs.loc.gov/folklife/2015/02/beyond-i-regret-to-inform-you/. Some relatives of POW/MIAs relate visits from chaplains who broke the news that a loved one was missing in a more personal way. See, for example, Jim Stockdale and Sybil Stockdale, *In Love and War: The Story of a Family's Ordeal and Sacrifice during the Vietnam Years* (Annapolis, MD: Naval Institute Press, 1990), 119–120.

12. For comparisons with World War II and Korea, see Allen, *Until the Last Man*, 2.

13. Figures from Allen, *Until the Last Man*, 17–18. Memo for the record by Samuel Krakow, Director, International Service, September 26, 1967, "American Prisoners in Vietnam," box 55, Group 5 (1965–79), RG 200.

14. ARC memo, January 24, 1972, box 55, Group 5 (1965–79), RG 200.

15. Allen, *Until the Last Man*, 170.

16. Dorothy Cameron Disney, "How P.O.W. Marriages Were Saved," *Ladies' Home Journal* (March 1974): 12; Craig Howes, *Voices of the Vietnam POWs: Witnesses to Their Fight* (Oxford: Oxford University Press, 1993).

17. Peter Arnett, "New Ordeal for Ex-POW – the Heartbreak of Divorce," *LAT*, April 22, 1973, 4.

18. Gerald F. Linderman, *The World within War: America's Combat Experience in World War II* (New York: Free Press, 1997), 311; Lieut. Col. Alfred Torrie, "The Return of Odysseus: The Problem of Marital Infidelity for the Repatriate," *British Medical Journal* 2, 4414 (August 11, 1945): 192.

19. Kushner quoted by Ken Ringle, "A POW Wife's Angry, Endless Wait," *Washington Post*, July 4, 1972, A1; William Claiborne, "POWs Get Better Reception," *Washington Post*, May 6, 1973, A16.

20. Stockdale and Stockdale, *In Love and War*, 135–137.

21. Major A. W. Gratch, USAF, Directorate of Personnel Services, Memo, "Mail Procedures – North Vietnam," n.d. (1967), box 55, RG 200.

22. Gratch, "Mail Procedures – North Vietnam." This memo is also quoted at length in a contemporary novel, based on substantial research, about POW/MIA wives that includes excerpts from several official documents: Joan Silver and Linda Gottlieb, *Limbo* (New York: The Viking Press, 1972), 43.

NOTES TO PAGES 154–158

23. On the reduction in size of the pro forma letter that Hanoi would permit, see Joe Kraft, Interview with US POWs detained in North Vietnam, July 1972, Folder 203D, Background Material PW Mail & Packages, box 1, Entry UD-O4W 151, Records of the Office of the Secretary of Defense, RG 330, NARA. On the television war and body counts, Daniel Hallin, *The "Uncensored War": The Media and Vietnam* (New York: Oxford University Press, 1989).

24. Allen, *Until the Last Man*, 38. For more on COLIAFAM, see oral history with Cora Weiss, Columbia University, https://static1.squarespace.com/static/575a10ba27d4bd5 d7300a207/t/57601b8d9f7266ebae932dbc/1465916301804/Weiss_Cora_2014.pdf.

25. Samuel Krakow, Director, International Service, Memo (not for circulation), n.d., box 55, RG 200.

26. Miller quoted by Thomas Fortune, "Surviving Controversy, Former POW Starts on New Life," *LAT*, December 16, 1973, 1.

27. Dorothy Gallagher, "A P.O.W. Wife's Dilemma," *Redbook* (July 1972): 138, 141. Many accounts state that six lines was the limit, but this doesn't appear to have been a universal rule. A magazine feature on Sybil and Jim Stockdale related that she was permitted to send letters using two pages of airmail stationary; Evan McLeod Wylie, "At Least I Know Jim's Alive," *Good Housekeeping* 170, 2 (February 1970): 218.

28. Mary Lou Loper, "Wives of POWs Fighting for 'Forgotten Americans,'" *LAT*, February 5, 1970, C8; John Saar, "Day of Drama for MIA Families," *Washington Post*, January 29, 1973, A19.

29. Nan Robertson, "P.O.W. Wives Await Peace with Joy and Dread," *NYT*, December 6, 1972, 32.

30. Powers quoted by Robertson, "P.O.W. Wives," 32.

31. Mrs. George S. Patton, letter to the editor, *Washington Post*, January 21, 1973, PC7. Patton's letter praised a long feature that the *Post* had carried some months earlier, Aileen Jacobson, "Waiting Wives," September 3, 1972, PO7.

32. Silver and Gottlieb, *Limbo*; *Limbo*, dir. Mark Robson, Universal Pictures, 1972. The movie did not garner critical plaudits: Charles Champlin, "*Limbo* Finds Its Own Limbo," *LAT*, February 28, 1973, H1. On Vietnam cinema, see Linda Dittmar and Gene Michaud (eds.), *From Hanoi to Hollywood: The Vietnam War in American Film* (New Brunswick, NJ: Rutgers University Press, 1990). Tellingly, this collection of essays makes no mention of *Limbo*.

33. Kathleen Reardon Boynton and W. Barnett Pearce, "Personal Transitions and Interpersonal Communication among Submariners' Wives," in *Military Families: Adaptation to Change*, eds. Edna J. Hunter and D. Stephen Nice (New York: Praeger Publishers, 1978), 130.

34. Most states set the limit at seven years; www.law.cornell.edu/wex/enoch_arden_doc trine. Anon., "Second Marriage and the Enoch Arden Laws," *Good Housekeeping* 148, 3 (March 1959): 133–134.

35. Both Homer's Penelope and Tennyson's Enoch Arden had earlier surfaced in World War II-era discussions and depictions of homecoming veterans and their marriages. See James I. Deutsch, "Piercing the Penelope Syndrome: The Depiction of World War II

Veterans' Wives in 1940s Hollywood Film," *Humboldt Journal of Social Relations* 16, 1 (1990): 31–42; Grace Sloan Overton, *Marriage in War and Peace: A Book for Parents and Counselors of Youth* (Nashville, TN: Abingdon-Cokesbury Press, 1945), 188.

36. On Tangee Alvarez, Zaretsky, *No Direction Home*, 48–49. On Charlie Plumb, Howes, *Voices of the Vietnam POWs*, 146. Plumb's wife filed for divorce on the grounds of "abandonment," a claim that Plumb's lawyer publicly rubbished, noting that his client had been away from home "by reason of forcible detention by the North Vietnamese"; UPI, "Citing 'Abandonment' POW Wife Asks Divorce," *Washington Post*, February 21, 1973, A12; Leroy F. Aarons, "Ex-POW: Re-entering a New World," *Washington Post*, February 18, 1973, A1. On POW divorces in captivity, see also "POW, Wife Try to Start Again," *Afro-American*, March 10, 1973, 1, 2.

37. Everett R. Holles, "U.S. Planned More Gradual Homecoming for POWs," *NYT*, September 30, 1972, 10; Loudon Wainwright, "When Johnny Comes Marching Home Again – or Doesn't," *Life*, November 10, 1972, 32–39.

38. On the ARC's role in these homecoming arrangements, see correspondence in folder 619.2 SEASIA, box 52, Group 5 (1965–79), RG 200.

39. Maj. Charles H. Schmidt and Capt. Thomas J. McNamara, "After Action Report on 'Operation Homecoming,'" April 11, 1973, box 10, Entry A1 1A, RG 247; Stahl, *Enlisting Faith*, 224–225.

40. Schmidt and McNamara, "After Action Report."

41. Schmidt and McNamara, "After Action Report."

42. Allen, *Until the Last Man*, n. 44, 326; Leroy F. Aarons, "Quiet Reception Awaits Returning POWs at California Base," *Washington Post*, February 13, 1973, A11.

43. Wainwright, "When Johnny Comes Marching Home"; Michael Getler, "Medical Personnel, Air Crews Alerted for POWs' Return," *Washington Post*, January 24, 1973, A7; Allen, *Until the Last Man*, 69–76.

44. Howes, *Voices of the Vietnam POWs*; Zaretsky, *No Direction Home*, 28.

45. D. Stephen Nice et al., "The Families of US Navy Prisoners of War from Vietnam Five Years after Reunion," *Journal of Marriage and Family* 43, 2 (May 1981): 431–437; Catherine L. Cohan, Steven Cole, and Joanne Davila, "Marital Transitions among Vietnam-Era Repatriated Prisoners of War," *Journal of Social and Personal Relationships* 22, 6 (2005): 777–795.

46. Dr. John Plag and Dr. Edna Hunter quoted by Dave Smith, "Vietnam POWs Rebuild Their Lives: Not All Have Trouble Adjusting to Freedom," *LAT*, September 8, 1976, 4.

47. Four of Brudno's letters to Deborah appear in facsimile form in Bernard Edelman's anthology, *Dear America: Letters Home from Vietnam* (New York: W. W. Norton & Company, 2002 [1985]), 265–268.

48. Wolfgang Saxon, "Despondent P.O.W. Apparent Suicide: New Yorker Was among First North Vietnamese Freed," *NYT*, June 4, 1973, 7; UPI, "Former POW Kills Himself – 'Life Is Not Worth Living,'" *LAT*, June 4, 1973, 2; AP, "POW – from 'Rebirth' to Baffling Suicide," *LAT*, June 5, 1973, A10; "Air Force Making 'Deep' Study of Suicide by Indochina P.O.W.," *NYT*, June 5, 1973, 6; AP, "Suicide's Tensions Revealed," *Washington Post*, June 6, 1973, A20. Rabbi David J. Jacobs' remarks were reported,

slightly differently, by AP, "Suicide's 'Dream' Soured: Former POWs Lay a Comrade to Rest," *LAT*, June 9, 1973, 5, and by Colman J. Sullivan, "Ex-POW, 'Overwhelmed' by Ideals, Is Buried," *Washington Post*, June 9, 1973, D6. See also Howes, *Voices of the Vietnam POWs*, 145; Allen, *Until the Last Man*, 75.

49. Peter Arnett, "In an 'Emotional Wringer': New Ordeal for Ex-POW – the Heartbreak of Divorce," *LAT*, April 22, 1973, 1; Steven V. Roberts, "P.O.W. Wives Who Chose New Life Face Dilemma," *NYT*, March 6, 1973, 10.

50. Washington Irving, "Rip Van Winkle," www.gutenberg.org/files/19721/19721-h/197 21-h.htm#RIP_VAN_WINKLE; Wainwright, "When Johnny Comes Marching Home," 36.

51. "Report of the DOD PW/MIA Rehabilitation/Readjustment Study Panel," January 1972, Tab C, p. 7, "Families of the Repatriates," Entry UD-O4W 151, box 1, RG 330.

52. MacIntosh, "Separation Problems." Constantine J. G. Cretekos, "Common Psychological Syndromes of the Army Wife," *Military Medicine* 138, 1 (1973): 36.

53. William C. Menninger, *Psychiatry in a Troubled World: Yesterday's War and Today's Challenge* (New York: MacMillan, 1948); Steuart Henderson Britt and Jane D. Morgan, "Military Psychologists in World War II," *American Psychologist* 1, 10 (October 1946): 423–437; Ellen Herman, *The Romance of American Psychology: Political Culture in the Age of Experts* (Berkeley, CA: University of California Press, 1995), chapter 4; Paul Wanke, "American Military Psychiatry and Its Role among Ground Forces in World War II," *Journal of Military History* 63 (1999): 127–46; Ben Shephard, *A War of Nerves: Soldiers and Psychiatrists 1914–1994* (London: Pimlico, 2002).

54. Reuben Hill, *Families under Stress: Adjustment to the Crises of War Separation and Reunion* (New York: Harper, 1949). See also the work of one of Hill's collaborators, Elise Boulding, "Family Adjustments to War Separation and Reunion," *The Annals of the American Academy of Political and Social Science* 272 (November 1950): 59–67.

55. Helene Deutsch, *Psychology of Women: A Psychoanalytic Interpretation* (New York: Grune and Stratton, 1944); Evelyn Millis Duval, "Loneliness and the Serviceman's Wife," *Marriage and Family Living* 7, 4 (November 1945): 77–81; Edward C. McDonagh, "The Discharged Serviceman and His Family," *American Journal of Sociology* 51, 5 (March 1946): 451–454; Edward C. McDonagh and Louise McDonagh, "War Anxieties of Soldiers and Their Wives," *Social Forces* 24, 2 (December 1945): 195–200.

56. McDonagh and McDonagh, "War Anxieties," 198. For a different appreciation, focused on GIs' psychology, of the pressures wives confronted to sustain the illusion that neither "home" nor they themselves had altered during their spouse's absence, see W. Edgar Gregory, "The Idealization of the Absent," *American Journal of Sociology* 50, 1 (July 1944): 53–54.

57. Susan L. Carruthers, *Cold War Captives: Imprisonment, Escape, Brainwashing* (Berkeley, CA: University of California Press, 2009), chapter 5.

58. Bowlby's insights derived from psychoanalytic work undertaken with children suffering from anxiety disorders in postwar London; John Bowlby, "Separation Anxiety," *International Journal of Psycho-Analysis* 41, 1–2 (1960): 89–113. Intriguingly, the

concept of "separation anxiety" had earlier been employed (around the time Bowlby began his work with infants) by Navy psychiatrists keen to decipher how and why some naval personnel exhibited anxiety about return to civilian life prior to separation from the service. Commander J. J. V. Cammisa and Commander James Clark Moloney, "Separation Anxiety," *Mental Hygiene* 31 (April 1947): 229–236.

59. Richard A. Isay, "The Submariners' Wives Syndrome," *Psychiatric Quarterly* 42, 4 (1968): 647–652; Chester A. Pearlman, "Separation Reactions of Married Women," *American Journal of Psychiatry* 126, 1 (January 1970): 946–950; Cretekos, "Common Psychological Syndromes"; Douglas R. Bey and Jean Lange, "Waiting Wives: Women under Stress," *American Journal of Psychiatry* 131, 3 (March 1974): 283–286.

60. Isay, "Submariners' Wives Syndrome," 649.

61. Bey and Lange, "Waiting Wives." On the strong social prohibitions against wives' infidelity in military communities, see also R. C. W. Hall and W. C. Simmons, "The POW Wife: A Psychiatric Appraisal," *Archives of General Psychiatry* 29 (November 1973): 690–694.

62. The Center's objectives are set out in Edna J. Hunter, "Families in Crisis: The Families of Prisoners of War," Report 77–45, Naval Health Research Center, 1977, 1–3. By the time of Operation Homecoming, researchers with the Center had personally interviewed over 50 percent of all POW/MIA families.

63. Holles, "U.S. Planned More Gradual Homecoming," 10.

64. M. McCubbin and H. McCubbin, "Family Stress Theory and Measurement: The T-Double ABCX Model of Family Adjustment and Adaptation," in *Family Assessment Inventories for Research and Practice*, eds. H. McCubbin and A. Thompson (Madison, WI: University of Wisconsin Press, 1987): 3–32.

65. Hunter, "Families in Crisis," 11.

66. Hamilton I. McCubbin, Barbara B. Dahl, Gary R. Lester, and Beverly A. Ross, "The Returned Prisoner of War: Factors in Family Reintegration," *Journal of Marriage and The Family* 37, 3 (August 1975): 477.

67. Loretta Stirm's letter quoted by Esper, "POW's Homecoming a Picture of Joy."

68. Edna J. Hunter, "Combat Casualties Who Remain at Home," *Military Review* 60, 1 (January 1980): 31; Hunter quoted by Smith, "Vietnam POWs Rebuild Their Lives," 4.

69. McCubbin et al., "Returned Prisoner of War," 477.

70. Zaretsky, *No Direction Home*, 44–49. At around 35–40 percent, the RPW divorce rate was "really not too different from divorce rates generally in the United States today," noted Dr. Hunter, "Combat Casualties," 31.

71. Esper, "POW's Homecoming."

72. Disney, "P.O.W. Marriages," 112; Larry Chesley, *Seven Years in Hanoi: A POW Tells His Story* (Salt Lake City, UT: Bookcraft, 1973).

73. Zaretsky, *No Direction Home*, 48.

74. Everett Alvarez with Anthony S. Pitch, *Chained Eagle* (New York: Donald I. Fine, 1989). On POW memoirists' discursive alignment of faithless wives with the North Vietnamese, Zaretsky, *No Direction Home*, 49.

75. Alvarez, *Chained Eagle*, 238–242. Elliott Gruner, *Prisoners of Culture: Representing the Vietnam POW* (New Brunswick, NJ: Rutgers University Press, 1993), 98. Alvarez later claimed that his publishers had urged him to play up this angle.

76. Ernest C. Brace, *A Code to Keep* (New York: St. Martin's Press, 1988), 252. See also Allen, *Until the Last Man*, 75, citing Stuart I. Rochester and Frederick Kiley, *Honor Bound: American Prisoners of War in Southeast Asia, 1961–1973* (Annapolis, MD: Naval Institution Press), 587.

77. Charlie Plumb and Glen H. DeWerf, *i'm no hero* (Independence, MO: Independence Press, 1973), 277–279. In Craig Howes's analysis of POW memoirs, *i'm no hero* delivered "the most calculated and relentless POW account of marital betrayal"; Howes, *Voices of the Vietnam POWs*, 146. Gruner, *Prisoners of Culture*, n. 23, 213–214.

78. UPI, "Former P.O.W. Divorced," *NYT*, June 24, 1973, 42; Ben A. Franklin, "Ex-P.O.W. Seeks Money Paid to Wife," *NYT*, June 30, 1981, A12.

79. Paul Farhi, "The Separate Peace of John and Carol," *Washington Post*, October 6, 2008.

80. Steven V. Roberts, "Prisoners: Thoughts on Reentering 'The World,'" *NYT*, February 18, 1973, 246.

81. Michael Satchell, "Half of POWs Face Divorces," *The Star*, August 4, 1973, clipping TTU VNCA. For an account of one African American RPW couple struggling with this issue, Kathy Sawyer, "Fighting for a Marriage," *Washington Post*, December 4, 1975, E1, E18.

82. Robert S. Andersen, "Operation Homecoming: Psychological Observations of Repatriated Prisoners of War," *Psychiatry* 38 (February 1975): 69.

83. Zaretsky, *No Direction Home*, 47.

84. Jerry Lembcke, *Hanoi Jane: War, Sex and Fantasies of Betrayal* (Amherst, MA: University of Massachusetts Press, 2010). On the politics of memory, see Allen, *Until the Last Man*; Patrick Hagopian, *The Vietnam War in American Memory: Veterans, Memorials, and the Politics of Healing* (Amherst, MA: University of Massachusetts Press, 2009). On the gender politics of Reagan-era revisionism, Susan Jeffords, *The Remasculinization of America: Gender and the Vietnam War* (Bloomington, IN: Indiana University Press, 1989).

85. On VIVA and conservative activism on POW/MIA issues, Sandra Scanlon, *The Pro-war Movement: Domestic Support for the Vietnam War and the Making of Modern American Conservatism* (Amherst, MA: University of Massachusetts Press, 2013). Stockdale and Stockdale, *In Love and War*; Dorothy McDaniel, *After the Hero's Welcome: A POW Wife's Story of the Battle against a New Enemy* (Chicago, IL: Bonus Books, Inc., 1991).

86. William Claiborne, "Ex-prisoner Denies Illegal Acts in Hanoi," *Washington Post*, June 29, 1973, A14. An earlier report suggested that political differences weren't the only contributory factors in this marital breakdown. Mrs. Miller had reportedly secured a restraining order against her violent husband on May 31; "Wife Charges Abuse: POW Named in Misconduct Action Faces Divorce Suit," *LAT*, June 23, 1973, C1.

87. Fortune, "Surviving Controversy."

88. *The Hanoi Hilton*, dir. Lionel Chetwynd, Cannon Film Distributors, 1987. On the trope of the adulterous POW wife-as-traitor in prisoner movies, see Gruner, *Prisoners of Culture*, chapter 4; Maureen Ryan, "Pentagon Princesses and Wayward Sisters:

Vietnam POW Wives in American Literature," *WLA: War, Literature and the Arts: An International Journal of the Humanities* 10, 2 (1998): 132–164.

89. Stephen Howard, "The Vietnam Warrior: His Experience, and Implications for Psychotherapy," *American Journal of Psychotherapy* 30, 1 (January 1976): 121–135; Emanuel Tanay, "The Dear John Syndrome during the Vietnam War," *Diseases of the Nervous System* 37, 3 (March 1976): 165–167.

90. Tanay, "Dear John Syndrome"; Bey and Lange, "Waiting Wives," 284. On public opinion and the war, John Mueller, *War, Presidents and Public Opinion* (New York: John Wiley, 1973); Hallin, *The "Uncensored War"*; Marilyn B. Young, *The Vietnam Wars, 1945–1990* (New York: HarperPerennial, 1991).

91. John M. Dell Vecchio, *The Thirteenth Valley* (New York: Bantam, 1983), 109; Kalí Tal, "The Mind at War: Images of Women in Vietnam Novels by Combat Veterans," *Contemporary Literature* 31, 1 (Spring 1990): 85.

92. Winston Groom, *Better Times Than These* (New York: Pocket Books, 1994 [1978]); Tal, "The Mind at War," 88.

93. W. D. Ehrhart, *Vietnam–Perkasie: A Combat Marine Memoir* (Amherst, MA: University of Massachusetts Press, 1995), 2, 131–136. On the pervasiveness of this trope in Vietnam veterans' memoirs, John A. Wood, *Veteran Narratives and the Collective Memory of the Vietnam War* (Athens, OH: Ohio University Press, 2016), 72.

94. W. D. Ehrhart, *Passing Time: Memoir of a Vietnam Veteran against the War* (Amherst, MA: University of Massachusetts Press, 1995 [1986]), 132.

95. Jane Whitbread, "How Servicemen's Marriages Survive Separation," *Redbook* 132, 6 (April 1969): 94.

CHAPTER 6

1. Winston Groom, *Better Times Than These* (New York: Pocket Books, 1994 [1978]), 368. Christopher Lehmann-Haupt, "Books of the Times," review of *Better Times Than These, NYT*, June 28, 1978, C24; William Fadiman, "With the 'Freshmeat' on the Vietnam Front," *LAT*, October 1, 1978, N8; L. J. Davis, "Dispatches from the Combat Zone," *Washington Post*, July 9, 1978, E5.

2. Dennis Wayne Nicks, interview with Martin Madert, n.d., AFC/2001/001/111483, VHP.

3. George S. Rostron, Jr., interview with Mike Farrar, May 8, 2012, AFC/2001/001/86408, VHP. For testimony recounting similar incidents from the Korean war, see Joseph Monteleone, interview with Charles Jennings, October 18, 2016, AFC/2001/001/106881, VHP; John Newsom, interview with Da Vinci High School Veterans at War Project, November 20, 2013, AFC/2001/001/93450, VHP.

4. Raymond Scurfield, *Vietnam Trilogy: Veterans and Post Traumatic Stress* (New York: Algora Publishing, 2004), 52. See also Richard A. Gabriel, *No More Heroes: Madness and Psychiatry in War* (New York: Hill and Wang, 1987), 53; Major Douglas R. Bey and S-5 Water E. Smith, "Mental Health Technicians in Vietnam," *Bulletin of the Menninger Clinic* 34, 6 (November 1, 1970): 363–371; Douglas Bey, *Wizard 6: A Combat Psychiatrist in Vietnam* (College Station, TX: Texas A&M University Press, 2006), esp. 93–94; James D. Johnson,

Combat Chaplain: A Thirty-Year Vietnam Battle (College Station, TX: Texas A&M University Press, 2001), 88, 147, 236, 237; Col. Joseph W. Cooch, "What Is Military Medicine?," *Military Medicine* 133, 4 (April 1968): 293. On self-mutilation and Dear John letters, Tracy Kidder, *My Detachment: A Memoir* (New York: Random House, 2005), 73.

5. Constantine J. K. Cretekos, "Common Psychological Syndromes of the Army Wife," *Military Medicine* 138, 1 (1973): 36.

6. Boyd quoted by Susan J. Matt, *Homesickness: An American History* (New York: Oxford University Press, 2011), 93. On Union soldiers and home more generally, Reid Mitchell, *The Vacant Chair: The Northern Soldier Leaves Home* (New York: Oxford University Press, 1993).

7. Matt, *Homesickness*, 96.

8. Union soldier Charles Mattock quoted by Matt, *Homesickness*, 93–94.

9. Frances Clarke, "So Lonesome I Could Die: Nostalgia and Debates over Emotional Control in the Civil War North," *Journal of Social History* 41, 2 (Winter 2007): 254. Clarke references Eric T. Dean, Jr., *Shook over Hell: Post-traumatic Stress, Vietnam, and the Civil War* (Cambridge, MA: Harvard University Press, 1997) and John E. Talbot, "Combat Trauma in the American Civil War," *History Today* 46 (1996): 41–47.

10. On the origins of the PTSD diagnosis and its association with the antiwar commitments of both veterans and psychiatrists, Patrick Hagopian, "The Politics of Trauma: Vietnam Veterans and PTSD," *Mittelweg* 36, 5 (2015): 72–87.

11. Matt, *Homesickness*, 94.

12. On masculinity in the Civil War era, Lorien Foote, *The Gentlemen and the Roughs: Manhood, Honor, and Violence in the Union Army* (New York: New York University Press, 2010); Stephen W. Berry, II, *All That Makes a Man: Love and Ambition in the Civil War South* (New York: Oxford University Press, 2002). On letter-writing, Clarke, "So Lonesome I Could Die," 268–270; Robert E. Bonner, *The Soldier's Pen: Firsthand Impressions of the Civil War* (New York: Hill and Wang, 2006), chapter 6; Christopher Hager, *I Remain Yours: Common Lives in Civil War Letters* (Cambridge, MA: Harvard University Press, 2018).

13. Rebecca Jo Plant, "The Veteran, His Wife and Their Mothers: Prescriptions for Psychological Rehabilitation after World War II," in *Tales of the Great American Victory: World War II in Politics and Poetics*, eds. Diederik Oostdijk and Markha Valenta (Amsterdam: VU University Press, 2006): 95–105.

14. Alice Fahs, *The Imagined Civil War: Popular Literature of the North and South* (Chapel Hill, NC: University of North Carolina Press, 2001), 107.

15. This was not a unanimously shared professional opinion. Some physicians thought married men more vulnerable to nostalgia, linking this malady to a strong libido and masturbation. They regarded the latter practice as indicative of men indulging in fantasies of the connubial lives they'd left behind; Matt, *Homesickness*, 95, 96.

16. Susan Zeiger, "She Didn't Raise Her Boy to Be a Slacker: Motherhood, Conscription, and the Culture of the First World War," *Feminist Studies* 22, 1 (Spring 1996): 6–39.

17. Ben Shephard, *A War of Nerves: Soldiers and Psychiatrists, 1914–1994* (London: Pimlico, 2002 [2000]), chapter 8.

18. Louis Faugeres Bishop, Jr., "Soldier's Heart," *American Journal of Nursing* 42, 4 (April 1942): 377–380. See also R. McN. Wilson, "The Irritable Heart of Soldiers," *British Medical Journal* 1, 2873 (January 22, 1916): 119–120; B. S. Oppenheimer and M. A. Rothschild, "The Psychoneurotic Factor in the 'Irritable Heart' of Soldiers," *British Medical Journal* 2, 3002 (July 13, 1918): 29–31; Bernard Rostker, *Providing for the Casualties of War: The American Experience through World War II* (Santa Monica, CA: RAND Corporation, 2013), 98.

19. Merrill Moore, ms. paper, "The Psychoneuroses of War: Some Personal Impressions," box D191, Merrill Moore Papers [hereafter MMP], LOC.

20. On the psychiatric profession in World War II, Shephard, *A War of Nerves*; Ellen Herman, *The Romance of American Psychology: Political Culture in the Age of Experts* (Berkeley, CA: University of California Press, 1995), 82–123; Hans Pols, "War Neurosis, Adjustment Problems in Veterans, and an Ill Nation," *Osiris* 22, 1 (2007): 72–92.

21. Bishop, "Soldiers' Heart," 377–378.

22. On Gold Star Mothers, see Frances M. Clarke and Rebecca Jo Plant, "'The Crowning Insult': Federal Segregation and the Gold Star Mothers Pilgrimages of the Early 1930s," *Journal of American History* 101, 4 (September 2015): 406–432; Erika Kuhlman, *Of Little Comfort: War Widows, Fallen Soldiers, and the Remaking of the Nation after the Great War* (New York: New York University Press, 2012), chapter 3; Lisa M. Budreau, "The Politics of Remembrance: The Gold Star Mothers' Pilgrimage and America's Fading Memory of the Great War," *Journal of Military History* 72, 2 (2008): 371–411. On "mom" and "momism," Philip Wylie, *Generation of Vipers* (New York: Rinehart, 1942). For a similarly negative appraisal of American "matriarchy," see Henry Elkin, "Aggressive and Erotic Tendencies in Army Life," *American Journal of Sociology* 51, 5 (March 1946): 410–411. On the monstering of mothers in interwar America, Rebecca Jo Plant, *Mom: The Transformation of Motherhood in Modern America* (Chicago, IL: University of Chicago Press, 2010).

23. Moore, "A Report on Morale," p. 28, box D188, MMP.

24. J. L. Henderson and Merrill Moore, "The Psychoneuroses of War," *The Military Surgeon* (November 1944), box 1314, Records of the Office of the Surgeon General (Army), RG 112 NARA. On "mother attachment," see also Roy R. Grinker and John P. Spiegel, *Men under Stress* (Philadelphia, PA: Blakiston, 1945); Commander J. J. V. Cammisa and Commander James Clark Moloney, "Separation Anxiety," *Mental Hygiene* 31 (April 1947): 229–236. For a critique, Plant, *Mom*, 98–99.

25. Eli Ginzberg, *The Ineffective Soldier: Lessons for Management and the Nation* (New York: Columbia University Press, 1959), 108; Henderson and Moore, "Psychoneuroses of War."

26. Ginzberg, *Ineffective Soldier*, 108.

27. Matt, *Homesickness*, 203.

28. Grinker and Spiegel, *Men under Stress*, 182; Gerald F. Linderman, *The World within War: America's Combat Experience in World War II* (New York: Free Press, 1997), 308–309.

NOTES TO PAGES 189–193

29. "A Morale Study in the CBI Theater," August 21, 1944, pp. 21–22, folder HD: 730 (Neuropsychiatry) MORALE STUDY. Section III General Morale Factors, box 1312, RG 112.

30. Merrill Moore, "Report," p. 21, folder HD 730 (Neuropsychiatry) Morale South Pacific. Misc Reports), box 1312, RG 112. Moore's psychiatric case notes from patients treated during his wartime period of service occupy several boxes, archived as Series D of his personal papers at the Library of Congress.

31. Maj. Theodore Lidz, "Report of Medical Department Activities Southwest Pacific Area," March 26, 1945, p. 25, folder HD: 730 Neuropsychiatry May 1945. Morale and Psychiatry. ASF Report No. 16, box 1313, Entry 31 (ZI), RG 112. On the relationship between broken homes and susceptibility to neuro-psychiatric complaints, see also Grinker and Spiegel, *Men under Stress*, 9.

32. Moore, "Report," p. 26, RG 112. See also McDonagh and McDonagh, "War Anxieties of Soldiers and Their Wives," *Social Forces* 24, 2 (December 1945): 195–200.

33. R. E. Peek, "Nervous in the Service," mimeographed pamphlet, folder HD 730 (Neuropsychiatry) Neuroses, box 1314, RG 112. Few clinical accounts written during World War II explicitly reference Dear John letters named as such. But for an account of psychiatric symptoms, seemingly precipitated by a Dear John received by a soldier while stationed at Guam in 1943, and which had persisted for thirty years, see Joseph Wolpe, "Behavior Analysis of a Case of Hypochondriacal Anxiety: Transcript of First Interview," *Journal of Behavioral and Experimental Psychiatry* 1 (1970): 217–224.

34. Ginzberg, *Ineffective Soldier*, 41.

35. McDonagh and McDonagh, "War Anxieties of Soldiers and Their Wives," 197.

36. ARC correspondence on requests for emergency furloughs can be found in folder 618.3, Family Problems and Disagreements, box 983, Group 3 (1935–46), RG 200.

37. Ginzberg, *Ineffective Soldier*, 49–50.

38. Grinker and Spiegel, *Men under Stress*, 187; Albert N. Mayers, "Dug-out Psychiatry," *Psychiatry* 8 (November 1945): 386.

39. Samuel Futterman, "Changing Sex Patterns and the War," *Marriage and Family Living* 8, 2 (May 1946): 29.

40. Grinker and Spiegel, *Men under Stress*, 188.

41. Shephard, *War of Nerves*, chapters 23–24; Franklin Del Jones and Arnold W. Johnson, "Medical and Psychiatric Treatment Policy and Practice in Vietnam," *Journal of Social Issues* 31, 4 (1975): 49–65.

42. Stephen Howard, "The Vietnam Warrior: His Experience, and Implications for Psychotherapy," *American Journal of Psychotherapy* 30, 1 (January 1976): 121–135. Howard wasn't alone in this judgment. Ralph Gabriel notes a connection between Dear John letters and what he terms "nostalgia-related conditions," *No More Heroes*, 54; Larry E. Morris, "Over the Hump in Vietnam: Adjustment Patterns in a Time-Limited Stress Situation," *Bulletin of the Menninger Clinic* 34, 6 (November 1, 1970): 352–362; Emanuel Tanay, "The Dear John Syndrome during the Vietnam War," *Diseases of the Nervous System* 37, 3 (March 1976): 165–167.

43. Howard, "Vietnam Warrior," 123–126; on pulp magazines and masculinity, Gregory A. Daddis, *Pulp Vietnam: War and Gender in Cold War Men's Adventure Magazines* (New York: Cambridge University Press, 2020).

44. Statistic from Peter G. Bourne, *Men, Stress, and Vietnam* (Boston, MA: Little, Brown & Co., 1970), 43. On the lavish "comforts of home" provided to men at the rear, Meredith H. Lair, *Armed with Abundance: Consumerism and Soldiering in the Vietnam War* (Chapel Hill, NC: University of North Carolina Press, 2011).

45. Bourne, *Men, Stress, and Vietnam*, 40–42. On primary groups, Edward Shils and Morris Janowitz, "Primary Groups in the American Army," in *Center and Periphery: Essays in Macrosociology*, ed. Edward Shils (Chicago, IL: University of Chicago Press, 1975).

46. Morris, "Over the Hump in Vietnam," 360–362.

47. Moskos highlighted the phenomenon of GIs not keeping in touch with one another when buddies rotated back to the United States, noting: "The rupture of communication is mutual despite protestations of lifelong friendship during the shared combat period." Charles C. Moskos, "A Sociologist Appraises the G.I.," *NYT Magazine*, September 24, 1967, 131. Howard, "Vietnam Warrior." See also John A. Renner, Jr., "The Changing Patterns of Psychiatric Problems in Vietnam," *Comprehensive Psychiatry* 14, 2 (March/April 1973): 176–177; Charles C. Moskos, "The American Combat Soldier in Vietnam," *Journal of Social Issues* 31, 4 (1975): 29–30.

48. Richard P. Fox, "Narcissistic Rage and the Problem of Combat Aggression," *Archives of General Psychiatry* 31 (December 1974): 807–811. Howard also observed that "when death arrives, mourning lasts only a few minutes if it occurs at all"; "Vietnam Warrior," 126.

49. On veterans' violence toward female partners, Robert S. Laufer and M. S. Gallops, "Life-Course Effects of Vietnam Combat and Abusive Violence: Marital Patterns," *Journal of Marriage and the Family* 47, 4 (November 1985): 839–853.

50. On GI drinking culture in World War II, Paul Fussell, *Wartime: Understanding and Behavior in the Second World War* (New York: Oxford University Press, 1989), 96–114; on so-called "3.2 beer," James J. Cooke, *American Girls, Beer, and Glenn Miller: GI Morale in World War II* (Columbia, MS: University of Missouri Press, 2016), 34–35.

51. V-mail from 1st Sgt. Albert E. Martin, IV Special Service Company, US Army, to Anne Gudis, September 16, 1943, folder 12, box 2, KFP.

52. Kenneth John Brown, "How I Became a Chaplain's Assistant," September 1, 1944, Camp Pendleton, CA; Kenneth Brown interview with Scott Turner, March 22, 2017, AFC/2001/001/108632, VHP.

53. The defection of these prisoners provoked considerable controversy in the 1950s and early 1960s. For some of the most prominent contributions to this debate, see Virginia Pasley, *21 Stayed: The Story of the American GI's Who Chose Communist China: Who They Were and Why They Stayed* (New York: Farrar, Straus & Cudahy, 1955); Eugene Kinkead, *In Every War But One* (New York: Norton, 1959); Albert D. Biderman, *March to Calumny: The Story of American POW's in the Korean War*

(New York: Arno Press, 1963). For scholarly analyses of the POW "brainwashing scare," see Susan L. Carruthers, *Cold War Captives: Imprisonment, Escape, and Brainwashing* (Berkeley, CA: University of California Press, 2009), chapter 5; Charles S. Young, *Name, Rank, and Serial Number: Exploiting Korean War POWs at Home and Abroad* (New York: Oxford University Press, 2014); Brian D. McKnight, *We Fight for Peace: Twenty-Three American Soldiers, Prisoners of War, and "Turncoats" in the Korean War* (Kent, OH: The Kent State University Press, 2014).

54. Carruthers, *Cold War Captives*, 189–190; "A Prodigal and His Kin," *Life*, November 2, 1953, 45; "There's Joy in Crackers Neck," *Newsweek*, November 2, 1953, 22–23; "One Changed His Mind," *Time*, November 2, 1953, 25.

55. Robert Alden, "G.I. Who Quit Reds Just 'Feels Great,'" *NYT*, October 22, 1953, 2.

56. John H. Thompson, "Write a Letter to Lonely GI and Cure His Monday Blues," *Chicago Daily Tribune*, August 25, 1952, 1.

57. *A Dear John Letter*, written by Johnny Grimes, owned by Lewis Talley and Fuzzy Owen, and performed by Jean Shepard and Ferlin Husky, Capitol Records, May 1953. On this song and its sequel "Forgive Me John," see Ivan M. Tribe, "Purple Hearts, Heartbreak Ridge, and Korean Mud: Pain, Patriotism, and Faith in the 1950–53 'Police Action,'" in *Country Music Goes to War*, eds. Charles K. Wolfe and James E. Akenson (Lexington, KT: University Press of Kentucky, 2005), 135–136.

58. UP, "Romance May Await GI in Virginia Mountains," *Washington Post*, October 22, 1953, 6.

59. UP, "Romance May Await GI"; UP, "P.W. Hints Girl Trouble Made Him Choose Reds," *New York Herald Tribune*, October 22, 1953, 1; UP, "Mom Says Reds Doped 'Change of Heart' PW," *Atlanta Constitution*, October 23, 1953, 1. See also McKnight, *We Fight for Peace*, 149.

60. AP, "G.I. Who Chose Reds, Then Quit, Is Seized in Court-Martial Case," *NYT*, January 23, 1954, 3. Richard L. Lyons, "Anacostia Students Shine in Quiz Series," *Washington Post*, December 13, 1953, 29.

61. Warren Unna, "Family of POW Who 'Spurned' Reds Sees the Sights," *Washington Post*, November 22, 1953, M23.

62. "Report on interrogation of Edward Dickenson," Tokyo, box 144, Records of the Army Staff RG 319, NARA. See also materials in RG 319, box 143.

63. AP, "G.I. Who Chose Reds, Then Quit, Is Seized in Court-Martial Case," *NYT*, January 23, 1954, 1.

64. UP, "Army Trial Hears 2 Psychiatrists," *NYT*, April 29, 1954, 21; Elie Abel, "Army Convicts Dickenson of Collaborating with Reds," *NYT*, May 5, 1954, 1. Fred L. Borch, "Lore of the Corps: The Trial of a Korean War 'Turncoat': The Court-Martial of Corporal Edward S. Dickenson," *Army Lawyer* (March 2014): 30–33. On Dickenson's cooperative character, "Interrogation at Disciplinary Barracks, New Cumberland, PA," box 144, RG 319.

65. AP, "Korea Turncoat Ends Jail Term," *NYT*, November 24, 1957, 21; AP, "Turncoat GI Finishes 3½ Years in Army Prison, *LAT*, November 24, 1957, 19.

66. "USARV Defector to Sweden, SP4 Mark A. Shapiro," July 21, 1968, folder 228–03, box 13, Entry A1 749, RG 472.

67. On Shapiro and other antiwar defectors in Sweden, Matthew Sweet, *Operation Chaos: The Vietnam Deserters Who Fought the CIA, the Brainwashers and Themselves* (New York: Henry Holt and Company, 2018). A Swedish filmmaker produced a documentary about Shapiro and other deserters; *Deserter, USA*, dir. Lars Lambert, Lars Lambert Filmproduktion, 1969.

68. HQ 26th Infantry Division to Commanding General, II Field Force Vietnam, "Methods to Reduce AWOL and Desertion Rates," December 28, 1969, box 3, Entry A1 749, RG 472.

69. AP, "Young Marine Charged with 5 Viet Murders," *LAT*, August 10, 1968, 7; William Tuohy, "The Incident at Van Duong Bridge: Why?," *LAT*, September 30, 1968, 1, 6, 7; William Tuohy, "'The Worst U.S. Atrocity in Vietnam': 7 Marines Stand Trial," *LAT*, October 1, 1968, A12. The *Los Angeles Times* devoted far more coverage to this story than other prominent national newspapers, with the *Washington Post* neglecting it altogether and the *New York Times* running only brief inside-page reports from wire services. Tuohy would win a Pulitzer for his reporting on the case.

70. On Seymour Hersh and the breaking of the My Lai atrocity story, see Susan L. Carruthers, *The Media at War* (Basingstoke: Palgrave MacMillan, 2011), 109–110, and on My Lai more generally, Howard Jones, *My Lai: Vietnam, 1968, and the Descent into Darkness* (New York: Oxford University Press, 2017).

71. Joe Allen quoted by Tuohy, "Worst U.S. Atrocity."

72. McMath quoted by Tuohy, "Worst U.S. Atrocity"; Gary D. Solis, *Marines and Military Law in Vietnam: Trial by Fire* (Washington, DC: History and Museums Division, HQ, US Marine Corps, 1989), 111–113.

73. I have given this defendant a pseudonym. AP, "Marine Acquitted in Vietnam Killings," *NYT*, January 24, 1969, 3.

74. AP, "More 'Dear John' Letters Blamed on War Backlash," *Austin Statesman*, April 29, 1969, 3.

75. Tanay, "Dear John Syndrome," 165, 167.

76. Tanay, "Psychiatric Evaluation in the Matter of Mark Gonzalez," October 30, 1968, 6, Emanuel Tanay Papers, Wayne State University, Detroit, MI [hereafter ETP].

77. Affidavit of Nguyen-Khoa-Lai, MD. Translated from French, 20 July 1968, ETP.

78. Transcript of Evaluation of Mark Gonzalez by Dr. Hermann Steinmetz; Lt. A. S. Halpern, Division Psychologist, 1st Marine Division, "Psychological Evaluation," July 11, 1968, ETP.

79. Steinmetz, Evaluation, ETP.

80. Statement of K. O'Neill, HM, etc., 14 August 1968; Statement of 2nd Lt. Roger G. Charles, USMC, 12 August 1968; Statement of Bruce L. Danto, M.D., Detroit, October 23, 1968, ETP.

81. Statement of Danto; Halpern, Psychological Evaluation; Steinmetz, Evaluation, ETP.

82. On the pervasiveness of extrajudicial killing in Vietnam, Nick Turse, *Kill Anything That Moves: The Real American War in Vietnam* (New York: Metropolitan Books/Henry Holt and Co., 2013).

83. For a contemporary psychiatric appraisal of another young soldier who had also committed murder in Vietnam, see Herman P. Langer, "The Making of a Murderer," *American Journal of Psychiatry* 127, 7 (January 1971): 126–129.

84. Tanay, "Psychiatric Evaluation in the Matter of Mark Gonzalez," October 30, 1968, ETP. Capt. Sandy McMath, defense counsel for Allen, quoted by Tuohy, "The Worst U.S. Atrocity."

85. AP, "Michigan Marine Awaits Verdict in Viet Killing of 4," *Detroit News*, January 22, 1969, clipping, ETP.

86. Letter from Emanuel Tanay to Mark Gonzalez, August 1, 1969, ETP.

87. George Lepre, *Fragging: Why U.S. Soldiers Assaulted Their Officers in Vietnam* (Lubbock, TX: Texas Tech University Press, 2011), 57.

88. Lepre, *Fragging*, 98.

89. Lepre, *Fragging*, 98–99.

90. Major General Lloyd S. Ramsey, The Provost Marshal General, memo, "Serious Incident Resulting in the Death of One Officer" to Chief of Legislative Liaison, April 29, 1970 [courtesy of Beth Bailey].

91. For a table of sentences bestowed on fraggers convicted of murder, see Lepre, *Fragging*, 229.

CHAPTER 7

1. Col. Ritchie quoted by Arline Kaplan, "Untreated Vets: A 'Gathering Storm' of PTSD/ Depression," *Psychiatric Times*, October 1, 2008 [online]. For a widely cited military study that posits a close correlation between relationship failure and suicide, see Joseph E. Logan et al., "Precipitating Circumstances of Suicide among Active Duty U.S. Army Personnel versus U.S. Civilians, 2005–2010," *Suicide and Life-Threatening Behavior* 45, 1 (February 2015): 65–77. For recent studies of suicide and the military, Rajeev Ramchand et al., *The War Within: Preventing Suicide in the U.S. Military* (Santa Monica, CA: RAND, 2011); Antoon A. Leenaars, *Suicide among the Armed Forces: Understanding the Cost of Service* (Windsor, Ontario: Baywood Publishing Company, 2013); John Bateson, *The Last and Greatest Battle: Finding the Will, Commitment, and Strategy to End Military Suicides* (New York: Oxford University Press, 2015); David Kieran, *Signature Wounds: The Untold Story of the Military's Mental Health Crisis* (New York: New York University Press, 2019).

2. This time-honored trope has not disappeared altogether from more recent war-writing. Andrew Carroll's collection of war letters includes a "last letter" from a soldier identified only as Leon, written from Korea on June 14, 1952, after he'd received a Dear John the previous day. Carroll notes that "two days later Leon single-handedly charged a Chinese machine gun nest on his own initiative. He was killed instantly in a hail of bullets," Andrew Carroll (ed.), *War Letters: Extraordinary Correspondence from American Wars* (New York: Washington Square Press, 2001), 341.

3. "Mary Haworth's Mail," *Washington Post*, July 12, 1944, 10; Letter from "D.W.P.," "Mary Haworth's Mail," *Washington Post*, July 18, 1944, 7.

4. V-mail from 1st Sgt. Albert E. Martin, IV Special Service Company, US Army, to Anne Gudis, September 16, 1943, folder 12, box 2, KFP.

5. Leon Uris, *Battle Cry* (New York: Putnam, 1953), 154–156. For a discussion of this literary trope, Gerald F. Linderman, *The World within War: America's Combat Experience in World War II* (New York: Free Press, 1997), 310.

6. Dennis W. Brandt, *Pathway to Hell: A Tragedy of the American Civil War* (Lincoln, NB: University of Nebraska Press, 2008), 168, citing Robert R. Lyman, *History of Roulet, Pa. and the Life of Burrel Lyman* (Couldersport, PA: Potter County Historical Society, 1967), 139. Bateson opens his study of military suicide with a vignette of Crapsey's life and death, but makes no mention of a Dear John letter; *The Last and Greatest Battle*, 1–4. Jacqueline Garrick refers to Crapsey's "Dear John" letter in presenting the same historical example: "Understanding Failed Relationships as a Factor Related to Suicide and Suicidal Behavior among Military Personnel" in *Intimacy Post-injury: Combat Trauma and Sexual Health*, ed. Elspeth Cameron Ritchie (Oxford: Oxford University Press, 2016), 109–121. On suicide in the Civil War more generally, Col. Gregory R. Lande, "Felo De Se: Soldier Suicides in America's Civil War," *Military Medicine* 176, 5 (May 2011): 531–536; Diane Miller Sommerville, "'A Burden Too Heavy to Bear': War Trauma, Suicide, and Confederate Soldiers," *Civil War History* 59, 4 (December 2013): 453–491; Larry Logue, *Heavy Laden: Union Veterans, Psychological Illness and Suicide* (New York: Cambridge University Press, 2018).

7. Rick Salde, interview with Thomas Smith and John House, n.d., AFC/2001/001/47921, VHP.

8. Tony Perry, "Rescue for At-Risk Marines: As Suicides Rise, the Corps Is Turning to the Buddy System to Help Those on the Edge," *LAT*, September 10, 2010, A4. See also Vernon Loeb, "Military Investigates 7 Suspected Suicides: Soldiers Deployed for War in Iraq," *Washington Post*, July 20, 2003, A20; Lisa W. Foderado, "Suicides Prompt Concern at West Point, a Place Known for Toughing It Out," *NYT*, February 22, 2009, 28.

9. Congressional Quarterly Transcriptions, "Rep. C. W. Bill Young Holds a Hearing on the Navy and Marine Corps Budget," May 7, 2013, LexisNexis.

10. The classic sociological analysis is Émile Durkheim, *Suicide: A Study in Sociology*, translated by John A. Spaulding and George Simpson (London: Routledge & Kegan Paul, 1952). For recent studies, see Maurizio Pompili (ed.), *Phenomenology of Suicide: Unlocking the Suicidal Mind* (Cham: Springer, 2018); Colin Tatz, *The Sealed Box of Suicide: The Contexts of Self-Death* (Cham: Springer 2019); Anne Cleary, *The Gendered Landscape of Suicide: Masculinities, Emotions, and Culture* (Cham: Palgrave Macmillan, 2019).

11. Sam Sachs, interview with George Briney, n.d., 2017, AFC/2001/001/111229, VHP.

12. Carl Banks recalls a comrade in Vietnam who "emptied a damn M-16 right through the top of his head because he got a Dear John letter," Carl Joe Banks interview with Dixie Ferguson, May 14, 2015, AFC/2001/001/99859/, VHP. Castel Allgood, an army Vietnam veteran, recalls a young staff sergeant putting an M16 in his mouth, because "his wife had told him she didn't want to see him no more," Castel Louis Allgood, interview with Mary Ann Sison, n.d., AFC/2001/001/30444, VHP. Likewise USAF veteran Chuck Creel recalls that many suspected suicides in Vietnam were associated

with Dear John letters, with soldiers especially prone to taking their own lives with an M16 over the holidays; Charles Edward Creel, Jr., interview with Hoffman and Gilmer, December 13, 2003, transcript, AFC/2001/001/12645, VHP.

13. Dr. Theodore Clifford Ning, interview with Gary Smith, October 26, AFC/2001/001/74032, VHP.

14. On guns and suicide, Elspeth Cameron Ritchie, "Suicide and the United States Army: Perspectives from the Former Psychiatry Consultant to the Army Surgeon General," *Cerebrum* (January 2012): 9.

15. The water tower incident is recounted by Richard K. Butters, interview with Branden Butters, September 9, 2012, AFC/2001/001/23823, VHP. On the unrecovered man overboard, see Richard Earl Blair, interview with Charles Deusner, March 30, 2017, AFC/2001/001/108700, VHP. For a similar story from Vietnam, see Sidney B. Baird, interview with Kelly Crager, November 2, 2009, OH0728, Mr. Sidney "Junior" B. Baird Jr. Collection, The Vietnam Center and Sam Johnson Vietnam Archive, Texas Tech University [hereafter TTU].

16. Paul E. Charest, interview with Dudley Dudley, n.d., AFC/2001/001/112754, VHP.

17. Lester W. Elam, interview with Regina Korthals, April 24, 2012, AFC/2001/001/88463, VHP. This method of ending one's life was prefigured by some suicidal men in World War II who walked into airplane propellors. See, for example, an incident recalled by Army Nurse Corps veteran Verla DeBeer; Verla Virginia Kallemeyn DeBeer, interview with Victoria Vernau, September 5, 2006, AFC/2001/001/74391, VHP.

18. Ilsa Hansen Cooper, interview with Joseph Panzarella, November 6, 2008, AFC/2001/001/72266, VHP. There's a growing literature on veterans' rehabilitation and its intersection with gender norms. See David A. Gerber (ed.), *Disabled Veterans in History* (Ann Arbor, MI: University of Michigan Press, 2012); and on World War II specifically, Christina Jarvis, "'If He Comes Home Nervous': US World War II Neuropsychiatric Casualties and Postwar Masculinities,' *Journal of Men's Studies* 17, 2 (Spring 2009): 97–115; Susan Hartmann, "Prescriptions for Penelope: Literature on Women's Obligations to Returning World War II Veterans," *Women's Studies* 5 (1978): 223–239. For Hollywood's most memorable demobilization drama, see *The Best Years of Our Lives*, dir. William Wyler, Samuel Goldwyn Productions/RKO Radio Pictures, 1946; David A. Gerber, "Heroes and Misfits: The Troubled Social Reintegration of Disabled Veterans in *The Best Years of Our Lives*," *American Quarterly* 46, 4 (1994): 545–574.

19. Letter from Calvin Chapman to "Dear Folks," October 14, 1965, folder 8, box 1, 0380108027, Dr. Calvin Chapman Collection, TTU. Chapman's psychiatric evaluation of this patient can also be found in this collection, "Analysis of Psychiatric Patient," October 13, 1965, folder 21, box 1. For another combat psychiatrist's experience treating enlisted men suicidally depressed by Dear John letters in Vietnam, Douglas Bey, *Wizard 6: A Combat Psychiatrist in Vietnam* (College Station, TX: Texas A&M University Press, 2006), 93–94.

20. John O'Connell Nugent, interview with Shaun Illingworth and Gerald Carlucci, October 5, 2011, transcript p. 54, https://oralhistory.rutgers.edu/interviewees/1484-nugent-john-o-connell, ROHA. Vietnam veteran Casper Everhard tells a story of sitting

on top of his tank for hours at night, "making a silhouette," after getting a Dear John from his girlfriend; Casper Everhard, interview with Shaun Illingworth, February 26, 2008, transcript pp. 43–44, ROHA.

21. I'm grateful to Brian McAllister Linn for directing me toward the motif of suicidal heroism. For Brooks's description of Siegfried Sassoon's life-endangering actions, "Siegfried Sassoon," World War One Online, https://firstworldwaronlinedotcom.word press.com/poetry/siegfried-sassoon/.

22. On suicide in ancient Greece, Elise P. Garrison, "Attitudes towards Suicide in Ancient Greece," *Transactions of the American Philological Association* 121 (1991): 1–34. Richard A. Gabriel discusses suicidal heroism with reference to Dear John letters, making particular reference to Farley Mowatt's World War II memoir, *And No Birds Sang* (Toronto: Bantam, 1979). See *No More Heroes: Madness and Psychiatry in War* (New York: Hill and Wang, 1987), 53–54.

23. Chuck Gross, *Rattler One-Seven: A Vietnam Helicopter Pilot's War Story* (Denton, TX: University of North Texas Press, 2004), 127.

24. Daniel E. Evans Jr. and Charles W. Sasser, *Doc: Platoon Medic* (Bloomington, IN: iUniverse, 2002 [1998]), 182.

25. James T. Lawrence, *Reflections on LZ Albany: The Agony of Vietnam* (Marietta, GA: Deeds Publishing, 2014), 120–121.

26. Some service members witnessed another man shooting himself after receiving a Dear John. For one such instance, see Fred Blanchard (Charlie Horse 23), "A Vietnam War Personal History," unpublished manuscript (1999), entry for September 22, 1970, Quang Tri army base, p. 18, 8870111001, folder 11, box 1, Michael Law Collection, TTU.

27. Elsie Theresa Fehst Hamaker, interview with Barbara Longoria, February 3, 2005, AFC/2001/001/28609, VHP.

28. Sachs interview with Briney.

29. Bryant Mitchell, interview with Shaun Illingworth, March 24, 2016, transcript p. 17, https://oralhistory.rutgers.edu/interviewees/1876-mitchell-bryant, ROHA; Banks interview with Ferguson.

30. Ronald Pica, interview with Janet Hammond, December 10, 2002, AFC/2001/001/09608, VHP.

31. Bateson dates this development to 2001, *The Last and Greatest Battle*, 22–23.

32. Jeffrey Hyman et al., "Suicide Incidence and Risk Factors in an Active Duty U.S. Military Population," *American Journal of Public Health* 102, Supplement 1 (March 2012): S145.

33. Orman quoted by Vernon Loeb, "Military Investigates 7 Suspected Suicides: Soldiers Deployed for War in Iraq," *Washington Post,* July 20, 2003, A20.

34. Roy R. Grinker and John P. Spiegel, *Men under Stress* (Philadelphia, PA: Blakiston, 1945).

35. See John Milne Murray papers, LOC. Col. Paul F. Eggertsen, USAF, MC, "Suicide, the Opaque Act," *Military Medicine* 132, 1 (1967): 9.

36. This term appears in the Southeast Asia Combat Area Casualties Database; David P. Adams et al., "Hearts and Minds: Suicide among United States Combat Troops in Vietnam, 1957–1973," *Social Science Medicine* 47, 11 (1998): 1687–1694.

37. Headquarters II Field Force Vietnam, Talking Paper, "Suicide as a Command Problem," n.d., Entry P 1750, box 41, RG 472.

38. Memo, II FFV Commanders' Conference, December 3, 1969, Entry P 1750, box 41, RG 472.

39. UPI, "1,163 GI Homicides in Vietnam War Reported," *LAT*, June 5, 1973, A4.

40. Stephen Howard, "The Vietnam Warrior: His Experience, and Implications for Psychotherapy," *American Journal of Psychotherapy* 30, 1 (January 1976): 128. The same point is made in almost identical language by Dale Reich, "One Year in Vietnam: A Young Soldier Remembers," *Wisconsin Magazine of History* 64, 3 (Spring 1981): 165.

41. Adams et al., "Hearts and Minds," 1689.

42. Hyman et al., "Suicide Incidence and Risk Factors," 145.

43. Alison Howell and Zoë Wool, *The War Comes Home: The Toll of War and the Shifting Burden of Care* (Providence, RI: Watson Institute for International Studies, 2011); Kenneth T. MacLeish, *Making War at Fort Hood: Life and Uncertainty in a Military Community* (Princeton, NJ: Princeton University Press, 2013), 226.

44. Leslie Kaufman, "After War, Love Can Be a Battlefield," *NYT*, April 6, 2008, ST1.

45. David Smith, "Divorces Inflict Home Front Damage on US Troops as Iraq War Drags On," *Observer*, June 1, 2008, 38.

46. David Finkel, *Thank You for Your Service* (New York: Farrar, Strauss and Giroux, 2013), 155.

47. Nancy Sherman, *Afterwar: Healing the Moral Wounds of Our Soldiers* (New York: Oxford University Press, 2015), 14–15.

48. Panetta quoted by Bateson, *The Last and Greatest Battle*, 68; see, for example, James C. McKinley, "Despite Army's New Efforts, Suicides Continue at Grim Pace," *NYT*, October 11, 2010, A11. Several studies found no positive correlation between deployment and elevated risk of suicide; see, inter alia, Mark A. Reger et al., "Risk of Suicide among U.S. Military Service Members Following Operation Enduring Freedom or Operation Iraqi Freedom Deployment and Separation from the U.S. Military," *JAMA Psychiatry* 72, 6 (June 2015): 561–569; Christopher J. Philips et al., "Risk Factors Associated with Suicide Completions among U.S. Enlisted Marines," *American Journal of Epidemiology* 186, 6 (September 2017): 668–678; Cynthia A LeardMann et al., "Risk Factors Associated with Suicide in Current and Former US Military Personnel," *JAMA* 310, 5 (2013): 496–506.

49. Ritchie, "Suicide and the United States Army," 3–4.

50. Mental Health Advisory Team (MHAT) V, *Operation Iraqi Freedom 06–08* (Washington, DC: Office of the Surgeon Multi-National Force – Iraq and Office of the Surgeon General United States Army Medical Command, 2008), 88. The *Military Medicine* study of Army suicides between 1975 and 1985 actually makes no mention of failed relationships as the leading precipitant of suicide: Col. Nicholas L. Rock, "Suicide and Suicide Attempts in the Army: A 10-Year Review," *Military Medicine* 153 (February 1988): 67–69.

51. On CSF, see the essays in a special issue of *American Psychologist*, 66, 1 (January 2011). For critiques of CSF and the "resilience" model of CBT on which it rests, Alison Howell, "The Demise of PTSD: From Governing through Trauma to Governing Resilience," *Alternatives: Global, Local, Political* 37 (2012): 214–226; Emily Sogn, "Throw a Survey at It," *Anthropology Now* 6, 1 (2014): 25–34; Beatrice Jauregui, "World Fitness: US Army Family Humanism and the Positive Science of Persistent War," *Public Culture* 27, 3 (2015): 449–485; Kenneth MacLeish, "How to Feel about War: On Soldier Psyches, Military Biopolitics and American Empire," *BioSocieties* 14, 3 (2018): 274–299.

52. John M. Gottman, Julie S. Gottman, and Christopher L. Atkins, "The Comprehensive Soldier Fitness Program: Family Skills Component," *American Psychologist* 66, 1 (January 2001): 54.

53. For an overview of military marriage-building programs, "U.S. Military Marriage Enrichment Programs," *Excellent Parent Magazine*, September 2020, 65. See also the marriage resources on Military OneSource, a DoD online resource for military personnel and their families: https://www.militaryonesource.mil/family-relationships/relationships/military-relationships-support/; and for the Army's Strong Bonds program, www.strongbonds.org.

54. Elizabeth M. Lorge, "Injured Soldiers Struggle to Maintain Relationships, Intimacy," May 23, 2008, www.army.mil/article/9393/injured_soldiers_struggle_to_maintain_re lationships_intimacy. On an earlier iteration of video training as a tool of suicide prevention in the USMC, see Hugo Martin, "War with Iraq: Suicide Too Frequently a Foe for Military," *LAT*, April 16, 2003, 8.

55. On army suicide prevention initiatives, Ramchand et al., *The War Within*.

56. Staff Sgt. Crista Yazzie, "USARPAC Suicide Prevention Goes 'Beyond The Front,'" March 5, 2009, www.army.mil/article/17846/usarpac_suicide_prevention_goes_beyond_the_front.

57. Gordon Lubold, "Army Uses Video Games in Suicide Prevention," *Christian Science Monitor*, November 26, 2008, 2; Bateson, *The Last and Greatest Battle*, 220.

58. Dear Abby, "Don't Send Soldier 'Dear John' Letter," *Deseret Morning News* (Salt Lake City), September 8, 2006, https://advance.lexis.com/api/document?collection=new s&id=urn:contentItem:4KV9-N0M0-TWHW-633D-00000-00&context=1516831. For the responses, Dear Abby, "Break Up Letter to Soldier Threatens His Life, Comrades," *Charleston Daily Mail* (West Virginia), October 25, 2006, https://advance.lexis.com/a pi/document?collection=news&id=urn:contentItem:4M6J-T730-TX2T-P32H-00000-00&context=1516831.

59. Dear Abby, "It's Better to Receive Dear John Letter in the Company of Comrades," *St. Paul Pioneer Press* (Minnesota), December 20, 2015.

60. Michael Russell, "Suicide and Suicide Prevention," in *When the Warrior Returns: Making the Transition Home*, eds. Nathan D. Ainspan and Walter Penk (Annapolis, MD: Naval Institute Press, 2012), 102.

61. MHAT V, 103.

62. Garrick, "Understanding Failed Relationships," 110.

63. Ibid.

64. Ibid., 111. On the need to explore further the "mechanisms by which romantic relationship dissolution may contribute to suicidality," see Jessica M. LaCroix et al., "Intimate Partner Relationship Stress and Suicidality in a Psychiatrically Hospitalized Military Sample," *Comprehensive Psychiatry* 84 (2018): 109–110.

65. See, inter alia, James Griffith, "Army Suicides: 'Knowns' and an Interpretative Framework for Future Directions," *Military Psychology* 24 (2012): 488–512; James Griffith and Craig J. Bryan, "Suicides in the U.S. Military: Birth Cohort Vulnerability and the All-Volunteer Force," *Armed Forces & Society* 42, 3 (2016): 483–500; M. K. Nock et al., "Suicide among Soldiers: A Review of Psychosocial Risk and Protective Factors," *Psychiatry* 76 (2014): 97–125.

66. Michael Schoenbaum et al., "Predictors of Suicide and Accident Death in the Army Study to Assess Risk and Resilience in Servicemembers (Army STARRS): Results from the Army Study to Assess Risk and Resilience in Servicemembers," *JAMA Psychiatry*, 71, 5 (2014): 493–503. On STARRS, www.nimh.nih.gov/health/topics/suicide-prevention/suicide-prevention-studies/army-study-to-assess-risk-and-resilience-in-servicemembers-army-starrs-a-partnership-between-nimh-and-the-us-army.shtml. Hyman et al. note an increased risk of suicide for service members with one or more deployments to Iraq or Afghanistan, "Suicide Incidence and Risk Factors," S139.

67. MacLeish, *Making War at Fort Hood*, chapter 1 and passim. In a similar vein, Jean Scandlyn and Sarah Hautzinger adopt a broad view of what they term "deployment stress" in their co-authored anthropological study of Fort Carson: *Beyond Post-traumatic Stress: Homefront Struggles with the Wars on Terror* (Walnut Creek, CA: Left Coast Press, 2014).

68. MacLeish, *Making War at Fort Hood*, 226–227.

69. See the critiques made by Howell, "Demise of PTSD"; Jauregui, "World Fitness"; MacLeish, "How to Feel about War"; Pat O'Mally, "Resilient Subjects: Uncertainty, Warfare and Liberalism," *Economy and Society* 39, 4 (November 2010): 488–509.

70. Sogn, "Throw a Survey at It," 31–32.

71. Robert L. Sinclair, Abby L. Paulson, and Lyndon Riviere, "The Resilient Spouse: Understanding Factors Associated with Dispositional Resilience among Military Spouses," *Military Behavioral Health* 2, 4 (2019): 376–390.

72. A recent review of civilian-focused literature about the nexus between suicide and failed relationships found a heightened risk of suicide among LGBTQ individuals; Dominique Kazan, Alison L. Calear, and Philip J. Batterham, "The Impact of Intimate Partner Relationships on Suicidal Thoughts and Behaviors: A Systematic Review," *Journal of Affective Disorders* 190 (2016): 585–598.

73. Military Relationships Support, www.militaryonesource.mil/family-relationships/relationships/military-relationships-support/#our-best-resources; www.strongbonds.org.

74. Wayne C. Booth, *My Many Selves: The Quest for a Plausible Harmony* (Logan, UT: Utah State University Press, 2006), 162–164. The threats of suicide made by a corpsman in Vietnam to extract more (and more effusive) letters from his nineteen-year-old bride are documented in a letter from Major M. P. Fleming, a chaplain at Fort Wainwright who had counseled the young woman, to Office of the Chaplain, Chu Lai, June 26, 1969, 1010102237, Rev. James Haney Collection, TTU.

75. Col. Thomas S. Stefanko, interview with Eileen Hurst, n.d., AFC/2001/001/102712, VHP. On internet pornography, Gottman, Gottman, and Atkins, "Comprehensive Soldier Fitness Program," 53.

76. C. Monson et al., "Military-Related PTSD and Intimate Relationships: From Description to Theory-Driven Research and Intervention Development," *Clinical Psychology Review* 29 (2009): 707–714; C. T. Taft et al., "'Strength at Home' Intervention to Prevent Conflict and Violence in Military Couples: Pilot Findings," *Partner Abuse* 5 (2014): 41–57; April A. Gerlock et al., "Comparing Intimately Violent to Non-violent Veterans in Treatment for Posttraumatic Stress Disorder," *Journal of Family Violence* 31 (2016): 667–678.

77. Garrick, "Understanding Failed Relationships," 118; on the phenomenon more generally, Thomas Joiner, *The Perversion of Virtue: Understanding Murder-Suicide* (Oxford: Oxford University Press, 2014).

78. Lizette Alvarez and Deborah Sontag, "When Strains of Military Families Turn Deadly," *NYT*, February 15, 2008, A14; Bateson, *The Last and Greatest Battle*, 242; Ann Jones, *They Were Soldiers: How the Wounded Return from America's Wars – the Untold Story* (Chicago, IL: Haymarket Books, 2014),123. On Fort Hood and Guillén's murder, Manny Fernandez, "A Year of Heartbreak and Bloodshed at Fort Hood," *NYT*, September 10, 2020.

79. Draft letter from Anne Gudis to Sam Kramer, November 1, 1943, folder 3, box 2, KFP. Letter from J. M. Sprinkel to Anne Gudis, September 27, 1943, folder 12, box 2, KFP.

80. Patton quoted by Adela Rogers St. John, *The Honeycomb* (New York: Doubleday & Co., 1969), 89.

81. R. M. Wingfield, *The Only Way Out: An Infantryman's Autobiography of the North-West Europe Campaign August 1944–February 1945* (London: Hutchinson, 1955), 174.

CONCLUSION

1. The path of the relationship can be traced through Anne and Sam's correspondence in the Kramer family papers at Cornell University library. It is also recounted by Judy Barrett Litoff and David C. Smith, *Since You Went Away: World War II Letters from American Women on the Home Front* (Lawrence, KS: University Press of Kansas, 1991), 53–63.

2. Casper Everhard, interview with Shaun Illingworth, February 26, 2008, transcript pp. 43–44, ROHA.

3. Ann Pfau, without having consulted the Kramer Family papers, relates that "most of the letters" Anne received were rebukes, "Allotment Annies and Other Wayward Wives: Wartime Concerns about Female Disloyalty and the Problem of the Returned Veteran," in *The United States and the Second World War: New Perspectives on Diplomacy, War, and the Home Front*, eds. G. Kurt Piehler and Sidney Pash (New York: Fordham University Press, 2010), 106. She cites the gloss put on the mail Gudis received by Litoff and Smith, *Since You Went Away*, 56. The archived letters attest that far more men wrote Anne because they wanted an explanation, a pen-pal, and/or the promise of a date than to chastise her; correspondence in folder 12, box 2, KFP.

4. On the retrospective construction of the "good war," see Michael C. C. Adams, *The Best War Ever: America and World War II* (Baltimore, MD: Johns Hopkins University Press, 1994); John Bodnar, *The "Good War" in American Memory* (Baltimore, MD: Johns Hopkins University Press, 2010); Kenneth D. Rose, *Myth and the Greatest Generation: A Social History of Americans in World War II* (New York: Routledge, 2008).

5. Statistic from Ellen Herman, *The Romance of American Psychology: Political Culture in the Age of Experts* (Berkeley, CA: University of California Press, 1995), 88.

6. On wartime strikes, James T. Sparrow, *Warfare State: World War II Americans and the Age of Big Government* (New York: Oxford University Press, 2011), chapter 5.

7. Howard Whitman , "Jilt in the Mail Gets Yank Down: 'Dear John' Letters Are Not Ones He Wants," *Chicago Daily Tribune*, May 31, 1944, 1.

8. Helena Goscilo, "Graphic Womanhood under Fire," in *Embracing Arms: Cultural Representation of Slavic and Balkan Women in War*, eds. Helena Goscilo and Yana Hashamova (Budapest: Central European University Press, 2012), 166.

9. Goscilo acknowledges the work of fellow feminist critic Susan Gubar, citing Cpl. John Readey's World War II poem about a Dear John letter, "A Woman's a Two Face," Susan Gubar, "'This Is My Rifle, This Is My Gun': World War II and the Blitz on Women," in *Behind the Lines: Gender and the Two World Wars*, eds. Margaret Randolph Higonnet et al. (New Haven, CT: Yale University Press, 1987), 246.

10. The manufacturer Verlinden is no longer in business, but these figurines continued to be sold on eBay at the time of writing. See www.ebay.co.uk/itm/Verlinden-1-35-Dear-John-US-G-I-Reading-Letter-in-Vietnam-Resin-Figure-420-/170653478233, last viewed on April 25, 2021.

11. David Kieran, *Signature Wounds: The Untold Story of the Military's Mental Health Crisis* (New York: New York University Press, 2019), chapter 3.

12. See, for example, views expressed by men serving in Iraq with the New Hampshire National Guard in *The War Tapes*, dir. Deborah Scranton, 2006. Literary articulations of this mood can be found in Ben Fountain, *Billy Lynn's Long Halftime Walk* (New York: Ecco, 2012); Phil Klay, *Redeployment* (New York: The Penguin Press, 2014); Nico Walker, *Cherry* (New York: Alfred A. Knopf, 2018); and in the long-form journalism of David Finkel, *Good Soldiers* (New York: Sarah Crichton Books/Farrar, Straus and Giroux, 2009) and *Thank You for Your Service* (New York: Sarah Crichton Books/Farrar, Straus and Giroux, 2013).

13. Council on Foreign Relations, "Demographics of the U.S. Military," July 13, 2020; www.cfr.org/backgrounder/demographics-us-military. Dave Phillips and Tim Arango, "Who Signs Up to Fight? Makeup of U.S. Recruits Shows Glaring Disparity," *NYT*, January 10, 2020, www.nytimes.com/2020/01/10/us/military-enlistment.html.

14. On Duckworth's indebtedness to Black folkloric tradition, Tyina Steptoe, "'Jody's Got Your Girl and Gone': Gender, Folklore, and the Black Working Class," *Journal of African American History* 99, 3 (Summer 2014): 251–274; Michael Hanchard, "Jody," *Critical Inquiry* 24, 2 (Winter 1998): 473–497.

15. Sandee Shaffer Johnson, *Cadences: The Jody Call Book, No. 1* (Canton, OH: The Daring Press, 1983), 15.

16. On the exploitation of servicemen's fears of infidelity by psychological warfare operatives on both sides, Lee Kennett, *GI: The American Soldier in World War II* (New York: Scribner, 1987), 76; John Costello, *Love, Sex and War: Changing Values, 1939–45* (London: Collins, 1985), 242. Examples of this type of wartime propaganda can be found at www.psywarrior.com/sexandprop.html.

17. Philip M. Taylor, *War and the Media: Propaganda and Persuasion in the Gulf War* (Manchester: Manchester University Press, 1992), 90.

18. Richard Allen Burns, "Where Is Jody Now? Reconsidering Military Marching Chants," in *Warrior Ways: Explorations in Modern Military Folklore*, eds. Eric A. Eliason and Tad Tuleja (Logan, UT: Utah State University Press, 2012), 79–98.

19. On misogyny and the military, Aaron Belkin, *Bring Me Men: Military Masculinity and the Benign Façade of American Empire 1898–2001* (New York: Columbia University Press, 2012); Carol Burke, *Camp All-American, Hanoi Jane, and the High-and-Tight: Gender, Folklore, and Changing Military Culture* (Boston, MA: Beacon Press, 2004); Cynthia Enloe, *Maneuvers: The International Politics of Militarizing Women's Lives* (Berkeley, CA: University of California Press, 2000); Joshua S. Goldstein, *War and Gender* (Cambridge: Cambridge University Press, 2001); Megan Mackenzie, *Beyond the Band of Brothers: The US Military and the Myth That Women Can't Fight* (Cambridge: Cambridge University Press, 2015).

20. Kenneth T. MacLeish, *Making War at Fort Hood: Life and Uncertainty in a Military Community* (Princeton, NJ: Princeton University Press, 2013), 10. On injury as war's most inescapable feature, see also Elaine Scarry, *The Body in Pain: The Making and Unmaking of the World* (New York: Oxford University Press, 1985).

21. MacLeish, *Making War at Fort Hood*, 165–172; Douglas K. Snyder et al., "Intervening with Military Couples Struggling with Issues of Sexual Infidelity," *Journal of Contemporary Psychotherapy* 41 (2011): 201–208.

22. Terri Tanielian and Lisa H. Jaycox (eds.), *Invisible Wounds of War: Psychological and Cognitive Injuries, Their Consequences, and Services to Assist Recovery* (Santa Monica, CA: RAND Center for Military Health Policy Research, 2008).

23. Zoë H. Wool, *After War: The Weight of Life at Walter Reed* (Durham, NC: Duke University Press, 2015).

Index

MILITARY, WAR, AND SOCIETY IN MODERN AMERICAN HISTORY

Series Editors
Beth Bailey, University of Kansas
Andrew Preston, University of Cambridge

Military, War, and Society in Modern American History is a new series that showcases original scholarship on the military, war, and society in modern U.S. history. The series builds on recent innovations in the fields of military and diplomatic history and includes historical works on a broad range of topics, including civil–military relations and the militarization of culture and society; the military's influence on policy, power, politics, and political economy; the military as a key institution in managing and shaping social change, both within the military and in broader American society; the effect the military has had on American political and economic development, whether in wartime or peacetime; and the military as a leading edge of American engagement with the wider world, including forms of soft power as well as the use of force.